THE DEATH PENALTY AND SEX MURDER IN CANADIAN HISTORY

PATRONS OF THE SOCIETY

Professor Constance Backhouse, University of Ottawa

Blake, Cassels, & Graydon LLP

Chernos, Flaherty, Svonkin LLP

Gowling WLG

Hull & Hull LLP

McCarthy Tétrault LLP

Osler, Hoskin & Harcourt LLP

Paliare Roland Rosenberg Rothstein LLP

Pape Chaudhury LLP

Torys LLP

WeirFoulds LLP

The Osgoode Society is supported by a grant from The Law Foundation of Ontario.

The Society also thanks The Law Society of Upper Canada for its continuing support.

THE DEATH PENALTY AND SEX MURDER IN CANADIAN HISTORY

CAROLYN STRANGE

Published for The Osgoode Society for Canadian Legal History by
University of Toronto Press
Toronto Buffalo London

Published by University of Toronto Press
Toronto Buffalo London
utorontopress.com
osgoodesociety.ca

ISBN 978-1-4875-0837-1 (cloth)
ISBN 978-1-4875-3810-1 (PDF)
ISBN 978-1-4875-3811-8 (EPUB)

Library and Archives Canada Cataloguing in Publication

Title: The death penalty and sex murder in Canadian history / Carolyn Strange.
Names: Strange, Carolyn, 1959– author.
Series: Osgoode Society for Canadian Legal History series.
Description: Series statement: Osgoode Society for Canadian Legal History series | Includes bibliographical references and index.
Identifiers: Canadiana (print) 20200286579 | Canadiana (ebook) 20200286641 | ISBN 9781487508371 (cloth) | ISBN 9781487538101 (PDF) | ISBN 9781487538118 (EPUB)
Subjects: LCSH: Capital punishment – Canada – History. | LCSH: Lust murder – Canada – History.
Classification: LCC HV8699.C2 S77 2020 | DDC 364.660971 – dc23

University of Toronto Press acknowledges the financial assistance to its publishing program of the Canada Council for the Arts and the Ontario Arts Council, an agency of the Government of Ontario.

Canada Council for the Arts
Conseil des Arts du Canada

Funded by the Government of Canada
Financé par le gouvernement du Canada
Canada

Contents

Acknowledgments

Considering the principal topics of this book – the death penalty and sex murder – it has been difficult to write. The evidence of these crimes and trials and the decisions of the executive were harrowing to read. Yet, the historical significance of these matters and their ongoing public policy relevance spurred the project's completion.

Many colleagues, research assistants, and institutions helped to make this book possible, and it is a pleasure to acknowledge them. Funding for the research came from an Australian Research Council Discovery project (DP150101798), a stipend from the Robarts Centre for Canadian Studies, and a period of outside studies leave from the Australian National University. I spent my leave as a visiting professor in the Faculty of Law, University of Toronto, whose staff and resources facilitated the completion of the first draft. Several researchers across Canada tracked down local newspapers and primary source material: Koral Lavorgna, David Kitai, Pauline Mercier, Stacey Hare Hodgins, Rhiannon Murphy, and Patrick O'Connor. I am grateful to my Canadian colleagues who recommended research assistants: Simon Devereaux, Mary Lynn Young, Lori Chambers, Jennifer Stephen, and Michael Boudreau. In Australia, it was a pleasure to work with Amy Thomas, who took charge of the statistical analysis and prepared primary material for an associated website.

Archivists at the Library and Archives Canada (LAC) often went out of their way to make files available during my research trips and to assist with access clearance: Richie Sue Allen, Michel Brideau, Michel Dufresne,

Yannick Clément, and Suzanne Lemaire. Paul Leatherdale, archivist at the Law Society of Ontario, was extraordinarily helpful in providing material from member lawyers' and judges' files. Stacy Kaufield of the Legal Archives Society of Alberta provided assistance in research related to members of the Alberta and Northwest Territories bars.

Conversations with fellow Canadian historians allowed me to refine my approach, and many colleagues provided valuable feedback: Sarah Carter, Joan Sangster, James Miller, Philip Girard, Constance Backhouse, and Shelley Gavigan. Donald Fyson, Jonathan Swainger, Hamar Foster, and Michael Boudreau lent not just their expertise and support; in addition, they shared primary sources and data. I also acknowledge the assistance of Hetoevėhotohke'e (Annita Lucchesi), who provided access, as executive director of the Sovereign Bodies Institute, to her database in progress on Missing and Murdered Indigenous Women and Girls in Canada and the United States.

The support the Osgoode Society for Canadian Legal History provides for scholarship is magnified by the expertise and acumen of its editor-in-chief, Jim Phillips. Over several decades, his sharp but encouraging editorial skills have become legendary, for good reason. The book's co-production through the University of Toronto Press allowed me to work again with Len Husband, whose advice as the book took shape was invaluable. The managing editor, Lisa Jemison, was patient, efficient, and affable in bringing the book to fruition. I am also grateful that two peer reviewers pointed out errors and provided insightful commentary, which allowed me to make improvements in the final draft.

When criticism comes with companionship and conviviality, it reminds us of scholarship's communal capacity. The School of History's book group took apart two drafts of the introduction and one of the later chapters, and Karen Downing generously read the penultimate full draft. Donald Fyson was unfailingly helpful at every stage of the project, and he freely shared his expertise in the history of criminal justice in Quebec. Fellow historian of violence and emotions, Robert Cribb, was always prepared to discuss the perils and imperatives of writing about traumatic events. He and Li Narangoa kindly allowed me to tag along on a writing retreat. Sociologist Lorna Weir was an interlocutor par excellence. Her hard questions and mind for methodology and theory were challenging in the best of ways, even better when delivered over many brunches.

Finally, I want to acknowledge the inspiration of Arthur Strange, a man whose thirst for knowledge far exceeded his formal education. Even though my father is gone, he is not forgotten, and therefore I dedicate this book to his memory.

THE DEATH PENALTY AND SEX MURDER IN CANADIAN HISTORY

1

The Politics of the Death Penalty and the Problem of Sex Murder

What fate should befall the convicted sex killer? Over most of Canada's history, the answer was simple: death. Every person over seven years of age and deemed to be of sound mind was subject to the mandatory penalty of death if found guilty of the offence.[1] Legislators narrowed the death penalty's scope in 1961, when capital punishment was confined to "planned and deliberate" killings, homicides committed in the course of another criminal act, and incidents causing the death of police officers and prison officials. Then, in 1967, a partial moratorium further restricted the death penalty to murders of law enforcement agents.[2] Before Parliament formally put an end to capital punishment in 1976, over 1,500 persons were sentenced to death,[3] sixty-one of whom were found guilty of sex murders.[4] Despite the small number of individuals in this subset, their significance in the death penalty's history is great. Convicted sex killers faced a high rate of execution – substantially greater than that of other convicted murderers.

From the vantage point of the early twenty-first century – a time of sex offender registers, sex predator laws, amber alerts, and victim impact statements – the harsh response to these sorts of murderers in Canada's past seems unremarkable.[5] The death penalty's abolition failed to staunch public support for capital punishment, particularly for murders involving sexual violence.[6] Recent polls indicate that over half of Canadians look enviously at US states that retain the death penalty and nostalgically back to the time when capital punishment was the sentence that awaited murderers in their own country.[7] These potent desires, frequently voiced by populist politicians, cannot be challenged without deeper research into the death penalty's history and a comprehensive understanding of the detection, prosecution, and punishment of sex murder. How did the Canadian public and policymakers approach such crimes and criminals when the mandatory penalty of death was in effect?

Wherever death has been set as the ultimate criminal penalty, the poor, minority groups, and stigmatized peoples have suffered disproportionately – more likely to be accused, convicted, and executed.[8] Historical evidence of the death penalty's enforcement contradicts apologists' claims that its application has been determined by "legitimate considerations, duly recognized, impartially and equitably enforced, and exemplifying the rule of law."[9] In the United States, opponents of capital punishment convinced the Supreme Court in 1972 that racial prejudice favoured white defendants and thereby put African Americans at greater risk of execution, particularly when victims of murder were white. The court agreed that the death penalty, under such conditions, amounted to "cruel and unusual" punishment; however, procedural changes introduced by the states led the court to reaffirm the constitutionality of the death penalty in 1976. Executions resumed the following year.[10]

In Canada, Parliament, not the Supreme Court, was the agent of change from the 1960s onward.[11] The movement that led to abolition also differed. In individual cases, petitioners pointed out biases against accused defendants who were not members of the Anglo-Celtic majority, but Canadian critics of capital punishment did not base their opposition on a critique of systemic racism.[12] Instead, abolitionists in Canada drew attention to a wide range of issues that distorted capital justice: the use of coercive police tactics; poor people's inability to fund their defence; the courts' strict definition of insanity; the impediments against criminal appeals; the lack of legal aid; and the vagaries and unaccountability of executive clemency.[13] Together, they charged, these ingredients constituted a recipe for irreversible miscarriages of justice. Had they studied the history of sex murder convictions, these critics would have discovered at least one of these elements at play in every capital case.

Inspired by the death penalty debates of the 1970s, criminologists and historians began to rake through historic records of capital cases and reports on executions and commutations, and they found that Canada's

Table 1.1. Outcome of Sex Murder Convictions by Race*

Offender Race	Executed (n)	Not Executed (n)	Rate of Execution (%)
White	32	20	61.5
All Others	7	2	77.8

*Race as defined by authorities and press accounts of trials.
Source: Lorraine Gadoury and Antonio Lechasseur, *Persons Sentenced to Death in Canada, 1867–1976: An Inventory of Case Files in the Fonds of the Department of Justice* (Ottawa: National Archives of Canada, 1994).

Table 1.2. Proportion of Male Murderers Executed by Type of Murder, 1867–1967*

Sex Murderers (%)	Robbery & Burglary Murderers (%)	All Other Male Murderers (%)
63.9	54.3	48.0

*Compared with the proportion of executions among males convicted of other forms of murder, the execution rate of sex murderers was statistically significant. Pearson's chi-square test determined a difference in proportions of .159 (p = .015).
Source: Lorraine Gadoury and Antonio Lechasseur, *Persons Sentenced to Death in Canada, 1867–1976: An Inventory of Case Files in the Fonds of the Department of Justice* (Ottawa: National Archives of Canada, 1994).

history of capital justice was riven with racism and ethnic biases (Table 1.1). Among the capitally convicted, Indigenous people, black Canadians, immigrants from non-English backgrounds, and francophones were executed more frequently than were white Anglo-Celtic persons.[14] In Canada, as in most other nations, males of all backgrounds were hanged at a higher rate than females, especially women convicted of infanticide, which remained a capital offence until 1948.[15] Yet, decision-makers also responded to the types of homicide men committed and the victims of their crimes, not just perpetrators' characteristics (Table 1.2).[16] For instance, men who committed murder in the course of robbery or burglary, often involving planning and the use of weapons, were executed more frequently than other male murderers.[17] Men found guilty of sex murder were considered still more deserving of death, and thirty-nine of these sixty-one offenders were executed, thirty-two of whom were white. Of the nine non-white men sentenced to death for sex murders, seven – four Indigenous, two black, and one Mauritian man – died on the gallows. In the white Dominion, these sex slayers fared worst.[18]

"Sex murder" is not a term that appears in historic Canadian criminal statutes; instead, it refers here to homicides that involved rape or sodomy as well as killings motivated, in the eyes of contemporaries, by perverted sexual desires or attempted assaults of a sexual nature.[19] The legal definition of sexual assault is too tight to capture the social meanings of these offences and the changing ways in which they struck historic actors, from police officers to news editors.[20] In 1948, Parliament came close to incorporating a broader conception of sexually motivated crime by creating a new category of offenders: "criminal sexual psychopaths." But the indeterminate sentencing regime it put in place applied only to persons charged with non-capital offences.[21] As far as the criminal law was concerned, murder was murder. The only type of culpable homicide defined by the victim's identity or the perpetrator's motivation (aside from infanticide) was treason, a grave threat to the sovereign or the state. Murders characterized by sexual coercion and violence were no less grave in the public mind. They violated moral norms and threatened the social order; they set communities clamouring for the identification and capture of the culprit. Anger and grief, amplified through the press, pressured police and prosecutors to ensure swift and severe punishment.[22]

Whether or not trial transcripts or judges' reports showed that rape, as defined by law, had taken place in addition to homicide, the file summaries that bureaucrats prepared for cabinet reviews clearly indicated the cases they considered to be murders of a sexual nature. From the moment investigators discovered a victim's body – skirts raised, trousers torn, bruising or cuts to the lower limbs, stains suggesting semen – these homicides were treated in ways that indicated they were distinctly disturbing. As late as the early 1960s, when commutations became de facto policy, the executive was acutely aware that locals, enraged by sex slayings, expected offenders to hang. Revulsion rocked the families of victims and community members; it reverberated in jury rooms, on the bench, in the offices of federal justice bureaucrats; and in cabinet chambers, it inclined decision-makers to severity.

Processing Capital Case Files

Every prisoner condemned to death was granted the right of executive review and the prospect of clemency. No legal appeal or sponsor was necessary. Upholders of the death penalty extolled executive discretion as a treasured attribute of British justice, benign and proper.[23]

The British North America (BNA) Act of 1867 assigned responsibility for capital case reviews to the federal government.[24] Formally, the governor general wielded the authority as the monarch's representative to grant or withhold mercy; in practice, and with few exceptions in the early decades of Confederation, royal appointees endorsed cabinet recommendations.[25] Staff in the Department of Justice supported the executive wing of government, and legally trained clerks managed the records of each capital case.[26] Ministers and cabinets came and went, with changes of personnel between and within government terms, as senior public servants helmed capital case reviews.

Invisible operatives in the machinery of capital justice, these bureaucrats processed each case to facilitate life-and-death decision-making. This procedure entailed combing through transcripts, judges' and medical experts' reports, petitions, and correspondence, official and otherwise. Hewitt Bernard, deputy minister of justice to his brother-in-law, Sir John A. Macdonald, was the first to undertake this task, and he standardized procedures for others to follow.[27] By the late 1870s, the department put the chief clerk in charge of capital cases, and it became customary for him to compose summary memoranda. The aptly named Augustus Power was head clerk from 1879 to 1891. With strokes of his blue and red pencils, he marked up passages of transcripts and any other documents he considered pertinent. No matter how much material ended up in a case file, Power set the tradition of sticking close to the trial judge's report to ensure that the cabinet knew his opinion on the deservedness of the death penalty.[28]

Bureaucratic memoranda on sex murder cases do not make for dry reading. Power, the most senior public servant under the deputy minister of justice, approached these files as moral tales. In his summary of an 1891 case concerning the rape and strangulation murder of two prepubescent sisters, he commented: "The evidence discloses a case of perhaps unparalleled atrocity."[29] The reports written by the men who filled Power's shoes conveyed similar impressions. Two chief legal clerks filled his role after his retirement – Pierre M. Côté and John D. Clarke – but the next man, Michael F. Gallagher, headed capital case reviews from 1924 to 1952.[30] Over his long tenure, Gallagher processed reports from a growing range of experts in the science of mind, yet his moral emotions prevailed.[31] Through his skillful editing of case file materials, he minimized any indication of ambivalence concerning convicted sex murderers' culpability, and he amplified the gravity of their offences. This framing encouraged the cabinet to allow the law to take its course.

Table 1.3. Sex Murder Capital Case Outcomes by Decade

Decade	Cases (n)	Executions (n)	Commutations (n)	Successful Appeals* (n)
1870s	3	1	2	0
1880s	0	0	0	0
1890s	3	3	0	0
1900s	4	4	0	0
1910s	3	3	0	0
1920s	5	4	0	1
1930s	5	3	0	2
1940s	16	10	1	5
1950s	13	10	3	0
1960s	9	1	7	1
Totals	**61**	**39**	**13**	**9**

*Appeals that resulted in non-capital convictions or acquittals after original conviction; verdicts set aside and new trial not proceeded; acquittal entered.
Source: Lorraine Gadoury and Antonio Lechasseur, *Persons Sentenced to Death in Canada, 1867–1976: An Inventory of Case Files in the Fonds of the Department of Justice* (Ottawa: National Archives of Canada, 1994).

Out of the twenty-nine sex murder case files Gallagher processed during his tenure in the Department of Justice, he recommended clemency for just two offenders, both of whom were teenagers.[32]

Petitions for mercy, presented by individuals or signed by numbers of concerned citizens, appeared in sex slayers' files, as they did in the files of others, but they were rarely persuasive. Although legal appeals delayed the final result, just nine of the sixty-one convicted sex killers were saved from the gallows by appellate court decisions (Table 1.3). For the remainder, the federal executive determined who might be spared. Defenders of these men, plus their advocates prepared to plead for clemency, swam against the tide of punitive sentiment. Homicides that involved child victims, torture, mutilation, or multiple victims were the most likely of sex murders to rouse merciless feelings.[33] Relatives of men sentenced to death and persons closely connected to them, including chaplains, sheriffs, and wardens, tried their best to humanize sex killers, sending letters that implored the executive to consider these convicts as flawed or mentally disturbed individuals, not incarnations of evil.[34] Religious believers could swing either way: for some, the extreme penalty was the only punishment adequate to demonstrate the sinfulness of murder; for others, God alone had power over life and death, and even the worst of criminals could be redeemed.[35] By the 1950s, prominent religious figures, mainly Jews and Protestants, became outspoken critics of the death penalty, and they added moral authority to secular abolitionists' portrayal of capital punishment as an outmoded penalty and ineffective deterrent.[36] Support for abolition broadened in Canadian society and spread within the major governing parties in the early 1960s, and executions became rare events.[37] Aside from Louis Fisher, the last man hanged for a sex murderer in 1961, men who would have been executed for these crimes in earlier decades were spared. The statutory suspension of the death penalty in 1967 merely formalized the government's de facto practice of universal clemency.

Approaching the Death Penalty

The "spectacle of the scaffold" has dominated academic and popular approaches to the death penalty's history.[38] This holds for Canada as well, where histories of capital punishment have taken aim at the myth of the "peaceable kingdom."[39] Yet, state violence was never absolute or uniform, and there was no point in Canadian history when everyone sentenced to death was executed. Discretionary justice lacks the drama of an execution, but the power executives held to determine who lived is no less critical to the analysis of capital justice.[40] In post-Confederation Canada, the administration of the death penalty was a drab remnant of the customs followed in pre-modern times, when kings and queens exercised the prerogative of mercy personally.[41] The sovereign's use of the pardon power dramatized his or her grace; it granted criminals facing execution their only hope of life. In the Dominion of Canada, mere commoners, elected to Parliament, determined the outcome of capital cases. Behind the doors of the cabinet chambers, ministers gathered around a large table, puffing tobacco and shuffling through papers as they considered capital cases amidst their other agenda items. Informed by the responsible minister (usually the minister of justice, sometimes the solicitor general), they reached a decision. Cabinet recommendations were then forwarded to the governor general, and once he approved, the government announced the capital offender's fate. The executive's review

Image 1.1 The members of Prime Minister William Lyon Mackenzie King's cabinet assembled around the table where they deliberated over capital cases and other ministerial business. LAC, C-009060.

of capital cases was opaque and unspectacular; however, bureaucratic discretion was every bit as consequential as it was in ancient times: a condemned criminal was about to live or die.

In Canada, as in other countries that kept capital punishment on the books until the late twentieth century, the policy of sentencing murderers to death jarred against the tenets of modern penal practice.[42] Most studies of punishment after the abolition of public hanging neglect the death penalty's retention, instead emphasizing the rise of discipline, correctionalism, and penal welfarism.[43] But these jarring practices and policies co-existed, creating discomfort for officials who administered criminal justice.[44] In public, the men who investigated, prosecuted, tried, and punished the crime of murder tried to dissociate themselves from their fellow Canadians who vented vengeful feelings toward murderers. During a debate on the death penalty's prospective abolition in 1924, the minister of justice, Ernest Lapointe, stated: "As far as my own personal feelings are concerned, by temperament and by instinct I would be inclined to vote for the bill, but from a high sense of duty I feel that I cannot do so, and that for the present we must retain capital punishment."[45] Recent work on emotions and criminal justice has prompted historians to challenge the impression that modern legal decision-making is characterized by cognitive reasoning.[46] Historians have no reason to presume that families and local communities found atrocious sex murders deeply disturbing, while uncritically taking judges, bureaucrats, and cabinet ministers at their word, based on their claims that they deliberated dispassionately.[47] Internal correspondence in capital case files shows that privately, at least, they were shocked and angered by sex murders.[48]

Abolishing the death penalty was a critical component in campaigns to resolve the discordant strains of modern punishment, and one of the most difficult challenges reformers faced was the problem of the sex killer. Abolitionists had always faced criticism that they were sentimentalists, coddling criminals, but starting in the early twentieth century, they fought back by promoting the promise of social and medical science.[49] If criminologists could prove that capital punishment was an ineffective deterrent, and if psychiatrists could unlock the mystery of criminal impulses, a civilized nation, such as Canada, could dispense with the death penalty. In the mid-twentieth century, the "psy" professions occupied a prominent place in the criminal justice system, but the role they played in decreasing faith in the death penalty is more complex than previous studies have suggested.[50] On the one hand, psychiatric evidence became a standard feature in capital trials and in post-conviction deliberations in the lead-up to abolition; on the other, the executive persisted in favouring psychiatric diagnoses that adhered to the legal concept of criminal responsibility. Over the 1950s and early 1960s, the government regularly called on Dr. John P.S. Cathcart to conduct post-conviction reviews in sex murder cases. In a magazine feature on his career, he told a reporter: "I'm a hard-boiled bird. Don't get any idea I'm a soft one."[51] The government's reliance on psychiatric expertise was less a mark of the profession's status and more a reflection of its effort to rationalize the growing number of cabinet commutations. The 1976 bill that abolished capital punishment – 130 votes for and 124 against – was a narrow legislative victory that papered over the division that remained in the public.[52] The law severed the death penalty from the Criminal Code, but most Canadians still believed that murderers, especially sex killers, could not be treated or reformed.

Capital Sex Murder: Patterns and Themes

The fate of each man sentenced to death for murder is documented in the Library and Archives Canada's repository of capital case files, preserved in boxes not far from the offices where Department of Justice clerks processed them and where cabinet ministers deliberated over the death sentence. Every person charged with murder was tried in a provincial or territorial criminal court, which meant that most decisions were made far from the places where murders had taken place. Rules of procedure, established in 1869 and codified in 1892, required judges in capital trials to send a report and transcript whenever they presided in a case that ended in conviction.[53] Cabinet members made their first decision about a condemned sex murderer in 1873. Joseph Auger's capital case file, like most from the early years of Confederation, is slim, containing a one-page report on the trial and sentence from the judge, a short handwritten summary of the trial, a petition from prominent citizens of Renfrew County, Ontario, and letters from two Catholic priests who pleaded for mercy. The judge commented that this trial was Auger's second one, the jury in the first having failed to reach a verdict. Against this possible reason for the executive to question his guilt, the crime – the rape, mutilation, and murder of an eighty-year-old woman – was unquestionably brutal. On 9 December 1873, the cabinet recommended that the law take its course, and Lord Dufferin, the vice regal, approved. Eighteen days later, the condemned man's execution augured the fate of almost two-thirds of convicted sex killers over the subsequent course of Canadian history.[54]

Over time, the contents of capital case files grew more voluminous and more varied. One reason was the growing length of murder trials, from one or two days in the nineteenth century, to several days in the early twentieth century, to a week or more in the mid-twentieth century. In 1950, Vancouverites were riveted for fifteen days as Blanche Fisher's accused killer (whom the judge later labelled a "psychopath of some description, with an inclination to sexual misbehaviour") stood trial.[55] In proceedings of this duration, transcripts run to hundreds of typed pages. Most files produced from the mid-twentieth century onward include crime scene photographs, coroners' reports, the mug shots and criminal records of the offender, plus his medical and psychiatric history. Another component, absent in earlier files, is correspondence concerning appeal court proceedings. The first appeal in a sex murder case (1908) was anomalous since it was filed by the trial judge. Certain that racial prejudice had led to an African American man's conviction, Justice Gordon Hunter referred the case to his brother judges on the Supreme Court of British Columbia.[56] In every subsequent appeal, lawyers acted for defendants, arguing that confessions were coerced, that pre-trial publicity prejudiced the jury, or that judges had misdirected jurors on circumstantial evidence or erred in admitting evidence. Few succeeded, as clerks in the Remission Branch invariably noted. Well before Dr. Cathcart's day, the government started to call for post-trial psychiatric examinations in sex murder case files. The first was ordered in 1914, after James Taylor's conviction for a murder of "fiendest cruelty," in which a boy had been subjected to an "unnatural offence."[57] In that instance, the examination was perfunctory, ordered at the last minute, and the psychiatrist's report was brief. By contrast, when cabinet ministers considered Louis Fisher's sentence in 1961, they reviewed four lengthy psychiatric reports, each presenting a different view of his sanity. Still, the outcome for both of these men was the same.

The number of sex murder capital cases occurred unevenly across Canadian post-Confederation history (Table 1.4). There were very few convictions for sex murders in the late nineteenth and early twentieth century, but a large cluster appeared in the 1940s and 1950s, when concern over "sex perverts" spiked. In the early years of Confederation, the state of criminal investigation was rudimentary, which made prosecutions of suspected sex murderers difficult, particularly in cases where the alleged perpetrator was a stranger to the victim. Criminal detection only became a branch of policing in the 1870s, and municipal forces (starting with Toronto) did not adopt fingerprinting until the early twentieth century.[58] Forensic analysis methods improved rapidly thereafter, particularly in Montreal, and dedicated laboratories in several other cities helped to identify suspects and analyse evidence by the 1920s.[59] Interprovincial police communications improved as well, and the establishment of the Royal Canadian Mounted Police (RCMP) and its national policing service made it easier to track down murder suspects who were drifters. Many of the convictions in the mid-twentieth-century cases were secured on the basis of shared information between police forces, nationally and internationally. Although criminal identification innovations multiplied and became more sophisticated over the twentieth century, few defenders of accused sex killers were able to capitalize on them or to contest the reliability of Crown evidence. Only one sex killer's conviction was overturned on the basis of questionable forensic evidence.

Table 1.4. Percentage of Sex Murder Convictions in Provinces and Provincial Percentage of Canada's Population (1871–1971)

Percentage (%) of Sex Murder Convictions in Provinces*								
Time Period	ON	QC	BC	AB	NS	MB	NB	NWT
1871–1971	46	11	16	5	3	7	10	1

Provincial Percentage (%) of Canada's Population by Decade								
Decade	ON	QC	BC	AB	NS	MB	NB	NWT
1971	36	28	10	8	4	5	3	.1
1961	34	28	9	7	4	5	3	.1
1951	33	29	8	7	5	6	4	.1
1941	33	29	7	7	5	6	4	.1
1931	33	28	7	7	5	7	4	.09
1921	34	27	6	7	6	7	4	.09
1911	35	28	5	5	7	6	5	.09
1901	41	31	3	1	9	5	6	.4
1891	44	31	2	n/a	9	3	7	2
1881	45	31	1	n/a	10	1	7	1
1871	44	32	1	n/a	11	1	8	1

*The Yukon Territory, Prince Edward Island, Saskatchewan, and Newfoundland are excluded, as no capital convictions for sex murder were recorded in these jurisdictions.
Source: Population figures adapted from Statistics Canada, Series A2-14, Population of Canada, by province, census dates, 1851 to 1976.

The profile of victims in cases of sex murder is both illuminating and deceptive. To presume that the total corresponds to the actual incidence of sex murder would defy decades of feminist criminological research on the under-reporting of sexual violence.[60] The 2019 report of the National Inquiry into Murdered and Missing Indigenous Women and Girls provides compelling evidence that many murders have gone undetected and killers have been allowed to go free as a result of racism and prejudice against victims marginalized by poverty, addiction, or homelessness.[61] Only three of the victims of convicted sex murderers were Indigenous women. Police, prosecutors, and jurors – all white, all men – were more inclined to treat men who murdered white victims as dangers to society, although people of European ancestry were the victims in seven of the sixty-one murders. Due to the lack of court records, it is not possible to track every sexual homicide in Canadian history prosecuted as manslaughter, murder trials that ended in convictions for manslaughter, or trials in which defendants were found not guilty by reason of insanity. And tragically, the number of unsolved sex murder cases is likely far greater than official records of uncleared homicide and missing persons cases will ever document.[62]

Men convicted of sex murders with child victims were reviled, and in some parts of the country, offences of this nature comprised the majority of capital cases.[63] Judges charged jurors to keep their emotions in check, but prosecutors routinely emphasized the depravity of child murders, many of which involved extreme bodily trauma. Courts in Quebec produced few sex murder convictions, but in that province, six of the seven cases concerned child victims, and the only adult victim was a woman raped and murdered by her father.[64] Four of those killings were attacks on boys, a factor that further alienated defendants from their communities.[65] In trials of alleged sex murderers, defence lawyers in all provinces tried to persuade jurors to find defendants guilty of manslaughter if the victim was a teenager or a woman, especially if she had been drinking or consorting with strangers. Yet, outside of Quebec, there were numerous cases in which jurors found defendants guilty of murdering adult women. In Ontario, the province that produced the most convictions, women were the victims in sixteen of the twenty-eight cases.[66] The province's urban and provincial police forces were large and comparatively well resourced, and its Attorney General's Department had a stable of nation-leading prosecutors, who may have presented more convincing evidence to jurors.[67] In British Columbia, the story was different. The number of convictions in that province also outstripped its population, although only by the late 1940s. At that juncture, British Columbia and Ontario were both centres of agitation over the prevalence of sex "perverts."[68] In that province as well, the number of adult victims – two of ten – was low. Across Canada, child slayings constituted the majority of sex murder convictions by the mid-twentieth century, when jurors came to consider that men who killed and sexually abused children were the most reprehensible of criminals. Unless those perpetrators were also youths, the cabinet concurred (Table 1.5).[69]

The executive was not aloof from the public's disgust toward sex murderers; if they were in any doubt, the newspaper clippings, which clerks pasted into case files, provided further evidence.[70] Canadians followed crime news primarily through print media, even after radio coverage began in the 1920s and television news started up in the 1950s.[71] Canadian wire services transmitted accounts of sex murders from coast to coast, turning local traumas into national headlines. In the late

Table 1.5. Sex Murder Case Outcomes by Age of Offender and Victim

Offender and Victim Age Categories*	Executed (n)	Not Executed** (n)	Execution Rate (%)
Child Victim	21	15	58.3
Adult Victim	18	7	72.0
Youth Offender	2	8	25.0
Adult Offender	37	14	72.5

*Youth defined as under twenty-one years of age; child defined as sixteen years of age and under. See Reflection on Sources and Methods for full analysis.
** Includes successful appeals and commutations.
Source: Lorraine Gadoury and Antonio Lechasseur, *Persons Sentenced to Death in Canada, 1867–1976: An Inventory of Case Files in the Fonds of the Department of Justice* (Ottawa: National Archives of Canada, 1994).

nineteenth century, the "Jack the Ripper" murders transformed the murderous mutilation of women into front-page fodder in England, but in Canada a code of propriety cloaked reportage.[72] Editors found ways to identify sex murders without being explicit. In 1896, the rape-murder of fourteen-year-old Annie Kempton in Bear River, Nova Scotia, was clarified by remarks that she had died "defending her honour."[73] When the body of eight-year-old Phillip Goldberg, his throat slashed, was discovered in Toronto's High Park in 1920, the Toronto *Daily Star* surmised that he must have been the "VICTIM OF MANIAC?," and the only hint that the killer had sodomized the boy came through the subtitle: "Police Believe Lad Was Done to Death Following Assault."[74] Press restraint loosened over the 1940s, when mainstream magazines published exposés on sexual psychopaths, scandal sheets dwelled on sex crime cases, and Canadian true crime magazines covered local sex murders. In Quebec, the racy Montreal weekly, *Allô Police*, delivered on its promise to publish the absolute truth.[75] Readers who opened the 8 August 1954 edition were confronted with images of Raymond Trudeau's dismembered body parts. The black and white reproductions did nothing to reduce the emotional impact of the eight-year-old's murder or the public's expectation that the man identified as his killer would be put to death. Defence lawyers regularly complained about the prejudicial nature of pre-trial publicity, but no appeal on those grounds was successful.

The rush to judgment and the compulsion to punish are evident in many of these cases, but just one wrongful conviction of a sex murderer sentenced to death has been confirmed – Steven Truscott's.[76] Convicted of the rape-murder of Lynne Harper in 1959, granted clemency and sentenced to life in prison in 1960, and released on parole in 1967, he was finally exonerated in 2007 when the Ontario Court of Appeal quashed his conviction and named it a miscarriage of justice.[77] Little is known about other accused sex slayers who were convicted under equally, if not more dubious circumstances. Most defendants had court-appointed lawyers who lacked the skill, time, or resources to raise reasonable doubt or to mount an insanity defence; several defendants were unable to comprehend the proceedings or instruct counsel; and three men, each of them white, were convicted and executed after trials without a lawyer to defend them. Yet, some public pariahs were saved from the hangman (and, in several cases, near lynchings), thanks to lawyers committed to the principle that every accused individual, no matter how loathsome his alleged crime, deserves the strongest possible defence against the prospect of execution. Sex murderers incited disgust and anger but also, occasionally, compassion.[78]

Sex Murder and the Death Penalty from Confederation to Abolition and the Legacy of Their Entanglement

Several of the sex murder cases in post-Confederation Canada have appeared in earlier works, most notably Truscott's; however, this study is the first to consider all sixty-one across the period when murder remained punishable by death[79] (Table 1.6). The chapters that follow weave these disturbing stories into the aforementioned patterns and themes to illuminate the death penalty's politics and the problem of sex murder. Each chapter focuses on a period distinguished by the incidence of sex murder convictions; the administration and administrators of capital justice; shifting legal, expert, and popular perceptions of sexual deviancy; the expansion of criminal appeal provisions; the holding of major crime and justice inquiries; and the legislative and political battles against and in favour of capital punishment.

In the first decade of Confederation, the majority of capital sex cases concerned the crimes of rape and carnal knowledge (sex with girls under the age of ten). None of the twenty-six men sentenced to death for these offences was executed, and the federal government decided in the mid-1870s to do away with a mandatory penalty that was never carried out.[80] By contrast, just two men convicted of murders involving sexual violence in the late nineteenth and early twentieth century, both white, received commuted sentences. Chapter two focuses on this

Table 1.6. Sex Murder Cases and Outcomes by Period

Period*	Sex Murder Convictions (n)	Executed (n)	Commuted (n)	Successful Appeals** (n)
1873–1914	13	11	2	0
1921–1942	12	8	0	4
1945–1952	17	11	2	4
1953–1959	10	8	2	0
1960–1966	9	1	7	1
Totals	**61**	**39**	**13**	**9**

*Gaps in years covered in the chapters correspond to periods in which no convictions for sex murder occurred.
**Appeals that resulted in verdicts set aside (new trial ordered and non-capital conviction or acquittal); verdicts quashed and new trial not proceeded; acquittal entered.
Source: Lorraine Gadoury and Antonio Lechasseur, *Persons Sentenced to Death in Canada, 1867–1976: An Inventory of Case Files in the Fonds of the Department of Justice* (Ottawa: National Archives of Canada, 1994).

period, when Augustus Power, following the system of capital case protocol established by Hewitt Bernard, processed the majority of the files concerning sex murders. Although his commentary maintained a tradition of stern moral judgment, which the executive followed, new approaches to sexual deviance and homicidal violence were emerging. Findings from the fields of psychiatry, sexology, and criminal anthropology appear in files by the late nineteenth century, as do newspaper clippings on the study of "sex fiends." Canadian coverage of the "Ripper" murders familiarized readers with terms such as "sexual sadism" and "sexual degeneracy," and accounts of several local sex murder cases referred to the work of international sexologists.[81] Yet, the condemnatory approach that Power and his successors took in summarizing sex murder cases held firm before the Great War. The judge's opinion of the defendant's culpability remained the reference point in memoranda, and cabinet ministers carried the M'Naghten rule into their deliberations, despite the unfettered nature of executive clemency.[82] Resistant to the possibility that sex slayers might be mentally ill or incapable of resisting psychological impulses, clerks and cabinet ministers also defaulted to ethnocentric and racist readings of culpability. When they viewed files of Anglo-Celtic men convicted of sexual murders, they approached them on an individual basis, but when it came to the others (in this period, Indigenous, black, Mauritian, and French Canadian), race-based notions of criminality prevailed. Despite the attribution of homicidal sexual violence to the proclivities of "lower races," identified as such in transcripts, judges' reports, and official memoranda, these characterizations did not translate into justifications for clemency.[83] In the elite white executive's eyes, the monstrosity of those sex killers made it imperative that their sentences be carried out.

In the interwar years, the rate at which convicted sex killers were executed dropped off, but this trend had to do with new rules concerning criminal appeals, not squeamishness toward the death penalty or the executive's receptivity to mental disorders as mitigating factors. Chapter three examines the impact of the legislation that reduced impediments against appeals. Prior to the 1920s, no defence lawyer filed an appeal after his client was sentenced to death for sex murder, although several were convinced that guilty verdicts were unjust. The Criminal Code of 1892 required that the trial judge reserve questions for the Court of Appeal concerning the conduct of the trial.[84] Not surprisingly, judges were indisposed to grant requests from defence counsel who challenged decisions from the bench – to admit or exclude evidence, to charge the jury on the distinction between murder and manslaughter, or to explain the defence of insanity. After the 1920s, the intent to appeal could be filed directly to courts of appeal on matters of fact as well as law. Out of twelve men convicted of sex murders from 1921 to 1942, eight filed appeals and half were successful. Not one was based on the defence of insanity or its interpretation, however. In some cases, evidence of prior treatment for sexual psychopathy or records of brain trauma from injury or war wounds resurfaced in clemency bids if appeals failed, as well as those in which no appeal was filed. But when pleas based on evidence of this ilk reached Michael Gallagher's desk, the chief clerk reached for his red pencil. At a point when criminal investigative bureaus and forensic laboratories were replacing the heroic lone detective of the nineteenth century, Gallagher and the cabinets he served considered that form of expertise more reliable than psychological understandings of abnormalities.[85] Nevertheless, two of the successful appeals challenged the reliability of forensic evidence, and one of them led to the exposure of a significant miscarriage of justice in the prosecution of a Catholic brother for the sex murder of a girl in Montreal in 1931. After the man was retried and acquitted in 1931, allegations of anti-clericalism and prosecutorial malfeasance surfaced.

The subsequent prosecution of the chief witness against the brother as the true killer fuelled further controversy, eclipsing the original tragedy.

In the mid-1940s, a spike in the number of convictions for sex murder occurred in Canada at a time when parents' groups and civic organizations urged the government to devise policies to fight the problem of sex crime. Pressed to act, Parliament introduced legislation that subjected persons who exhibited a pattern of sexual offending, and who appeared unable to stem their impulses, to indeterminate detention. The lobbying efforts that led to the passage of the criminal sexual psychopath law of 1948 signalled that the concept of sexual psychopathy had become part of public discourse and policy. Chapter four examines the impact of this post-war atmosphere on the fate of the seventeen men sentenced to death for sex murders between 1945 and 1952. This period was a time when reformers, including future prime minister John Diefenbaker, anticipated that experts were close to being able to detect and treat sexual disorders that might lead to homicide. But retributivism prevailed, as government-ordered public opinion polls confirmed.[86] The hard-line Michael Gallagher remained head clerk over that period, and he worked closely with his counterparts in "Indian Affairs" to ensure the death penalty's administration cohered with the government's "civilizing" mission.[87] Although courts of appeal continued to offer hope to the condemned (four men sentenced to death for sex murders filed successful appeals), only two of the other thirteen condemned men were granted commuted sentences in this period. In these cases, even Gallagher was moved to recommend clemency for teenagers; however, neither the chief clerk nor cabinet ministers were willing to spare men previously hospitalized for mental illness, Indigenous men prosecuted by authorities who failed to follow basic protocol, or defendants who were represented by incompetent counsel.

Although the federal government sponsored a series of inquiries into the nature of crime and the purpose of punishment in the 1950s, they played a minor part in turning the executive away from severity toward sex murderers. Chapter five shows how cabinets that reviewed the sentences of men convicted of these crimes in this period were unswayed by abolitionist stirrings, despite some ministers' personal convictions. Between 1953 and 1959, eleven males were executed for sex slayings, and the two whose sentences were commuted were youths. Prior to the 1950s, one federal inquiry into capital punishment was conducted in 1937, when parliamentarians contemplated a range of alternatives to hanging (electrocution and gas were the prime contenders).[88] Although the custom of death by rope was preserved, the government appointed another group of parliamentarians in 1953, a Special Joint Committee of the House and Senate, to consider whether Canada might abolish the death penalty. Several members of Parliament (MPs), mainly from the Co-operative Commonwealth Federation (CCF) and a handful from the major parties, introduced private member's abolition bills after the committee recommended that capital punishment be retained.[89] Two further government inquiries in this period – one concerning the insanity defence and the other struck to review the country's criminal sexual psychopath law – suggested the government was prepared to consider granting medical and psychiatric expertise greater authority in guiding its policies toward all persons who committed acts of sexual violence. However, the psychiatrists whom the Department of Justice relied upon in capital case reviews persisted in pronouncing men convicted of sex murders as sane within the definition of the law, including men who sexually assaulted and tortured young children. The election of John Diefenbaker's Progressive Conservatives in 1957 brought a former criminal defence lawyer with misgivings over the death penalty to head cabinet meetings, but this changing of the guard left the executive's harsh approach to sex killers in place.[90] Until 1960, men who committed sex murders continued to be executed at a disproportionately high rate.

Sex murder cases were not just determined by the death penalty's administration; by the 1960s, they also shaped it. Trials of sex murderers in the early 1960s occurred as the federal government made its haltered way toward partial abolition. The anger and disgust that sex slayings had always stirred found a new target: the federal executive, which commuted sentences in case after revolting case. Within the cabinet, abolitionists argued against supporters of the death penalty, and minutes of their meetings provide accounts of their skirmishes. These records (called "Cabinet Conclusions") show that ministers were troubled by the scrutiny their decisions attracted. They also reveal the ministers' growing discomfort over capital punishment.[91] Chapter six draws on these records to show how the public's reaction to several controversial commutations of sex killers' sentences prompted the Conservative government to introduce degrees of murder in 1961 (with the mandatory penalty of death applying only to "capital murder") and to pare back the discretionary powers of the Parole Board. Commutations in two sex murder cases involving child victims – Léopold Dion's in 1963 and Kenneth Meeker's in 1964 – put the new Liberal government under a burning spotlight. Dion's prior record for rape exposed the ineffectiveness of Canada's criminal sexual psychopath law, which neither reformed sex offenders nor prevented their release on parole. These widely condemned commutations added further pressure on the government: if it proposed to incarcerate sex killers rather than execute them, could the penal system be trusted? Several provincial leaders, especially in Quebec, denounced Ottawa's federal parole system and the Parole Board's unhampered discretion. The government responded by eroding the right of prisoners serving commuted death sentences to apply for parole, a concession granted to prop up sinking confidence in public security. The second concession – to restrict the death penalty in 1967 to murders of guards and police officers – occurred over the objection of some politicians, who felt that sex murders were more serious. It took journalist Isabel LeBourdais's well-timed exposé of the questionable police practices and local prejudices that led to Steven Truscott's conviction to convince a critical mass of parliamentarians to pass the legislation. Whether or not they cared to admit it, the legal titans who led the abolitionist movement knew that, without this woman's book, the powerful police lobby and retentionist politicians may well have carried the day.

Over the nine years between the first partial moratorium and capital punishment's formal abolition in 1976, no other convicted sex murderer confronted what the sixty-one men before them had faced: the strong likelihood of dying on the gallows.[92] Pressure to reinstate the death penalty continued to roll in waves, many of them set off by sex murders. The epilogue traces how public anger over these crimes has led to demands that the government hold referenda on capital punishment and reinstate the death penalty. Thus far these calls have been unheeded, although they have inspired legislation that has increased the penalties for sex offenders and denied the hope of early release for persons serving life sentences. Abolition is not set in stone: at any point, the statute that abolished the death penalty could be amended. Accordingly, this book on the past is a cautionary tale for today and the future.

2

Sex Fiends and the Death Penalty at the Turn of Canada's Century

As Canada's Century dawned, Sir John A. Macdonald's National Policy gave way to Prime Minister Wilfrid Laurier's bold effort to populate a polity with the capacity to make the most of the country's resources.[1] Nation planners encouraged immigrants from Britain and Europe to settle and solidify the white Dominion; simultaneously, the federal government imposed head taxes on Chinese immigrants and rejected African Americans on "climate" grounds.[2] Consolidating the white Dominion was the objective that led to the carving up of Indigenous lands and the paternalistic regulation of First Nations peoples through the administration of reservations, all part of a program of assimilation.[3] But not without opposition. In the Northwest, resistance took the form of uprisings, which were suppressed by military force and followed by the use of capital punishment.[4] Despite an attempted insanity defence and post-conviction campaigns for clemency, principally from Quebeckers and French Catholics, Métis leader Louis Riel was executed in 1885 for treason and eight Cree men were hanged for murder before a crowd corralled by the victors.[5] The politics of executive discretion were stripped bare at that sharp point of central Canadian imperialism. Yet, every time the prime minister and his cabinet met to determine whether the law should take its course, they exercised sovereign power, authorized by the governor general.

In the late nineteenth and early twentieth century, men convicted of sex murders stood little chance of escaping the gallows. Between 1873 and 1914, thirteen men were condemned to death for sex murders, and the executive, advised by the chief clerk in the Remission Branch of the Department of Justice, recommended that eleven of them serve their sentence.[6] The only two granted clemency were co-accused Anglo-Celtics wealthy enough to hire a topnotch lawyer, who used his influence to secure their early release from their life sentences. White privilege and high social station were signal advantages in the executive discretion stakes, but First Nations peoples and the "strangers" allowed within the white Dominion's "gates" were not the only people subject to injustice in capital case reviews.[7] The men who were hanged (seven of whom were white) were all outsiders – regarded as such through the politics of class, gender, ethnicity, race, and national origin, but also through moral disgust over their crimes.[8]

This period saw the emergence of psychiatric readings of violence and deviant sexual behaviour, distinct from religious-based notions of evil and from the prevailing legal definition of insanity. Defined in 1843, the M'Naghten rule affirmed that every defendant was sane unless the defence could convince a jury that the accused person's reasoning at the time of the offence was defective. If the jury decided that imbecility or a disease of the mind had rendered a defendant incapable of knowing the nature and quality of the act, or its wrongfulness, they could reach a verdict of not guilty by reason of insanity.[9] However, some psychiatrists and sexologists argued that the law's organic and cognitive definition of insanity failed to take uncontrollable impulses into account. Psychopathy (literally, sick mind) and sadism could drive individuals to commit heinous acts of sexual violence without making a person insane under the law.[10] In sex murder trials, judges instructed juries to discount such diagnoses, even in cases where homicides involved gross mutilations and sexual acts carried out on dead bodies. The executive and the experts they consulted were equally dismissive. If jurors agreed that a sex murderer was sane, and if the judge considered the verdict sound, the law took its course.

The possibility to alter the fate of a condemned offender through the courts increased in 1892, when the Criminal Code allowed appeals "on the ground that the verdict was against the weight of evidence" or because the minister of justice "doubt[ed] whether such person ought to have been convicted." However, requests from the defence to reserve questions of law for the consideration of courts of appeal and applications to file appeals in sex murder cases were unsuccessful in the pre-war period. The first such attempt occurred in 1895, when a lawyer tried to save a French Canadian man, Almeda Chattelle, accused of a grotesque child murder in southwestern Ontario. During his trial, the defendant had refused representation and rambled incoherently throughout the proceedings, but the judge refused to consider any ground on which to question the verdict.[11] Joseph Bennett benefitted from an unusually robust defence, represented by a King's Counsel (KC). Ironically, because the accused sex murderer was a "status Indian" (and consequently a "ward" of the state), the Department of Indian Affairs funded his defence.[12] Bennett's barrister challenged the Crown at every turn, called alibi witnesses, and raised reasonable doubt. After the trial, he filed an appeal pro bono, charging that the evidence did not support the verdict. He failed. The only appeal initiated by a trial judge also failed. In 1908, the chief justice of British Columbia stated a case for appeal because he believed that prejudicial witness identification led to the conviction of James Jenkins, an African American man. The Supreme Court of British Columbia decided that the jury's decision was more reliable than the judge's belief.

When petitioners attempted to save men condemned for sex murders, most took the conventional route: they wrote and wired the executive, pleading for mercy. Both Bennett's and Chattelle's lawyers petitioned after their appeals failed, joining the cue of supplicants. Most requests for clemency highlighted the difficulties that hampered the defence, primarily lack of time to prepare and insufficient funds to hire experts. Since it was so difficult to marshal experts after the countdown to execution began, defence lawyers typically repeated what they had asked jurors: surely none but a "maniac" could commit such a crime?[13] The chief clerks and the cabinet swept that question aside until 1914, when the lawyer for James Taylor presented evidence that persuaded the Department of Justice to hire a psychiatrist to examine the man, convicted of sodomizing and murdering a young boy near Brantford, Ontario.[14] Following the legal definition of insanity, based on the M'Naghten rule, the psychiatrist pronounced the man sane. Taylor was a "degenerate," the expert thought, but that did not amount to insanity. With this assurance, petitions for clemency fell on deaf ears.

Occasionally, editorials raised the possibility that offenders were not criminally responsible on the basis of mental abnormalities, but on balance, the legitimacy of convictions in sex murder cases was unquestioned. In the late nineteenth century, Canadian press coverage of the crimes attributed to "Jack the Ripper" led to heightened coverage of local sex murders, particularly in the metropolitan press.[15] Reporters scrambled for scoops on grisly murders, spinning stories of frantic searches and the nail-biting capture of suspects. News editors rarely questioned the police or their tactics: as soon as detectives had "their man," they pronounced the suspect guilty.[16] In Canada's white-owned newspapers, men of unconventional appearance or habits and those whose racial, ethnic, or religious characteristics diverged from the Anglo-Celtic norm were shaped into monsters and fiends. Catholic French Canadians accused of killing English Protestants were also considered outsiders. In the aftermath of Chattelle's execution, a journalist pronounced it proper to "sacrifice" doomed sex killers "on the altar of outraged decency."[17] The newspaper clippings Department of Justice clerks pasted into the capital case files for cabinet members' consideration document their concern to monitor public opinion. In the late nineteenth and early twentieth century, internal memoranda, judges' reports, the findings of medical men, and the headlines in Canada's newspapers all supported an unstated policy of stark moral judgment of killers whose crimes involved sexual violence.

The Administration and Administrators of Executive Discretion

The first man to put his stamp on the Department of Justice's processing of capital case files was Prime Minister John A. Macdonald's trusted former secretary and brother-in-law, Hewitt Bernard.[18] The second man in the post did not bear the title of "Deputy Minister," as Bernard did, but Augustus Power's duties were greater.[19] As head clerk, he headed the Remission Branch, which was responsible for processing requests for releases from federal penitentiaries as new institutions were added over the 1870s. The passage of the Ticket of Leave Act in 1899 (governing federal prisoners) added responsibility for processing parole applications.[20] The Dominion Police, another branch of the federal Department of Justice, assisted Power's staff by providing information on convicts' backgrounds.[21] Amidst his myriad duties, the chief clerk had the special job of communicating with judges and petitioners as well as the minister to whom he reported. In every capital case file Power processed, evidence of his work remains. He reviewed all the material that ended up in case files, digested it, and wrote a summary, which, more often than not, included his own view on the prospect of clemency.[22]

Power cued the cabinet's reading of capital cases through his typology of condemned criminals and their crimes: some murders were inspired

Image 2.1 The Privy Council Chambers (c. 1886), the epicentre of executive discretion as it appeared during Augustus Power's tenure as chief clerk. LAC, MIKAN 3192916.

by revenge or jealousy; others were motivated by the expectation of gain; there were also spousal killings, and murders sparked by rivalry. These classifications distilled the unique features of individuals, relationships, and crimes into tales of guilt and desert. If offenders and victims were Anglo-Celtic, Power's memoranda never mentioned race, although they sometime referred to ethnicity. By contrast, he never failed to make note of Indigenous and black condemned men, as well as offenders originally from eastern or southern Europe.[23] Power was not unusually prejudiced or intolerant. In turn-of-the-century white Canada, his attitudes were consistent with the views of the political leadership of his day. In many instances, he was less overtly racist than the judges who passed the sentence of death in sex murder cases.[24] However, as chief clerk he was in a unique position to influence executive discretion through his advice and emotive descriptions. The men who served in cabinet over the late nineteenth and early twentieth century shared Power's disgust and his ethnocentrism.

Clemency and Insider Status

Just prior to August Power's appointment as head clerk, the executive granted clemency to two co-accused sex killers. It was an unusual case on multiple levels, starting with the fact that the victim, Mrs. Ellen Bennett of Whitby, Ontario, a small town east of Toronto, lived long enough to give a dying declaration. She stated that two local men, Thomas Burk and John McPherson, were the assailants who broke into her home while her husband was away in July 1877. After they covered her mouth and nose, she passed out, but she recalled hearing one of them say: "Never mind, she had two young ones before she was married, and she can stand two men well enough." When she came to, she discovered her night dress pushed up and "considerable blood over my bed and bed clothes." Two weeks after Mrs. Bennett described the assault, she succumbed to cellulitis, a bacterial infection cause by the assault, according to the Crown.[25] Under the prevailing definition of culpable homicide, the jury could find the pair guilty of murder if the prosecution could establish a direct link between the sexual assault and the victim's death.[26]

As the son of a respectable and well-off farmer, McPherson and his labourer friend likely expected the men of the jury to acquit them, especially because it was so dark that Mrs. Bennett could identify the men only by their voices. There were no witnesses to corroborate her account. And she died a full fortnight after the alleged attack. However, once the woman's ante mortem statement was ruled admissible, it could not be challenged. The judge, Chief Justice Robert Harrison, was most emphatic on this point in his charge to the jury. The victim had suffered an alarming assault and a painful death, he reminded them, and they must keep in mind the violence done to her body: "You have in her testimony the fact of an outrage having been committed upon her of a most diabolical character … treated by two men in a manner worthy of demons, and the result of that treatment was her death." After he briefly reviewed the evidence for the defence, Justice Harrison reiterated that the defendants were accused of an "outrage … of a serious and aggravated character."[27] In the trial report he sent to Ottawa after their conviction, Harrison maintained this stern posture. Although he noted that the jury had attached a recommendation to mercy, Harrison stressed he did not share the jurors' sentiment. The judge could not have sent a clearer message to the executive: he saw no reason for "not carrying the sentence of the court into effect."[28]

The Canadian cabinet rarely deviated from judicial advice in capital cases, but in this instance a formidable defence lawyer made the difference. Mr. McPherson Senior, whom the Whitby *Chronicle* described as a "well-to-do farmer," may have had to mortgage his assets to hire the best legal talent money could buy, but his investment in Matthew Crooks Cameron was astute. An outstanding legal mind and courtroom performer, Cameron had appeared for the defence in the 1868 trial of Patrick J. Whelan for the murder of politician D'Arcy McGee. Although the convicted assassin was executed, the case provided Cameron with a crash course in the management of high-profile capital cases and the ways he might approach post-trial petitioning.[29]

In this murder trial, Cameron chose the tactic defence lawyers used regularly in rape cases – discredit the reputation of the alleged victim and cast doubt on the motives of her relatives, in this case, the victim's father and husband.[30] But the jury found the Crown's evidence persuasive. Convinced that the conviction was a travesty, Cameron did not file an appeal. Instead, he complained to Zebulon Lash (the deputy minister and the man who had briefly served as the Department of Justice's chief clerk before Power took over in 1879).[31] Speaking as if he were lodging an appeal, Cameron said he was of the "strongest opinion the conviction was wrong, the evidence being insufficient to establish the alleged crime of rape resulting in [the] death of [the] deceased." In the 1870s, the only way to appeal a verdict legally was to file through the Judicial Committee of the Privy Council, so the experienced barrister chose an alternative strategy that relied on his stature within the profession. At the same time, Cameron's appeal, although personal, anticipated the reforms that would be introduced in the Criminal Code, which allowed the minister of justice to reconsider the legitimacy of the jury's verdict.[32]

Cameron's intervention may also have induced the judge to reflect on the evidence that had sealed the men's conviction. After Justice Harrison submitted his trial report, he received a letter from the Office of the Secretary of State (the department that handled administrative matters for the governor general) to remind him that a copy of the trial transcript was required as well. This approach led the judge to reassess the medical evidence.[33] In addition, rumours had begun to swirl, alleging that Crown witnesses had committed perjury and that the victim was not as virtuous as her family claimed. Harrison still believed the defendants had raped Mrs. Bennett, but now he wondered if perhaps she had died of natural causes. In an irregular move, the judge submitted a second report with an altered recommendation: "The demands of Justice will be sufficiently met by the imprisonment of the convicts for life."[34]

McPherson and Burk's term of imprisonment turned out to be much shorter, thanks, again, to Cameron. Shortly after the murder trial, Cameron was elevated to the provincial Court of Queen's Bench, and his new status lent additional authority to his request for further clemency.[35] Now a judge, Cameron contacted the new minister of justice, fellow Conservative James McDonald, to familiarize him with the case. It was certain that "somebody" had visited the woman on the night in question, but Cameron thought it doubtful that the encounter "was of the character alleged." He then circled back to the allegation that the victim was on "intimate terms" with men other than her husband. The verdict, Cameron concluded, was "surprising" for what amounted to an "alleged murder." The wealthy McPherson family was anxious that their son be released after two years in prison, but Justice Cameron made it clear that neither man should remain in prison: "I shall be glad to see the prisoners receive the Royal Clemency."[36] Several months later, the minister of justice obliged, and his recommendation strongly suggested that this action would remedy a miscarriage of justice: "The sentence of imprisonment for life cannot justly be sustained and I recommend that the prisoner be ~~discharged~~ pardoned."[37] Freed from the Kingston Penitentiary late in March 1881, McPherson and his mate returned to society after they had served less than three years for murder.[38]

None of the other eleven men sentenced to death for sex murder in the late nineteenth and early twentieth century (or indeed, over the entire period when the death penalty was in effect) had the finances, social capital, or community support that aided the two convicts in the Whitby case, and only a few were represented by a lawyer of Cameron's acumen. The judge's misgivings, possibly under political pressure, were also singular. And normally, the chief clerk emphasized a judge's disinclination to recommend mercy, as occurred after the convictions of the other eleven men tried for sex murders in this period.

"A Tramp Suspected": Outsiders and Outrage

Harshness toward racial and ethnic outsiders in the Anglo-Celtic–dominated white Dominion is evident in the profile of the men executed for sex murders in the early decades of Confederation.[39] Yet, to isolate racism as the root cause of severity in sex murder cases discounts the emotions that added force to the belief that these sex murderers deserved death. The age, respectability, and social status of the victim also informed impressions of the offender's blameworthiness. In the other cases, all but one of the victims were girls or elderly or feeble women.[40] By contrast, scurrilous rumours about Ellen Bennett's reputation made their way from Whitby's taverns to the cabinet chambers through a chain of correspondence between men. Jurors, judges, and cabinet ministers appraised the character of accused sex murderers, their reputation and prior offences, and the nature of the violence they were accused of inflicting.[41] With the exception of one woman, every victim was white, a fact that suggests that police and prosecutors took crimes against non-whites less seriously. But whiteness did not equate automatically to respectability or credibility, as the Bennett case showed. Outsiders of all types – including five Anglo-Celtic men in this period – were most vulnerable to arrest, prosecution, conviction, and execution when murders roused grief and anger. On several occasions, sex murders roiled communities and stirred the impulse to lynch. Although the men who appraised capital cases sat at desks far away from these volatile scenes, the bureaucrats who bent over documents in the tweedy atmosphere of the Department of Justice and the ministers who assembled in the smoke-filled Privy Council Chambers to render decision were not immune to feelings of disgust and outrage.

Five of the men executed in the late nineteenth and early twentieth century had no family ties to the locales where the offence took place, and their rootlessness robbed them of the resources that helped save even the poorest of men condemned to death. They were men on the move, seeking employment on farms and in forests and coal mines. The economic forces and racial discrimination that perpetuated and fostered inequality meant that men without steady work or stable homes were readily identified as suspects. The most marginal were men whom the press described as "tramps," a figure strongly associated with criminality and defiance of social responsibility in the late nineteenth century.[42] Once arrested and convicted, drifters became special objects of fear and loathing, not pity, in the eyes of the public and in the deliberations of the cabinet.[43]

Concern over the mobility of criminals was one of the reasons why municipal authorities professionalized police forces in the mid-nineteenth century.[44] Working with the country's expanding network of penitentiaries and reformatories after Confederation, police looked for more effective ways to identify habitual criminals through the use of photography and the description and measurement of bodies.

By cataloguing the skin, eye, and hair colour of arrestees, along with their height, weight, scars, and tattoos, they sought to fix and sort an unstable population of people, mainly shiftless and shadowy men. The Dominion Police Force, which operated as an investigative arm of the federal government, combined in 1873 with the Royal Northwest Mounted Police, whose activities focused on the frontiers of white settlement; these police organizations shared with the provincial police forces this ambition of tracking down the shiftless. These new layers of policing, densest in Ontario, augmented the Crown's capacity to gather the evidence necessary to pin responsibility for sex murders and to convince the executive that the weight of that evidence sustained the verdict of guilt.[45]

Each of the men executed for sex murder around the turn of the century lived in impoverished circumstances, and some also had records of drunkenness, quarrelsomeness, or petty crimes. But one defendant stood out as a prototypical tramp: Almeda Chattelle. When he was captured, the Toronto *Daily Mail*'s 20 October 1894 edition introduced its story of the "outrage and murder" of a white farm girl in southwestern Ontario with the headline, "A FIEND'S CRIME: A Tramp Suspected."[46] The blamelessness of the victim – fourteen-year-old Jessie Keith – enraged her Anglo-Celtic community, leaving the entire district with the sense that it had suffered an undignified assault.[47] With the aid of a provincial detective, an arrest was made, giving the community a target for their rage. Months later, when the official reports concerning the crime and Chattelle's conviction, plus a handful of appeals for clemency, appeared on Augustus Power's desk, he could find no "reason for interference with the due course of the law," despite considerable evidence in the transcript that the condemned man was likely insane and that he had been denied a fair trial.[48]

The nature of the injuries inflicted on Jessie Keith would have been grotesque and shocking in any era, but the girl's murder occurred in the autumn of 1894, several years after a series of mutilation murders that claimed the lives of at least five women in London's East End.[49] Although these murders occurred an ocean away from Canada, the transatlantic cable system, in place by the 1870s, allowed Canadian readers to keep up with the latest stories and images. The Metropolitan Police's inability to capture the man or men responsible for these murders kept interest in the case alive and speculation rife.[50] The culprit, colloquially known as "Jack the Ripper," was possibly still at large, but where in the world was he? Had he escaped to Canada and taken up his horrible craft? As soon as the nature of Keith's injuries became known, Canadian reporters connected her murder to the Ripper's crimes and circulated the theory that the killer was either the mysterious man or a criminal inspired by the London murderer.[51]

The victim in this case was set upon while she was out walking, but she was nothing like the destitute East Enders whom "Jack" preyed upon. Jessie Keith left her modest farmhouse on a warm October day to conduct an errand in town, and her failure to return led to a search that ended with a ghastly discovery: the girl, naked aside from a petticoat tied around her neck, had deep gashes to her neck, and her internal organs were missing. These violations were alarming yet familiar to newspaper readers: "The crime stands quite on a par with the hideous Whitechapel murders, inasmuch as the body was so grossly mutilated, doubtless after the commission of an outrage."[52] Further exploration of fields where searchers had come upon Keith's body turned up her clothing and her "private parts," gouged from her body.[53] Reports from several witnesses of a suspicious character in the district led police to telegraph posters across the country and to US authorities. Without a clear suspect, newspapers noted that "plusieurs vagabonds ont été arrêtés" and that a sweep of "presque tous les gueux" (tramps) had been conducted to "trouver l'auteur de ce crime affreux."[54] Local police questioned several tramps, but they released them all. Then provincial detective John Wilson Murray took over the search, and with his help Chattelle was arrested and indicted.[55]

From the moment of Chattelle's apprehension his execution was expected. Indeed, it was demanded. An editorial in the Toronto *Daily Mail* commended the use of provincial resources to capture a killer worse than Frankenstein's monster, "the most frightful fiend [Shelley's] mind could put in human shape." If Chattelle was a monstrous madman, and therefore of "unsound mind," it was possible he would be spared prosecution. But authorities were anxious to see the man put on trial for murder and convicted, lest the "vengeance of the mob" enact a "barbarous way of dealing out justice." The only way to restrain these "avengers," a Toronto paper advised, was "to punish the culprit."[56] Canadians prided themselves on their restraint and their trust in the legal system, but both crumbled once Chattelle was identified. Even after his conviction, the threat of mob violence remained, pressuring the executive to deny clemency.

Canadian newspapers reported on lynchings far more frequently than they covered sex murders, and they came across those stories from

6 O'CLOCK EDITION

THE EVENING NEWS.

CIRCULATION ON TOP

READ OUR WANT ADS

TORONTO, SATURDAY, OCTOBER 27, 1894.

ALMEDA CHATTELLE.

THE SELF-CONFESSED MURDERER OF JESSIE KEITH.

Image 2.2 An angry crowd threatened to lynch the "Hairy Man." Numerous newspapers speculated that Almeda Chattelle, aka Amedé Chatelle, might be Jack the Ripper. Toronto *Evening News*, 27 October 1894.

the United States. Most editorials, like judges' sentencing statements, condemned the practice as an outcome of weaknesses in the American criminal justice system.[57] Rough justice had no regard for the rights of suspects, which meant that the innocent were punished along with the guilty. Fortunately, lynching did not happen in the "peaceable kingdom," where the principle of fairness and equality before the law was upheld.[58] But the failure of the police to make a swift arrest created a combustible ingredient, and the long-awaited identification of the suspect exploded into a near lynching. Detective Murray did not help matters when he boasted to reporters that "the chain of evidence was completed" and Chattelle "was the right man." He tried to reassure the small southwestern Ontario community that they could rely upon the criminal justice system; the Crown attorney went further, stating: "Unquestionably he is the man we are after. There is no doubt about it."[59] But authorities still feared that Chattelle might be lynched. To avert that prospect, police intercepted the train that took the accused from the county seat of Stratford (where he had been detained and questioned) to Listowel, where the inquest was to be conducted. With the suspect in tow, they made haste to the town hall, managing to arrive just before a hostile crowd, estimated at 600, rushed for admittance.[60] The inquest into "the most awful crime ever perpetrated in Canada" was about to commence.[61]

Without counsel to advise him, Chattelle confessed his guilt after the coroner's jury found him responsible for the murder, and this finding led to his committal for trial. But what to do with the defendant? Local authorities, who had to return their prisoner to Stratford, knew that a "clamorous surging mob" was throwing stones at the town hall and uttering "inflammatory cries and threats." The "infuriated crowd" chased the hack as it raced off toward the station, a reporter recounted:

> With passionate cries of "Lynch him," "Hang him," "Here's the rope," "Throw him under the train" ... a determined attempt was made to get him ... and the mob made a dash at him. In the melee Constable Thomas McCarthy drew a loaded revolver and held the glistening weapon above his head, prepared to shoot the first man that interfered ... Wild threats were still made ... One man on the [rail]car, evidently an American, did much to incite the crowd by telling them that they were a lot of fools for not dealing with the prisoner when they had him.[62]

This show of force, and further assurances from Detective Murray and local police that Chattelle would be tried in a court of law, defused the situation.[63] However, as the trial opened, it differed little from the lynching authorities had suppressed.[64]

Chattelle was one of two men convicted for sex murder at the turn of the century after trials in which they were not represented by defence counsel. The murder of Jessie Keith was evidently "the work of a human brute," but the defendant's sanity was not appraised before, during, or after his trial.[65] When Louis Riel was prosecuted, he rejected the defence's strategy of entering an insanity plea, which would have turned his political leadership into a symptom of messianic delusion.[66] After the Métis leader's conviction, Prime Minister Macdonald commissioned an inquiry into his sanity, but the alienists (mental experts) appointed found him to be sane, and he was hanged on 16 November 1885.[67] Chattelle was no political leader, but he was a Catholic French Canadian on trial for his life in Anglo-Protestant–dominated Ontario.

Chattelle's brother, who learned about the case through the Quebec press, paid a Toronto-based lawyer to represent his sibling. Harry M. East, like Riel's lawyers, decided it was best to argue that his client was insane.[68] But Chattelle refused to cooperate with East, and he declined his lawyer's services. Rather than delay the trial or appoint another member of the bar to take the case, Chief Justice John D. Armour allowed the trial to proceed.[69]

The trial of the tramp became a peculiar sham, which opened with the judge informing the defendant of his right to question Crown witnesses and "to give evidence as a witness on his own behalf."[70] The Crown, John Idington, QC, opened the prosecution's case by bringing the horror of the event back to the jurors' minds five months after the victim's body was discovered. He presented further medical evidence, incomplete at the time of the inquest, which indicated the girl's "private parts" showed evidence of tearing and fluid of an undetermined nature.[71] Neither East (who remained in court) nor the defendant presented any evidence. There were no challenges to possible contradictions in Crown witnesses' testimony, no expert testimony concerning the defendant's sanity, and no summation of the case for the defence. The jury performed as expected and found Chattelle guilty with no recommendation to mercy. Before he sentenced the man, Justice Armour followed the protocol of asking the defendant if he had anything to say. All he received in response was an incoherent statement. The sentence of death was duly pronounced, and Armour told the convict to prepare for his execution. But Harry East was determined to act for the client who had rejected him. In the realm of discretionary executive justice, he did his best to save a doomed man whom he believed to be insane.

Sexology and the Sex Killer

By the 1890s, European, British, and American researchers began to study and label a host of sexual deviations. In doing so, they challenged long-standing moral and religious interpretations of sex murderers, but they did not supplant them, as the response to Jessie Keith's killer demonstrated. In the Toronto region, where Harry East based his law practice, numerous medical men were early readers of Richard von Krafft-Ebing's *Psychopathia Sexualis*, first published in German in 1886 and released in English in 1893, just before the trial.[72] According to the Toronto *Daily Star*, East had planned to call two medical men to testify because they were conversant with "cerebral paresthesia sexualis."

This term, coined by Krafft-Ebing, described the pathological perversion of the male sexual instinct, one manifestation of which was the inclination to wear women's clothing.[73] Since Chattelle was wearing women's underclothes when he was arrested, East believed the man suffered from this condition and was consequently not responsible for the murder: "Psychopathic states may lead to crimes against morality, and at the same time remove the conditions necessary to the existence of responsibility."[74] After the trial, East asked Justice Armour to reserve a question for the Court of Appeal regarding Chattelle's capacity to plead and inform his counsel. The resourceful advocate also solicited statements from eight Canadian experts in psychiatry, which he hoped would prompt the minister of justice to order a commission (similar to the one ordered after Riel's conviction) to assess Chattelle's sanity. Justice Armour denied East's request, and no commission was ordered. However, the expert evidence East had amassed reappeared in his bid for clemency. Chattelle's last chance lay in his rejected lawyer's attempt to prevent the execution of a man who suffered from a newly diagnosed form of abnormality.[75]

The medical affidavits East assembled in his petition for mercy landed in Augustus Power's pigeonhole, along with the transcript and Justice Armour's report, which conveyed his dismissive appraisal of the psychological evidence. The judge considered the diagnoses of Chattelle's behaviour ill-founded and distasteful, particularly the one written by a doctor who stated that the girl's rape was "very doubtful."[76] When Power reached the section of Armour's report where he stated the only issue was the defendant's capacity to understand "the nature and quality of his act" and his knowledge "that it was wrong," he pencilled "the legal test" in the margin.[77] Ignoring the fact that Chattelle had refused East's service, Justice Armour criticized the lawyer for failing to defend the man on the basis of a plea of insanity, which would have made the jury the appraisers of his legal responsibility, not the executive. The recently minted Criminal Code's definition of criminal insanity was uppermost in Power's and Armour's minds. It set a higher bar for proof of insanity than the M'Naghten judgment of 1843. After 1892, to be considered not criminally responsible, the defence had to establish that the accused was "labouring under natural imbecility or disease of the mind, as to render him incapable of appreciating the nature and quality of the act or omission, and of knowing that such an act or omission was wrong."[78]

The only hint that Chattelle's conviction troubled Justice Armour was his suggestion that the executive explore another section of the Criminal

Code. Under section 748, the minister of justice could, after an "application for the mercy of the Crown," order a new trial.[79] Power, the most senior bureaucrat in the Department of Justice, who had participated in the drafting of the 1892 Code, could have highlighted this option when he prepared his memorandum for Charles Tupper, the minister of justice. Instead, his memorandum highlighted the judge's belief that Chattelle was legally responsible: "This murder was a most cruel and revolting one, and the evidence, though circumstantial, appears to be ~~justifiably~~ irresistibly conclusive of the prisoner's guilt."[80] His opinion clear, Power included an editorial clipped from *Le Monde*, a pro-Conservative paper, when he forwarded the file to the minister. The column bolstered Power's opinion, and it endorsed the subhuman murderer's execution: "Chatelle ne mérite aucune sympathie. On se débarrasse des monstres, des bêtes féroces et des chiens enragés."[81] The glaring lack of legal representation for a defendant in a capital trial vanished in the course of the clemency review.

"Atrocious Crime, Committed by a Tramp": Race and the Reinforcement of Outrage

Although Chattelle belonged to the French "race," a term that was used widely in this period to refer to whites of different ethnicities, most newspapers referred to him as a beast or monster.[82] In Detective Murray's memoir, he dubbed Chattelle the "Hairy Man" and likened him to a gorilla or a "baboon when it rises on its hind legs." But the hirsute murderer's tanned skin (probably from life on the road over the summer) deepened his repulsiveness: "he was very dark."[83] The association of darkness with criminality and sexual violence gained credibility over the nineteenth century, as criminology and anthropology reproduced and authorized hierarchical racial thinking.[84] The rate of lynching also increased in this period, claiming hundreds of lives annually in the United States, frequently in response to alleged sexual attacks on white women.[85] In Canada, no man suspected of committing a sex murder was lynched, but racial prejudice undermined dark-skinned men's chances of fair trials. It also lowered the likelihood of clemency if they were convicted. And if defendants also lacked community roots or religious ties, the prospect of mounting a strong defence or clemency petition was minute, as James Jenkins's execution demonstrated.

When Jenkins, an African American drifter, was accused of a sex murder involving a respectable woman in British Columbia, every component of the criminal justice system worked on behalf of the dominant white majority. Readers of the Victoria *Colonist* learned on 10 June 1908 that Mrs. Mary Morrison and her eight-year-old daughter had been set upon by a man who had attacked the woman, then fled. As the wife of a prominent rancher and mother of five children, she had matronly claims to respectability, distinct from Jessie Keith's, whose virginal condition made her death honourable as well as tragic.[86] In this case, however, there was an eye witness – the victim's daughter. The girl, May Morrison, ran for help after she saw the man attack her mother, which made her testimony critical to the capture and prosecution of any suspect. At first she told police the assailant was a "young white man" with a dark complexion, but local authorities quickly decided they were after a "half-breed negro," possibly "mulatto" or "coloured."[87] The police doubted that any local white man could be the killer. The "hoboes and tramps" who rode the rails and camped rough in the border district made better suspects, and local officials sent the girl's modified description to US and Canadian police forces.

"Watch all tramps and suspicious looking characters," the BC Provincial Police reward poster advised. In the immediate aftermath of the murder, men in the district formed an armed posse. Although they failed to capture a suspect, they disparaged the local "parlour" police. The amount of the official reward – $1,000 for the "arrest and conviction" of the murderer with "possibly negro blood" – encouraged a gang of rail workers in Washington to identify James Jenkins as the wanted man. The sheriff in Bellingham apprehended the suspect and notified Canadian authorities.[88] When a provincial constable brought the victim's daughter to Washington, she identified the "half-witted tramp," which triggered James Jenkins's extradition, whereupon Canadian justice took over in New Westminster.[89] At Jenkins's preliminary hearing in July 1908, he was not represented by a lawyer, although he pleaded not guilty to the charges presented by the provincial attorney general. The trial occurred at the Fall Assizes, and it was only at that point that the court assigned the defendant a lawyer. The man who took the case, G.M. McQuarrie, was an experienced barrister, but the defence he put together was insufficient to counter the racism and moral outrage that engulfed the trial.

Unlike Chattelle, Jenkins did not resist his lawyer's request for a lunacy commission to determine his client's fitness to stand trial. The presiding judge, Chief Justice Gordon Hunter, granted the request, but the five men he appointed to assess Jenkins's sanity agreed the man was fit to plead, albeit mentally dull.[90] In light of the crime's "atrocity," Jenkins's lawyer told the jury that it "must have been the work of an insane man." McQuarrie based his defence on questioning the reliability of the Crown's evidence, but he had nothing to counter it aside from cross-examining witnesses. By the time he reached his closing address, he dissociated himself from the defendant. The jury must bear in mind that he was "compelled to undertake the defence of [the] accused at short notice and much against his wish."[91]

The judge who presided over the trial shared the defence's doubt over Jenkins's guilt, and this prompted him to conduct a controversial courtroom experiment. During a recess, Justice Hunter called for another black man to be brought to the courtroom and placed in the prisoner's dock. When the proceedings resumed, he tested little May Morrison's capacity to identify the man who had murdered her mother by asking her to point out the culprit. The girl's identification of the stand-in caused a sensation: "Child Positively Identifies Negro Placed in Prisoner's Box as Substitute for Coloured Man Accused of Murder."[92] On top of this, McQuarrie reminded the jury that the police had questioned numerous suspicious characters but released them, without thoroughly checking their alibis. But Jenkins had no alibi to prove he was elsewhere when the offence took place. Notwithstanding these substantial grounds for reasonable doubt, the jury, all white men, found Jenkins guilty.

Justice Hunter delayed his report to Ottawa in order to reserve a question of law for his brother judges.[93] In a stated case before the Supreme Court of British Columbia, he contended that the evidence did not support the verdict. Robert Cassidy, KC, the Crown counsel in Jenkins's trial, and McQuarrie argued either side of the point Hunter had raised before the court.[94] Craftily, Cassidy argued that McQuarrie's failure to present evidence meant there was "no power to grant [an appeal] on the ground that the verdict was against the weight of evidence when there was no evidence called by the defence."[95] In other words, Jenkins could not be granted a new trial *because* he had been defended by a lawyer who had no time or funds to find alibi witnesses or expert witnesses. Justice Hunter's colleagues were unreceptive to the allegation that racism was a factor in Jenkins's arrest and conviction. The Supreme Court justice acknowledged that Jenkins was the only "coloured man brought before [the victim's daughter] for identification" in the line-up of men paraded before May Morrison, but they "did not consider the defendant's identification to be unsound."[96] Justice Irving, who delivered the

Image 2.3 Chief Justice Gordon Hunter (1863–1929; photo c. 1910) presided over the 1908 trial of African American James Jenkins for the sex murder of a white woman, Mary Morrison, but the judge was unsuccessful in his efforts to expose the role of racism in the conviction. City of Vancouver Archives, AM1616-: CVA 136–185.

court's reasons for denying Hunter's request, rejected the inference that the white jurors were "prejudiced against the accused on account of his being a negro." The fantasy that anti-black racism was an American, not a Canadian, problem inspired Irving to add: "I cannot believe any such prejudice did exist."[97]

The BC Supreme Court's dismissal of Justice Hunter's request on 23 November 1908 set the post-conviction clemency review wheels into motion on a course that veered toward execution. Had the file reached Augustus Power's desk immediately after the trial, accompanied by pleas for mercy submitted by Jenkins's reluctant lawyer, the prospect of the commutation of his sentence would have been negligible. However, the court's explicit rejection of Hunter's contention, compounded by his courtroom stunt, convinced the country's chief law clerk to consider the verdict sound. The trial judge's abuse of a child witness, which required that she step directly in front of the prisoner's dock and point at the man she thought had murdered her mother, led some of his BC colleagues to question Hunter's fitness and to report him to the federal executive.[98] The press was certain the chief justice had been drinking heavily during the Fall Assizes, and the attorney general, W.J. Bowser, wrote to the minister of justice to complain that Hunter's trick amounted to deception. Power agreed: "It amounted to a deliberate mis-statement made to the child ... [C]ounsel are not permitted to make false statements even in cross-examining witnesses."[99] In Power's opinion, the judge's comment that the Crown's direct evidence was "valueless" was the most questionable aspect of the case, not the compelling evidence of racism in the defendant's identification. After he read over the transcript, the dismissed reserved case, and the correspondence questioning Hunter's fitness to preside, Power concluded: "There can be no doubt that a murder of a particularly brutal character, probably accompanied by rape or an attempt at rape, was committed," and he was equally certain about the identity of the man responsible.[100] On 18 December 1908, the Dominion executioner placed Jenkins, an Asian man, and another "coloured" man together on the trap door that opened with a crash in the New Westminster Provincial Gaol.[101] Only one black flag was hoisted.

Shiftless Degenerates and Heinous Crimes

Although the crime of vagrancy remained in the Criminal Code in the early twentieth century, psychiatrists, sexologists, criminal anthropologists, and eugenicists came up with novel explanations for habitual criminality, shiftlessness, and immorality.[102] Religious-coded notions of evil and condemnation lingered, however. One of Canada's leading medico-legal authorities, Dr. Daniel Phelan, brought these various perspectives together. In his presidential address to the American Association of Prison Surgeons in August 1909, he spoke of his experience as the Kingston Penitentiary's surgeon. "Drawing from his years of experience, study and observation of criminal insanity, criminality and anthropology," he determined that true criminals were distinct from those who committed crime driven by rage or revenge: "The degenerate, the vicious, the habitual, the incorrigible criminal ... is depraved and never improves, is dangerous, designing, cunning and is marked clearly with the stigmata of moral and physical degeneration."[103] This blend of folk wisdom and eugenic theory was widely shared in professional circles, including Canada's legal fraternity. Augustus Power, the veteran clerk who turned sixty in 1907, was more receptive to criminal anthropological approaches; nevertheless, he and Phelan could agree on the matter of criminal responsibility. The association president informed his audience of fellow prison surgeons that the government frequently asked him to examine "criminals under sentence of death where insanity was set up as a defence." The truly insane could not be held accountable for committing criminal offences, Phelan acknowledged, but persons with "criminal instincts" must pay the consequences of their "evil deeds."[104]

When Phelan distinguished between wrongdoers and degenerates, he followed the diagnostic categories introduced by English sexologist Havelock Ellis.[105] He also shared the view of criminal anthropologists that criminality was more prevalent in "lower races."[106] Although degeneracy was considered a problem within British and French racial stock (the majority of images in Ellis's *The Criminal* were of white British men), early criminologists, particularly Cesare Lombroso, contended that criminal traits, including violence and hypersexuality, were passed on by primitive types who lacked a moral sense.[107] In Canada, these theories reinforced anti-Asian and anti-black sentiment, and immigration policy increasingly singled out these people as undesirables. In this hostile atmosphere, the capture of a black man in 1909 for the rape and murder of an elderly white woman in her homestead near Stratford, Ontario, fortified white prejudice.[108]

Frank Roughmond was Canadian born, but this fact did not make him an insider in the eyes of the white farming community. To these locals, he was a dangerous alien. Like Jenkins, the man seized for sexually assaulting and murdering a white elderly woman was described as "the negro murderer" before any legal process began.[109] Southwest Ontario had one of the largest communities of people of African descent, but Roughmond was born in Quebec, and he had no stable connection to the region. His liminal status made him a choice target for summary justice. The victim's sons and her neighbours did not need a posse to search for the suspect, since they found Roughmond in the basement of Mrs. Mary Peake's home. After the men came upon her bruised and bloodied body, they discovered the man, asleep. These "brawny and incensed" farmers were in an "infuriated state," according to the Stratford *Herald*. As they tied up the suspect, impatient for the police to arrive, "murmurs of lynching" created an electric atmosphere in the house. Some newspapers, including the Toronto *World*, which reported the crime, opined that this "dangerous looking negro" deserved to be lynched. However, the *Herald* underscored the need to follow the law of the land. Of course, Roughmond was "probably guilty" of this "heinous crime," but "in this country," the editor intoned, "the vilest criminal is given a fair trial for his life."[110] Once again, the public expected the Canadian criminal justice system to serve up retributive justice as a bargain for turning over a black man to the courts.

The judge who presided over Frank Roughmond's trial in Stratford at the Spring Assizes of 1909, William Renwick Riddell, took a keen interest in medico-legal matters and the subject of criminal insanity, but neither he nor the defence could see past the defendant's "race."[111] Whether he was innocent (as J.J. Coughlin for the defence attempted to prove) or possibly insane (as the judge considered), Frank Roughmond was a "negro." The defence was just as convinced as the Peake boys that the defendant's race could explain the crime, but Coughlin drew the white jurors' attention to Roughmond's physical appearance to discourage them from finding him guilty of murder. By describing the defendant as "not a good looking man, even for a negro," Coughlin offered his ludicrous theory that the "sudden appearance of a man of the black race" might have frightened Mrs. Peake "to death."[112] If so, the defence asked the Crown's medical witnesses, was it possible that this crime could not amount to murder? Although Coughlin's question failed to raise sufficient doubt for the jury to find Roughmond innocent, it did cast doubt on the planned and deliberate nature of the attack.

Prior to the trial, Roughmond's eccentricities – picking up money on the road by performing card tricks, conducting phrenological exams, and reading palms – prompted Justice Riddell to order a pre-trial examination by two of Ontario's leading experts in sanity, Dr. C.K. Clarke (of the Asylum for the Insane in Toronto) and Dr. Bruce Smith (provincial inspector of Prisons and Public Charities).[113] The men's short visit with the suspect led them to the same conclusion, which had a Lombrosian ring: the prisoner was a "well-developed negro" who was not insane but merely "a man of low type who is somewhat addicted

FARMER'S WIFE MURDERED

FOUND BY HER SON IN CELLAR OF HOME.

NEGRO DRUNK BESIDE HER

Tragedy Near Stratford — Frank Roghmond, a Vagrant, Accused of Having Choked and Assaulted Mrs. Wm. Peak.

ALONE IN THE HOUSE WHEN CRIME OCCURRED.

STRATFORD, Sept. 30.—(Special).—A terrible tragedy occurred this afternoon at the rural home of William Peak, a farmer living at lot 11, con. 1, Downie, about two miles from this city.

While the husband and two sons were absent from the house a tramp negro named Frank Roghmond entered the house and, it is believed, outraged Mrs. Peak, she being found about four o'clock lying dead on the cellar floor.

Roghmond was also lying in a sleeping condition in the cellar, his hands, face and clothing spotted with blood, while blood covered the face of the victim. Marks would indicate that the woman had been choked and that a hemorrhage resulted.

The tragedy happened between noon and four o'clock. Mr. Peak had gone to the Herman farm a mile or two distant, while the boys, George and John, went to work in the fields about 300 yards from the house. About four o'clock, John returned to the house to get a jug of cider, and arriving at the cellar he saw the form of the sleeping negro and, in the dim light, what he mistook to be the form of another negro. Rushing to the field he informed his brother that two negroes were asleep in the cellar. Both returned to the house, when the horrible discovery was made that their mother was lying dead with a portion of her face covered with blood.

George hurried across the road to a neighbor's Robert McIntosh, saying "Hurry over, Bob, I believe mother is dead." Other nearby neighbors were soon on the scene, while John Peak was despatched to Stratford for Chief McCarthy.

Before the chief arrived, however, the negro awakened and tried to escape from the house. He was pounced upon by the brawny and incensed farmers, while Robert Fuller placed the noose of a heavy rope over his body, pinioning his arms to his side.

He was securely bound and carefully watched until the arrival of the chief. The crowd of farmers were entertained by protestations of innocence by the captive, who told them a very unlikely story to the effect that he had been carried to the cellar by three men and robbed of $15.

When found the body of Mrs. Peak was flat on the back, with limbs outstretched. Indications point to her having been criminally assaulted after

REV. ANDREW TAYLOR.

Phila. May Fill Pulpit At Cooke's

Congregation Have Decided to Call Rev. Andrew T. Taylor of Gaston Memorial Church, That City.

At a meeting of the congregation held last night, Dr. McTavish presiding, in the lecture room of Cooke's Presbyterian Church, it was decided unanimously to extend a call to Rev. Andrew T. Taylor of Gaston Memorial Church, Philadelphia, to be their pastor.

There is probably no other church in Canada so well known in Presbyterianism as Cooke's for its influence among the young people in the downtown district of Toronto. The largest young people's society of Christian Endeavor in the world assembled here weekly during Dr. Patterson's pastorate. Men of such standing as Dr. Gregg of Knox College and the late Dr. Robb of Belfast were among its

Image 2.4 The apprehension of Frank Roughmond for the sex murder of an elderly white woman, Mary Peake, unleashed racist fury. Toronto *World*, 1 October 1908.

to the use of alcohol, and who belongs to the very large class of tramps found wandering about the country." At Riddell's request, the same doctors re-examined the prisoner after his conviction, but they stuck to their original diagnosis. "While it is true that Roughmond is a man of the lowest type mentally and morally, yet it is also true that he does not show any evidence of mental disease, and cannot be classified as an insane man." Characteristics that would otherwise be considered evidence of psychological deviance in a white man were considered normal for men of his "race," as the doctors' joint report concluded: "He conforms to the ordinary type of common negro, and is probably a man of brutal instincts; he is also superstitious and ignorant."[114] Both the medical experts and the judge knew that race was not a legal defence. They were also aware that their assessments helped to seal Roughmond's fate.

When the transcript and judge's report reached Ottawa in May 1909, Augustus Power, soon to retire, was doubtless relieved to find a case so easy to summarize. "The prisoner, a negro," he opened his memorandum, had killed Mary Peake "by ravishing her with considerable violence. The facts are few and simple."[115] He did not trouble the minister of justice with details from the transcript, which showed that Justice Riddell had appointed Roughmond's lawyer one day prior to the trial. In his report, Riddell complimented Coughlin on his honourable service, even though his defence consisted of the brief cross-examination of several witnesses and a short closing statement, in which he returned to his racial fright theory.[116] No witnesses were called on the defendant's behalf, and no family members or clerics came to his aid. But the transcript does indicate that Roughmond stood up for his rights. The white men who tied him up testified that their captive had protested that "he was a Canadian" and that "we [have] a law in this country and a King."[117] The man's use of the inclusive "we" asserted a common national identity as much as it expressed his desperation to avoid a summary execution. By contrast, the Canadians who determined his fate, including the cabinet members who decided the law must take its course, expressed no fellow feeling for a "negro tramp."

The Irony of Incorporation: Indian Status and Capital Justice

Resistance to the incorporation of "coloured" peoples was one of the founding stones of the white Dominion. The first enslaved Africans in British North America, the black Loyalists who fled after the American

Revolution, the people who escaped slavery prior to the Emancipation Proclamation, and blacks who attempted to migrate northward after the American Civil War all encountered resistance and hostility. At the same time, the federal government imposed concerted policies of assimilation and sequestration on First Nations. Until Indigenous peoples were absorbed into the wider community, or died out, as many Canadian authorities projected in the late nineteenth and early twentieth century, Ottawa would act in a position of stewardship, particularly in regard to people the government defined as "status Indians." The state categorized such people as wards, and protection was packaged with regulation. Consequently, whenever a "status Indian" was accused of committing a capital crime, the Department of Indian Affairs (DIA) provided funds to hire defence counsel, in keeping with paternalistic government policy.[118] After Confederation, such arrangements occurred on an ad hoc basis at the discretion of provincial attorneys general, and judges occasionally persuaded senior counsel to defend Indigenous accused, in part to tutor communities in the superiority of British justice. In the early phase of contact and colonization, judicial recommendations to mercy and the granting of clemency to Indigenous convicts were common, designed to give the assertion of sovereignty a benevolent gloss.[119] However, this strategy began to shift in the longer-settled regions of the country by the early twentieth century, as the first DIA-funded defence of an accused sex murderer in 1905 dramatized.[120]

Joseph Bennett, a member of the Grand River Reserve of the Six Nations, was accused of killing a physically disabled middle-aged woman from the same community. After the coroner's inquest, held at the Six Nations Council House, determined that Betsey Jacobs had met her death at the hands of Bennett, the local Indian superintendent urged the federal government to fund the man's defence.[121] The DIA responded positively, and the offer of federal funding tempted an experienced local KC based in Brantford, the town west of Toronto that sat within historic Six Nations territory.[122] Nothing in the history of Louis F. Heyd's practice indicated he was particularly concerned about the welfare of local First Nations. Like J.J. Coughlin, whose racist representation of Roughmond was his chief line of defence, the man who defended Bennett shared the anti-Indian prejudices prevalent among whites in Brant County (named after Mohawk military and political leader Joseph Brant). Although the defence in this case was far stronger and better resourced, the stereotype of the savage and duplicitous "drunken Indian" was stronger still.

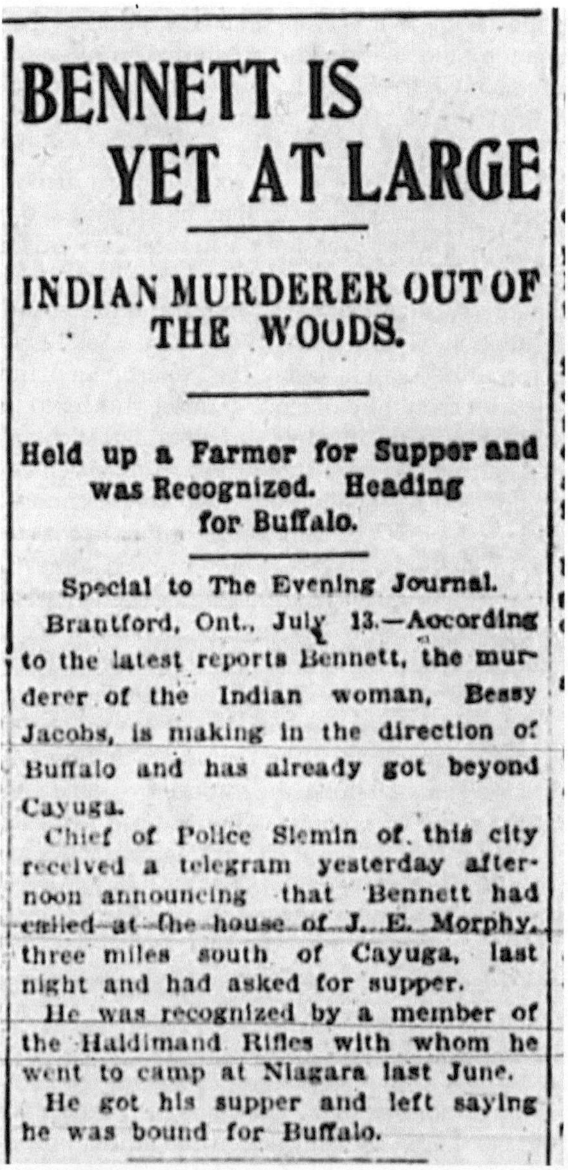

BENNETT IS YET AT LARGE

INDIAN MURDERER OUT OF THE WOODS.

Held up a Farmer for Supper and was Recognized. Heading for Buffalo.

Special to The Evening Journal.

Brantford, Ont., July 13.—According to the latest reports Bennett, the murderer of the Indian woman, Bessy Jacobs, is making in the direction of Buffalo and has already got beyond Cayuga.

Chief of Police Slemin of this city received a telegram yesterday afternoon announcing that Bennett had called at the house of J. E. Morphy, three miles south of Cayuga, last night and had asked for supper.

He was recognized by a member of the Haldimand Rifles with whom he went to camp at Niagara last June.

He got his supper and left saying he was bound for Buffalo.

Image 2.5 The press's colonialist identification of the suspect (Joseph Bennett) and the sex murder victim (Betsey Jacobs, aka Bessy and Betsy) as "Indians" persisted from Bennett's capture to his execution. Ottawa *Evening Journal*, 22 July 1905.

As in most trials that involved unwitnessed homicides, the Crown's case against Bennett depended on forging a chain of circumstantial evidence. The Crown, Methodist Willoughby S. Brewster, KC, painted a scenario in which the defendant had arrived at the humble two-room house where Betsey Jacobs lived with her mother, who was away from home to pick berries. On 9 July 1905, in the middle of the night, Bennett crawled through a window, then beat and strangled the woman. Frail, and suffering from a diseased hip, she was no match for the "husky" thirty-three-year-old, who committed a "fiendish crime."[123] Crown medical witnesses' confirmation of the presence of sperm in the deceased's vagina and bloody handprints on her upper thighs, together with the discovery that her night dress was raised, supported the Crown's theory that the killer was motivated by lust. The most damning evidence against Bennett, apart from his swift exit from the district directly after the murder, was a letter addressed to him, which was found beside the woman's body.

The defence countered by pointing out the weak links in the Crown's theory and providing the basis for an alibi, giving his client a far better chance of acquittal than most indigent defendants had. Heyd used his DIA funding to search for numerous witnesses who were prepared to testify that Bennett was elsewhere at the time of the murder. He questioned medical witnesses to raise doubt that a rape had occurred. And Heyd also took the risk of calling his client to the witness stand. The defendant insisted he was innocent, and he claimed that the letter had been planted to implicate him. But once Heyd reached his closing statement, he fell back on paternalistic convention, presenting the "Indian" defendant to the jury as an object of pity.

The closing address of the defence drew on racist notions of "Indian" womanhood as well as manhood. Heyd spoke to the jury as fellow white men. Ever since he took the case, he confided, he had carried a "great weight on his shoulder." If Bennett had committed the deed, the failing was not so much the defendant's as the entire First Nation of which he was a member. From this point of view, he challenged the Crown's theory that Bennett had raped the victim and killed her to cover up his crime. Surely, Heyd explained, the rape theory was implausible in a community that did not adhere to the values of white Canadians. Considering the "looseness of morals on the reserve," he queried, could any white juror believe the motive was "lust"? Not content to tar an entire community by implying that promiscuity was rife, Heyd then denigrated the victim: "The woman Jacobs was poor and crippled and not the kind to stimulate passion, though it had been established that one man on the Reserve had paid attentions to her."[124] If the white men who served on the jury found this version of events credible, they could find the defendant guilty, at worst, of manslaughter. But the Crown prevailed. After a three-day trial, the jury found Bennett guilty of murder, and the countdown started on 29 September 1905 for the convicted sex killer's execution.

Whether or not Heyd was motivated by the hope of further DIA funding, he did not abandon his client after the conviction.[125] The Ontario Court of Appeal accepted Heyd's motion to file an appeal through the attorney general. On his authority, he moved that the court consider requesting the trial judge to grant a stated case. Despite the attorney general's support, the appellate justices dismissed his request.[126] Without the opportunity to argue that the evidence did not support the verdict and that the judge had misdirected the jury on the probative value of the circumstantial evidence, Heyd turned to the federal minister of justice, hoping that he might use his discretion to order a new trial. This request, too, was denied, leaving Heyd with his final option: a plea for mercy.[127]

Up to that point, Heyd had corresponded with bureaucrats in the DIA, the agency set up for the purported welfare of Canada's Indians; now he dealt with the head clerk in the Department of Justice, who had no such brief. Augustus Power received word from local law enforcement agents, who confirmed that the condemned man had been arrested on six prior occasions, mostly for drunkenness and vagrancy but also for theft. In his summary for the minister, Power highlighted this petty criminal record. Although he considered that Bennett had been "well defended by able counsel," he thought Heyd's claim, that his client had been framed, "incredible." To Power, the Crown's theory was more convincing: Betsey Jacobs had been "ravished," and there was "little doubt, if any, as to the motive of the murder." Power gave no consideration to the possibility that Bennett might be mentally dull, a degenerate, or a sufferer of sexual paraesthesia.[128] This brutal crime simply confirmed he was a "bad Indian." In the end, the chief clerk concurred with the trial judge, who stated he was "entirely satisfied with the verdict returned by the jury."[129] The minister of justice, Charles Doherty, agreed with the judge and Power's recommendation that he deny the defence lawyer's request for a new trial.[130] The cabinet declined to interfere with the sentence. It was necessary that this "Indian" be held accountable for murder. In this long-settled and semi-urbanized region of Canada, the era of "savage mercy" was long over.[131]

The Limits of Whiteness and Inferior Stock

Augustus Power's convention of introducing capitally convicted offenders in his case summaries by their race and colour extended to their ethnicity. He distinguished between Italians, Finns, Galicians, and Ukrainians and also between Welsh, Scottish, Irish, and English offenders. By the early twentieth century, concerns over the quality of Canada's immigrants applied to a much broader range of individuals than analysts of racist immigration practice typically emphasize.[132] Eugenically minded physicians, including Dr. Phelan and, most notably, Dr. C.K. Clarke, frequently vented their frustration over Canada's acceptance of British immigrants of inferior "stock."[133]

Immigration schemes, which brought orphans from England's slums and subsidized the migration of poor women and men to work in domestic and farm labour, offered opportunities for advancement, but they also exposed impoverished youth to native-born white Canadians' snobbery and vilification.[134] These social tensions could play out at a micro level, when individuals who considered themselves true Canadians encountered the white immigrants the government hoped would transform the West into a profitable breadbasket.[135] When thirty-six-year-old Georgina Brown, the single mistress of a farm household near Brandon, Manitoba, called her farmhand a "dirty English brat" for failing to wash before dinner, her jibe was not just a personal insult but a slur against his status. Lawrence Gowland's response – to slash the woman's throat and rape her – set in motion a legal process that exposed the low regard for the principles of fairness that judges regularly exalted in capital trials.

From the discovery of Georgina Brown's body on 22 May 1907, no one, including Gowland, disputed he had killed her.[136] But without a lawyer to defend him, the only men who considered the question of his criminal responsibility were the Crown and the trial judge. Gowland, aged nineteen, admitted he had fatally stabbed the victim, after which he attempted to take his own life by cutting his throat. His feeble suicide attempt followed the frenzied attack, which left the victim "horribly mutilated and … ravished."[137] When a provincial constable and a doctor questioned Gowland in hospital after his recovery, he told them he had assaulted the woman knowing that her brother was away from the farmstead. The trial opened on 23 October 1907, and Gowland pleaded guilty to murder. The presiding judge, Justice Frank Hedley Phippen, indicated he could not accept that plea as Gowland faced a capital charge. Was the defendant represented by counsel? "No sir." Did he have the funds to hire a lawyer? "I would have one if I could," Gowland replied.[138] Although Phippen had recently been appointed to the Manitoba Court of Appeal, he allowed the trial to proceed, and the Crown presented evidence that established the defendant's commission of the crime. The judge interrupted from time to time with a question from the bench. The entire trial took less than one hour.

As a poor immigrant, Gowland had no means to hire a lawyer, and his family in England was in no position to help. Normally, judges who presided over criminal assizes cast their eyes over the courtroom to see if any barrister present might take on a capital case if the defendant was indigent, but in Morden, Manitoba, population just over 1,000, the pool of candidates was nothing like it was in Canada's large cities.[139] Gowland spent a long time in prison, from Georgina Brown's death in May 1907 to his trial in October, due to the schedule of the circuit courts in the province's regions, and this hiatus left ample time for a barrister to step forward on his own initiative. Prior to the trial, Justice Phippen had requested assistance from the attorney general of Manitoba, but the province turned down his request that a barrister be hired. To explain the situation, Phippen told Gowland:

> The province is too poor to see [that] in such cases the court has proper assistance. I do not know a case where a prisoner has been tried without counsel having previously occurred in Canada. I am afraid we shall have to try you without counsel. We shall have to do the best we can.[140]

Evidently, Phippen was unfamiliar with the Chattelle case, in which Justice Armour had allowed a capital trial to proceed without defence counsel.[141] In this perfunctory trial, the judge was more concerned about the province's imposition on the court, as he complained. It was always difficult to try a capital case, but it was a "much greater responsibility where [the judge] has to try an undefended prisoner."[142] In Phippen's report on the trial, he did not suggest that the province's penury may have violated the principle of fairness for a man on trial for his life. On the contrary, the judge concluded that he could find "no palliating features whatever in connection with the whole case."[143]

In his ministerial memorandum on the Gowland case, Augustus Power demonstrated unusual concern for the condemned man, but not on the basis of his lack of legal representation. Two local ministers were certain that Gowland had been denied his right to a fair trial, and they wrote to the minister of justice asking him to intervene. Gowland's spiritual advisor, Methodist Reverend C.W. Finch, noted that the trial had opened and closed with "not a word offered in his defence." Had a lawyer represented Gowland, evidence might have come out that the youth was "not wholly accountable for the awful crime." Reverend Arthur S. Wiley, another cleric who visited Gowland in prison, found him "dull and ill educated, and apparently a person of a violently passionate nature." But he was not "of the criminal class or type," in the cleric's opinion. To Wiley, it seemed that Gowland's offence had occurred "in a fit of mad frenzy, brought on by the frustration of overmastering desire."[144] Both ministers raised the question of the defendant's sanity, and they pointed out that no psychiatrist had examined the lad. In this small town, the local doctor was accepted as an authority on mental illness. When the Crown asked the doctor who treated Gowland if he had observed "any signs of insanity" after Gowland attempted suicide, the witness replied: "None whatsoever."[145]

Justice Phippen categorically set aside the possibility that the convicted murderer was insane. Instead, he diagnosed him a moral failure, and Power quoted the judge in his case summary: "From what I should opine the prisoner [is] one of those unfortunates with little moral responsibility, whose passion and temper when roused are beyond their control, but who are nevertheless fully responsible for their acts."[146] Although Power described the province's failure to fund a lawyer "unfortunate," he assured the minister he was confident "the young Englishman" had been convicted after a "perfectly fair trial."[147] His report left out the legal points the Manitoba ministers had raised (including the judge's dismissal of manslaughter as a possible verdict). Power also declined to mention that one of them feared that Gowland's mother, a "devout Christian," would likely "die of a broken heart" if he were executed.[148]

From time to time, Power did respond to petitioners in order to inform them about the standard clemency review process and to address the specifics of the cases that concerned them. Without disclosing his steering role in curating the contents and formulating a narrative that tilted for or against clemency, he assured advocates for condemned men that no request for clemency was ignored and that "all capital cases are carefully considered by His Excellency in Council." In his response to Reverend Finch, written on the minister's behalf, Power advised the cleric that "all the circumstances connected with this case," including "any features of mitigation," would be investigated as long as they were

Image 2.6 Augustus Power (1847–1912), long-serving chief clerk in the Department of Justice. William Cochrane, *The Canadian Album: Men of Canada, Or, Success by Example, in Religion Patriotism, Business, Law, Medicine, Education and Agriculture; Containing Portraits of some of Canada's Chief Business Men, Statesmen, Farmers, Men of the Learned Professions and Others*, vol. 5 (Brantford, ON: Bradley Garretson and Co., 1896), 40.

brought to the attention of the Department of Justice.[149] But Gowland lacked the support necessary for a trial lawyer, let alone one willing to draft and circulate a petition, seek affidavits, or file an appeal. And because the prisoner lacked the counsel to request the court to order an inquiry into his sanity, the department made no effort to pursue this possible ground for clemency after his conviction. With no other source of support from the Manitoban farming community where he had found work, the young Englishman suffered the same fate as Roughmond and Jenkins. Whiteness was no buffer from severity for the sex murderer of a respectable white woman, not when mixed with poverty and disconnectedness from community and judged by locals incensed over a crime "too horrible for thought."[150]

"This Murder Case Is a Revolting One"

Augustus Power's adherence to a strict notion of criminal culpability was consistent with his mid-nineteenth-century education in a Jesuit seminary, capped by his law degree.[151] If his night-time reading included the latest tomes on sexual pathologies, there is no evidence he was persuaded that mental abnormalities or dullness of mind could ever excuse men convicted of sex murders. The man he groomed as his successor prepared capital case file memoranda with a similar mix of emotion-laden commentary and technical legal advice. Pierre M. Côté, the longest-serving of the six legal officers who worked under Power, made his way up from clerk, third class, in 1883 to the top position as head clerk after his superior retired in 1911.[152] The new man faced a mountain of work, due to a significant increase in the volume of capital cases in the early twentieth century. Between 1912 and 1913, for instance, Côté assessed the files of fifty-four persons sentenced to death, a task that required him to digest over 10,000 pages of evidence.[153] Only a tiny fraction of those cases concerned sex murders, but they stood out in Côté's mind, as they did for Power, as crimes that called for the death sentence.

The first case of a sex murderer to arrive in the Department of Justice after the veteran chief officer's retirement blended the old and the new in legal and medical terms. In 1911, the venerable Sir William Glenholme Falconbridge (born in 1846) presided over the trial of Edward Jardine; after Jardine's conviction, the judge made his thoughts clear to the minister of justice that he considered the man's fate appropriate: "I will not recommend commutation of the sentence." Falconbridge was impressed by the Crown's medical witnesses (Toronto's Dr. Bruce Smith, Dr. C.K. Clarke, and Dr. Arthur Jukes Johnson), who testified that the defendant was "of low mentality and a confirmed masturbator" but agreed he was "perfectly capable of appreciating the nature and quality of the act."[154] In this case, Elizabeth Anderson, aged seventeen, was found dead with her throat slit from ear to ear. Although there was no physical evidence of a sexual assault, the victim was found in a pool of blood in a cellar, her body naked and her clothes slashed away. This "act of brutality" indicated the victim had died in a "desperate struggle," according to the Toronto *Globe*, and it also signalled that Anderson was the victim of a sex murder.[155]

The victim and accused were acquaintances, and both had attended the fall fair at Goderich on the night of her murder. Once apprehended, Jardine told Dr. Bruce Smith (in town, making a routine visit to the prison) that he had led the teen to an abandoned house on the fairgrounds for a sexual assignation. He admitted that he "had a spend" (ejaculated) when she tripped down the stairs. As she lay stunned, he attacked her: "Suddenly, the devil got possession of me," Jardine recounted. A local lawyer, Loftus E. Dancey, agreed to defend the accused killer. Although he was a seasoned member of the bar, he built his defence on the latest psychiatric theories of sexual deviancy, rather than the Christian notion of evil that Jardine had articulated.[156]

The line-up of experts in Jardine's trial was unusually even: on the side of the defence, Dancey found three local doctors who considered the prisoner "a degenerate and not criminally responsible;" however, the Crown's Toronto experts informed that jury that such deviates were legally sane.[157] The chief justice reminded the jury that the onus was on the defence if insanity was claimed. In this case, the defence had not produced convincing evidence that the defendant was seized with a fury over which he had no control. "It was lust passion that seized the prisoner," Falconbridge stated in his charge, and "lust passion [is] by no means insanity, as regarded by law."[158] So instructed, the jury found Jardine criminally responsible and guilty of murder. Dancey's request that the judge reserve a stated case for the Court of Appeal, concerning the admission of Jardine's statement to Dr. Smith, was rejected. This refusal left Jardine's lawyer to work through the channels of clemency, now under Côté's direction.

"This murder case is a revolting one, both on account of the cynical way it was perpetrated and the depravity of the lustful criminal who committed it." With this condemnatory opening, Côté prepared one of his first memoranda for Allen Aylesworth, the minister of justice. He dispensed quickly with the matter of law, which Dancey had raised. During the trial, Dr. Smith testified that he had attended Jardine in prison officially to treat his injured leg. During the procedure, he noticed the twenty-year-old's penis in an "abnormal condition," which led the doctor to reprove Jardine for masturbating: "You have been guilty of practices which make you what we term a sexual pervert," the doctor told his patient. When Smith made a second visit, he brought along Dr. Clarke (his partner in the Roughmond case). Together, they drew out the prisoner's tale of sexual desire leading to a murderous frenzy. Justice Falconbridge (a former law partner of Aylesworth) refused to grant a stated case, but he advised Dancey to request that the government appoint alienists (psychiatrists) to reassess after the trial. However, Côté followed the judge's report, in which he stated that George Tate Blackstock, the renowned forensic performer, had demolished the defence experts' claim that sexual perverts' "moral and mental standards" were so low that they could not discern right from wrong. Accordingly, Côté advised the minister that Dancey's request for further examinations "by experts in mental diseases" was "almost irrelevant."[159] The cabinet's final decision, that the law should take its course, indicated that Aylesworth and his fellow ministers agreed.

In the nineteenth century, many medical experts connected masturbation and insanity (as a cause of it, as well as a symptom), but that association had weakened by the time that Lizzie Anderson's murder was investigated.[160] In any event, the contention that onanists were insane was rejected in criminal courts unless further evidence of insanity was adduced.[161] In Blackstock's grandiose closing statement for the Crown in Jardine's trial, he warned the jury to reject "all this talk of 'sexual perverts' and 'brain storms'" as "mere speculation." If Canadian courts were to accept sexually fired rage as an excuse for "atrocious" crimes, "there would be no law in this land."[162]

Degenerate Desire at the Turn of the Century

The moral outrage sex murders generated was not confined to farming communities or small towns in turn-of-the-century Canada. It appeared in the statements uttered from the raised daises where judges donned a black cap and gloves to deliver the sentence of death. It scented the air in the offices where top-ranking civil servants advised their ministers. And it kept the cabinets of Conservative and Liberal governments steering clear of clemency. The revulsion expressed toward men accused of murders motivated by lust or "degenerate" desire was most intense when children were victims or if assaults included mutilation. The only men granted clemency in this period were the pair found guilty of a murder involving a woman whose cause of death was disputed. Burk and MacPherson's top-drawer lawyer represented them with added political sway, although he trafficked in the grubby business of attacking the victim. In the other cases, outsider status and the incapacity to mount a strong defence made the Crown's work easier and the defence's task more onerous. As an Indigenous man, Joseph Bennett was the ultimate insider, one of the continent's first peoples, but in the white Dominion he was branded as a "status Indian." Although the federal government reimbursed Bennett's counsel for his work, the barrister was no different from the Crown, the judge, or the government departments in viewing this murder case through the prejudicial lens of race.

Prior to the 1920s, every trial for a sex murder took place in Anglo-Celtic Canada (none took place in Quebec), where communities distinguished themselves from defendants on the basis not just of race, but of ethnicity, religion, and immigrant status.[163] When Justice Riddell charged the jury in the Roughmond case, he complimented white locals on the restraint they had shown. As a result, a black assailant ended up where he belonged: "in the hands of the law in the regular administration of the law."[164] Each of the lawyers who defended a sex murderer whom juries convicted was Anglo-Celtic, and this distinction factored into clemency appeals on behalf of men whose ethnicity, complexion, and national origins differed from their own. Pronouncements from the bench about the fairness of British justice, uttered in the course of sentencing defendants to death, invoked the royal prerogative of mercy, which granted every offender, no matter what his station, the possibility of clemency. The nine men hanged for sex murders in the late nineteenth and early twentieth century discovered that the granting of mercy was for others.

The common law principle that insane persons could not be held criminally responsible was another hallmark of British justice, which Canadian criminal law incorporated, but sex murder trials and clemency reviews included the consideration of mental conditions that had not been named, let alone studied, when the M'Naghten rule was formulated in 1843. Unless a man who forced sex upon a victim and strangled, beat, or slashed her to death appeared to be a lunatic, bereft of reason, the defence struggled to portray defendants as anything other than evil. Yet, starting in the late nineteenth century, experts in psychology, psychiatry, and criminal anthropology analysed sexual violence and deviant desires according to criteria beyond the law's definition of criminal insanity.[165] The new expert diagnoses of men who committed sex murders had no influence over Augustus Power and his successor, Pierre M. Côté. Whether a convicted killer was a "psychopathic sadist," a "defective degenerate," or a man who suffered from "sexual paraesthesia," he was criminally responsible. These murderers were not the romanticized killers of dime novels or melodramas: they were real-life fiends. The majority of Canada's leading psychiatric authorities agreed. Defendants might be "dull" or men of a "low type" without suffering a diagnosable disease that would render them incapable of forming criminal intent.[166]

On paper, the 1892 Criminal Code's new provisions for criminal appeals reduced the risk that community prejudice might careen into miscarriages of justice. In practice, the most poorly defended men convicted of sex murder were least likely to have the means to appeal, and the two cases in which courts agreed to consider reserved questions – one filed by a judge and the other by a lawyer paid by the government – ended in dismissals. Trial judges denied requests to reserve questions that challenged their conduct of trials. And none of the men who served as minister of justice used his power, under the Code, to address an apparent miscarriage of justice by requesting a new trial or by referring questions to a court of appeal in a sex murder case, including the two trials in which men were sentenced to death without legal representation.

By the onset of the Great War, there was little appetite in the legal or medical profession to make the punishment of men who committed sex murders less certain or severe. In the war's aftermath, the study of sexual disorders began to move from consultation rooms, asylums, and prisons into clinics connected to courts and universities, where researchers sought scientific solutions and modern forms of treatment. The law also began to change by the 1920s, as the proclaimed fairness of Canadian criminal justice was placed on firmer footing with amendments to the Criminal Code that expanded the scope for appeals. A brief campaign to abolish the death penalty occurred over the war years, garnering little support, but it left a question for Canadians to ponder over the following half century: how could a country that executed criminals, with the penalty reviewed by faceless bureaucrats and determined by politicians protected by cabinet secrecy, consider itself civilized?

3

Contesting Convictions and Questioning Culpability between the Wars

As Canada followed England into the Great War, domestic skirmishes erupted on the divisive issue of conscription. Over the war years, smaller battles broke out in Parliament against capital punishment as MP Robert Bickerdike introduced four abolition bills. Despite the failure of his crusade and its unsuccessful revival in 1924, debate over these bills publicized two critical issues: inequities in the fate of persons accused of murder and the fallibility of capital justice.[1] "We find that if a man commits murder and he is very wealthy, he is adjudged insane and saves his neck," Bickerdike proclaimed. Only the poor faced "the full effects of the law." He also alleged that innocent Canadians had been convicted, "hanged on circumstantial evidence which has afterwards been disproved."[2] Although Canada retained the death penalty, Parliament expanded the scope for appeals against verdicts in criminal cases in the 1920s and 1930s. Sex killers numbered among the convicted murderers who sought relief through courts of appeal: six of the twelve cases over the interwar period. Three of those appellants had their verdicts set aside; in addition, in one ruling, the Court of Appeal entered a verdict of acquittal, a decision that took the case to the Supreme Court of Canada where the decision was upheld. Yet, there was no change in the executive's severity toward sex killers in the post-war decades, despite considerable shifts in expert analyses of mental abnormalities.[3] The six men who did not file appeals and the two whose appeals were dismissed were all executed.[4]

After the Great War, the involvement of psychiatrists in sex murder cases became common, not just as expert witnesses in trials but also as assessors of fitness to stand trial. Psychiatric evaluations of condemned men informed the executive's consideration of the death sentence, whether or not courts had considered insanity as a possible defence. Evidence of mental disorders or impairment that did not meet the legal standard of proof of insanity played a more prominent role in the post-war period, including consideration of the emerging notion of sexual psychopathy.[5] American researchers were at the forefront of research in that field, and Canadians began to catch up in the 1920s.[6] No matter which diagnostic label experts and petitioners applied to convicted sex killers – defective delinquent, feeble-minded, sadist, psychopath – such diagnoses carried no weight in post-trial case reviews, including those in which convicted sex murderers allegedly suffered from war psychosis.[7] Even the multiple sex murderer Earl Nelson, who suffered a serious skull injury as a child and spent several years in a hospital for the criminally insane, was executed in 1927, declared sane by the government-appointed psychiatrist. None of the clemency appeals based on claims of mental disorders resulted in the commutation of the death sentence in the interwar period.[8]

The rise in the number of sex murder convictions after the Great War was likely due to significant advances in forensic science, combined with improved coordination between police forces. When the Royal Canadian Mounted Police (RCMP) formed in 1920, it enhanced communications between provincial forces, which every province instituted by the 1920s. Montreal was the country's first capital of forensic scientific expertise. In other cities, university-based scientists assisted police in the identification of fingerprints, blood, hair, fibres, and bite marks.[9] Like psychiatrists, forensic experts expected to be paid, which put them out of reach for most barristers working pro bono. Only the most astute and avid defence lawyers, undeterred by convictions, successfully challenged forensic evidence. In 1937, John Comba's lawyer convinced the Court of Appeal of Ontario that the prosecution's physical evidence was so poor that the judge erred in failing to caution the jury on its unreliability. Another ruling, this one with express political undertones, occurred in 1931, when Quebec's Superior Court set aside the conviction of a Catholic brother for the sex murder of a seven-year-old Montreal girl. The defence argued that the forensic evidence was open to question and that the police had failed to take seriously the prospect that another man, the chief Crown witness, was the killer.

Although the brother, Albert Nogaret, was acquitted in his second trial, rumours of anti-clericalism and allegations of police corruption clung to the case, which took a dramatic turn in 1939 when the man who had testified against Nogaret was indicted for the murder. In the midst of his trial, the judge halted the proceedings to consider the defendant's sanity, and the jury found him unfit to stand trial. No one was found criminally responsible for Simone Caron's murder, and the promised provincial inquiry into the affair was never held.

In the Department of Justice, the administration of the death penalty altered when Michael F. Gallagher was appointed its new head law clerk in 1924, but the close relationship between the executive and the bureaucracy continued to be critical to the disposition of capital cases.[10] Gallagher headed the department's Remission Branch, the section responsible for managing capital case decision-making as well as parole applications and violations.[11] Throughout his extraordinary three-decade career in the branch, Gallagher's capital case memos, like Augustus Power's, were dismissive of claims that convicted sex murderers were sexual psychopaths or unable, for any reason, to control their criminal impulses. His internal correspondence confirms that he shared his predecessors' ethnic- and race-based biases.[12] He also drew principally on judges' reports to inform his advice. Gallagher had no constitutional authority to determine whether condemned offenders' sentences should be carried out; nevertheless, every minister of justice (nine of them during Gallagher's career as branch chief) acted on his opinion concerning the death penalty's deservedness for sex murderers.[13]

Is the Sex Killer Insane?

As the fields of psychiatry, sexology, and psychology moved forward in the early twentieth century, the law regarding the definition of criminal insanity in Canada remained frozen in 1892. Through their connections with practitioners in the United States, Britain, and Europe, Canadian experts and interested amateurs explored an ever-increasing range of sexual behaviour, compulsions, and disorders.[14] Trials of men accused of sex murders exposed the widening chasm between medical and legal notions of responsibility, including cases that did not involve the insanity defence.[15] No matter how grotesque or gruesome a crime was, every defendant was considered legally responsible for criminal acts unless proven otherwise. But proof was unpersuasive unless experts provided it, and that took time and money. When lawyers defended capitally charged offenders pro bono, with only hours to prepare, most stuck to the strategy of claiming that no sane man could commit such a loathsome act. In cases that ended in capital convictions, lawyers for the defence took advantage of the opportunity to frame a convict's history of mental abnormality as a mitigating factor without having to follow the rules of evidence, but the informal court of clemency was hostile to such approaches. In a Toronto case involving the sex murder of a boy, the presiding judge took a keen interest in the defendant's deviant behaviour as well as his diagnosis of tertiary syphilis. Yet, these factors did not amount to insanity under the law. The defendant was criminally responsible for failing to control his impulses. Gallagher and the executive agreed.[16]

The judge who presided over the 1922 trial of Frederick L. Davis was a veteran of the High Court of Justice in Ontario, and he dealt with numerous cases of murder. Justice William Renwick Riddell was the judge in the 1908 trial of Frank Roughmond, the itinerant black man ultimately executed for the rape and murder of Mary Peake.[17] In that case, he went to considerable effort to have the defendant's sanity evaluated, but the government's psychiatrists concluded that Roughmond was just a "low type" of "negro," not insane. Since Davis was an Anglo-Celtic man, Riddell considered that the offence that had led to the indictment – the 1920 murder and sodomization of Philip Goldberg, aged eight – might be attributable to sexual disorders unconnected to Davis's ethnicity.[18] Sodomy was a serious criminal offence, irrespective of consent, and the nature of the victim's rectal injuries and his slit throat indicated that the murderer must be "unnatural." Justice Riddell, a member of the Royal Society of Canada, the International Medico-Legal Association, and the American Association for the Advancement of Science, must have relished the opportunity to preside over a trial that tested theories of the impulses that drove men to commit horrid and bizarre acts of sexual violence. He found the murder so intriguing that he published an article after Davis's execution: "A Case of Supposed Sadism."[19]

Initially, the police followed the theory that a stranger, probably a "foreigner," had enticed the boy in order to commit sodomy, but they came to believe the killer knew Goldberg, who lived in Toronto's inner-city Jewish neighbourhood.[20] Davis, a forty-six-year-old tool maker, had roomed nearby in 1920, and he disappeared across the US border immediately after the boy's body was discovered in a "lonely spot" in Toronto's High Park.[21] A reward of $1,000 from the Toronto police

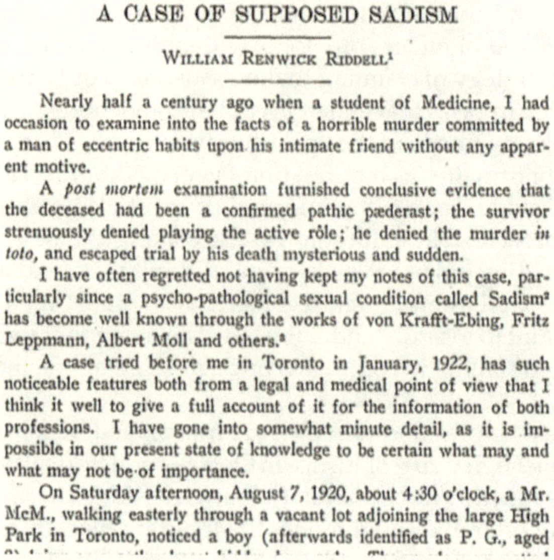

A CASE OF SUPPOSED SADISM

WILLIAM RENWICK RIDDELL[1]

Nearly half a century ago when a student of Medicine, I had occasion to examine into the facts of a horrible murder committed by a man of eccentric habits upon his intimate friend without any apparent motive.

A *post mortem* examination furnished conclusive evidence that the deceased had been a confirmed pathic pæderast; the survivor strenuously denied playing the active rôle; he denied the murder *in toto*, and escaped trial by his death mysterious and sudden.

I have often regretted not having kept my notes of this case, particularly since a psycho-pathological sexual condition called Sadism[2] has become well known through the works of von Krafft-Ebing, Fritz Leppmann, Albert Moll and others.[3]

A case tried before me in Toronto in January, 1922, has such noticeable features both from a legal and medical point of view that I think it well to give a full account of it for the information of both professions. I have gone into somewhat minute detail, as it is impossible in our present state of knowledge to be certain what may and what may not be of importance.

On Saturday afternoon, August 7, 1920, about 4:30 o'clock, a Mr. McM., walking easterly through a vacant lot adjoining the large High Park in Toronto, noticed a boy (afterwards identified as P. G., aged

Image 3.1 Justice William Renwick Riddell (1852–1945) used the trial of Frederick L. Davis for the 1920 sex murder of eight-year-old Philip Goldberg to explore his interest in sexual sadism and "pederasty" (man-boy sexual relations). William Renwick Riddell, "A Case of Supposed Sadism," *Journal of the American Institute of Criminal Law and Criminology* 32, no. 1 (May 1924): 32–41.

led to a tip-off in 1921 that Davis had frequented Mrs. Goldberg's illegal liquor business and was the likely suspect.[22] With the assistance of prison officials in New York State, where Davis was serving a four-year sentence for theft, he was arrested on an extradition warrant.[23] Quoting the telegram that Toronto's sergeant of detectives wired to headquarters, the Toronto *Daily Star* reported the welcome news: "We got our man. It is Fred L. Davis without a doubt."[24] The initial suspect, possibly a foreign maniac, turned out to be an unremarkable-looking small-statured white man.

The murder of Philip Goldberg was not the first case in Canada to involve the sex killing of a male child, but it was the first in which witnesses, lawyers, and the judge raised the prospect that sexual psychopathy might account for the commission of the crime. In 1913, a similar murder occurred near Brantford, Ontario, where twelve-year-old

Charlie Dawson's body was discovered with his throat cut and his body bearing twenty stab wounds. Further injuries and the disturbance of his trousers indicated he had been sexually assaulted anally. A local white man, William Taylor, confessed to the murder (as did Davis). With one day to prepare for the trial, the young lawyer who accepted the case, Archibald M. Harley, argued that the defendant was incapable of forming criminal intent to murder because he was intoxicated.[25] The jury, unconvinced, returned a guilty verdict with no recommendation to mercy. After Taylor's conviction, Harley informed the executive that it was impossible, under pressure of time, to inquire into the man's past "or have a medical examination by competent parties." Respectfully, he asked the Department of Justice to provide an expert to assess his client's sanity. "Clemency in the usual sense of the word is not asked for," Harley pleaded, "simply an investigation to ascertain if Taylor is insane to such a degree as would warrant an amelioration of the death penalty."[26] He was more emphatic when he approached his local MP for support: "The State has a duty to perform in satisfying itself that the death penalty is not being inflicted on an insane person."[27]

Shortly before Taylor's scheduled execution, the government granted Harley's request. The Remission Branch had never before considered a sex murder case in which a boy was the victim, and in 1913 the protocol for expert reviews of condemned criminals had yet to be firmed up. Pierre M Côté, the recently promoted chief, hastily arranged for Dr. R.W. Bruce Smith (Ontario's inspector of Prisons and Public Charities) to examine Taylor, and the psychiatrist provided his report on the day before Taylor was to be hanged: "From the revolting details of the crime … I do not believe that there was uncontrollable impulse resulting from disease of the brain, or that the prisoner has that form of mental disease known as 'Sadism.' He is an ordinary, illiterate degenerate."[28] When Côté wrote his memorandum to the minister, he avoided the doctor's sexological terminology, writing instead in the language of moral condemnation: "The murder was one of fiendist [*sic*] cruelty and was accompanied [by] the heinous unnatural offence of sodomy."[29]

Almost a decade passed between Taylor's and Davis's cases, and over that period psychiatry began to be incorporated in several government departments (particularly the Department of Veterans Affairs), aided by the role it had played in the screening of recruits for physical and mental disorders and the treatment of war-related disorders.[30] Riddell was aware of this work, and he kept up with research in the United States and Europe into violent and sexually deviant behaviour.

The Davis trial provided an opportunity for him to demonstrate his expertise. At numerous points, the judge interrupted the Crown, Gordon Waldron, KC, to ask his own questions concerning the nature of the crime and the motivations behind it. In the midst of the medical examiner's testimony for the Crown, Riddell leaned in to inquire whether a certain category of criminal found gratification in sodomy:

Q: Is there a well recognized class of men who are given to acts of this kind and also given to violence on the loved object?
A: Yes, there are sadists.
Q: Sadism is a well recognized condition?
A: Yes.
Q: Psychopathic condition?
A: Yes, psycho-sexual fiend.
Q: Knowing perfectly well what he is doing, knowing perfectly well it is wrong?
A: Yes, a mental pervert.[31]

In Davis's capital case file, this passage is marked in red and blue pencil, which indicates that the reader, most likely Gallagher, was struck by these psychological neologisms and colloquial terms for abnormality.[32] Justice Riddell's trial report gave an exhaustive account of Davis's psycho-sexual and medical records, but it skipped quickly over his criminal past. Riddell, who had served as president of the Health League of Canada, established in 1919 to combat venereal disease, was most concerned about Davis's diagnosis of tertiary syphilis. Authorities had shown that this grave disease could produce "sadism, a psychopathic condition," he stated. Yet, the judge was unequivocal in his conclusion: "There can be no doubt of the criminal responsibility of the convict under the Criminal Code." Sexual sadism, Riddell underlined, was merely an "impulse" that "can be and generally is resisted."[33] Gallagher, whose signature and comments appear in Davis's case file, advised that the cabinet could consider the murder "without having recourse to the theory of sadism." If they were in any doubt over the death sentence, his disgust sufficed: "The crime itself was a most revolting one and without a single redeeming feature."[34]

The barrister who defended Davis, Basil W. Essery, KC, was more prominent and experienced than Taylor's lawyer, and his campaign for clemency was more assertive.[35] In the trial, he raised considerable doubt over the reliability of the Crown's circumstantial evidence, and it was his cross-examination of medical witnesses for the prosecution that revealed that Davis suffered from syphilis. As he later explained: "I tried to show in this man's defence that his mental condition was such that he could not realize his responsibility in committing so vicious and terrible an offence."[36] Essery's tactic may have backfired, however. The men who served on the jury had possibly reached their verdict before they left their seats, as they returned after just two minutes. Rather than attempt an appeal, Essery followed the same route he had taken late in 1921, when he had petitioned successfully for the commutation of the sentence received by an Armenian man, David Harri, sentenced to death for his part in a taxi driver's murder in the course of a robbery. In pleading for mercy in Davis's case, he emphasized that tertiary syphilis was incurable, which meant that the condemned man likely faced imminent death. Combined with his "general make-up" of "idiocy," there were surely grounds for clemency, Essery added. The cabinet was unmoved. On 1 May 1922, Essery received a cable informing him that Davis's sentence would be carried out.

Frustrated by the government's announcement, Essery framed an eleventh-hour appeal for clemency on the grounds of racial politics. In a direct address to the minister of justice, Sir Lomer Gouin, he asked how the government could have commuted the death sentence of the Armenian "while an Anglo-Saxon not responsible through mental condition and physical condition, destroyed through whiskey, is condemned to die." Essery was also of the opinion that "a great portion of the citizens of Toronto" were "astounded that Harri should receive the consideration he did."[37] Neither the medical nor the xenophobic strain of the peremptory clemency plea worked. The minister replied that the two cases were "considered with equal care."[38] However, the sex killer was the one who was hanged in Toronto's Don Jail on 9 May 1922. As Gallagher explained to a member of the public opposed to capital punishment, the difference between the two was that Davis's case was "revolting."[39]

Broken Hero or Villain?

Despite a lack of consensus over the effects of shelling on the mental condition of combatants, the Great War introduced Canadians to diagnoses of battle-induced neurosis and psychosis in men who had seen action. Psychiatrists disagreed over the issue of underlying psychopathic tendencies, and many asserted that mental and emotional aberrations were unlikely in healthy individuals.[40] The experts the Canadian government hired to assess the sanity of condemned men were averse to attribute homicidal sexual violence to war trauma, as the case of Harry D. Williams illustrated. A wounded veteran, he was convicted of the sex murder of his half-niece in 1925. During his trial, he became melancholic and declared he wished that "one of Fritz's bombs had struck him, as he would not have gotten into this trouble."[41] Neither psychiatrists nor the executive would get him out of trouble after his conviction for murder.

Williams's capital trial was held in Fredericton, New Brunswick, but doubts over his sanity emerged shortly after it commenced.[42] Justice Arthur T. LeBlanc, who appeared anxious to assist the defence, halted the proceedings to conduct a sanity trial to determine the defendant's sanity.[43] Frederick H. Peters, the lawyer appointed to represent the defendant, had only one day to prepare, so the judge's move granted the defence the opportunity to come up with medical witnesses who testified that the defendant suffered from dementia and "confusional insanity." One doctor stated that the defendant suffered from hallucinations and mental confusion, and another described Williams's form of dementia as "a total absence of proper mentality."[44] The Crown, a prominent barrister who worked closely with the attorney general in New Brunswick, subjected the defence's experts to a withering cross-examination. In closing the sanity trial, P.J. Hughes stated that the defendant was play acting, and these gullible doctors had been duped.[45] In forty-three minutes, the jury reached the same conclusion, and they declared Williams fit to stand trial.

The former Mrs. Williams (whom the defendant had abandoned) was prepared to testify for the defence. The defendant had shot and raped fourteen-year-old Cynthia Foster and shot her younger sister, ten-year-old Neacia, but Mrs. Williams thought these crimes were out of character. Williams had "served four years in the Canadian army without any letup, almost always in the trenches." He had always been a "quiet, unassuming, kind-hearted" man, she recalled, but the "terrible war" changed him: "I cannot believe he did it in his right mind."[46] The grieving Foster family disagreed.[47] The girls' father considered the attempt to attribute the crime to the psychological impact of war distasteful: "No, insanity pleas cannot excuse Williams. He had a bad streak in him."[48] After the insanity defence faltered, the jury found the defendant guilty of murder, and they declined to recommend mercy. Williams accepted the decision: "I am willing to make the admission [I] outraged Cynthia Foster," he wrote shortly before he was hanged, "and that act causes me more grief than the actual murder and I hope I will be Forgiven."[49] The government's expert assessor of criminal responsibility, Dr. Daniel Phelan yet again, considered Williams "perfectly sane," particularly in view of his expressions of shame and remorse.[50]

Considered from the perspective of Christian forgiveness and humane justice, those emotions could be seen in a more positive light, several petitioners argued, especially in view of Williams's wartime sacrifice. Professor Wilfred Currier Keirstead, an ethicist with a doctorate in religion and philosophy from the University of Chicago, wrote the minister of justice, Ernest Lapointe, imploring that Williams's war record should "lead to the greatest clemency." In the professor's opinion, psychiatric evaluations of sanity were irrelevant: what mattered was that "exceptional experiences of war may affect a man's character and moral equilibrium and bring that instability of impulses and habits that could lead to the action that he has committed."[51] The Canadian Prisoners' Welfare Association shared this viewpoint. A representative of the advocacy organization claimed that the government should apply a simple formula when considering capital convictions: the "more heinous a crime of this nature the more likely is it that there is mental derangement."[52] The spirit of revenge could be countered if the executive followed this advice. But local newspapers and the community of Fosterville were consumed with moral outrage. "Two innocent children were cruelly murdered to gratify the lust of a beast," the Fredericton *Daily Gleaner* reported shortly after the girls' bodies were found.[53] Enemy bombardment had spared the ex-soldier in France and Belgium, but the Canadian government resolved that he should hang, unmoved by the possibility that invisible war wounds might explain Williams's outburst of sexual violence.[54]

Canada's Greatest Manhunt

A court's request that a member of the bar represent an indigent man accused of a sexual murder was a risk and a temptation. For a junior barrister, accepting the challenge could earn him respect and admiration if he could prise out weak spots in the Crown's case and argue points of law. Even when pro bono lawyers lost cases at trial, a thorough defence helped to pave the way for a well-grounded appeal. But defence counsel also risked being seen by the public as impediments to justice. Sex murders stirred retributivist emotions and stoked expectations of harsh punishment, no matter what the perpetrator's race.

During the Williams trial, Frederick H. Peters received a menacing letter that warned he was putting his own life, not just his client's, in danger by defending the man: "Sir. – Stop now, you are trying to defeat justice, and encourage crime by the same old plea of insanity, and if you succeed you will have to answer for Williams' crime. This is your warning. Beware. K.K.K."[55] The letter arrived in an envelope with a postal stamp from a town 100 kilometers south of the New Brunswick village, where local men had reluctantly handed over the suspect after they captured him. Similarly, James H. Stitt, the barrister appointed to defend Earle Nelson, charged in 1927 with strangling and sexually assaulting a married woman and a teenaged girl in Winnipeg, felt the "weight of public opinion." He tried to build an insanity defence with expert testimony that his client suffered from "constitutional psychopathy."[56] But as soon as the verdict was announced, Stitt informed the press he would not file an appeal, due to the distress caused by the "scurrilous phone calls and anonymous letters" he had received.[57] Although he proceeded down the avenue of executive clemency by reprising evidence concerning Nelson's insanity, Stitt was blocked by the sentiment most Canadians and Americans shared: this monstrous "strangler" was "not worth saving."[58]

Unless murder trials occurred in their home provinces or ridings, clerks in the Department of Justice and cabinet ministers were rarely familiar with capital cases before reports arrived in Ottawa. Earl Nelson's case was an exception. An account of his case, "Canada's Greatest Manhunt" appeared in the September 1927 edition of *The Canadian Police Bulletin*, and scores of newspapers in Canada and the United States covered the case through to Nelson's trial in November.[59] From the announcement of the "strangler's" capture in Winnipeg in June 1927, Canadian law enforcers crowed that they had caught a repeat offender, who had allegedly strangled and raped over twenty women in half a dozen US cities between 1925 and 1926 before he made his way to the Prairie provinces. Continent-wide police bulletins were issued early in 1927, and reports of similar cases helped Winnipeg police identify Nelson, a white man of European heritage, as the killer of Mrs. Emily Patterson and fourteen-year-old Lola Cowan. Described by the Winnipeg police as "swarthy" in complexion, Nelson appeared more menacing to the public through press headlines that warned Canadians about the "dark strangler" and the "gorilla man" who subdued his victims with his inhumanly strong grip.[60] In Winnipeg, the captive was indicted for two counts of murder, and Stitt accepted the court's request to defend the man.[61] But Nelson was condemned by print and radio media across North America long before his trial opened. The defence faced staggering odds, since "the jury's verdict was written by the newspapers for them."[62]

Although Michael Gallagher knew that Nelson was not indicted for a series of murders, he opened his memorandum as if he were announcing an episode of a radio serial: the condemned man was the murderer "popularly known throughout the continent as 'the strangler.'"[63] As usual, Gallagher thoroughly read the transcript, which showed that Justice Dysart had excluded evidence of Nelson's treatment over several years in psychiatric hospitals. Psychiatrists at the Napa State Hospital for the insane in California diagnosed Nelson in 1921 as a "constitutional psychopath with psychosis." After several months, the medical staff considered his condition as "improved," but the hospital did not authorize his release. Nelson escaped from Napa in 1925, and soon after a cluster of strangulation and sexual assault murders occurred in cities across the country. Now the culprit appeared to be snared. With no funds to hire an expert for the defence, Stitt tried to support his insanity defence by calling Nelson's ex-wife and aunt, who confirmed that his behaviour was so threatening and aberrant (including responding to voices and seeing faces) that they had had him institutionalized. The Crown rebutted this evidence by calling Dr. Alvin T. Matthews, the director of the Winnipeg Psychopathic Hospital and one of the province's leading psychiatric authorities.[64] Under cross-examination, Matthews admitted that Nelson was quite likely insane in 1921 and that psychosis could flare up periodically. But he considered Nelson sane when he examined him in 1927, and he was rock solid on the prisoner's criminal responsibility.[65]

In Stitt's appeal for executive clemency, a twenty-eight-page screed sent to the minister of justice, Ernest Lapointe, he quoted numerous medico-legal texts to support his contention that Nelson was not criminally responsible. But his emotional pitch rose when he referred to higher ideals: the values for which the Great War had been fought and the Christian ideal of mercy. Stitt, who had served for three years as a lieutenant with the Canadian Field Artillery and had been severely wounded, reminded Lapointe of their countrymen in France, who died "in an assault at arms to vindicate the message of the Prince of Peace to a world of men weary of injustice." If the cabinet granted mercy to Nelson, these martyrs could rest in peace, knowing the "principles for which they died are pure and eternal." Stitt likened his defence of Nelson in the face of "public displeasure" to his service in the face of the enemy. Ultimately, war had taught him that "the taking of a human life

HOME EDITION

The Winnipeg Evening Tribune

NELSON FOUND GUILTY

Murderer Of Mrs. Patterson Sentenced To Die

AS HIS TRIAL ENDED

200 DEATH TOLL IN GREAT FLOOD IN NEW ENGLAND

PREMIERS ARGUE CONSTITUTION, SENATE REFORM

DEATH SHIP'S LOG TRACES HORROR OF OCEAN DRIFT

Image 3.2 Earle Nelson's capture by the Winnipeg police was a coup in law enforcement circles, after police in several US states had failed to arrest the man deemed responsible for a score of murders involving the strangulation of women. The *Canadian Police Bulletin* described the case as "Canada's Greatest Manhunt." Winnipeg *Evening Tribune*, 5 November 1927.

is an act far better left to the Giver of All Life Himself." Confident that he addressed a fellow Christian in Ernest Lapointe, Stitt reminded him of Christ's teaching that beneficence be "extended unto every man – even the least of these my brethren."[66] What must Gallagher, who screened this letter before it reached Lapointe, have made of this homily? The "X" he pencilled on the final page of Stitt's letter spoke louder than the lawyer's sermon on mercy.[67]

Appealing against Conviction

During the debate on Robert Bickerdike's first abolition bill, the MP for Laval, Charles A. Wilson, requested information from the Department of Justice concerning instances in which "appeal has been made on behalf of the persons convicted of capital offences ... for the exercise of the Royal prerogative of mercy." The concept of appeals to superior courts based on points of law was not a component of his request because Canada balked at following the "Mother Country," which established a court of criminal appeal in 1908.[68] Instead, Canadian lawmakers considered the right to plead for mercy sufficient, since the executive's prerogative was unfettered. Nevertheless, criticism of the existing legislation, which depended on judges' willingness to reserve questions of law, grew after the First World War. Had Earle Nelson's appointed counsel requested leave to file a legal appeal, the Criminal Code provided new options thanks to several amendments in the early 1920s. As of 1920, persons convicted of an indictable offence were allowed to appeal to the Supreme Court from a decision of a provincial court of appeal if the decision to confirm a conviction differed from a judgment in a similar case. A year later, courts of appeal were granted the power to review the "fitness" of a non-mandatory sentence. Then, in 1923, the most significant change took place. Thereafter, the Criminal Code permitted defendants to appeal convictions for indictable offences by right on questions of law alone or by leave on "any ground of appeal which involves a question of fact alone or a question of mixed law and fact."[69] Courts of appeal could set aside any verdict they considered "unreasonable" or verdicts that appeared unsupported by the evidence. Furthermore, a judgment could be set aside if the court determined "a miscarriage of justice" had occurred.[70] However, the 1923 amendment included a notwithstanding clause. Having determined there were grounds for appeal against conviction, a court of appeal could still dismiss an appeal if it considered that "no substantial wrong or miscarriage of justice ha[d] actually occurred."[71] None of these modifications came close to eroding the doctrine of finality (as traditionalists feared). However, these amendments did facilitate successful appeals in the cases of four capitally convicted sex killers in the two decades that followed.[72]

Was it just to execute a man whom police records indicated had been hospitalized for head trauma or diagnosed as criminally insane? This question, pertinent in the Williams and Nelson cases, could have been considered by courts of appeal under the revised statute of 1923, which stated that a guilty verdict could be quashed if the offender "was insane at the time the act was done ... so as not to be responsible according to law for his actions." Had Williams's sanity trial, held within his murder trial, confirmed he was insane, the judge could have sentenced him to be kept in "strict custody" on an indefinite basis.[73] In Nelson's case, the

Crown's own expert stated under cross-examination that the defendant was "a constitutional psychopath – in the borderland – one who might be subject to psychic storm – and which storms might render the individual irresponsible."[74] A Winnipeg-based lawyer, Conservative Senator Lendrum McMeans, supported the 1923 amendment and worked further to move Canada in the direction of England, which had recognized the need to provide legal means to rectify miscarriages of justice.[75] But Canada's limited amendments failed to provoke a sudden upsurge of verdicts set aside in favour of the defence. Provincial courts remained hesitant to grant leave to appeal, especially when insanity was at issue. As a default position, courts of appeal considered it more appropriate for juries to determine a defendant's sanity.[76] And there was no provision in the amended Criminal Code to appeal against the sentence of death for murder, since it was "fixed by law."

The Politics of Miscarriages of Justice

Critics of capital punishment and advocates of persons condemned to death chipped away at the myth that capital cases were treated equally, as the minister of justice informed Frederick Davis's lawyer. In the course of trying to save his client, Bertram Essery attempted to tap into anti-immigrant sentiment and accused the government of treating an Anglo-Celtic man with undue harshness. These were not the sorts of arguments that the revised criminal appeal provisions allowed, although appellants could argue that the evidence adduced did not support the verdict. Generally, appellants continued to focus on questions of law, particularly the judge's decision to include or exclude evidence, or the errors or omissions in his charge, and courts of appeal were reluctant to challenge the convention that jurors were the best judges of fact. In 1931, a narrow technical ruling concerning a breach of protocol in the trial of Albert Nogaret, convicted of the sex murder of a Montreal girl, was typical in these respects. However, the political dimensions of the case were unique. Nogaret was retried and acquitted, but the defence's theory that the police had arrested the wrong man and allegations of anti-clericalism and prosecutorial misconduct continued to float around until 1939, when the Crown's chief witness was put on trial for the murder. When the court determined the man was unfit to stand trial, the fairness of Quebec's criminal justice system appeared doubtful. The investigation and prosecution of this murder left the police, prosecutors, and the premier, Maurice Duplessis, tarnished.

Initially, the case, which was heavily reliant on circumstantial evidence, appeared open and shut. In July 1930, seven-year-old Simone Caron disappeared from home; two months later, the partially decomposed body of a girl was discovered in the basement of a nearby Catholic college. On identifying their daughter's clothes, her parents were distraught – the father "ébranlé" (shocked) and the mother "inconsolable" over her loss.[77] The coroner's report was inconclusive on the question of sexual assault, but Dr. Wilfrid Derome, founding director of the Laboratory of Forensic Research in Montreal and one of North America's premier medico-legal experts, testified that the victim had likely suffered an "intervention sexuelle" prior to being fatally stabbed.[78] Albert Nogaret (brother Dosithée of the Sacré Coeur) was a middle-aged, hearing-impaired man who worked in the kitchen and garden at the Académie Roussin, and he assisted police in the early phase of the investigation. But after a detective from the Sûreté du Québec questioned the brother, he transformed from an important witness into "l'accusé."

Working at the request of the police, Dr. Derome determined that one of the knives owned by Nogaret had a blade that matched nicks in the child's ribs. A possible motive was supplied by the testimony of neighbourhood children, who told police the "gros Frère" (as they taunted him) had offered Simone apples and sweets. The Crown interpreted this evidence as a ploy the brother had used to lure the girl to her death.[79] But the most significant testimony came from Antonio Godon, a general labourer who washed dishes and worked closely with Nogaret. The judge, former MP Charles A. Wilson, had to halt the proceedings to accommodate Godon's bouts of crying on the witness stand, but the nineteen-year-old managed to tell the court he had seen the cook hide the bag containing the girl's body.[80] After a week-long trial, owing to a vigorous defence and several mid-trial twists and turns, the jury returned a verdict of guilty with an added wish for "la clémence du tribunal."[81]

Nogaret had one thing in his favour: his membership in a religious order that supported their fellow brother.[82] By pooling their resources, the Brothers of the Sacred Heart assembled a defence team that included Lucien Gendron, an ambitious KC and criminal defence specialist, who had previously defended an abbé accused of killing his brother.[83] Nogaret's conviction was unjust, Gendron was convinced, and he raised twenty-nine grounds in the appeal he filed in the Quebec Court of

King's Bench.[84] Taken together, they amounted to an argument that the verdict was not supported by the evidence. The judge failed to draw the jury's attention to reasonable doubt, put unwarranted weight on circumstantial evidence, and unduly favoured the prosecution through his praise for the diligence and truthfulness of the police. Justice Wilson had also turned down the defence's request that the jury visit the site of the body's discovery, which prevented them from testing whether Godon could have seem Nogaret move the bag. Gendron was also concerned that the Crown, Ernest Bertrand, KC, and the judge both commented that the defendant (who had profound hearing loss) had not taken the witness stand to declare his innocence. In addition, Justice Wilson, who had a reputation as a hanging judge, commented negatively in his charge about the brothers of the academy, inferring that they had used their influence to protect one of their own from conviction. In the midst of the trial, while the defendant was locked in Bordeaux Prison, the provincial police received a letter that claimed Nogaret was innocent, and the writer (who confessed to the crime) enclosed a bloody ring, which belonged to the victim. This discovery caused a sensation, but Justice Wilson ruled that it had no relevance to the case. As for the disturbed behaviour of the prosecution's key witness (who attempted suicide after the body's discovery and gave his statement to the police from a hospital bed), the judge did instruct the jury to question the veracity of his testimony.[85]

Gendron had one more ground in his appeal: a court officer's interference in the jury's deliberations. The principle that jurors must reach their verdict in secret was compromised in this trial, Gendron discovered after the conviction. The warden of the jury admitted he had responded to a request concerning the possibility that they might recommend mercy by telling them that "verdicts of this kind" had occurred in earlier cases. Compared to allegations of perjured testimony, anti-clericalism, and the prospect that the real sex slayer was on the loose, the ground on which the Court of King's Bench, Appeal Side, granted the appeal – jury interference – upheld a legal principle. The Criminal Code dictated that the jury must be sequestered during their deliberations. If any questions arose, the judge alone was authorized to address them.[86]

Although the Court of Appeal set aside Nogaret's guilty verdict, the judges found the jury's recommendation of mercy ill-informed. Curiously, Justice Hall stated that the trial judge would have "had to tell the jury that they could not return such a verdict." Justice Galipeault speculated that the jury must have believed their "recommendation of clemency would

Image 3.3 Albert Nogaret (c. 1883 to 1938) was initially sentenced to hang for the murder of seven-year-old Simone Caron in 1931. After a successful appeal and retrial, he was acquitted. He died shortly before the chief Crown witness was put on trial for the girl's murder in 1939. *Le Mémorial du Québec*, tome V, *1918–1938* (Montreal: La Société des éditions du Mémorial, 1980), 216.

be forwarded to the Minister of Justice, who might have commuted the sentence [to] one of life imprisonment." Even Gendron stated that the "legal idea of clemency" existed only when the judge could exercise sentencing discretion.[87] Although the jury's reference to the "tribunal" (meaning court) was likely an inexpert misunderstanding of the prerogative of mercy, Chief Justice LaFontaine put great weight on it:

> If [Nogaret] is guilty, his crime is one of the most odious that can be imagined, and the jury recommendation to the leniency of the court is not understandable. If the accused is not guilty, it is the conviction that has no reason to exist, and the recommendation ... would be a poor palliative, completely insufficient.[88]

The judges did not bother with the other grounds for appeal, referring to them as a "number of more or less serious grievances."[89] The court's order of a new trial was simply "in the interest of justice."[90]

Concerns over the tactics police used to secure evidence against the Catholic brother played a more significant role in Nogaret's second trial. This time Gendron flanked himself with two KCs, and he called witnesses who raised doubt about Antonio Godon's comings and goings on the day of the girl's disappearance.[91] A nine-day replay of the first trial took place with the defence facing the same opponent, Crown Attorney Ernest Bertrand. However, the disturbed dishwasher became even more histrionic in his second appearance, and Gendron's cross-examination caught him in a web of contradictions.[92] Amidst fainting spells and bouts of tears, Antonio Godon claimed, as he did in the first trial, that he had attempted suicide because the brothers at the Académie Roussin had commanded him to take poison on the day the girl's body was discovered. The Crown's case unravelled with every question from the defence, and the jury acquitted Nogaret.[93] But the not-guilty verdict left the mystery unsolved: if the brother did not murder Simone Caron, who did?

A seismic shift occurred in Quebec political life in the years that followed Nogaret's trials. In 1936, the provincial Liberals, in power since 1897, were routed by the Conservative coalition with L'Union Nationale (L'UN). Lucien Gendron, a supporter of Maurice Duplessis, L'UN's leader, was rewarded with a new role of special Crown prosecutor in the Office of the Attorney General.[94] Earlier in the decade, when he was defending Nogaret, Gendron accused the Crown of prosecuting the wrong man, and Duplessis (who also held the portfolio of attorney general) agreed. They believed that a Catholic brother (like the abbé whom Gendron had defended in 1924) made an easy target during the Liberal regime.[95] As Quebec's premier from 1920, Louis Taschereau had angered clerical nationalists by encouraging private enterprise, which threatened the ethno-religious basis of collectivism.[96] Now, under the new pro-Catholic regime, Gendron had the L'UN premier's backing to go after Godon.

"Star Witness Is Under Arrest," the headline that greeted readers of the Quebec press on 15 November 1938, offered hope that the mystery of Simone Caron's murder would finally be solved. At the preliminary hearing in December, two handwriting experts testified that the confessional letter and ghoulish blood-smeared ring could have been sent by Godon.[97] His trial for murder opened in January 1939, and Gendron, as prosecutor, was supported this time by another leader of the criminal bar, Antoine Rivard, one of the organizers of the Conservative Party in the 1930s.[98] The court learned that undercover detectives had obtained a writing sample and induced Godon to confess after befriending him and finding him a job in the Laurentians in the summer of 1938. However, officers and jail officials testified that Godon's behaviour was bizarre. He frequently bayed at the moon, raved at night, and wept copiously. This testimony prompted the judge, Justice Wilfrid Lazure, to call a halt to the proceedings. If the "decidedly queer" defendant was insane, he should not be tried for the murder.[99] Against the objections of the defence (which did not present an insanity defence), Dr. Daniel Plouffe, superintendent of the Criminal Insane Asylum at Bordeaux Prison, and Dr. Émile Legrand, a psychiatrist employed by two of Montreal's largest hospitals, examined Godon.[100] Neither man offered a clinical diagnosis, but they agreed he had the "mentality of a ten-year-old, and a marked weakness which permits him to be easily influenced and a tendency to tell falsehoods."[101] Having heard this evidence, the jury (convened in the insanity trial within a trial) found the defendant not criminally responsible. This verdict terminated the murder trial, and Justice Lazure sentenced Godon to be held at his majesty's pleasure in Plouffe's institution.[102] But "l'affaire Godon" quickly flared into a political scandal, which the opposition Liberals ignited and Premier Maurice Duplessis vigorously fanned, then quietly let die.

The collapse of the Godon prosecution presented an opportunity for the Liberals to expose the provincial government's direct hand in the pursuit of a deranged man. The leader of the Quebec Liberal Party, Léon Casgrain, accused the man serving as premier and attorney general of having authorized police entrapment.[103] He also alleged that Gendron knew the accused killer was insane and should have had him examined prior to the trial.[104] Duplessis shot back: during the previous Liberal regime, Nogaret's arrest and trial was the nefarious work of a government hostile to Catholicism.[105] In April 1939, the premier went to the extraordinary length of introducing a bill in the Quebec Assembly to authorize an inquiry into the "inhuman treatment of a member of a religious order." The hounding of Nogaret by the Liberals, Duplessis thundered, amounted to "Bolshevist and anti-clerical proceedings."[106] Casgrain agreed that it was appropriate to launch an inquiry, but he demanded that the probe include the conduct of the police and the Crown in the subsequent Godon case.[107] Furor over the Nogaret-Godon prosecutions on both sides of the legislature dissipated over the following six months in the lead-up to the election of October 1939, which saw the Liberals return to power. The grand standing and point scoring of the party leaders had more to do with provincial politics than the murder of a small child. However, Casgrain and Duplessis, bitter opponents, could agree on one matter: "the brother was innocent."[108] Unfortunately, Albert Nogaret never heard this news, as he died at the age of fifty-one, just prior to Godon's trial.[109] More tragic, still, was the horrible death of Simone Caron, unsolved but not unmourned.

"One of the Strangest Murder Cases in [the] Legal History of the Dominion"

Between Nogaret's acquittal in 1931 and the derailed prosecution of Godon in 1939, a similar case occurred in Ontario – a girl disappears; her body, showing signs of sexual assault, is found by a man who helps police; the police charge him with murder; he is convicted and sentenced to death; an appeal court decision alters his fate.[110] Yet, a different set of political rivalries and tensions filtered into the successful appeal of John Comba's conviction. In this instance, questions of judicial competence were linked to anti-Catholic sentiment, a factor that may have encouraged the majority of justices on the Anglo-Protestant–dominated Court of Appeal to quash the conviction and substitute an acquittal.[111] In the midst of the Depression, when the rate of execution in Canada peaked, the outcome was surprising, but the response to the court's ruling made it unique: it was bitterly contested by the dissenting judge and appealed by the Crown to the Supreme Court.[112]

The case began in the summer of 1937, when thirteen-year-old Ethel Hedderwick went out to pick cherries in the bush near Renfrew, Ontario. When she failed to return home, Boy Scout troops and local townsfolk hunted for the girl. Comba, a twenty-six-year-old Renfrew man, was the searcher who stumbled over the girl's battered body. The doctor who conducted the autopsy confirmed that "the child had been violated," both vaginally and anally, before she died from a blow to the skull, bashed with a chunk of granite.[113] Comba was a long-time resident of the town from a respectable family of Polish heritage, and he told the police that he had come upon the body by chance. But the police had their suspicions, prompted by reports that Comba had been seen in the area earlier on the day in question. Members of the Criminal Investigation Bureau of the Ontario Provincial Police (OPP) came from Toronto to assist local officers, and Comba was subjected to four rounds of questioning over several days. Although he accounted for his movements and repeatedly denied responsibility for the victim's murder, the police charged him with Hedderwick's murder, anticipating that forensic evidence would confirm their suspicions.

The attorney general considered the case sufficiently significant to appoint a special prosecutor, T.M.J. Galligan, KC.[114] The younger man who defended Comba, James A. Maloney, was a local, whose Irish Catholic family was prominent in the Conservative Party.[115] He crafted a well-informed and incisive defence that attacked the prosecution's case, which hinged on testimony from children (who identified Comba as the man they had seen) and circumstantial evidence. Maloney strongly objected to the judge's admission of Comba's statements to police (before he had been cautioned), but he failed to convince the jury to return a verdict of not guilty.[116] At the trial's close, Maloney was so certain the judge had erred that he immediately announced he would appeal for a new trial: "I think there has been a serious miscarriage of justice," he told the press, and he felt "duty bound" to have it rectified.[117]

In April 1938, the court ordered that Comba's death sentence be quashed, a ruling that appeared to surprise Maloney as much as it did the Crown and Justice Latchford, who dissented.[118] A further amendment to the Criminal Code's appeal provisions in 1930 set up the legal framework for the Crown's subsequent appeal against the decision. The Code's revised section clarified and affirmed that appellants had the right to appeal against convictions and acquittals on questions of law plus questions of fact (under limited circumstances); additionally, it enlarged the Supreme Court's capacity to hear criminal appeals from provincial courts of appeal, including appeals filed by the Crown.[119] Although it took some time for lawyers to acquire the confidence to act on this "new freedom," thirty-three-year-old Maloney (assisted by a highly skilled senior barrister, R.H. Greer, former Crown attorney of York County) presented a convincing case.[120]

In its majority ruling, the Court of Appeal subjected the trial judge to criticism. Anglo-Protestant snobbery may have inflected their view that Justice Edgar-Rodolphe-Eugène Chevrier had mishandled the trial. Although the French Canadian Catholic was fifty years old at the time of Comba's trial, it was one of his first capital trials since his appointment to the bench in 1936 (a reward for twenty-six years' service as Liberal MP for Ottawa East).[121] In addition to his decision to admit unsworn statements from the defendant into evidence, the grounds for appeal included Chevrier's recall of two expert witnesses after the jury retired, without allowing the defence to cross-examine them. Maloney also argued that the forensic evidence was flawed and that Crown experts had failed to distinguish hairs taken from the murder scene and the suspect's hair samples. In this case, like Nogaret's, Maloney came across disturbing news after the trial concerning the jury, who had access to newspapers during the proceedings. In sum, Justice Chevrier had failed to ensure the jury had reached their decision based on the evidence. The Court of Appeal agreed that the verdict could not be sustained and directed that a verdict of acquittal be entered.

Justice Middleton, who delivered the unanticipated decision, considered that the judge had failed in his duty to charge the jury that there was no evidence to convict the accused. He also criticized Chevrier for his mishandling of a case based "exclusively on circumstantial evidence." Referring to the Supreme Court's 1936 ruling in Fraser v. The King, Middleton stated that inculpatory facts must be incompatible with the accused's innocence in order to infer guilt, and must also be incompatible with any other rational inference.[122] That decision referred to Hodge's rule, derived from a reported English case of 1838 in which the judge charged the jury that "a single circumstance which is inconsistent [with guilt] is of more importance than all the rest, inasmuch as it destroys the hypothesis of guilt."[123] Accordingly, Middleton insisted that this decision did not make new law.[124] On the contrary, he proclaimed that the majority had fulfilled the highest aims of the law: "to grant the [acquittal] is to advance the cause of justice; to refuse it is to send a man to the gallows."[125]

The chief justice, Francis Latchford, dissented in a lengthy, acid-tongued decision.[126] Nearing the end of his life, he blasted his fellow judges for overstepping their authority. At most, he thought, a second trial was warranted. The attorney general of Ontario, Gordon Conant, was also stunned by the court's decision, and Latchford's dissent provided a base for the Crown to appeal the decision in the Supreme Court. This case marked the first time in Canadian history that the Crown appealed a decision to substitute an acquittal on a charge of murder.[127] The Hedderwick and Comba families were left in suspense as the country's highest court deliberated. Almost two years after the girl's murder, the Supreme Court unanimously upheld the decision, and it further "censored" Justice Chevrier. The judge ought to have "told the jury that in view of the dubious nature of the evidence it would be unsafe to find the prisoner guilty."[128]

When John Comba heard that the acquittal would stand, he was unaware that the ruling had made legal history. "I'm so glad it's all over," he told reporters.[129] Each of the appellate court justices, including Latchford, asserted that he had acted on principle concerning the rights of the accused, the laws of evidence, and the rules respecting appeals. But the Supreme Court's decision was final. Although it brought relief to the once-condemned man and his family, it offered nothing to Ethel Hedderwick's loved ones, left with "deep sorrow" and an unanswered question: who sexually assaulted and murdered their girl?[130]

"Unnatural Desires" and Forensic Certainty: The Murders of Ruth Taylor and Henry Doto

The murder and sexual violation of prepubescent children invariably evoked horror, but crimes of this nature began to raise questions about the psychological make-up of every sex killer by the 1930s. When Fritz Lang's chilling film *M* was released in 1933, Canadians sat glued to their seats in movie theatres as they watched the police try to catch an elusive killer, only to be outsmarted by denizens of the underworld who devised more effective ways to track down the eerie man. In the movie scene where their captive faces a mock trial, he pleads: "I can't help myself! I haven't any control over this evil thing that's inside me … [T]here's this evil force inside me … It's there all the time, driving me out to wander through the streets."[131] The sordid compulsions of the killer called for the actor who portrayed him to bulge his eyes and grimace for maximum dramatic effect. But could real men who hunted vulnerable children and women, committing sexual attacks and murder, mask their twisted tendencies? This was the question a Toronto jury pondered in 1936 as they deliberated over the evidence against Harry O'Donnell, charged with the murder of Ruth Taylor.

In this sex murder, the victim was a young clerical employee from a respectable working-class home in Toronto's east end. O'Donnell lived in the same neighbourhood and was married, the father of a newborn baby. Although a Catholic in a Protestant-dominated city, the twenty-five-year-old mechanic was not an affiliate of a religious order, a member of a persecuted racial minority, or a man who had suffered serious physical or mental ailments. But Taylor's murder caused a wave of fear in Toronto, matched by outrage against the killer. The victim – white, dutiful, and virginal – had been snatched off a rain-soaked street, dragged into a ravine, sexually assaulted, and bashed to death with a rock.

O'Donnell's lawyer chose the same defence strategy that Maloney used in Comba's case: attack the circumstantial evidence the police used to link the suspect to the crime. Frank Regan, KC, acting pro bono, argued that the Crown's evidence was unreliable, and he found experts to challenge it; however, he also urged the jury to consider that the police had concocted evidence against his client and overlooked leads. There was no question that Taylor met a violent end after she finished a late shift in a downtown office and alighted from a streetcar several blocks from her home.[132] But perhaps it was a secret beau, Regan suggested, who had become violent. Or was it another stranger? The defence expressly accused the police of dismissing other possible suspects once they had O'Donnell in their sights. Torontonians familiar with Regan's career were not surprised by his defence strategy. One of Toronto's most colourful lawyers, he was a fierce critic of the police.[133] In 1932, he exposed the Toronto force's botched attempt to frame a man with a criminal record by entrapping him in plans for an armed robbery. This disclosure led to a provincial royal commission in 1933, in which Regan represented the robber, while James C. McRuer, KC, represented Toronto's chief detective.[134] The commissioner's conclusion – that the police were guilty of corruption, incompetence, and cover-ups – left Regan the victor in that round.[135] But the trial of Harry O'Donnell turned the tables: McRuer acted for the Crown, backed by a phalanx of forensic experts.

Regan's theatrical courtroom antics and his testy objections delighted the press but irritated the judge. By contrast, the methodical McRuer

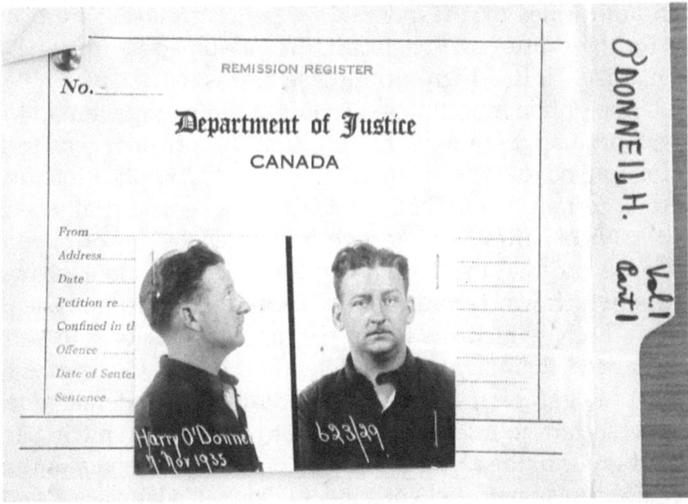

Image 3.4 Harry O'Donnell, the man arrested for the murder of Ruth Taylor, was neither "dark" nor "monstrous" in appearance, but a long-time resident of Toronto's working-class east end. His history of sex offences and violent attacks was revealed after his execution. LAC, R.G. 13, Volume 1601, volume 1, part 1.

built up his case brick by brick and called up an unusually large number of witnesses.[136] The Crown's scientific experts presented their analyses of blood samples, fingerprints, hairs, fibres, and plant materials and testified that this evidence linked O'Donnell to the crime.[137] Regan managed to hire several experts for the defence, and they reached different conclusions, raising doubt that O'Donnell had come into contact with Taylor on the night she was killed.[138] A battle of experts ensued. One scientist later referred to his appearance in the O'Donnell trial as "the most difficult, exacting and delicate thing I have ever undertaken. The nervous strain was terrific."[139] The eyes of the city and its pack of reporters were fixed on the trial, which stretched over an extraordinarily long twelve days. On 15 February 1936, readers of the Toronto press and its affiliated papers learned that the jury found the defendant guilty. O'Donnell was convicted of "one of the most fiendish lust murders in criminal history," the usually restrained Toronto *Globe* reported. The paper also predicted the case would "go down in Canadian criminal annals as the 'Scientific Murder Case.'" It was "dramatic in the extreme."[140]

When authorities first responded to Taylor's murder by posting a reward for the capture of the culprit, they assumed he must be "some sort of maniac."[141] In a high-profile case of this nature, which "greatly alarmed" the public from the first report of the young woman's death, there was little appetite for a finding that the prisoner was insane.[142] Regan focused on matters of law when he filed an application to appeal the verdict, certain that O'Donnell deserved a second trial. He argued that Justice Nicol Jeffrey had improperly charged the jury on circumstantial evidence and that the Crown had exceeded the allowable number of experts (which was technically true). On top of this, morgue photos of Taylor's body, which the judge had allowed McRuer to show the jury, prejudiced them against the defendant.[143] The Court of Appeal's dismissal of Regan's appeal and the Supreme Court's denial of leave to appeal forced him to redirect his efforts to a clemency pitch, based on a different ground: the convict's history of abnormal sexual impulses.

In an effort to spare his client's life, O'Donnell's lawyer moved from portraying the man as a victim of police malfeasance to providing evidence that contended he was not responsible for his actions. Regan persuaded Mrs. O'Donnell to provide an intimate affidavit, in which she attested to her husband's frequent nocturnal absences and his preference for non-penile sexual stimulation. As in Ethel Hedderwick's murder, the pathologist who examined Taylor's body found no evidence of semen in her remains. O'Donnell's seven-page confession, penned in the Don Jail several days before he was to be executed, was the most sensational document in Regan's petition package. Although O'Donnell admitted his guilt, he attributed the murder to his sexual compulsions. In a matter-of-fact manner, O'Donnell narrated his long history of voyeurism and coercive sexual acts, including a conviction in 1929 for attempted rape (the criminal record that had led the police to question him, but evidence unknown to the jury).[144] When Michael Gallagher received this extraordinary set of papers, he granted Regan his request for a meeting to discuss the possibility of commutation. The opportunity to appear before the chief remission officer was unusually generous, and it was likely granted because the minister of justice, Ernest Lapointe, was absent when O'Donnell's case came up for consideration.[145]

To avoid any chance that an insane man might be executed during the short period he served as acting minister of justice, J.A. Cardin, the minister of public works, authorized a psychiatric examination.[146] Dr. Harvey Clare, head of the Ontario Hospital for the Insane, accepted the request to assess O'Donnell. The prisoner had unusual sexual impulses, the doctor confirmed, but he was capable of resisting them. He was also plainly capable of planning attacks and evading capture. Clare's brief report dwelled on the stealth O'Donnell had used to stalk his victims (including the woman he murdered) and to cover up his crime, which showed he did not suffer "any such disease of the mind as would justify his being classed as irresponsible." Nevertheless, the prisoner was "a sexual pervert." Dr. Clare reached this diagnosis partly because O'Donnell had used his hands to sexually assault Ruth Taylor (as he confessed and as the autopsy suggested). The nature of this assault confirmed that the prisoner's "sexual adventures" were prompted by a desire to "gratify unnatural desires."[147] Without expressly advising the executive on its course of action, Dr. Clare cleared any doubt that may have crossed the acting justice minister's mind as he conferred with his fellow ministers. Gallagher's recommendation was clearer still: the law could take its course. In the mid-1930s, neither Mackenzie King's Liberals nor Bennett's Conservatives hesitated to endorse capital punishment as a deterrent, and executive clemency was in short supply.[148] The man who admitted responsibility for the sex murder of Ruth Taylor was hanged.

Despite O'Donnell's confession, and the psychiatrist's diagnosis of his perverted sexuality, all of his victims were female. Men who pursued women for sexual gratification without inflicting serious violence were considered normal, and those who were accused of rape were often defended on the basis that alleged victims had consented to sex.[149] However, men who pursued males for sex were both unnatural and criminal, whether or not they inflicted violence. In the report of the 1938 Royal Commission to Investigate the Penal System of Canada (the Archambault Commission), "homosexual perverts" were the only sex offenders singled out as a class of prisoners.[150] Over the 1930s, the conflation of homosexual desire and sexual predation firmed, particularly in the United States where, in 1937, FBI director, J. Edgar Hoover, declared "war on the sex criminal."[151] In one of the accounts he sent to the nation's press under the banner "For a Crime-Free America," he claimed that local law enforcement agencies' lax approach to homosexuals had led to an alarming increase in the number of sex murders. Looking into the pasts of men arrested for such "loathsome" crimes, Hoover found that most had begun by committing minor offences, which authorities should have recognized as a "blazing signpost pointing to a future of torture, rape, mutilation and murder." Instead, local police typically told petty sex offenders to move along, and when these "fiends" were arrested, state parole boards released them back into society.[152]

Drawing by G. Patrick Nelson

WAR ON THE SEX CRIMINAL!

The safety of America's women and children is menaced by the most loathsome member of the vast crime army—but private citizens can help end his reign of terror. The third article in a series, "For a Crime-Free America!"

by J. EDGAR HOOVER
Director of Federal Bureau of Investigation

The sex fiend, most loathsome of all the vast army of crime, has become a sinister threat to the

sentences—none of which deters him in the slightest degree from other and more serious offenses. And every sex

Image 3.5 Many Canadians criticized the federal government for lagging behind the United States, which was waging war against the sex criminal, led by FBI director J. Edgar Hoover. Los Angeles *Times Magazine*, 26 September 1937.

Two years after Hoover published his declaration of war, the FBI director played a supporting role in the prosecution of a homosexual sex killer caught in Canada. Because twelve-year-old victim, Henry Doto, and the man arrested for murdering him were residents of Buffalo, New York, Canadian prosecutors turned to US officials to document the suspect's criminal history.[153] As it transpired, Stewart Nighswander, aged twenty-five, had a prior history of sexual "perversion." His prosecution on a charge of murder could have served as the coda for Hoover's alarmist account of sex criminals' frequent slide from minor sexual offences to homicide.[154]

Doto's body was discovered in a wooded area just across the international border on the outskirts of Fort Erie, Ontario, in the summer of 1939. The attorney general of Ontario sent the province's top forensic pathologist, Dr. Edgar R. Frankish (one of the Crown experts in the O'Donnell case), to conduct the post-mortem. The boy was found nude, battered, and slashed multiple times with a sharp blade. Surgical tape bound his ankles and wrists, and a strip of cloth had been used to strangle him. Investigators first arrested Nighswander for attempted suicide, because he turned up in a nearby hospital on the day of the victim's disappearance. While he was being treated for razor wounds to his arms, a medical attendant heard him state he had just committed a murder, and the police quickly connected him to Doto.[155] Welland police, the OPP, the RCMP, and their counterparts in the FBI worked together to make the charge stick. Inquiries in New York revealed that Nighswander had one previous arrest for "impairing the morals of a boy." However, a Buffalo City Court judge had liberated the prisoner before he was technically eligible for parole on his promise to support his bedridden mother, recently widowed.[156] That promise, Nighswander subsequently admitted, allowed him to keep seeking out boys for sex.

On both sides of the border, the press followed the salacious trial closely. Within days of Nighswander's arrest, a young Welland barrister, John D.S. Cromarty, agreed to tackle the challenge of representing the accused homosexual killer.[157] Aged twenty-seven and only recently admitted to the bar, Cromarty faced the attorney general's biggest gun, the director of public prosecutions, William B. Common, appointed to assist the local Crown attorney.[158] The prosecution correctly anticipated that Cromarty would attempt an insanity defence, which led Common to emphasize that the murder was meticulously planned. In the weeks prior to Doto's death, Nighswander had treated the boy to ball games, purchased tickets to the movies, and taken him on long bicycle rides. The final trip, a ferry ride across the Canadian border, was the one the defendant had planned as "a final orgy of sexuality" before taking his own life. Common was emphatic that behaviour of this nature could not support the notion that Nighswander was insane: he was simply "an abnormal man with the jitters from his excesses."[159] The defence agreed the man had "abnormal sexual tendencies," but Cromarty faced an uphill battle to convince the jury that these afflictions rendered him not criminally responsible.

Stewart Nighswander's trial was the second sex murder case in which Justice Chevrier sat on the bench, and in this instance, he was spared criticism from the Court of Appeal since Cromarty did not file an appeal.[160] To support an insanity defence, the judge allowed the defence to enter Nighswander's criminal record into evidence, and the defence also called the Buffalo psychiatrist who had tried to treat the young man as a witness. Dr. Matzinger testified that Nighswander, troubled by his impulses, had approached him to help conquer these "unnatural tendencies."[161] In the American expert's opinion, the defendant was a "psychopathic personality of the sexual type."[162] But when William Common pressed Dr. Matzinger on cross-examination, he admitted that the defendant was sane according to Canadian law. The experts the Crown called to rebut the insanity defence agreed that the defendant was legally sane. In another blow to the defence, Justice Chevrier refused Cromarty's request to enter into evidence a landlady's observations of Nighswander's sexual deviancy and abnormal behaviour on the ground that a lay witness could not give "opinion evidence."[163] This ruling left the defence to appeal to the jurors' common sense and to tap their emotions. Unlike Frank Regan, who objected to the Crown's use of disturbing morgue images, Cromarty waved glossy photos of Henry Doto's lacerated nude body before the jury and asked: "Could a man in his right mind commit this crime?"[164] The men who served on the jury appeared to contemplate the question, as they deliberated for nine hours after the six-day trial. In Justice Chevrier's post-trial report, he concluded that the jury believed Nighswander was sane before and after the homicide; however, the foreman had requested further instruction over "what caused them some trouble was, was he able 'to appreciate &c' at the very same moment that he did the act, that resulted in death."[165] Nevertheless, the judge found the jurors' confusion over insanity at the time of event, versus in the past or present, unworthy of comment. For the second time in three years, E.R. Chevrier sentenced a convicted sex killer to death.

When Michael Gallagher looked for a government expert to assess Stewart Nighswander's mental state before the cabinet met, he selected the same psychiatrist who had diagnosed Harry O'Donnell as a sexual pervert whose modus operandi demonstrated his capacity to plan his attacks and to evade capture. During the trial, Cromarty had attempted to prove that Nighswander suffered from schizophrenia in an effort to explain why he could hold a job and appear normal but succumb to deviant impulses. Dr. Clare differed. Nighswander had attempted suicide, rather than tried to escape, but this murder involved considerable forethought (the rental of bicycles in Buffalo, the packing of the tape and straight razor used in the attack, the trip across the border). Although Clare knew that Henry Doto had not been sodomized, he categorized the murder as a sex killing on account of the man's history of "vicious sexual habits," by which he meant homosexual encounters with boys.

More broadly, he classified Nighswander as one of many "cases suffering from perversions [who] are always abnormal and peculiar types of people." Yet, these abnormalities did not amount to insanity, and he thought that no diagnosis of mental illness (dementia praecox, general paresis, manic depression) could explain the prisoner's crime. Still, Clare shaded his conclusion by stating that Nighswander's unnatural practices had weakened his willpower to the extent that he "would not, or could not, control himself in a normal way."[166] When Michael Gallagher prepared his memorandum for the minister, he made no effort to capture the expert's ambivalence: "[Dr. Clare's] conclusion is that the prisoner is not insane, nor a suitable person for treatment." The branch chief's advice rested more squarely on the judge's recommendation that "the law may well be allowed to take its course."[167]

Drunken Sex Maniacs or Loose Women?

There was no question in the minds of medical and psychiatric authorities in the 1930s that homosexual desire and conduct were not just deviant but morally corrosive at a social scale. Experts differed over the question of the "pervert's" threat to others, but all were agreed that heterosexuality was the norm. This consensus made it possible for defence counsel in opposite-sex murder cases to suggest that accused men had engaged in consensual sexual encounters without murderous intent. Some lawyers who defended sex killers of women also suggested that victims were eager sex partners, partially responsible for their fate. In the trial of Harry O'Donnell, Frank Regan made little headway by suggesting that Ruth Taylor may have planned an assignation on the night she was murdered. A paragon of respectability – a dutiful daughter helping to support her family, a responsible worker willing to take a night shift, a church-going Protestant, and as the autopsy confirmed, a virgin – Taylor was the prototype of the blameless victim. Young women who met their death after consorting with strangers, drinking and dancing with men in public venues, did not fit the rigid mould of innocence that Taylor filled perfectly. Canadian scandal magazines, such as *Hush*, published hundreds of articles in the 1930s about young "beauties" who brazenly flirted with danger, only to find themselves in the clutches of "maniacal prowlers."[168]

In trials for the crime of rape, defence lawyers typically encouraged jurors to empathize with drunken defendants who became sexually aggressive after buying a woman drinks.[169] Yet, there were limits to jurors' tolerance of sexual attacks if they ended in a pick-up's death.[170] By the mid-1930s, Prohibition was repealed in the United States and all but a few locales in Canada, but the common law doctrine did not change: drunkenness was not a defence. Some medical authorities contended that drunkenness could be so extreme as to be "pathological," but Michael Gallagher had a low opinion of them. In his review of capital cases involving men convicted for sex crimes committed under the influence of alcohol, he kept his moral compass oriented to criminal responsibility, as did the cabinet.[171]

In Fort William, Ontario, an early spring night in 1936 brought an eighteen-year-old telephone operator, Susan Mildred Johnston, into the company of Arthur Bliss, ten years her senior and the son of a railroad accountant. The pair were casually acquainted, but a dance hosted by the Elks Lodge allowed them to become intimate. Although the young woman arrived with friends, she made a fateful decision to return to the Bliss home on her own at 1 a.m. A party was underway, the man lied to her. As Bliss exited the cloakroom, an attendant overheard him say he'd been looking for a girl all night and "now he had one."[172] Bliss made advances as soon as he reached home, and Johnston repulsed them. Then he became violent, striking the woman numerous blows on her head with a wrench. After he stupefied and raped her, he found the woman had died. Bliss made no attempt to cover up his crime; indeed, he called the police, told them he had been drinking, and that he had killed the woman: "She resisted me and I hit her." Because Bliss's frank admission was odd, the local Crown attorney ordered a psychiatric examination before proceeding to trial (unlike the prosecutors in Godon's case, who proceeded to trial without assessing the defendant's sanity). Two psychiatrists concurred in their view that the prisoner was sane. They considered Bliss a spoiled, ne'er-do-well son from a respected family – a lazy young man, prone to alcoholic sprees and given to indulging his lust with a "lower type of women."[173] The confessed killer attributed his violent act to alcohol: "I did it, but was drunk, and did not know what I was doing."[174] But drunkenness was not insanity. Bliss was criminally responsible, and he was indicted for the murder.

Unlike most men convicted of sex murder, Bliss came from a family with the means to hire a local KC, Fred Babe. But the young man insisted on pleading guilty, and Babe never used his forensic skills.[175] In the preliminary hearing, the coroner confirmed that Susan Johnston was a virgin (not a "lower type") and that the injuries to her body confirmed she had been raped. When Bliss's trial opened, he continued to insist he was responsible for killing the woman. Justice Nicol Jeffrey, who had recently pronounced the death sentence in the trial of Harry O'Donnell, was reluctant to proceed under the circumstances. In his report to Ottawa, he described his dilemma, admitting he was "exceedingly worried as to whether or not [the defendant's] plea of guilty should be accepted." Justice Jeffrey asked the defence if he thought his client might be insane, but Babe disagreed, based on the psychiatrists' reports. And rather than argue his client was so drunk "as not to be able to form the necessary intent," the defence lawyer replied that Bliss had consumed just a few drinks and was sober on the night of the murder.[176] Jeffrey decided he had no choice but to sentence the accused to death. Based on the Criminal Code, which stated that persons charged with murder were "liable" for punishment, whether by "verdict or on confession," and on the English courts' practice of accepting "a judicial confession of guilt" as sufficient to "sustain a conviction," Jeffrey justified his decision.[177] Without a jury of Bliss's peers to charge at the close of evidence, Jeffrey advised Bliss to prepare for his execution, which he set for 5 January 1938. When Michael Gallagher read the judge's report, which arrived without a trial transcript, it was plain that the case was "out of the ordinary," but the absence of a jury verdict did not warrant clemency in his view.[178] Fred Babe, a devout Anglican, as were Bliss's parents, did petition for clemency, but again, he did his client no favour.[179] By describing the man as "courageous and honest enough" to confess to his crime, Babe's moralistic pitch was off-key.[180] "There has been no clement feature disclosed which would warrant commutation of the death sentence in this case," Gallagher concluded.[181]

The actions of Bliss's lawyer foreclosed the prospect of appealing this irregular verdict, but the editor of the *Dominion Law Reports* asked the Crown attorney if he might provide commentary. Cecil L. Snyder leapt at the opportunity, since he had prepared to prosecute the case. But the trial had opened and closed in thirty minutes, and he had said nothing. Since he was building his reputation as a Crown prosecutor in murder trials, Snyder was confident that the minister of justice should know his view of the case.[182] The ambitious Crown attorney confirmed the judge's impression that Bliss had "appreciated the nature of his confession and the consequences resulting from it." He also underlined that the case was "unique in Canada," since the court had accepted the defendant's confession. Although the editor of the *Reports* agreed to publish Snyder's account, he considered the outcome unjust. "Is a plea of guilty proof of guilt" sufficient for a conviction? he asked. How could

ACCEPTS MURIER GUILT PLEA

Said to be without precedent in Canada, Mr. Justice Jeffrey accepted the plea of guilty made by Gordon Bliss (above), of Fort William, and immediately sentenced him to death for the murder of Mildred Johnson last spring. It is expected an appeal will be made.

Image 3.6 Arthur Bliss's family was sufficiently wealthy to hire a KC to defend him, but his decision to plead guilty to the sex murder of Susan Mildred Johnson was accepted by the court, and his lawyer's appeal for clemency failed. Calgary *Herald*, 2 January 1936.

this be so if a plea of innocence is not considered proof of innocence? True, no "miscarriage of justice" had occurred under the law; yet, a larger issue was at stake: "Is there not conflict between the Criminal Code and that cardinal principle as commonly understood rather than as 'legally' interpreted – A man is innocent until proven guilty?" The editor condemned Bliss's conviction as it violated the ideals of "scientific and humanitarian jurisprudence" and was contrary to "British justice."[183] Gallagher had no such misgivings. Even in cases where judges suggested clemency or expressed discomfort over the sentence, as Justice Jeffrey did, he advised that the executive was under no obligation to grant clemency.[184] In Bliss's case, the law took its course.[185]

Public Safety and Cruel Severity

The status of medical authority in the fields of Canadian welfare and criminal justice rose in the interwar period, but it did not reduce the execution rate of convicted sex murderers. One reason for this was the improvement in police communications and investigative techniques, which enhanced the capacity to solve stranger homicides. By the 1920s, every man executed for a sexually related murder (with the exception of Arthur Bliss, who saved the Crown the trouble of presenting evidence) was identified and convicted through scientific means of detection. The psychiatrists whose involvement in capital sex cases made the greatest impact were primarily the professionals who worked for the Crown and the Department of Justice. Under Michael Gallagher's watch, the Remission Branch cast psychiatric diagnoses of uncontrollable abnormal sexual behaviour in a dim light, and ministers of the government, both Conservative and Liberal, followed his recommendations that the law take its course. In 1915, when MP Robert Bickerdike implored his fellow members to do away with the death penalty, he claimed: "There is a demand all over this country for a little more mercy and a little less law."[186] What little demand there was over the following two decades made no impact in Parliament's East Block, where the cabinet deliberated over capital cases.

Advances in the science of criminal detection allowed police to connect suspects to victims and crime scenes through the analysis of physical evidence.[187] However, Bickerdike was wrong: new laws governing appeals against verdicts in criminal cases saved more convicted sex killers than executive clemency in the 1920s and 1930s. Amendments to the Criminal Code provided greater means to challenge the certainty of convictions, including those in which the Crown had used government analysts. But improved prospects for appealing criminal convictions could not on their own rectify the inequities of capital justice. David Cromarty's clemency plea on behalf of Stewart Nighswander, which objected to the judge's exclusion of evidence, was "properly a matter for an appeal," he asserted. He would have appealed, but "there were absolutely no funds so to proceed." Cromarty, a future judge of the Superior Court of Ontario, also complained to the minister of justice that the definition of insanity, based on M'Naghten's case, was outdated: it was "not adequate to meet present day knowledge." Citing a list of authorities (Krafft-Ebing, Jung, and Freud), he concluded that the law's cognitive definition of insanity lagged behind psychological understandings of sexuality.[188] However, the legal notion of criminal responsibility held, and none of the men convicted of sex murders was granted clemency on the basis of mental impairment or abnormality.

Despite parliamentarians' unwillingness to dispense with capital punishment, the report of the Archambault Commission in 1938 indicated that reform-minded Canadians were concerned that the need to protect society be counterbalanced with measures to encourage prisoner rehabilitation. In the administration of justice, the report concluded, there was no place "for weak sentimentality or for cruel severity."[189] It also recommended that "provision should be made for psychiatric services at all penitentiaries" and that all "insane prisoners" ought to be treated in medical facilities, not the country's penitentiaries.[190] However, there was no specific reference to sexually motivated criminals in the report, nor did it mention the treatment of sex killers who were abnormal according to medical experts but sane in the eyes of the law. Within a decade of the report's release, these matters shot to the top of the parliamentary agenda and provoked unprecedented public concern over the sexual psychopath.

4

Sexual Psychopathy and Penal Severity in the Post-War Era

By the mid-1940s, cheap, glossy productions delivered regular doses of crimes committed by ruthless robbers, crazed killers, and sex maniacs.[1] The country's more buttoned-down dailies reinforced the assumption that violent sex crime was out of control by increasing their coverage of sex crimes and rape murders.[2] Reports of unsolved "sex slayings," plus a spike in the number of convictions, flagged that Canada, like its neighbour to the south, had been battered by a post-war wave of "sex crime."[3] Between 1945 and 1952, an unprecedented number of sex murder trials – seventeen – ended in capital convictions, including four cases of homosexual slayings.[4] The volume of these crimes, one senator observed, "has created considerable alarm among the public in general and parents in particular."[5] Sensing this escalation of public anxiety, the Liberal government felt bound to respond.[6]

The passage of a law respecting criminal sexual psychopaths gave the impression that Canada was moving toward a therapeutic model of correctionalism. The 1948 statute provided for the indeterminate segregation (subject to psychiatric review) of offenders whose history of sexual misconduct indicated they were incapable of controlling their sexual impulses.[7] However, the law did not apply to persons charged with sex murders: like any other capital offender, they faced the mandatory penalty of death. More significantly, the legislative recognition of the criminal sexual psychopath had no impact on the fate of the seventeen men convicted for sexually related murders between 1945 and

1952: eleven were executed, and rulings by courts of appeal changed the fate of four. In the Remission Branch and the cabinet, youth was the sole factor that prompted clemency, and the only two offenders whose sentences were commuted were under the age of twenty. By contrast, Indigenous men were singled out for severity. At a point when expert inquiries into the motives of sex killers became routine in capital cases involving Euro-Canadians, long-standing racist readings of "the Indian mind" persisted, from the courtrooms at the nation's "distant edges of authority" to the Department of Justice in Ottawa.[8] The assimilationist objectives of the post-war period found grim expression in the executions of the three Indigenous men convicted of sex murders, confirming that the earlier era of colonialist clemency had come to an end.[9]

Public opinion about the problem of the sex criminal was similarly mixed, incorporating the aspiration to cure and the impulse to condemn. The men responsible for sex attacks on males were reviled as menacing perverts in the late 1940s, and fear of heterosexual "maniacs" also grew after the war.[10] Sympathy toward the families of sex killers' victims became more prominent in the mainstream press, boosted by front-page photos of funerals and interviews with grieving relatives. Some parent and teacher organizations, as well as civic groups such as the Kiwanis, tried to channel grief and outrage into a call for scientific means to detect and cure sexual deviance, especially in young and first offenders.[11] Support for such treatment, if successful, could reduce the number of sex murders. Canadians who fully embraced the correctional ethos complained that the nation was "fettered by an outdated and inadequate system of dealing with sex perversion."[12] Viewed from this modern perspective, the sex killer was a social problem, not an object of punishment.

The administration of capital justice aligned more closely with the majority of Canadians who felt that murders deserved death, not treatment.[13] Government opinion polls, commissioned for the first time in the 1940s, confirmed that seven in ten Canadians supported capital punishment, and the post-war Liberal government maintained that the death penalty was a necessary deterrent against murder.[14] After the British House of Commons voted in 1948 to suspend capital punishment (blocked by the House of Lords), the minister of justice assured Parliament there was "little demand in Canada for any alteration of the present system."[15] Michael F. Gallagher, who remained in charge of the Remission Branch until 1952, would certainly have sided with the majority if a pollster had solicited his opinion.[16] The government endorsed the treatment of sex offenders by amending the Criminal Code, but the same authority retained the death penalty as the mandatory punishment of murder. Additionally, the fate of sex killers condemned to death still lay in the hands of cabinet ministers.

For a fortunate few, courts of appeal saved men from execution.[17] Lawyers who filed appeals against convictions pro bono acted in accordance with professional ethics as they had always done. But many barristers were dissatisfied that Canada was content to leave legal aid to bar associations, rather than follow the United States and Britain in developing public defender programs and administering legal aid for persons accused of criminal offences.[18] Believing that "every reasonable precaution must be taken to protect [defendants] from an unfair trial or an excessive punishment," leading bar members put themselves forward to defend accused murderers before trial courts and courts of appeal.[19] Twelve of the seventeen men convicted of sex murder between 1945 and 1952 were represented by counsel who appealed the verdict. Three guilty verdicts were set aside, and in one case – that of the Windsor "Slasher" – the conviction was quashed.[20] These legal contests focused increasingly on the rights of the accused: no matter how vicious the offender or how ghastly the murder, defendants deserved a fair trial and legal representation to contest unfair verdicts. As Canada was proudly aligning itself with the modern "free world," this message took on deeper meaning. But the review of capital convictions was governed by an ancient prerogative. Clemency was still an act of grace, unbound by rules that distinguished fairness from unfairness.

The Criminal Law and the Criminal Sexual Psychopath

In a retrospective on the formation of the Canadian Psychiatry Association in 1951, a member observed that "a remarkable expansion of psychiatric fields of interest" had occurred over the previous decade. The prime reason was "the extension of psychiatric services in the armed forces for the selection of recruits and the treatment of psychiatric disorders."[21] No expert better illustrated psychiatry's place at the centre of government than Dr. Brock Chisholm, a specialist in "preventive" psychiatry and a member of the University of Toronto's medical faculty. In 1942, he became the Canadian Army's director general of medical services, where he established a program that tested the mental health of recruits. Statistics from Chisholm's screening program, published after the war, painted a gloomy picture of Canadian manhood:

the army had rejected almost 50 per cent of recruits, the majority of them on the grounds of "mental retardation and temperamental instability."[22] This "astounding proportion" was "a lesson to heed," according to the Toronto *Globe and Mail*. Since Canada had invested wisely in the physical health of its troops, the peacetime government must not backslide by neglecting the nation's mental fitness.[23] Although the Great War ushered psychiatrists into the criminal justice system, they gained a stronger foothold after the Second World War, accompanied by psychologists, sociologists, and social workers.[24] A new army of credentialed experts began to mass, armed with tweed jackets, white coats, and clip boards, buoying hope that sexual psychopathy could be prevented, detected, and treated.

The work of these professionals was no longer confined to academic studies. Journalists promoted and popularized research on the causes of criminality and introduced the public to studies of sexual psychopathy.[25] One magazine article (titled "The Truth about Sex Criminals") described existing penalties for sexual offences – particularly whipping as a penalty for rape and attempted rape – as "vindictive" measures, built on "hatred and repugnance." Canada's laws could become more humane and effective if they were informed by modern studies of the psychosocial aetiology of abnormality.[26] By the war's end, Canada trailed several US states, which had begun to subject men diagnosed as unable or unwilling to curb violent or deviant sexual impulses to indeterminate segregation.[27] It was long past time to catch up.

Canadian parents' organizations, social clubs, and local women's groups played a critical role in pressuring the federal government to amend the Criminal Code, but they needed parliamentary allies. Howard C. Green, the Progressive Conservative MP for Vancouver South, was an early and passionate supporter of measures to combat the rise in moral offences against children.[28] Speaking on behalf of his alarmed electorate in 1947, he called for federal legislation to tackle all forms of sexual offending "due to a psychopathic condition."[29] The minister of justice, James L. Ilsley of Nova Scotia, dragged his feet, since he knew that professionals differed on the question of psychopathy: "extremists" claimed psychiatrists could solve the sex crime problem, whereas skeptics considered it impossible to predict which sex offender might reoffend or commit homicides.[30] Yet, the government decided it must do something to address these concerns. In 1948, in the final months of William Lyon Mackenzie King's tenure as prime minister, the Liberals introduced a criminal sexual psychopath (CSP) amendment to the Criminal Code.[31]

Although it was a government measure, the parliamentarian most committed to the bill was Conservative backbencher and future prime minister, John G. Diefenbaker.[32] Reports on the impact of CSP statutes in US states were inconclusive at best, Diefenbaker acknowledged, but he felt that Canada needed such a law to ensure that "a pervert" on trial for a sexual offence "should receive such remedial treatment as is provided for."[33] Arthur L. Smith, a fellow Progressive Conservative (and like Diefenbaker, an experienced criminal lawyer), agreed: "Let us place first the curative idea." Smith could recall several capital cases in which men had been hanged for murder "and who, it occurred to me, were under an impulse, an urge or something of that kind which they were quite unable to resist."[34] Late on the night of 14 June 1948, the debate in the House ended with an agreement on the wording of the amendment, which authorized the segregation of criminal sexual psychopaths on the advice of two government-appointed psychiatrists.[35]

Despite the CSP statute's endorsement of modern correctionalism, countervailing forces were at play in government ranks and amidst the broader public. After the amended Criminal Code received royal assent on 30 June 1948, some commentators were disappointed that criminals had first to be found guilty of a sexual offence before a judge could impose an indefinite sentence.[36] In Parliament, one of the government's own party members, Jean-Francois Pouliot of Quebec, considered the legislation preposterous.[37] Why endorse untested scientific theory when the penal law had proven itself perfectly adequate? "In my view," he thundered, "the death penalty is a rampart against crime." As a member of the bar, he saw no reason to treat sex criminals differently from other violent offenders: "So long as the death penalty exists, I do not see why we should have compassion for these men who act like brutes, who attack young children and who kill them." To Pouliot, this new law hoisted the rights of "the bestial criminal offender" above the rights of innocent children and alarmed parents.[38] Justice Minister Ilsley disabused the outspoken backbencher of the notion that "anything is to be relaxed here."[39] The minister, his fellow cabinet members, and the chief of the Remission Branch were all committed to manning Canada's rampart against sex murderers.

"Sex-Crazed Fiend" or Youth "with the Mind of a Child"?

Between the allies' victory in the European theatre in June 1945 and the revision of the Criminal Code in 1948, twelve capital cases concerning men condemned to death for sex murders required the attention of the

Remission Branch.[40] The summary reports Gallagher prepared for the minister of justice and his fellow members of Prime Minister Louis St. Laurent's cabinet referred, in most cases, to psychiatric assessments. Defence lawyers with resources sufficient to hire psychiatrists, in the course of trials or afterwards, submitted diagnoses of mental impairment, psychological disorders, or subnormal intelligence to support clemency bids. Many of these men had prior histories of sex crimes and aberrant sexual behaviour, which had not been treated or cured despite periods spent in mental hospitals. Yet, evidence of a "course of misconduct in sexual matters" and "a lack of power to control his sexual impulses" was not dispositive in the final phase of capital justice.[41] Whether or not convicts appeared to suffer from sexual psychopathy, these killers were unworthy of clemency. In the early post-war years, the only ground for compassion was youth.

Armand Proulx and the girl he was convicted of raping and murdering, Barbara Smith, were both in their teens. In the true crime account of the murder, "The Bloody Knife Points to Death," the hack writer took his readers back to a warm mid-summer evening in Winnipeg. The Smith family felt no qualms about allowing their fifteen-year-old daughter to attend the pictures downtown without an escort late at night. But she never made it home. According to the *Daring Crime Stories* feature, a "hot panting beast" seized the girl, and his "groping hands told her the worst." Unable to subdue her, the "sex-crazed fiend" stabbed her numerous times, then fled. Further details (her skirt was raised and torn pieces of "a pair of panties Barbara had worn" were found near the body) made it clear to readers that this was a sex murder.[42]

The story, published two years after the trial, praised the sleuthing that led the police to arrest Proulx and the prosecution that ended in his conviction. This tale fulfilled the requirements of the genre – a mystery solved, and a culprit brought to justice – but it cut out the life-and-death drama of executive discretion. The contents of Proulx's case file, assembled by Remission Branch clerks, include documents that point to three contentious issues that arose in the disposition of capital sex cases after the war: the criminal responsibility of youth, the tactics police used to extract confessions, and the culpability of persons found to be mentally deficient or defective.

Winnipeggers who jostled their way into the courtrooms where Proulx was arraigned and put on trial learned more about Barbara Smith's death than did readers of the true crime story.[43] When the trial judge summed up the case, he referred to police testimony that Proulx had

Youth Named In Smith Murder Case

ARMAND PROULX

Joseph Henri Armand Proulx, 16, 277 Dufferin ave., is the juvenile charged with stabbing to death Barbara Marion Smith, 15, shortly after midnight Saturday, July 28, it was disclosed following his appearance before Judge F. A. E. Hamilton in St. Boniface juvenile court this morning.

Judge Hamilton had the case transferred to St. Boniface police court, where the youth will appear later today.

Barbara Smith was murdered just after midnight July 28 in a moonlit field not more than 60 yards from her home, 505 Notre Dame ave., St. Boniface. She was on her way home at the time.

Within six hours after she died, St. Boniface and Winnipeg police apprehended Proulx at his home. The youth is being held in St. Boniface jail now.

When he appears in the adult court, police say, he will be charged with the murder, and the date for his hearing will be set.

Clifford W. Brock, K.C., is acting on behalf of Proulx. Crown prosecutor is E. J. Thomas.

Image 4.1 Although Armand Proulx could have faced trial in Winnipeg's juvenile court, the judge's decision to transfer the case to adult court meant that the sixteen-year-old would face the death penalty if convicted of Barbara Smith's murder. Winnipeg *Tribune*, 14 August 1945.

freely confessed he had "followed the girl, tried to force her down – in other words, tried to rape her – and she resisted and he let her have the knife," stabbing her three times in the chest. Because the defence was argued on the basis of insanity, the judge reminded the jury that Proulx was a youth of subnormal intelligence, whom the police had allegedly tricked into confessing. Justice A.K. Dysart, the same man who had presided in the trial of the "Strangler" almost twenty years earlier, charged the jury to consider carefully the defendant's responsibility: did Proulx's "mental deficiency" excuse his actions?[44] The jury was uncertain.

The judiciary often frowned upon jury recommendations to mercy, since they could possibly indicate disagreement. In Quebec, the Court of Appeal raised this concern when Albert Nogaret appealed his murder conviction in 1931. The difference in Proulx's trial was the judge's encouragement of the jury to indicate their wish that the youth be spared. During their deliberations, the foreman asked Justice Dysart whether they could recommend mercy. "By all means," he replied. Not only that, he assured them: "Any recommendation which you wish to give will be gladly received." The jury delivered their guilty verdict with a recommendation that the death sentence be commuted on the ground of Proulx's "confused mental condition." The veteran judge commended their decision and boldly predicted that "leniency ... will almost surely be exercised." Dysart also told the jury that he would add his own recommendation.[45] The judge's prediction of leniency was confirmed on 28 December 1945, when the executive announced the commutation of Proulx's death sentence.[46]

Canadians who read the news had no idea of the complex of factors behind the cabinet's decision, including the expert-supported case constructed by Proulx's defence counsel, the judge's support of penal welfare ideals, and the government's discomfort over the execution of a youth. Locals knew that Proulx was Métis (the Remission Branch summary stamped him as a "French half breed"), but they would not have known how advocates of clemency, including his lawyer, used this racist terminology to identify the young man's family.[47] However, this was not the only rationale presented as a possible reason for the commutation of Proulx's sentence.[48] Calls for clemency drew much more attention to his mental impairment, his frequent drunkenness, his poor upbringing, and above all his age. Proulx was one of fourteen children, raised in the sort of family pathologized in social surveys and psychiatric reports that traced delinquency and sexual deviance to crowded living conditions, poverty, and lack of schooling.[49]

Although the Proulx family was indigent, the lawyer Justice Dysart called upon to defend Armand Proulx was likely the man best suited to take on the task.[50] Clifford Wallace Brock was not just a local KC but the former provincial chairman of the Executive Committee of the Canadian Welfare Association's Prisoners Aid Division.[51] In this capacity, he kept abreast of scientific research into the mental and physical causes of delinquency. Using his connections, he convinced two of the province's most respected psychiatrists to testify that Proulx was mentally impaired, and both men pegged the defendant's mental age at no more than a ten-year-old's.[52] This testimony did not meet the legal test for insanity, but Brock anticipated it might save his client from death if he were convicted.

After Proulx's conviction for Barbara Smith's murder, his chronological age became more salient than his mental age. Dysart's report confirmed that Proulx's first appearance to face the murder charge occurred in Winnipeg's juvenile court, but the case was transferred to adult court.[53] At the trial in adult court, Wallace Brock referred to the defendant repeatedly as a "boy," a "lad." Clerks in the Remission Branch, working with local authorities, managed to pin down Proulx's age for Gallagher's memorandum, noting his age at the time of the crime, at his conviction, and at the date set for his execution (seventeen years and four months). His age raised a question Gallagher could readily answer: was the government prepared to execute a teenager with the "mind of a child?"[54] In the 1930s, half of the capital offenders aged twenty and under were executed, but that rate tailed off by the early 1940s.[55] Backed by the judge's "hearty concurrence" with the jury's recommendation, Gallagher advised that the "boy's" death sentence "may well be commuted to life imprisonment," and the executive agreed.[56]

Victimizer or Victim?

The recognition of youth as a transitional period between childhood and adulthood led to the establishment of juvenile courts and reformatories in numerous countries around the turn of the twentieth century. The Canadian criminal justice system followed that trend, aiming to divert youth from a path of criminality.[57] The Juvenile Delinquents Act of 1908 applied to persons over the age of criminal responsibility (seven) but not fully adult (under twenty-one). On account of their youth, "delinquents" were spared the penalties adults faced under the criminal law.[58] This legal apparatus was critical in Armand Proulx's prosecution. Had he faced trial in Winnipeg's juvenile court, he could not have been sentenced to death, but because juvenile court judges had the option to transfer youth aged over fourteen, charged with indictable offences, to adult criminal courts, his conviction led to his capital sentence.[59] As the Proulx case suggests, the heyday of the child-saving movement was starting to fade by the 1940s.[60]

Public perceptions of juvenile crime and criminals grew more complex and contradictory in the post-war era. On the one hand, psychologists and psychiatrists emphasized childhood and youth as a critical phase in psychosocial development, to be carefully managed through a course of frank but wholesome sexual education; on the other hand, many commentators believed that Canada's young people were veering perilously from pre-war higher moral standards. The period's cheap amusements – spicy pulp magazines and novels, lurid comics, and racy Hollywood movies – pandered to teenagers' base taste and encouraged unnatural desires.[61] In January 1946, Ontario's deputy attorney general observed that murders committed by young men had greatly increased, many of them "extremely brutal attacks."[62] Little did he know then that the person whom police would arrest later that year for a series of stabbing murders in Windsor, Ontario, would turn out to be a teenager, immersed in that culture. The case of Ronald Sears, unlike Proulx's, would raise a different question concerning culpability: was the perpetrator of a homosexual sex murder a victimizer or a victim?

Sears, an avid watcher of horror films and reader of pulp crime literature, was seventeen years old when detectives in Windsor arrested him in 1946. Over the previous year, the city had been on high alert as the number of knifing victims mounted with no suspect arrested. The "Slasher" (the press's name for the mystery killer) targeted adult males, not the typical victims of sex attacks, and each assault had occurred at insalubrious spots on the waterfront. Although the crimes began in the summer of 1945, the assaults were not connected until they resumed midway through 1946, when police picked up similarities in the victims' backgrounds. Local and national newspapers joined the hunt, and they revealed that each victim was a known homosexual, whom the Slasher had likely attacked during sexual assignations. Prior to Sears's arrest, the Windsor *Star* informed its readers that "experts in psychology" had shown that murders by homosexuals were motivated by "senseless blood-lust," which meant they could have been committed only by "someone with a perverted mind."[63] The effort to identify that "someone" received a boost after two victims, who survived near-fatal assaults, gave police a description of the attacker and his weapon.[64]

Until the press published this information, Sears lived a quiet life in town with his respectable white Protestant family.[65] As soon as Sears's sister-in-law saw the descriptions, the family decided to contact the authorities.[66] Under intense questioning without parental supervision, Ronald Sears confessed to numerous attacks, and Windsor detectives used that evidence to charge the youth with two counts of murder and three counts of attempted murder. Although he admitted his guilt, Sears stitched an exculpatory motive to his confession. Over the past year, he had been "on the lookout for men seeking abnormal sexual relations" because a "pervert" had sexually abused him as a child.[67] The defence tried to exclude this confession from evidence in Sears's trial and to present the defendant as mentally abnormal, but the two psychiatrists who testified for the Crown deemed the youth sane. The jury agreed and pronounced the defendant guilty on 18 September 1946. However, the defence, the trial judge, the Crown psychiatrists, and many observers of the trial were convinced that Sears was "far from normal."[68]

Aware that an appeal against the conviction was underway, the Remission Branch's preparation of Sears's capital case file proceeded until 20 November 1946, when the Ontario Court of Appeal set aside the verdict and ordered a new trial.[69] The murder trial, which attracted voluminous press coverage across Canada and the United States, was Justice Dalton Wells's first capital case. His decision to rule the defendant's confession admissible was a keystone in the Crown's case, but Wells worried that the defendant was not mentally competent. In his post-trial report, he stated: "Sears falls very far short of the moral responsibility for his acts which might be expected … and in my opinion his general intelligence is below normal." The Crown-appointed psychiatrists who pronounced the young man sane were equally concerned about Sears's fate, and they contacted Wells privately after the trial to inform him that Sears "suffer[ed] from sexual aberrations, probably of a homosexual and sadistic character." Wells also reminded the minister of justice of the prisoner's age: "Sears is hardly more than a boy in years."[70] Some members of the public were concerned about the impending execution of a "boy." In a letter addressed to Prime Minister Mackenzie King, a high-minded citizen advised that granting clemency would "fortify the sacredness of the immortal principle that the soul of Youth is precious and more susceptible to the temptations and influences of modern society than the soul of the hardened adult." This writer underscored

★ ★ ★

He Must Hang

Ronald George Sears, 18, confessed "slasher" of Windsor, Ont., shown above shortly after he was sentenced to death for knife murder of Canadian soldier on December 3. (Acme Telephoto.)

* * * * * * * *

Windsor Slasher Is Sentenced to Hang

WINDSOR, Ont., Sept. 19 (AP)—Mild-mannered, 18-year-old Ronald George Sears must pay with his life for the knife murder of a Canadian soldier.

He was sentenced to hang December 3 by Justice Dalton Wells of the Ontario supreme court immediately times and his throat was slashed, crown witnesses testified.

Sears was arrested last July 6 after his sister-in-law identified as her property a butcher knife that was found in the back of Joseph

See KILLER — Page 8

Image 4.2 The much-feared Windsor "Slasher" turned out to be a clean-cut, Anglo-Celtic youth. He confessed to stabbing men he enticed into sexual assignations because a man had sexually abused him as a child. Lansing *State Journal*, 19 September 1946.

that compassion was appropriate in any case of "mental or physical injury or defect." From the mysterious and greatly feared "Slasher," Sears transformed into an object of "benevolence."[71]

Had the Court of Appeal not quashed the verdict and ordered a new trial, the judge's recommendation and the cabinet's recent decision to commute Proulx's sentence would have inclined the executive toward clemency. The matter at the heart of Sears's appeal against conviction was the improper questioning of the suspect. Sears's working-class family had no means to fund an appeal, but the case's notoriety drew a highly accomplished barrister. Goldwin Arthur Martin had put his name forward for pro bono work, and the Ontario Court of Appeal requested his service in arguing the appeal.[72] Martin notched his first successful appeal in a murder case at the age of twenty-six, and he was the country's "only lawyer of first-class talent" in the mid-1940s to dedicate his practice to criminal defence.[73] In his oral argument in the Sears case, Martin contended that the confession was false and coerced. The convicted youth was not a murderer but a "boy" with a "morbid imagination," which the police had exploited in their desperation to find the killer. "I also suggest that there is evidence that he saw too many horror movies," Martin added.[74]

Every justice on the appeal court bench agreed that Windsor's detectives had failed to extract a voluntary confession. "To take a boy into custody and question him for eight hours and then for him to collapse from exhaustion ... doesn't sound like justice to me," Justice Laidlaw grumbled as he challenged the Crown. The chief justice, Robert Spelman Robertson, criticized the "formidable force" the police had used "to arrest the boy," and another member of court asked why the police had refused to allow the suspect "to see his father."[75] Martin's construction of Sears as a fragile youth, intimidated by bullying detectives, put authorities on notice: the methods used to apprehend and prosecute sex murderers could undermine convictions. A new breed of criminal lawyer was ready to pounce on law enforcers' "third-degree" tactics in order to defend civil liberties.[76]

Tué dans circonstances révoltantes: Hunting and Hanging Child Killers

The Windsor "Slasher's" victims – men whom the police and the public considered "perverted" – enflamed Canadians' fear and loathing of homosexuals in the post-war years.[77] Some members of the public, who considered Sears's death sentence unjust, approved of his murders: "I understand the police know where most Sexual Perverts are and yet nothing is done until they have done something terrible ... In my opinion they need stabbing."[78] Revulsion over homosexuality put police under intense pressure whenever murders appeared to be the work of "perverts." In the immediate post-war period, when the number of reported child homicides increased, the police used every tool at their disposal to arrest suspects. The men they charged with the murder of children to gratify deviant sexual desires were irredeemable in the eyes of most Canadians, whether or not they suffered from sexual psychopathy. Concern over civil liberties took a back seat whenever the public heard the welcome news: child killer caught.

The murder of nine-year-old John Benson left Montrealers reeling between "sickened horror and furious indignation."[79] Unlike the adults the "Slasher" attacked, Benson was a tragic victim, "a most attractive boy of sunny disposition and good character," according to the Montreal *Gazette*. His murder took place in daylight, in the heart of the city's winter playground on Mont Royal. Blood stained the snow where Benson was attacked, an infrequently travelled stretch of the park dubbed "the jungle." The police were familiar with the denizens of this heavily wooded area – drunks, prostitutes, and "perverts."[80] Frequenters of the jungle and known sex offenders were the first suspects questioned. The *Gazette*'s editor complained that this tragedy was the result of "a somewhat lax policy" on the part of the police toward "sexually perverted and mentally unbalanced persons." Because authorities had a policy of toleration toward these offenders, and since courts let them off with light sentences, they were "free to indulge their distorted inclinations." So long as "men of this type are left free to corrupt young children of both sexes," shocking murders were bound to occur.[81]

Press coverage of the boy's funeral on 17 February 1945 emphasized the emotional impact of the crime on his family and those concerned about their welfare, a feature in common with stories and images of Winnipeggers who shared in the grief of Barbara Smith's family.[82] *La Presse*'s reporters described the open-casket ceremony and commented that women, who dominated the crowd, filed by the body in silent tears: "tous réunie en cet endroit pour sympathiser avec M. et Mme Victor Benson dans leur terrible épreuve."[83] Over the two months that followed the crime, communal grief turned to anger, as detectives questioned 150 suspects without solving "one of the toughest cases on the police blotter."[84]

LA PRESSE

LE PLUS GRAND QUOTIDIEN FRANÇAIS D'AMÉRIQUE

PAGE 3

Aux funérailles du jeune John Benson

Une foule considérable de parents, d'amis et de citadins a assisté hier après-midi, en la chapelle William Wray, 2075, rue Université, aux obsèques du jeune John Benson, tué dans des circonstances révoltantes samedi après-midi sur le flanc de la montagne. Les photos ci-haut ont été prises à l'issue du service et avant le départ du cortège pour le cimetière du Mont-Royal. A gauche, on remarque M. et Mme Victor Benson, le père et la mère de la petite victime, ainsi que ses deux petites soeurs, à gauche l'aînée Juliette, et la cadette Phoebe, en avant à droite. — La photo de droite montre la sortie du cercueil, précédé du révérend Nathaniel Noseworthy, de l'église anglicane S.-Alban, qui a dit le service. — Enfin, dans le médaillon, la photo du garçonnet inconnu que la Sûreté municipale a posté dans une voiture face à la porte des établissements funéraires, dans l'espoir qu'il reconnaîtrait le sadique qui l'a accosté jeudi dernier dans la montagne en lui donnant rendez-vous pour le samedi suivant à l'endroit et à l'heure même du meurtre. Cette photo a été prise à l'improviste, à travers la glace de la portière de l'auto des détectives. — (Clichés la "Presse").

Image 4.3 The grieving family of John Benson (inset) was highlighted in the coverage of the murdered boy's funeral. *La Presse*, 28 February 1945.

After the Brotherhood of Policemen in Montreal posted a $100 reward for leads, a resident from an indigent men's shelter identified one of his neighbours. Ronald Charles Chassé made a likely suspect, having served time in Alcatraz and Leavenworth penitentiaries in the United States. Their captive had never been convicted of a sexual offence, but they discovered that he had spent time in the 1930s at the federal Hospital for Defective Delinquents in Springfield, Missouri, where doctors had tried but failed to cure his homosexual urges.[85] Deported from the United States after his release from Springfield, Chassé returned to Canada and tried to enlist in the Canadian Army. Although he was accepted, he became one of the thousands of men the forces pronounced "unfit," and the army discharged him on account of his "anti-social" personality.[86] After Chassé was charged with Benson's murder, the police and prosecution were determined to make the charge stick.

Chassé, a French Canadian man with no ties to family or friends, also lacked the resources to support his defence, and like most capitally accused persons in the period before legal aid, he depended on a court-appointed lawyer. The man who represented him was a promising young Montreal criminal lawyer, and like Harry O'Donnell's feisty defender, he was a thorn in the side of the city's police. Jean Drapeau, the firebrand who later launched a campaign to combat police corruption and the tolerance of immorality in the city, pressed the same issue that led the Court of Appeal to quash Sears's conviction: the abuse of police powers out of desperation to find a culprit.[87] Although forty-three-year-old Chassé was not a vulnerable youth, Drapeau charged that the police had cowed their suspect into confessing.

During the trial, detectives admitted they had found the suspect "terribly depressed." As soon as they accused Chassé of the crime, the man's speech became disjointed, and the force's chief medico-legal advisor told the police they should call upon Dr. Plouffe, the psychiatrist in charge of the Bordeaux Prison's Criminally Insane facility. But the police persisted until Chassé confessed. During the voir dire phase of the trial (concerning the admissibility of his client's statement), Drapeau put the defendant on the stand in order to demonstrate how the police had intimidated him: "Ils ont fermé les lumières, ils m'ont tourmenté; ils m'on crié dans les oreilles," Chassé claimed, despite his repeated denials of guilt.[88] But Justice Wilfrid Lazure ruled in favour of the Crown and admitted the confession into evidence. The jury took thirty minutes to reach its verdict: guilty, with no recommendation to mercy.

In his post-trial report to the minister of justice, the tone Justice Lazure adopted could not have differed more from Dysart's "hearty endorsement" of mercy in Proulx's case. Because Chassé had committed such an "abominable crime," the judge declared, he "well deserved the death penalty."[89] But Jean Drapeau was determined to fight to the end. Having lost the case at trial, he filed an appeal to the Quebec Court of King's Bench, Appeal Side, which protracted the case's resolution for eight months. Drapeau argued numerous points, but his greatest concern was the large number of vulnerable suspects whom the police had questioned, but let go, before they pinned responsibility on Chassé. The court dismissed the appeal on 30 November 1945, but it granted Drapeau's request to reset the execution date, which left him time to plead for clemency.[90]

As the Remission Branch began its work, it requested police background reports on Chassé, and these revealed his long history of sexual offending and psychiatric institutionalization. Despite this evidence,

Gallagher did not issue the usual call to investigate the prisoner's mental state. For the branch chief, Chassé's documented history of sexual abnormality, similar to "the dark strangler's," was not a prompt for clemency but rather evidence that deepened the deservedness of the death sentence, as the judge indicated.[91] The execution of Chassé vindicated Montreal's detectives and the methods they used to catch a "sadistic derelict," whom no one mourned.[92]

Self-Diagnosed Sexual Psychopathy

Chassé was one of five sex killers put to death for murders of children between 1945 and 1952, despite defence lawyers', psychiatrists', and even judges' claims that such senseless depravity must indicate some form of mental abnormality. The diagnosis of sexual psychopathy gained widespread currency in Canada, as talk of sexual perversion and compulsions spread beyond medical journals and the records of parliamentary debates. Along with watching Hollywood film noir, Canadians were avid consumers of true crime magazines and low-brow scandal sheets that were filled with tales of homosexual "perverts" and sadistic "psychopaths." It was only a matter of time before men arrested for child sex murders, conscious that they faced execution if convicted, began to diagnose themselves as sexual psychopaths who required treatment.

The murder and sexual assault of Garry Billings in Vancouver's Stanley Park was one of several unsolved sex murders of boys that sent a chill across Canada in the summer of 1946.[93] In Winnipeg, another boy, Roy McGregor, had suffered a similar fate the previous January. Then, three weeks after Billings's death, six-year-old Donnie Goss went missing in Calgary. On 24 July, his distraught family learned that their son had been stabbed, beaten, and sodomized. As the local police in Winnipeg and Port Arthur, Ontario, worked with the RCMP on the Winnipeg cases (another boy was found dead in September 1946), the Vancouver, Lethbridge, and Calgary police shared intelligence to pin the Goss murder on Donald Staley.[94] An ex-serviceman, Staley had drifted across the country until he ended up in the Lethbridge jail, charged with shop-breaking. According to his jailers, he confessed he had murdered the Goss boy under a bridge that spanned a Calgary playground. The police cleared up another mystery when he admitted he was also responsible for Billings's death in Vancouver.[95] "Now that I have started to kill," Staley projected, "I will not be able to stop unless something is done to take away the urge to kill and commit sodomy." He added his

Image 4.4 Through time spent in prisons and psychiatric hospitals, as well as from popular crime literature and films, accused criminals, such as Donald Staley, picked up terminology to describe what drove them to commit sex murders. LAC, R.G. 13, Staley, Volume 1660, volume 1, part 1.

psychiatric history to support his claim: "I have been affected with the desire to commit sodomy for a long time but the urge to kill has grown stronger as time passed."[96]

Staley's criminal record, compiled by the RCMP, confirmed he had served time for sodomy and indecent assault before he signed up with the Canadian Army in 1939. Despite racking up more arrests for indecent assault in the course of his overseas posting, he was not dismissed.[97] Evidently, neither criminal penalties nor the armed forces' psychological screening had steered the twenty-nine-year-old from his inclination to sexual violence. As he stood before Calgary's police magistrate at the initial hearing, faced with a charge of murder, Staley suggested he should be treated in the medical system, not tried in a criminal court: "I am guilty sir, but I am not responsible for my actions. I wish to be interviewed by a psychiatrist."[98] Although the magistrate granted Staley's wish by ordering that he be sent to Alberta's Provincial Mental Hospital for observation, the psychiatrists at that institution pronounced the defendant fit to stand trial.[99]

Publicity in the lead-up to Staley's trial did not match the coverage of the "Slasher's" capture, but it made it impossible for the lawyer appointed to defend Staley to convince the jury that his client was not responsible for this "sadistic slaying."[100] Even the Crown attorney, C.S. Blanchard, KC, admitted that Goss's murder had generated "wide and sensational publicity" in the press and on local radio.[101] From the discovery of the victim's body in St. George's Island Park, Calgarians eagerly followed the police hunt for the "fiendish killer," the "sex killer," the city's "most cold-blooded killer."[102] Now he faced trial. Staley was fortunate to be represented by John S. Mavor, KC, a plucky lawyer with a reputation for taking on unpopular causes, including a brief from the Swiss government to defend two German prisoners of war who had attempted to escape from their Alberta camp in 1945. Although they were captives, they had a recognized right to seek freedom, Mavor had argued.[103] In Staley's trial, Mavor based the defence on the common law principle that no insane man ought to be convicted of a criminal offence. However, in the hostile climate of abhorrence over the crime, mixed with an outpouring of sympathy for the victim's family – all respectable Anglo-Celtic Canadians – that principle wilted.

Had Staley not confessed, the trail left by the killer would likely have gone cold; with Staley's confession, which Chief Justice William R. Howson admitted into evidence, the Crown had a solid case.[104] Still, the question of the defendant's criminal responsibility for his acts remained to be settled. The expert whom Mavor hired to support the insanity defence and the psychiatrist who testified for the Crown both agreed that Staley suffered from a sexual disorder of the mind; they differed, however, over the criteria for the judgment of insanity. In his testimony for the defence, Dr. Wesley Robert Read stated that Staley, orphaned and institutionalized from the age of three, had a long history of committing sodomy and sexual assaults. This pattern of behaviour confirmed he had a "psychopathic personality." The psychiatrist who headed the mental hospital where Staley was assessed disagreed. The man's perverted behaviour did not amount to insanity under section nineteen of the Criminal Code: he could appreciate the nature and quality of his vile act, and his efforts to stalk the victim and to evade detection proved he knew it was wrong. Mavor's decision to call Staley to the stand, where he claimed he had blacked out during the assault, was likely the wrong move, since the defendant appeared to be trying to wriggle free. Forty minutes of deliberation was all it took for the jury to find Donnie Goss's killer guilty of murder. Justice Howson emphatically supported the verdict: "I cannot recommend that Royal Mercy should be shown to this man; the law should be allowed to take its course."[105]

The Alberta Court of Appeal's refusal to consider Mavor's appeal against conviction left the executive to determine the case's final outcome, and Michael Gallagher did little more than rubber stamp the trial judge's report. Although "the circumstances of this trial" prompted the remission chief to request that a government psychiatrist examine the prisoner in this case, he disingenuously reported that the expert witnesses' testimony was "contradictory."[106] In fact, the Crown's psychiatrist agreed with the defence's expert that Staley had "definite psychopathic tendencies and was suffering from a mental disease." More significantly, Gallagher knew that the cabinet did not require a confirmed finding of insanity to grant clemency.[107]

When a Vancouver woman heard the news of Staley's conviction, she implored the government to spare the man, since he was clearly a "sexual pervert." Possibly a constituent of Howard Green's, she explained her reasoning to the minister of justice, Louis St. Laurent: "The pervert is a victim as are those who may become his prey." In this "enlightened age," the writer advised, authorities should treat the "gruesome behaviour" of men who committed "child rape, sadism, indecent exposure, homosexuality, sex murder etc." not as crimes but as symptoms of "mental illness."[108] Despite her plea for a therapeutic alternative, the woman added an unsettling postscript: "If we must admit that we have no highly efficient psychiatric laboratory to cope with the needs of this minority group, let us be at least as humane as the Germans and grant painless death by lethal chamber."[109] Writing in 1946, the author was likely conversant with Nazi eugenic atrocities, which makes her suggestion chilling. Yet, her letter reflected the contradictory character of post-war policy toward sexual psychopathy. The Remission Branch and the Liberal cabinet had no compunction about the execution of psychopaths, while Parliament supported a statute that held out the possible cure of men such as Staley.

The Dilemma of the Sexual Pervert

James C. McRuer, one of the appointees on the Archambault Royal Commission on penal reform in 1936, the year in which he prosecuted Harry O'Donnell for the sex murder of Ruth Taylor, had risen in stature over the 1940s, as he went from serving on the Ontario Court of Appeal to sitting as the chief justice of the Ontario High Court. So when

McRuer admitted he faced a sentencing dilemma, the press listened. In the course of sentencing a seventeen-year-old for attempted rape in 1947, he stated that Canada's prison system was established "for [the] purpose of treatment of normal persons," and mental asylums operated to treat and cure the insane. Yet, there were no specialized institutions for "those guilty of sex perversion." McRuer sentenced the youth (convicted for an attack on a girl of thirteen) to two years in a reformatory, but he feared the young man "will be more likely to commit crime and repeat an offence of this character."[110] Or worse. Psychiatric expertise had made significant strides by the mid-twentieth century, but the legal definition of insanity, a cognitive construct from the previous century, remained in place, not just in courtrooms but in the minds of the men who reviewed capital convictions. Under the aging Gallagher's watch, youth was the only ground on which commutations were granted for sex killers. Unlike McRuer, the chief of the Remission Branch and the cabinet members who served in the early post-war years did not find determining the fate of sex killers a dilemma, particularly if they preyed on children.

Murders of girls by adult men who subjected them to sexual attacks could ignite as much community outrage as did boys' murders. This community anger occurred in Owen Sound, Ontario, in 1947, when the discovery of Betty Playford's body, bludgeoned and "criminally assaulted," sent "angry residents" in search of a "fiend." The local Police Commission posted a $1,000 reward for information leading to an arrest for the eleven-year-old's murder.[111] Like John Benson, who left home for a day of recreation, the girl was out on a play date on a warm late-summer Sunday when a chance encounter led to her murder. Hundreds of people from the small resort town turned up at her funeral and "paid tribute to the memory" of the "school pupil."[112]

The Criminal Investigation Bureau of the Ontario Provincial Police took charge of the investigation, but it was a lucky break, not police work, that produced a suspect. In a bizarre turn of events, a reporter from the Montreal *Herald* informed authorities in Ontario that a twenty-three-year-old naval veteran had contacted him to confess to the murder. Frederick Bussey, an itinerant carnival worker, was a textbook outsider.[113] He told the reporter he was driving aimlessly in central Ontario in a borrowed car when he came upon the girl. He lured her into the car and killed her, although he denied having had "improper relations." The detectives who transferred the man from Montreal to the local Grey County jail kept the suspect's arrival time secret, fearing

TORONTO DAILY STAR

3c PER COPY, 18c PER WEEK

FIND HAMMER IN MURDER HUNT

BUSSEY MAN WE WANT' POLICE OFFICIAL SAYS MOB VIOLENCE FEARED

HOME AND SPORT EDITION

REFUGEES PUT UP FIGHT ONE KILLED, NINE HURT ERE NAVY SEIZES SHIP

DREW MEAT TALK ENDS IN FAILURE STAND ON RIGHTS

PREDICTS NEW LOW FOR FOREST FIRES

QUINTUPLETS BORN TO RUSSIAN MOTHER

PAIR HELD IN DINER HOLD-UP AFTER CHASE AT 80 M.P.H.

GIRLS, 17, 19, HELP SAVE 3 IN FIRE RETURN FOR BABY

COURT-MARTIAL TRIAL QUASHED BY JUDGE

'STRANGLED ONE FREE VOICE' ITALY SOCIALISTS QUIT BLOC

EIGHT BOYS AT TIME CHINA WOMAN'S SCORE

TITO HOLDS TRIO, YANKS SAY FREED LAST NIGHT—BELGRADE

PLAN SUNDAY MOVIES EDUCATIONAL TYPES

LABOR ADDED $1.87 COAL UP $5, CHARGE

CLOSELY GUARDED IN CELL BUSSEY PLAYS GIN RUMMY

CHARGE SOVIET AIDS JEWISH IMMIGRATION

LA GUARDIA LEAVES HIS WIDOW $20,000

PRINCESS APPROVES FOOD AS GIFT IDEA

U.S. FLIES MEDICINE TO EGYPT'S CHOLERA

Short of Sleep All Summer? Gain Back That Hour Tonight

TOMATO CROP HURT MILLION BY FROST

THE WEATHER

INDIA PLANE CRASHES KILLING 14, INJURING 1

Image 4.5 Mob violence was feared after Frederick Bussey's arrest for the sex murder of Betty Playford. His lawyer requested a change of venue, due to local prejudice against his client. Toronto *Daily Star*, 27 September 1947.

"angry mobs."[114] No disturbances occurred, but townsfolk, and the provincial government, expected the state to convict and punish the man.

An experienced but harried criminal defence lawyer, Louis Isaacs, accepted the challenge of defending the accused child killer. On the day the press reported Bussey's confession, Isaacs was in the midst of another sex murder trial in St. Catharines, Ontario. In that case, he had filed an appeal against Sydney Chambers's conviction for the sex murder of a nine-year-old girl, Marion Rusnak. The verdict was set aside, but the second trial, which closed on 3 October 1947, ended with the same verdict. Although Isaacs did not file a second appeal, he took on Bussey's defence with little time to prepare.[115] On 11 November, he appeared in court for the third time in 1947, defending a man convicted of a child sex slaying. Six days later, Bussey's trial ended in a verdict familiar to Isaacs's ears: guilty, with no recommendation to mercy.

The attorney general was sufficiently concerned about Playford's murder that he sent one of the province's top prosecutors, Clarence P. Hope, KC, to serve as the Crown.[116] In anticipation of an attempted insanity defence, Hope asked two psychiatrists to determine whether the defendant was criminally responsible.[117] Neither Dr. Charles S. Tennant (the Ontario Department of Health's forensic psychiatry specialist) nor Dr. William Arthur Cardwell (of the Ontario Institution at Whitby) found any mental defect or disorder when they examined the prisoner.[118] Another government-sponsored expert, the director of the Mental Health Clinic of the Ontario Hospital at Hamilton, sat in on the trial, and without examining the defendant, he testified that "he did not consider Bussey a psychopathic personality."[119]

When Hope addressed the jury in his closing statement, he spoke in conventional moral language, not medical terms. The motive was "a 'sex attack and nothing else,'" and the "cruel murderer" was a man of "unbridled lust."[120] Isaacs, acting pro bono, tried to counter this portrayal of his client with medical evidence from Bussey's service in the naval reserves. The doctor who testified for the defence was prepared to interpret reports of the defendant's dishonourable discharge and his long history of sexual offending, but the judge ruled that evidence inadmissible, since the witness had not diagnosed the defendant himself. By contrast, Bussey's confession to the Montreal reporter (who netted the reward money), and his later statement to police, were admitted into evidence.[121] Backed with further circumstantial and forensic evidence, the Crown persuaded the jury to convict the defendant, and Justice Daniel P.J. Kelley immediately pronounced the death sentence.

For the second time in two months, Isaacs tried to save a convicted sex killer from execution, but this time he went the clemency route, which left him free to define Bussey as a sexual psychopath. Further inquiries into the man's record confirmed "there was a decided history of psychopathic personality in the boy." Isaacs substantiated this claim by referring the minister of justice to the British and American psychiatrists' wartime reports on Bussey, which the judge had ruled inadmissible. These army experts had used a variety of terms for his condition ("constitutional psychopathic disorder," "anxiety hysteria," "psychopathic personality"), which Isaacs summed up as "abnormality ... over which the boy had no control."[122] The condemned man's family in Regina attempted to help by writing that they had tried to seek treatment for their son, who had exhibited deviant tendencies from an early age. But they had faced the same problem that frustrated Justice McRuer: despite their repeated requests in local courts for some form of treatment, no magistrate had helped.[123]

Michael Gallagher was familiar with Isaacs, since he had recently dealt with him in the Chambers case, and his response to the lawyer's post-trial evidence of sexual psychopathy was perfunctory. His staff had done some digging of their own into Bussey's service records and his earlier convictions (five in total) in Saskatchewan. That province's Corrections Branch had requisitioned a "psychiatric social history" of Bussey, but Gallagher found the report of little use. It catalogued the man's childhood and provided profiles of his parents' and sibling's personalities, only to conclude that the young man had a "psychopathic personality." As far as Gallagher was concerned, this submission (prepared by a female social worker) was mumbo jumbo.[124] "Nothing here in our opinion ... to warrant conclusion of 'impaired mentality,'" he scrawled under her signature. Another female social worker, who had known Bussey as a student, pleaded for mercy: "Fred Bussey committed a serious crime BUT SOCIETY IS EQUALLY GUILTY in that his crime is the TOTAL PRODUCT OF OUR NEGLECT of Fred Bussey." When Gallagher read her letter, he simply pencilled "seen."[125]

The chief remission officer sought more trustworthy professional advice by turning to Dr. John P.S. "Jock" Cathcart, the neuropsychiatrist in charge of war veterans and an expert on the psychological effects of military service. In the first of nine sex murder cases in which he would provide diagnoses for the Department of Justice, Cathcart reassured Gallagher that Bussey could tell right from wrong: "The responsibility of the 'psychopathic personality' is the same as that of a normal person."[126]

Sexual Psychopathy or the "Savage" Mind?

The 1948 CSP amendment provided for the separate confinement and psychiatric assessment of non-capital offenders with a history of sexual offending and inability to resist aberrant sexual behaviour. The incorporation of a psychiatric diagnosis to label a subset of inmates was unmistakably modern, the product of expert knowledge deployed in the welfare state.[127] At the same time, prejudicial policies, rooted in white supremacist beliefs, produced distinct outcomes for Indigenous peoples. Treated as colonized minorities and subjected to violence, land seizure, and sequestration on reservations, Indigenous defendants suffered disproportionately in the criminal justice system.[128] Those whom the government defined as "status Indians" under the federal Indian Act were subject to paternalistic regulation, but it came with government responsibility for their defence if they faced capital charges, as the 1905 Bennett case demonstrated. However, the character of colonization transformed in the post-war era as the federal government attempted to recalibrate its "civilizing" mission.[129] In the context of post-war reconstruction, Ottawa questioned the expense of treating Indians as wards, while the racist treatment of Indigenous peoples as "savages" persisted in the criminal justice system.[130]

Between 1946 and 1948, a Special Joint Committee examining the Indian Act held hearings to harvest evidence and canvass opinion on the state of Native affairs.[131] Although it focused on health, welfare, schooling, and the management of resources, witnesses also testified about the handling of criminal cases involving Indigenous people. The committee's minutes do not refer to specific cases, but over the course of the hearings, two Indigenous men were tried for sex murders. In 1946, Davis Houston, a Squamish man with mixed European heritage, was sentenced to death, and Richard Rivers, an Ojibway from Blind River, Ontario, suffered the same fate in 1948. Unlike the trial of Armand Proulx, the prosecution, defence, and post-trial disposition of Houston's and Rivers's cases revolved around Euro-Canadian notions of "the savage mind." Because neither man was legally a "status Indian," the cabinet's decision that both men should face the death penalty could carry out the government's grim strategy of punishing Indigenous people equally, while obscuring the legacies and enduring effects of colonization.

In the post-war era, the Canadian press continued to "see red" when papers published descriptions of Indigenous defendants.[132] Some welfare agencies, ethnologists, and liberal-minded supporters of Indian progress made inroads in countering negative stereotypes, but for most Euro-Canadians, Indians were sneaky, dishonest, and given to "debased afflictions associated with the body (such as sexual debauchery, alcoholism, and capricious violence)."[133] Consequently, reports that a middle-aged Anglo-Celtic woman had been raped and murdered in an isolated logging camp late in 1946 were shocking, whereas the announcement that the man arrested for the crime was "an Indian" confirmed Euro-Canadian prejudice.

Beatrice Smith did not stand a chance against her attacker, one of the all-male crew employed at a logging camp that floated in Belize Inlet, British Columbia. The forty-year-old divorcee worked as the cook, and she was the only woman in the camp.[134] Petroglyphs marked the region as Nakoaktok First Nation territory, but at Erikson's logging camp, anyone willing to work was hired, including a twenty-nine-year-old Squamish man, Davis Houston, and his father, Ernest. On a Saturday night in November, the pair left camp by boat for a party. As day broke on Sunday and the camp stirred, no breakfast awaited the men. The discovery of Smith's dead body in her quarters prompted the loggers to summon a doctor from Alert Bay, who confirmed she had been raped and beaten to death. A corporal in the BC Provincial Police, who accompanied the doctor, conducted a quick investigation that led him to arrest Houston Junior, whom he presented before a stipendiary magistrate of the "unorganized" territory.[135] With no legal representation for the suspect, the preliminary hearing took place and justice moved swiftly. Davis Houston went on trial for his life in January 1947.

As the attorney general of British Columbia arranged for a lawyer to represent the logger, the federal government's Indian Act Committee heard complaints from provincial representatives about the costs of public assistance for Indians living off reservations. The man who accepted Houston's defence, C. Walter Hodgson, was a white lawyer based in Vancouver.[136] The province compensated him for his service in Houston's defence, but his efforts to save the "non-status Indian" exceeded the $250 fee he received.[137] Hodgson attempted to uphold the principle of equality before the law, which included calling on the state to account for its treatment of Indigenous people, including defendants accused of horrific crimes.[138] After Houston was sent south to New Westminster for trial, the first jury could not reach a verdict; however, a second trial, held three days later, ended in a guilty verdict. Hodgson filed an appeal, and he convinced the BC Court of Appeal that Chief Justice Wendell Farris had erred in admitting the accused's statement to the corporal. At the third trial in June 1947, Hodgson's decision to put the defendant on the stand backfired, as it so often did in murder trials. The accused man claimed that he had incriminated himself (smearing blood on his clothes) to protect the real killer – his father.[139] But the third jury of white men found the tale of filial self-sacrifice unbelievable, and

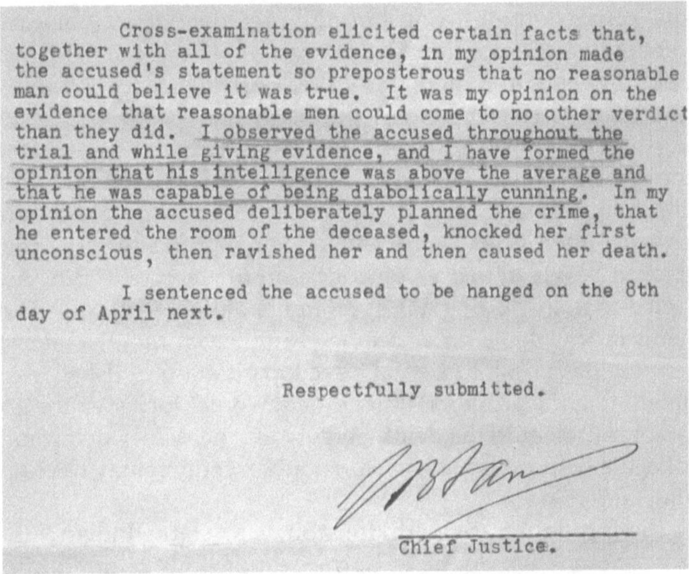

Cross-examination elicited certain facts that, together with all of the evidence, in my opinion made the accused's statement so preposterous that no reasonable man could believe it was true. It was my opinion on the evidence that reasonable men could come to no other verdict than they did. I observed the accused throughout the trial and while giving evidence, and I have formed the opinion that his intelligence was above the average and that he was capable of being diabolically cunning. In my opinion the accused deliberately planned the crime, that he entered the room of the deceased, knocked her first unconscious, then ravished her and then caused her death.

I sentenced the accused to be hanged on the 8th day of April next.

Respectfully submitted.

Chief Justice.

Image 4.6 In Chief Justice W.B. Farris's report on the trial of Davis Houston, he described the convicted sex murderer as "cunning," using a racist stereotype of Indigenous peoples. LAC, R.G. 13, Volume 1663, volume 1, part 1, 24 January 1947.

the Court of Appeal dismissed Hodgson's second request for leave to appeal, closing the last legal door for relief.

In the final transcript and the reports of the two trial judges, which made their way to Ottawa after the convictions, references to Houston's Indian identity occluded any consideration of mental illness. Justice Farris, who presided over the second trial in January, reinforced the jury's verdict with negative stereotypes about "Natives." These jurors of good conscience (it went without saying they were Anglo-Celtic) could see through this defendant, whom Farris considered "capable of diabolical cunning."[140] Gallagher's mark-up of the trial transcript, made with his red pencil, highlighted passages he later quoted in his memo for the minister, which recommended against clemency: "[The prisoner] is described as a halfbreed, apparently raised on a reservation, and of poor reputation," the branch chief opened. Despite the condemned man's previous conviction for "contributing to the delinquency of a minor," on top of evidence, submitted by Hodgson, that Houston's father had spent eleven years in a mental asylum, Gallagher declined to order a psychiatric evaluation.[141]

Hodgson still insisted that his client had told the truth: his father was the man who had raped and killed Beatrice Smith. He wired an eleventh-hour clemency pitch to Justice Minister Ilsley: "All the circumstances surrounding this unfortunate incident tend to show that [the son] should be given every consideration for mercy."[142] But the cabinet elected to follow Gallagher's recommendation, and Davis Houston was hanged at Oakalla on 1 October 1947. Seven months later, in the debate over the criminal sexual psychopath statute, Ilsley reassured Parliament that the proposed amendment would not lessen the government's commitment to the death penalty as a necessary deterrent.[143] As he spoke, the memory of Davis Houston's execution may have crossed the minister's mind.

Had the Indian Act defined Houston as a "status Indian," the federal government would have borne responsibility for funding his defence. Confirmation of this policy emerged during a fiery session at the hearing of the Special Joint Committee early in May 1947, when a Squamish chief, Andrew Paull, testified as founder of the North American Indian Brotherhood.[144] "Under the economic domination and strangulation of the antiquated and unjust laws of the white man," he charged, Indian people faced annihilation. An outspoken opponent of assimilation, Paull told the committee he made a practice of providing legal aid for Indigenous accused, despite the provincial bar's refusal to admit him.[145] Defying his racist exclusion from the profession, he proudly stated he had advised three of nine Indigenous men indicted for murder or manslaughter between 1946 and 1947, one of them possibly Houston.[146] When federal bureaucrats from the Department of Justice and the Indian Affairs Branch testified, they explained the joint management of Indians who faced capital charges. They also confirmed that Indigenous people who relinquished their status (or whose ancestors had done so) in order to become enfranchised citizens did not qualify for federal funding. These assimilationist rules put non-status indigent defendants in an invidious position: in court, in the Euro-Canadian press, and in clemency reviews they were "Indians"; yet, as far as the federal government was concerned, the non-status Indian was "in the same classification as a white before the courts."[147]

"Facilitating the Crime of Rape": The Stereotype of the Drunken Indian

Despite ample evidence that Davis Houston and his father had consumed many drinks on the night of Beatrice Smith's death, his lawyer had eschewed a defence of drunkenness. C. Walter Hodgson would not have found it difficult to convince a white jury that his client was intoxicated, but he knew that the Criminal Code recognized drunkenness as a defence only if the jury believed the defendant was so intoxicated that he could not have formed criminal intent. However, the Code also defined culpable homicide as murder if "grievous bodily injury [was inflicted] for the purpose of facilitating the commission of rape."[148] These subtle legal distinctions were central to the fate of another Indigenous man, Richard Rivers, found guilty in 1948 of the sex murder of his sister-in-law, May Rivers. His trial and conviction in Sault Ste. Marie, Ontario, foregrounded the difficulties of defining intoxication, but the decision that led to his execution exposed the connections between the criminal justice system and the inner mechanisms of mid-twentieth-century colonialism.

Was Richard Rivers so drunk on the night in question that he could not have intended to murder the victim? Witnesses confirmed that in July 1948 the defendant returned from fighting forest fires on the outskirts of Blind River in northwestern Ontario. Arriving at a hotel, he consumed a considerable amount of beer and whiskey with May Rivers. The following morning, staff in the hotel where they had stayed found her dead body, unclothed, strangled, and covered in blood. When inspectors sent up north by the Ontario Provincial Police interrogated Rivers about her death, he responded: "Maybe I done it and maybe I didn't. It's all a blank to me."[149]

The stereotype of the "drunken Indian" was far older and more insidious than the notion of the criminal sexual psychopath, just recently incorporated into the Code.[150] The Sault Ste. Marie barrister who represented Rivers pro bono, Ian Munro, was a former mining executive, and his opposite side was Sault Ste. Marie's Crown attorney, Arthur A. Wishart, recently honoured as a KC.[151] Throughout the trial, the defence, the Crown, and the judge referred to Rivers as "an Indian," but this label was a social, not a legal term. Because his father had chosen to seek political enfranchisement before the defendant was born, Rivers Senior was no longer a "status Indian" under federal law, and nor were his children.[152]

Prior to the trial, with approval from the attorney general, Wishart had requested that Dr. John M. Senn, the superintendent of the Ontario Hospital at Hamilton, assess Rivers's mental state. This strategy anticipated a possible defence of insanity. Because the province's expert attended the trial, Munro decided to take advantage of the psychiatrist's presence by having him testify for the defence. However, Dr. Senn told the court that Rivers was mentally "dull" but capable of distinguishing right from wrong.[153] In his summation, Munro switched strategies. After having raised doubt in cross-examination about the number of hotel guests who could possibly have committed the murder, he argued that Rivers should not be considered criminally responsible due to the volume of alcohol he had consumed. Consequently, Justice G.A. Gale had to inform the jury of the inculpatory and exculpatory aspects of intoxication under the law. After nine hours of deliberation, punctuated by two requests from the foreman for clarification on the question of criminal intent in rape-homicide involving intoxication, the jury finally agreed that May Rivers was murdered by Rivers, the "type" of Indian to be feared, not pitied. "FIND OJIBWAY INDIAN GUILTY OF MURDER" sufficed to inform white Canada that the convicted murderer was to be hanged on 9 December 1948.[154]

The post-trial disposition of the Rivers case was administered through the Department of Justice's Remission Branch, but another federal authority, the Department of Mines and Resources' Indian Affairs Branch, was called in to assist. As of 1936, federal management of Indigenous peoples was shunted into this department as a cost-saving measure.[155] Yet, senior Indian Affairs administrators continued to manage their portfolios as if they were colonial governors.[156] Gallagher regularly consulted his counterparts in Mines and Resources when cases involving condemned Indigenous persons crossed his desk, whether or not they were legally defined as "status Indians." That department's secretary, T.R.L. MacInnes, was Gallagher's respected and trusted colleague on whom he relied to confirm Rivers's status.[157] MacInnes confirmed that Richard's father (a member of the Manitoulin Island Unceded Band) had relinquished his status, which meant his son was not a ward under the Indian Act. Nevertheless, he described the condemned man as an Indian "for general purposes in the public mind and in the minds of the Indians in the district involved." This definition also suited MacInnes's purpose: to turn Rivers's conviction into an opportunity to assert Canadian sovereignty through severity. MacInnes was concerned that Indigenous men who killed "their" women were

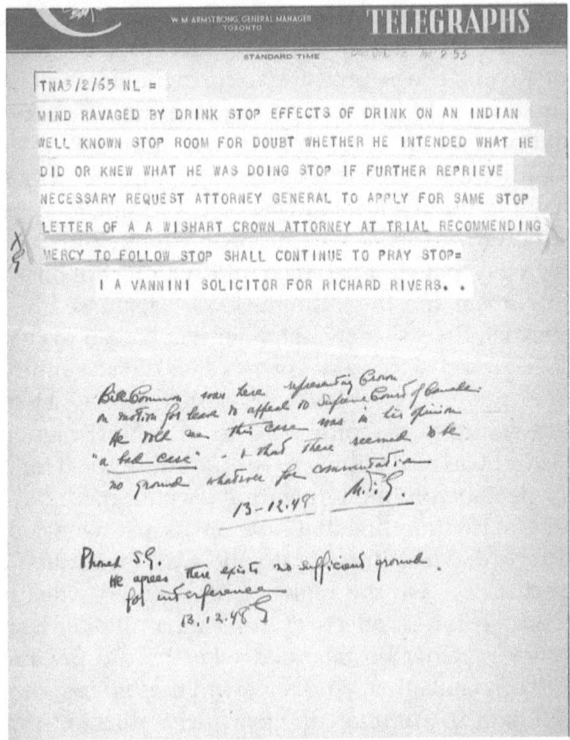
TELEGRAPHS

W M ARMSTRONG GENERAL MANAGER TORONTO

STANDARD TIME

TNA3/2/65 NL =

MIND RAVAGED BY DRINK STOP EFFECTS OF DRINK ON AN INDIAN WELL KNOWN STOP ROOM FOR DOUBT WHETHER HE INTENDED WHAT HE DID OR KNEW WHAT HE WAS DOING STOP IF FURTHER REPRIEVE NECESSARY REQUEST ATTORNEY GENERAL TO APPLY FOR SAME STOP LETTER OF A A WISHART CROWN ATTORNEY AT TRIAL RECOMMENDING MERCY TO FOLLOW STOP SHALL CONTINUE TO PRAY STOP=

I A VANNINI SOLICITOR FOR RICHARD RIVERS. .

13-12.48

13.12.48

Image 4.7 The clemency plea by Richard Rivers's lawyer invoked the stereotype of "the drunken Indian." Michael Gallagher's marginalia defined the murder as "a bad case." LAC, R.G. 13, Rivers, Volume 1672, volume 1, part 1, 13 December 1948.

frequently found guilty of manslaughter, rather than murder, including in homicides committed with "great brutality." He despaired that these crimes had multiplied: "The effect upon the morale of criminally inclined Indians has been bad." Accordingly, he advised Gallagher that "the consideration of exemplary punishment in the present case" was "important from the viewpoint of Indian administration."[158]

Many Euro-Canadians, including the men who had a hand in Richard Rivers's conviction, espoused more paternalistic beliefs about Indigenous people. For them, his case illustrated the need to deal with

Indians mercifully. A concerned Toronto citizen, speaking as "John Public," wrote the minister of justice shortly after the trial to request clemency for Rivers. It was unjust to enforce the death penalty, simply "because a man is an Indian and perhaps [of] no means or amount of wealth, social position or other drag to help him along."[159] The writer also urged that Rivers be retried, but a major Toronto firm was already on to this, having found a local lawyer, I.A. Vannini, to appeal the conviction.[160] Although he filed leave to appeal, Vannini did not request that Ottawa order a psychiatric assessment of Rivers.[161] But once the provincial Court of Appeal and the Supreme Court dismissed his attempt to appeal the verdict, Rivers's new defender was forced to change tack.[162]

As the clock ticked down on Rivers's last days, Vannini contacted the foreman of the jury, who had telegraphed Gallagher to "urgently request death sentence be commuted to life imprisonment." Crown Attorney Wishart was also willing to support the appeal for clemency.[163] Finally, three days before the impending execution, Vannini wired the governor general to underline that Rivers was just twenty-one and had no criminal record. Most importantly, he was "an Indian … brought up on a reservation." On the night of May Rivers's death, his mind was "ravaged by drink … effects of drink on an Indian well known … room for doubt whether he intended what he did or knew what he was doing."[164] But Gallagher, who reviewed these pleas, considered the opinion of William B. Common, the province's director of public prosecutions, more compelling: this was "a bad case."[165] Two branches of the federal government made Richard Rivers an example of "equal" justice. The Lethbridge *Herald*'s headline on 16 December 1948 was stark: "Indian Killer Gets Noose."[166]

In 1948, the Joint Committee on the Indian Act presented its report, and the Canadian Parliament endorsed the indeterminate sentencing of criminal sexual psychopaths. The disposition of the Rivers and Houston sex murder cases occurred in parallel with these post-war policy reviews, but modern-day colonialism, not correctionalism, coloured the outcome of their cases. There is no evidence that public outrage spurred the cabinet's decision that these men should be executed, as it did in cases involving white child victims, although one local paper hinted at the grief May Rivers's step-father felt as he identified her body: "Oh my God: That's my girl alright."[167] Racist stereotyping identified Houston and Rivers as "Indian," but the fact that neither man was legally a ward of the state meant the federal government could administer capital justice, like enfranchisement, in the interest of assimilation. For the men at the helm of government in mid-twentieth-century Canada, "the Indian mind" was not a puzzle for modern psychiatric science to solve but an accepted transhistorical truth.[168]

Sex Murder and the Death Penalty after the Criminal Sexual Psychopath Amendment

As Canadian parliamentarians considered amending the Criminal Code to include provisions for the imprisonment of criminal sexual psychopaths, the British House of Commons voted in favour of suspending capital punishment.[169] By that point, Canadian criminal defence specialists, notably Arthur E. Maloney (whose firm had contacted Vannini) and G. Arthur Martin, as well as several members of Parliament (foremost Ross Thatcher) publicly declared their opposition to the death penalty; however, the Canadian government held on to capital punishment.[170] The Liberal cabinet's decisions in sex murder cases in the late 1940s and early 1950s showed the government did not consider men who committed such crimes sick, and the passage of the CSP amendment made no impact. Three sex murder cases appeared before Louis St. Laurent's cabinet for consideration after 1948, and two of the condemned men were executed: Victor Beaulieu, a Chippewan, hanged in Fort Smith, Northwest Territories, in 1952; and Frederick Ducharme, a self-described "lone wolf," hanged at BC's Oakalla Prison in 1950. In the third case, the government followed the precedent of clemency on the ground of youth when the cabinet spared the life of sixteen-year-old Frederick Sykes, whom a jury convicted in 1951 for the murder of a thirteen-year-old schoolgirl. Disquietude over executing juveniles outweighed any concern that clemency might be warranted on the grounds of indigeneity or sexual psychopathy as an illness.

The cabinet's recommendation that Victor Beaulieu, aged twenty-three, should hang for the murder of a mother and two of her children in the Northwest Territories in 1951 indicated that little had changed since the Special Joint Committee on the Indian Act had presented its final report in 1949.[171] Representatives of Indigenous people, such as Paull, argued that his people must retain their status and enhance self-governance, and they railed against coercion and interference in band affairs. However, the committee endorsed assimilation as a sound policy. Despite the minor amendments made to the Indian Act in 1951, the government still assumed "the purpose of Indian policy was the end of the Indians."[172] Euro-Canadian authorities proceeded to govern according to two contradictory beliefs: Indigenous people were infantile, in need of tutoring to be integrated into civilization; and Indians were brutes who required severe punishment.

The conviction of Beaulieu, a non-status Indian under the Indian Act, gave the central government another opportunity to colonize through capital justice. Back in 1921, Albert Le Beaux, a Slavey Dene in Fort Providence, Northwest Territories, was executed for the murder of his wife and son. Although the jury had recommended mercy in that case, officials in Ottawa feared that a commutation would have a bad effect on others of the defendant's "race" and on the government's mission to impose Canadian sovereignty.[173] Thirty years later, the conduct of a similar trial, before six Euro-Canadian jurors, was bungled, and the post-trial proceedings were shambolic.[174] However, the federal Remission Branch compensated, ensuring that discretionary justice supported the assertion of sovereignty in the North.

The stipendiary magistrate of the Territorial Court for the Northwest Territories was John E. Gibben, a fastidious man who showered after sittings, especially cases involving sexual matters.[175] In this trial, the testimony was sordid. Beaulieu was charged with the sex murder of Mrs. Mary Madeline Norn and the murder of her two children; the chief evidence against him was his confession that he had killed the woman after she told him he "was not going to fuck her for nothing." The Crown claimed that the sexual "attack" had possibly taken place after the woman's death. In his report to the secretary of state, the magistrate confirmed that Beaulieu had been sent to Edmonton for a psychiatric assessment, but he was pronounced fit to stand trial. Gibben complimented the defence, despite the fact that Beaulieu's court-appointed lawyer, John Hagel, had argued a defence of insanity without calling any witnesses. The magistrate concluded by stating his agreement with the jury's verdict, that the defendant was sane and responsible for his crime.[176]

Irregularities in conviction procedures led officials to improvise. Magistrate Gibben neglected to set an execution date, and this omission set off a round of unseemly bargaining between the territory, the province of Alberta, and Ottawa about the appropriate date and venue for Beaulieu's hanging.[177] The magistrate wrongly assumed it was up to federal authorities to determine the execution date, and it took authorities almost six months after the conviction to sort out the arrangements. Finally, the date of 15 February 1952 was set, but where should the hanging take place? Under the terms of the Criminal Code, the location

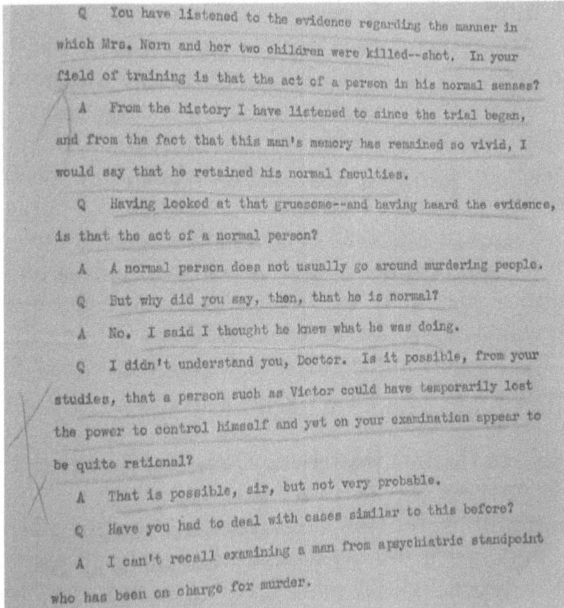

Q You have listened to the evidence regarding the manner in which Mrs. Norn and her two children were killed--shot. In your field of training is that the act of a person in his normal senses?

A From the history I have listened to since the trial began, and from the fact that this man's memory has remained so vivid, I would say that he retained his normal faculties.

Q Having looked at that gruesome--and having heard the evidence, is that the act of a normal person?

A A normal person does not usually go around murdering people.

Q But why did you say, then, that he is normal?

A No. I said I thought he knew what he was doing.

Q I didn't understand you, Doctor. Is it possible, from your studies, that a person such as Victor could have temporarily lost the power to control himself and yet on your examination appear to be quite rational?

A That is possible, sir, but not very probable.

Q Have you had to deal with cases similar to this before?

A I can't recall examining a man from apsychiatric standpoint who has been on charge for murder.

Image 4.8 Michael F. Gallagher marked up the transcript of the trial of Victor Beaulieu to highlight the defence counsel's cross-examination of the Crown's psychiatric expert, who found the defendant legally sane. LAC, R.G. 13, Volume 1688, part 3.

of the offender's imprisonment determined the site of execution.[178] However, a local RCMP corporal contacted the deputy commissioner of the force's Criminal Investigation Bureau to request the hanging be conducted elsewhere, since the people of Fort Smith might take a "sadistic interest" in the execution.[179] Another RCMP officer contacted the attorney general of Alberta concerning an alternative venue, and he offered Fort Saskatchewan, northeast of Edmonton. An exasperated Gallagher put his foot down when he learned of these dealings: capital justice protocol must be followed uniformly, without exception.[180]

The federal government approached Victor Beaulieu's death sentence as a matter of Indian policy, as it did when it determined Richard Rivers's fate. In this case, the commissioner of the Northwest Territories provided Gallagher the advice to let the law take its course as a way to nail a plank in the subarctic region's colonization.[181] The chief remission officer's recommendation against clemency for the "half-breed" quoted from the commissioner's letter, including his remark that "there is no public sympathy whatever for the prisoner." Local authorities confirmed that Beaulieu had made himself unpopular by attempting to force himself on other women in the hamlet, but this information did not prompt a call to Dr. Cathcart to determine if Beaulieu might be mentally disturbed or a sexual psychopath. As the commissioner had projected, to hang this man "would be serving the best interests of the administration of justice in the Territories."[182] At a point when Arctic colonization was accelerating in the interests of fighting the Cold War, the cabinet agreed that this condemned man would pay the price for those interests.[183]

"A Strong Sex Instinct Which He Does Not Bother to Control"

Far from Fort Smith, in the home town of the MP who had spearheaded the call for a change in the treatment of sexual perversion, the Vancouver trial of repeat sexual offender Roger Ducharme for the murder of Ferne Blanche Fisher revolved around the question of the "sex maniac's" mind and his motives, not his racial or ethnic status.[184] In November 1949, the discovery of the woman's battered nude body, her pubic hair shaven, was a salacious mystery that stumped Vancouver police until they received reports of a man, semi-clad, running through the streets at night. Upon investigation of the odd loner's squalid shack on the False Creek mudflats where her corpse had washed up six weeks earlier, they found articles of Fisher's clothing and belongings, enough evidence to charge Ducharme with murder. From his arrest in December to his lengthy trial in March 1950, the city's newspapers fed Vancouverites a steady drip feed of lurid details concerning the man's genital abnormality and his penchant for cross-dressing. While in custody, Ducharme contributed to the coverage by sending letters to the press in which he expounded psychological theories to help solve the mystery of the woman's murder.[185]

Ducharme's bizarre behaviour and social marginality were matters of public interest, not his French heritage or Roman Catholicism.[186] His trial of fourteen days – the longest of any sex murder defendant up to that point – and the protracted post-trial deliberations his case generated kept returning to the question of the man's mental and moral make-up. In Victor Beaulieu's case, the Remission Branch referred cabinet to an RCMP constable's report, which commented on the man's "primitive and cunning nature … [H]is mind appears not to be fully developed."[187] By contrast, the cabinet's determination of Roger Ducharme's fate boiled down to a decision over a white sexual psychopath's criminal responsibility.

Prior to the start of the trial, Ducharme's sanity was evaluated over eight days, and every expert agreed the man was mentally aberrant; yet, the jury, the trial judge, and the justices of the British Columbia Court of Appeal, plus the psychiatrist who conducted his post-trial review, considered him capable of distinguishing right from wrong.[188] As a suspect and later on the witness stand, Ducharme (who had four previous convictions for sexual exposure and indecent assault) gave contradictory accounts, flipping from admitting he had "intimate relations" with the woman (a white, single, church-going department store seamstress with an impeccable reputation) to denying he had any contact with or knowledge of her. Unlike Bussey, the carnival worker saddled with an overworked criminal lawyer with a losing track record, Ducharme was defended by Dugald McAlpine, a dogged Vancouver lawyer from a prestigious law firm.[189] The Crown was represented by an intimidating adversary, the burly future provincial Supreme Court justice, Thomas G. Norris, KC.[190] The judge, Alexander Manson, was perhaps more interested than most in eliminating all doubt over the verdict. Back in 1924, when he was British Columbia's attorney general, he had tarnished his reputation by covering up prosecutorial improprieties in a murder case. Since then, Manson had presided over Davis Houston's third trial and spent his subsequent career building a reputation as a "hanging judge."[191]

After the lengthy trial, the jury took ninety minutes (during which they broke for lunch) to find Ducharme guilty without adding a recommendation to mercy. The defence's own expert witness, Dr. William Dobson, was unwilling to declare the defendant insane, and the Crown's experts had agreed. McAlpine immediately launched an appeal in the provincial system, and an Ottawa firm followed with an application for leave to appeal to the Supreme Court of Canada, but neither bench saw merit in McAlpine's claim that Justice Manson had erred in admitting police evidence of Ducharme's behaviour on his arrest and his contradictory statements to police.[192] Executive clemency would determine the case outcome, supported by the government's own psychiatric expert.

As the appeal process ground along in the early months of 1950, the Remission Branch reviewed and responded to Justice Manson's

Image 4.9 A mixed crowd of men and women wrapped around the block in front of Vancouver Courthouse, hoping for a glimpse of Frederick Ducharme on the final day of his fourteen-day trial for the sex murder of Blanche Fisher. Vancouver Public Library, accession number 81198, 22 March 1950.

report. Although the judge considered the verdict sound, he advised that further inquiries be made: "The man is definitely a psychopath of some description, with an inclination to sexual behaviour." Alternatively, Ducharme might be "both amoral and immoral, with a strong sex instinct which he does not bother to control." In either case, Manson thought the government should enlist "the very best of medical men" to provide "the fullest information" well before the execution date.[193] Gallagher took the judge's advice and called on Dr. Cathcart, "our expert in capital case work." As he explained to the solicitor general, "the feature of impaired mentality will have a direct bearing upon the advisability of recommending commutation."[194] Dr. Cathcart reported that he visited Ducharme in June 1950 and found the prisoner intriguing but culpable: a "clever bluffer" who showed "no obvious indication of any psychotic state." He concluded that Ducharme's attitude toward civil authority was "too near that of the average criminal to have any psychiatric significance."[195]

Despite McAlpine's further efforts to save his client from execution (an appeal to the Supreme Court and a request that the minister of justice order a new trial based on new alibi evidence that could exonerate Ducharme), Dr. Cathcart's blunt assessment provided a solid wedge against commutation.[196] On 13 July 1950, after the Supreme Court dismissed the application for leave to appeal and the day before the scheduled execution, Gallagher telegrammed McAlpine to inform him the cabinet had decided not to interfere with the law.[197] After months of publishing shocking accounts of the crime and the voluble defendant, the Vancouver *Province* reported Ducharme's hanging with little flourish: "The execution in the death room at Oakalla Prison Farm was performed with precision."[198]

The Sex Offender "Society Created"

Just when it seemed that the Liberal government, re-elected in 1949, was set to maintain its tough stance against sex murderers, the commutation of Francis Sykes's death sentence confirmed that it was sensitive to accusations of heartlessness. The decision to commute the Anglo-Celtic youth's death sentence, after a jury in New Westminster, British Columbia, found him guilty of a sex murder, was influenced by psychiatric assessments, but the cabinet's qualms over putting a youth to death played a greater role. In 1933, England passed a law that prohibited the execution of young persons convicted of murder if they were under eighteen years of age at the time of their offence.[199] In Canada, there was no statute to prevent Sykes's execution, but there was executive discretion. After the British Columbia Court of Appeal dismissed the appeal filed by the defence, the capital case review process became the focus of efforts to save Sykes, a politicized clemency campaign that spread from British Columbia's lower mainland across the country.

By the early 1950s, social welfare and criminological professionals defined youth as a phase of psychological development in which offenders could not be held fully accountable for their crimes. Even supporters of the death penalty for adults expressed qualms over the execution of teenagers. In Parliament, the MP for Burnaby–Richmond (who visited Sykes in Oakalla) stated that he believed "the boy" did not "realize the immensity of his offence." He also felt that "his community, his church and his school" had failed to instill a strong sense of morals.[200] If "society" had created this sex offender, could the government rightfully execute him? This question raised the stakes of this case, prompting the Remission Branch and the cabinet to turn it into a tightly managed political matter.

For the second time in two years, Justice Manson presided over a trial in which a defendant faced execution for a sex killing. In contrast to the loquacious and flamboyant Ducharme, Sykes struck the judge as a "cool" character.[201] A high school student from Mission, British

Image 4.10 Alexander M. Manson (1883–1964), appointed to the Supreme Court of British Columbia in 1935, presided over numerous murder trials, including the sex murder trials of Davis Houston, Frederick Ducharme, and Francis Sykes. He appears here in his garb as grand master of the Masonic Lodge of British Columbia, c. 1926. "Alexander M. Manson," Grand Lodge of British Columbia and Yukon, http://freemasonry.bcy.ca/grand_masters/manson_a/manson_a.html.

Columbia, he was sixteen in September 1950, when Laura Grant's naked and bruised body was discovered in a field near her home. Witnesses who recalled seeing Sykes on the scene led the police to question him. Initially, he claimed innocence, but police stated he later confessed that he had engaged in consensual sexual relations with the thirteen-year-old, after which she passed out and died. Marks of strangulation and considerable contusions on the girl's inner thighs suggested a sinister encounter. At Sykes's trial, the Crown, John L. Farris, one of his prominent legal family's rising stars, convinced the jury that Sykes was guilty of murder.[202] There was no recommendation to mercy.[203]

In his report to Ottawa, Justice Manson went much further than he did in the Ducharme case to urge the executive to consider clemency. The "powerfully built" young man (his Anglo-Celtic heritage was a given) did not flinch at the verdict. Perhaps he was "oversexed or maybe amoral as well as immoral." But Sykes's age was most significant to Manson. He stopped short of stating that no "boy of his years" should be hanged for murder, but he urged the cabinet to approach this case as a matter of "public policy."[204] John S. Burton, the Vancouver criminal law specialist who defended Sykes, filed a notice of appeal, and the court revised the original date for the prisoner's execution to mid-December 1951.[205] But the British Columbia Court of Appeal unanimously dismissed the appeal on 4 October 1951, with an added note of condemnation: "The appellant knowingly and deliberately engaged in a series of acts for which civilized man exacts the highest penalty."[206] Burton's announcement that he would not seek special leave to appeal to the Supreme Court left the cabinet responsible for the final decision.

Members of the public, numerous newspapers, and several MPs confirmed Justice Manson's interpretation of the case was correct: Sykes's conviction presented a challenge for public policy. The editors of the *British Columbian* and the Vancouver *Sun* strongly advocated that the teenager miss his date with the executioner, while Ross Thatcher, the MP for Moose Jaw, asked the minister of justice, Stuart Garson, about the likelihood of clemency: "Will the government consider commuting this sentence to life imprisonment" on account of the boy's age?[207] Garson was familiar with Thatcher, who had introduced a private member's abolition bill in 1950, so he took care to craft a response.[208] Remission Branch staff produced three drafts of the letter before they came up with a version the minister was prepared to sign. Since it was "most unusual" for the death penalty to be carried out in cases where the condemned was so young, Garson reflected, Thatcher could "rest assured that [Sykes's] youth is an important factor which will be most carefully considered by Cabinet Council."[209] Members of the public, especially residents of British Columbia, addressed the federal government with greater passion. A Miss Frances Menzies of Vancouver, who claimed she had spoken with Justice Manson, urged clemency, since the "youth of Canada" were "bombarded by movies that make crime so commonplace that it's little wonder that [they] almost automatically do something which they have seen." Rather than respond in his usual

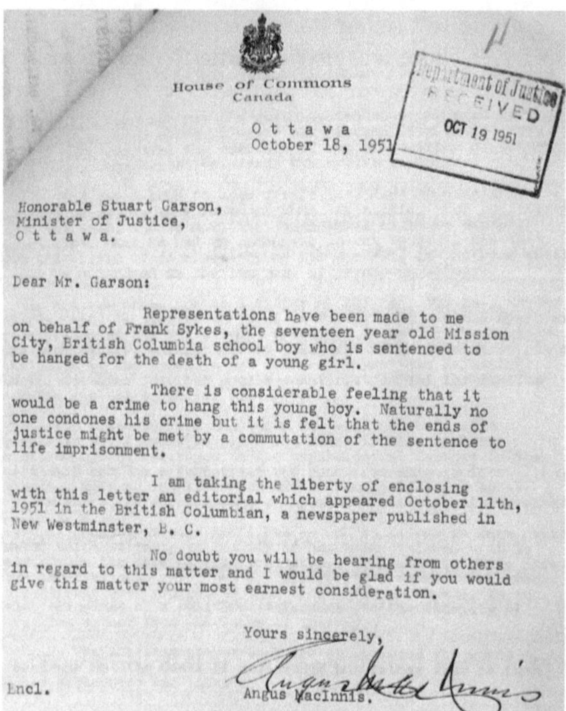

House of Commons
Canada

Ottawa
October 18, 1951

Department of Justice
RECEIVED
OCT 19 1951

Honorable Stuart Garson,
Minister of Justice,
Ottawa.

Dear Mr. Garson:

Representations have been made to me on behalf of Frank Sykes, the seventeen year old Mission City, British Columbia school boy who is sentenced to be hanged for the death of a young girl.

There is considerable feeling that it would be a crime to hang this young boy. Naturally no one condones his crime but it is felt that the ends of justice might be met by a commutation of the sentence to life imprisonment.

I am taking the liberty of enclosing with this letter an editorial which appeared October 11th, 1951 in the British Columbian, a newspaper published in New Westminster, B. C.

No doubt you will be hearing from others in regard to this matter and I would be glad if you would give this matter your most earnest consideration.

Yours sincerely,

Encl.

Angus MacInnis.

Image 4.11 House of Commons letterhead attracted keen attention in the Remission Branch. CCF MP Angus MacInnis called for the commutation of Francis Sykes's death sentence, warning of political fallout if the "school boy" were to be hanged. LAC, R.G. 13, Sykes, Volume 1697, volume 1, part 1, 18 October 1951.

measured manner (all submissions were "carefully reviewed"), Gallagher replied to the woman with an incautious prediction: "I would presume that the question of youth would figure prominently among the clement features which already have been urged in favour of an exercise of the Royal prerogative."[210]

Six weeks in advance of the date set for Sykes's execution, the government announced the commutation of his death sentence. In most capital cases, the government issued a press release several days before, or as little as one day prior, to scheduled hangings, but in Sykes's case, public and parliamentary pressure induced it to reach a decision more quickly.[211] Within a week of the court's dismissal of the appeal, the Vancouver *Sun* published numerous letters to the editor in favour of quick clemency: "If the department of justice does not intend Sykes to hang it should not keep him in cruel suspense." The following day, a hard-hitting editorial charged: "To take this young life, before the available resources, of psychiatric diagnosis and of treatment, have been brought to bear ... is to convict ourselves of a positive preference for the finality of destruction rather than the labor of therapy."[212]

As news of these demands reached Ottawa, clerks in the Remission Branch were ordered to conduct a search of their records to determine whether executing a youth (Sykes was now seventeen) would follow or diverge from recent practice. But Gallagher already knew the answer, after decades of service. When he submitted his report on 13 October 1951, he repeated the trial judge's remark concerning the case's policy dimensions, and he confirmed the results of the branch's search: no offender under the age of eighteen years had been executed since Confederation.[213] The cabinet acted on Gallagher's and Justice Manson's advice that mercy was the best policy, a decision that came at minor cost to the government of the day.

The Evils of Modernity

By the early 1950s, the majority of Canadians still approved of capital punishment for murder, and some took exception to the Liberal cabinet's rare acts of clemency. One writer (identified as "Scotty") criticized a woman who had written a letter, published by the Vancouver *Sun*, which expressed pity for Sykes and his family: "Doesn't she think that rape and murder of a 13-year-old girl also touches the heart of every decent person?"[214] In post-war Canada, the vulnerability of children to "perverts" was politicized as never before, but concerned citizens and their political representatives expressed their anxieties in divergent ways. Parents' groups that anticipated advances in mental sciences found representatives in Parliament who were prepared to back the CSP amendment in 1948. But there was no consensus concerning the meaning of sexual psychopathy, let alone the prospect that it could be predicted, diagnosed, or treated. The psychiatrists whom the Department of Justice consulted numbered among the pessimists. Hired to assess the mental state of condemned sex murderers, they maintained that these killers must be held accountable. The "Scotties" of Canada could rest assured that the post-war government faithfully manned the rampart against mercy.

As a new round of abolition bills began after a long hiatus in parliamentary activism, defenders of capital punishment emphasized that persons accused of murder were "given every opportunity to defend themselves, irrespective of the cost to the public."[215] On the face of things, they were right. None of the men prosecuted for a sex murder in the years following the Second World War faced trial without legal representation, and in most cases, lawyers whose clients were convicted proceeded with appeals. Some of the nation's leading criminal defence barristers put a spotlight on the strong-arm tactics of the police, desperate to finger suspects in sex murder cases that stirred public outrage.

Appeals on matters of law affirmed the capacity of courts to correct errors, but they did not address the structural disadvantages connected to poverty, racism, and the ongoing work of colonization. And courts of appeal could decide that "no substantial wrong or miscarriage of justice" had occurred, notwithstanding the presence of legitimate grounds for appeal against conviction.[216] "That clause has been the bête noir of every appeal," one senator lamented in 1952. "It has been the cause of very loose work by appeal courts."[217] In post-war Canada, the free world was not a world of equality before the law.

Post-trial clemency reviews also dismissed documented histories of abnormal sexual behaviour as possible grounds for clemency. The murder trials of men such as Chassé, Staley, and Bussey uncovered disturbing evidence of sex criminals who might have been stopped from committing horrid crimes had they been properly treated earlier in their lives. But the CSP amendment of 1948 lacked support in the courts and the penal welfare system, and it left Canadians feeling no safer. How could medical professionals and the criminal justice system prevent sex slayings when most people – including psychiatrists – considered sexual psychopaths "very bad," not mad?

The capital justice record in this period confirms that men convicted of sex murders were more likely to be executed than male murderers whose crimes were of a different nature. The rise of modern psychiatry inspired the Criminal Code's amendment, but the text of the statute retained the moral term "evil."[218] Politicians, such as Pouliot, spoke for many people in Canada who named sex offenders as "monsters whom society cannot endure."[219] Yet, by the mid-1950s, a small but articulate cohort of parliamentarians and lawyers began to campaign for a more radical revision of the Criminal Code to do away with the death penalty, even for sex killers.

5

Sexual Psychopathy, Insanity, and the Death Penalty under Scrutiny in the 1950s

Despite the tendency to associate the 1950s with conservatism, it was a time of considerable optimism in Canada's criminal justice system as ideas for reform that had hatched in the late 1940s matured and took flight.[1] The most comprehensive overhaul of the Criminal Code since its adoption in 1892 was finalized in 1954, five years after the Liberal government committed to the task.[2] Many leaders of the bar and judiciary, as well as psychiatrists and social scientists, encouraged the government to increase its modernizing momentum in areas directly relevant to the treatment of capital sex criminals.[3] The final report of the committee appointed to devise a new Criminal Code identified capital punishment and the defence of insanity as issues "of such paramount importance" that they required separate study in light of advances in the diagnosis of mental disorders and abnormalities.[4] The government responded with alacrity and commitment.[5] In 1954, two royal commissions got to work – one to review the law concerning criminal insanity and the other to evaluate the 1948 criminal sexual psychopath (CSP) statute. Justice James "Vinegar Jim" McRuer, chief justice of the High Court of Ontario, had acquired a national profile by publicizing his dissatisfaction over Canada's outdated approach to the mentally disordered offender. Almost twenty years had passed since McRuer had prosecuted repeat sex offender Harry O'Donnell, hanged for murder in 1936.[6] Perhaps the time had come to consider whether such offenders were incapable of controlling their violent sexual impulses and possibly responsive to expert treatment.[7]

The government also established a Special Joint Committee of the House and Senate in 1954 to consider whether Canada should retain the death penalty. The year before, MP W. Ross Thatcher, the CCF representative for Moose Jaw–Lake Centre, introduced a private member's abolition bill for the second time.[8] Like his first attempt in 1950, this one failed, but it flushed out supporters, including fellow CCF member Harold Winch. Both men were appointed as members of the committee, but as abolitionists, they were in the minority. In its final report, delivered in 1956, the Joint Committee advised that the death penalty be retained and meekly suggested that the policy be revisited in the near future.[9] While that committee conducted its hearings, the government set up a parallel inquiry to review the Remission Service and "the exercise of clemency."[10] This advisory committee, headed by Supreme Court Justice Gérald Fauteux, noted that a significant change had occurred in the branch in 1953: a new man replaced the long-serving chief, Michael F. Gallagher.[11] The position Gallagher had held for three decades also changed in response to the Fauteux Committee's report. In 1959, the government established a new national parole system, which replaced the Ticket of Leave Act. The old branch was renamed the Criminal Law Division (CLD), but it continued to support the executive in its review of death sentences by processing capital case files and advising cabinet on the prospect of clemency.

Although Prime Minister Louis St. Laurent's Liberals set these inquiries into motion, the Progressive Conservatives' landslide victory in 1957 raised rather than deflated expectations that reform in the realm of capital justice would proceed.[12] John Diefenbaker, a key supporter of the CSP statute and a critic of the death penalty, became prime minister in June of that year. Depending on their stance on capital punishment, Canadians had reason to fear or hope that the execution of murderers might soon become a thing of the past. A growing number of newspaper editors and outspoken members of the criminal bar encouraged the country to embrace more effective and humane means to prevent and treat individuals inclined toward violence and abuse. However, an undertow of fear and anxiety pulled against the current of correctionalism. The death penalty remained on the books and in effect during this period of penal optimism, and sex murderers were treated with singular severity: between 1953 and 1959 ten of the twelve males condemned to death for sexual murders were hanged.[13]

The first CLD director, Allen J. MacLeod, became a champion of parole and an exponent of correctional modernization toward the end

Image 5.1 The cabinet of Louis St. Laurent's Liberal ministry in 1953, just before the government initiated royal commissions and inquiries into capital punishment, the defence of insanity, the criminal sexual psychopath, and the Remission Service. LAC, MIKAN 3535436.

of his career.[14] Yet, Michael Gallagher's replacement did not diverge from the old chief's approach in cautioning the cabinet against clemency, including those cases in which there was significant doubt about a sex killer's sanity.[15] MacLeod made concerted use of unsuccessful appeals against guilty verdicts to lend weight to his recommendations that the law take its course. However, like Gallagher, he advised against the death penalty's infliction if those who were convicted of sex murders were youths. One spared sex killer was a twenty-year-old whom a jury convicted but recommended to mercy, and the other, aged eighteen, had the good fortune to be defended by Torontonian Arthur Maloney, one of the country's top defence lawyers. The energetic barrister's work on behalf of persons charged with murder, most of them unable to pay for his services, led him to take a leadership role in the embryonic abolition movement, both within his profession and as a member of Diefenbaker's Conservative government.[16]

The problems of sexual psychopathy, criminal responsibility, and the prospect of the death penalty's abolition grew into public policy issues over the 1950s, but each conviction of a man for sex murder demanded a separate answer to the question: should this criminal be executed? Committed abolitionists asserted that "retribution and punishment were artefacts of an earlier, less rational age,"[17] but Diefenbaker's government did not steer away from that historic course until 1959. As the records of cabinet meetings indicate, ministers quickly realized that commuting sex killers' death sentences while retaining the death penalty satisfied neither side of the simmering debate over capital punishment.

Insane within the Meaning of the Law

The year before his appointment as chairman of the royal commission on Canada's CSP sentencing provisions, Justice McRuer presided over the trial of a man with a history of violent crimes and sexual offences. Mervyn Hutson was convicted and executed for the rape-murder of three-year-old Susan Hutchins in North Bay, Ontario, in the spring of 1953. The crime was as shocking as any in the judge's recollection, a "crime of great bestiality" that left the girl mutilated.[18] The convicted culprit was a twenty-nine-year-old ex-army man who worked as a cook on a railway gang. After the Ontario Provincial Police tracked him down, Hutson admitted he had walked some distance with the girl, whose mother had asked him to mind her; after that point he had an epileptic fit, he claimed, leaving him with no memory of harming the toddler.[19]

In the nineteenth century, most psychiatrists categorized epilepsy as a form of insanity.[20] Although experts moved away from this understanding by the mid-twentieth century, courts continued to accept that certain forms of the condition were "sufficient to deprive the accused of all control over his actions at the time of the crime."[21] The North Bay lawyer who defended Hutson, George E. Wallace, took the case under the auspices of the Law Society of Upper Canada's new profession-run legal aid plan, established in 1951.[22] His defence rested on evidence that Hutson had suffered a gunshot wound to the head two years prior to the girl's murder. His life had been saved by an operation to remove the bullets, but doctors had to prescribe phenobarbital to treat Hutson's post-operative seizures. A well-respected expert witness testified for the defence, Dr. Arthur M. Doyle of the St. Michael's Hospital (Toronto) psychiatric clinic. Hutson's brain injury could explain his capacity to commit an assault with no awareness of its criminal nature or consequences.[23] But the two psychiatrists called by the Crown disagreed with Doyle. As McRuer reported, they were "emphatic" that no person experiencing an epileptic seizure could have murdered and sexually assaulted a child and then covered his tracks. The jury considered Hutson criminally responsible, and they found him guilty of murder with no recommendation to mercy.[24]

Justice McRuer's report supported the verdict, but the case left him uneasy over the appraisal of Hutson's responsibility under the Criminal Code's restrictive definition of insanity.[25] The sexual assault and murder of Susan Hutchins made McRuer "wonder whether a man who is sane could commit it." To settle his mind after the trial, the judge conferred with each of the psychiatrists who had testified, and he reported that he found the defence's expert the most persuasive. Dr. Doyle reiterated that Hutson was "unbalanced and his mental condition is questionable. He is firm that he ought not to be allowed to be at large again."[26] Hutson had a history of sexual offending (a charge that he had sexually molested a boy, which the police dropped), and McRuer also learned that Hutson had faced trial in 1948 for the axe murder of his mother. Had that earlier jury not been "extremely lenient," he despaired, the child's murder might have been prevented.[27] However, McRuer could not treat Hutson as a criminal sexual psychopath, since the CSP statute did not cover persons convicted of murder.[28]

Because Justice McRuer claimed there was "a pattern of conduct" in Hutson's crimes, he advised the Department of Justice that a "further examination and report as to the prisoner's mental state should be conducted."[29] The judge's request was granted, and the reliable Dr. John P.S. Cathcart, the government psychiatrist, was dispatched to examine the condemned man. Although he did not regard criminal psychopathy as grounds for clemency, Cathcart's report on Hutson was uncharacteristically guarded, as the nature of the prisoner's epilepsy was unclear.[30] In the memorandum MacLeod prepared for cabinet review, he ironed out Dr. Cathcart's hesitation to pronounce Hutson sane. Without reference to the psychiatrist's request for further clinical tests of the man's brain waves, MacLeod stated simply that he had carried out the judge's request for a psychiatric review.[31]

Mervyn Hutson was hanged on 9 February 1954, one month before Stuart Garson, the minister of justice, set up two royal commissions to interrogate whether the criminal law relating to the defence of

Image 5.2 James C. McRuer (1890–1985) lectured in criminal procedure at Osgoode Hall Law School until 1935. A Liberal, he was chosen to head the Royal Commission on the Criminal Law Relating to Criminal Sexual Psychopaths and the Royal Commission on the Law of Insanity as a Defence in Criminal Cases. Law Society of Ontario Archives.

insanity and the law concerning criminal sexual psychopaths "should be amended in any respect and, if so, in what manner and to what extent."[32] The Liberals put their faith in Justice James C. McRuer to chair both inquiries. In 1947, journalist Sidney Katz had used "His Lordship's" public admission – that he found the sentencing of sex offenders a dilemma – to open his *Maclean's* magazine article "The Truth about Sex Criminals." The confronting story referred to recent sex cases, including Roland Chassé's conviction in 1946 for the murder of

John Benson, and it concluded: "The truth is that sex deviates act under an overpowering compulsion."[33] But Canadian criminal law (unlike the statutes in numerous American jurisdictions) did not recognize "irresistible impulse" as a defence to murder outside of evidence of insanity (imbecility or disease of the mind).[34] Mervyn Hutson's trial and execution would likely have been uppermost in McRuer's mind as he took up his considerable responsibilities in the spring of 1954.[35] For the next four years, as he led the country's first official inquiries into the murky matters of sexual psychopathy and criminal insanity, seven men were condemned to death for sex murders. Despite a significant drop in the level of public support for capital punishment – from 71 per cent of Canadians in favour of its retention in 1953 down to close to 50 per cent in 1958 – each of these men was hanged.[36]

Inquiring into the Criminal Responsibility of Sex Offenders

The royal commission that studied the 1948 CSP sentencing provisions confirmed what every person directly involved in the field knew: they were seldom applied. The commission's inquiries revealed that, from 1948 to 1955, judges across Canada had sentenced just twenty-three men to serve indeterminate sentences on the application of Crown attorneys, supported by the diagnoses of two psychiatrists.[37] McRuer and his two fellow commissioners, Dr. Gustave Desrochers of Quebec City's St. Michel Hospital and Helen Kinnear, Canada's first federally appointed female judge serving in Ontario's County Court system, travelled the country to determine how the statute was operating. After canvassing advice and opinion from experts and interested organizations, McRuer had to report that experts were no closer than they had been in 1948 in reaching a definition of sexual psychopathy. However, the commission could make a clear recommendation that the statute be modified to broaden the capacity to impose preventive detention.[38]

Of the 169 witnesses who testified in eighteen public hearings, almost half were psychiatrists, psychologists, and medical professionals. Representatives from the Department of Justice, including A.J. MacLeod, gave evidence, and twenty-one members of the legal profession appeared. Although the two cohorts represented different fields of expertise, there was more division within the groups than between them. Among the psychiatrists who testified, the most dismissive of the capacity to predict the likelihood of sexual reoffending was Dr. John M. Senn, the expert who examined Arthur Bliss and pronounced him sane prior to his truncated trial in 1936. In that report, Senn described the prisoner as a "not attractive" man, who had "made no attempt to restrain" his "sexual appetites."[39] When he testified before the McRuer CSP Commission, Senn shot down the suggestion that sex killers were unable to restrain themselves: "He did not believe in irresistible impulse, he believed impulses were just uncontrolled."[40] The psychiatrists who worked in mental institutions were less categorical in their testimony, but most derided colleagues who claimed that psychopathy could be diagnosed to determine the likelihood of future offending.[41]

The attorneys general who appeared before the commission explained why so few sexual offenders were subjected to indefinite detention. Most psychiatrists doubted that sexual offenders were compelled to attack victims, and judges, with few exceptions, were loathe to place rubbery medical theory above common law jurisprudence on criminal responsibility. Considering that many psychiatrists did not recognize sexual psychopathy as a mental disorder, it was hardly surprising that judges were averse to apply the CSP statute. But most of all, the lack of treatment facilities in penitentiaries and secure hospitals deterred judges from experimenting with indefinite detention.

Nevertheless, there were clear patterns in the CSP sentences that judges did impose. Seventeen of the twenty-three men (there were no women) had a history of offences against females, and all but a few had been charged with sexual offences against children.[42] Evidently, the concerns that propelled the passage of the Criminal Code's 1948 amendment – anxiety over the sexual abuse of minors – also motivated Crown attorneys and judges to act. To assist the commission, MacLeod's department worked with penitentiary staff and police to prepare anonymized case summaries of men sentenced as CSPs. The first offender to be subjected to indefinite detention was a twenty-five-year-old man. His conviction in 1949 for the brutal rape of an adult woman, plus two previous convictions for indecent assault, had prompted the Crown to present the offender as a man with uncontrollable sexual aggression. Two psychiatrists traced a pattern of "anti-social acts" in the past, and they agreed the convicted rapist was "unable to control his abnormal tendencies" when intoxicated. The judge concurred. But when the offender learned he was sentenced to three and a half years' imprisonment plus an indefinite period set aside for his possible treatment, he vowed: "I'll kill the little bitch when I get out."[43] The commission's final report highlighted the need for greater understanding of the sexual psychopath: "There is urgent need in Canada for research in all aspects

Image 5.3 Liberal MP Stuart Sinclair Garson (1898–1977) exerted considerable influence over the reform of the criminal law and criminal procedure during his tenure as attorney general and minister of justice from 1948 to 1957. LAC, MIKAN 3215918.

of sexual deviation, with a view to development of means of correction and prevention." Yet, the commissioners offered no clear recommendation about the possible treatment of sex murderers with a history of sexual offending.[44]

The Royal Commission on the Law of Insanity as a Defence in Criminal Cases operated in parallel with the CSP Commission, but it presented its report two years earlier in 1956. It also focused more closely on the executive's administration of capital cases, since the review of death sentences frequently considered evidence of mental aberrations or abnormalities. When Stuart Garson, the man who established the commission, was asked to give evidence about the cabinet's appraisal of psychiatric evidence, he responded with the standard assurance.[45]

In every capital case, not just ones in which insanity pleas had been argued at trial, the cabinet took into consideration "much evidence ... that could not be presented in court under the rules of evidence governing courts in Canada." Although a convicted murderer might not be insane from a legal point of view, Garson testified, medical or psychiatric evidence, submitted during or after the trial, could prompt clemency if it appeared that the condemned person suffered from some form of mental deficiency or illness. "We weigh the evidence as carefully as we can and then we seek independent psychiatric experts to assist us in deciding the conflicts in the evidence before us," the minister stated. He also claimed that the cabinet always took into account any evidence that offenders were weak-minded or mentally disturbed. "The point that I wish to make," Garson emphasized, "is that no detail is ever considered to be too trivial, where the life of a condemned person is concerned, to merit the most comprehensive inquiry and investigation."[46]

The Insanity Commission's final report endorsed the justice minister's claims without checking them against the record of capital case dispositions. However, it did recommend that Canada adopt a rule to oblige the executive to review the mental condition of any person under sentence of death if there was any suspicion the prisoner suffered a disease of the mind, a provision that England had adopted back in 1884.[47] Had McRuer been able to examine the capital case files of convicted sex murderers over the period in which his twin commissions operated, he would have found that condemned men's records of prior sexual offences and diagnoses of mental illness did not incline the cabinet to clemency. He would also have seen that the government's foremost post-conviction psychiatric consultant upheld Canada's legal definition of insanity. Dr. Cathcart agreed with Dr. Senn that it would be dangerous to adopt the American notion of "irresistible impulses."[48]

"Only an Insane or Crazy Person Would Do That"

While members of national commissions, committees, and inquiries questioned witnesses and prepared reports pertinent to the disposition of sex murder cases over the mid-1950s, MacLeod and his CLD staff handled seven sex murder cases. Judges' reports confirmed that jurors who found defendants guilty of killing children rarely added a recommendation to mercy. In any event, the men who served in cabinet disregarded jury recommendations unless the trial judge supported them. In six of these cases, the victims ranged in age from six to thirteen – five girls and two boys. Moral outrage over the sex slaying of children was not new, nor were crimes of this nature. But advances in policing over the mid-twentieth century raised expectations that all sex murders could be solved and killers caught. When local police were out of their depth, provincial authorities and the RCMP sent reinforcements.[49] Most police forces also maintained files on known sex "perverts," which provided a ready source of suspects to question whenever sex murders occurred.[50] And there was no doubt that the police were in favour of the death penalty. Among the country's most vocal supporters of capital punishment as a deterrent to murder, the law enforcers who testified before the inquiries of the 1950s urged the government against abolition, and the government listened.[51] But not even the police called for the execution of insane persons.

Defenders of men charged with sex murders of small children often claimed they were mentally disturbed; however, in cases of attacks on adult women, lawyers for the defence frequently suggested that the victim had somehow invited her assailant's attention or that she had engaged in sexual relations with another man.[52] In the murder of Calgary woman Gharda Middlestad, the press and local radio stations initially portrayed her in an unflattering light, since she met her death after leaving a beer parlour in March 1953.[53] However, sympathy for the married woman of fifty-six, a Norwegian immigrant, grew after her respectability was confirmed and news of the savage beating and rape she had suffered became public. The viciousness of the attack convinced locals that a sex slayer was on the loose, threatening the entire city, and the police offered a reward for the man's capture.[54] Over the following six months, Calgary police questioned more than fifty men, and the city remained on edge until Mrs. Robert Sim contacted authorities to report her unemployed husband.[55] Brought into custody, the twenty-three-year-old suspect confessed: "I might as well tell you I killed the woman." Calgary police quoted Sim's confession when they announced they had caught the "sex criminal."[56] But the man claimed his memory was hazy, since he had consumed approximately ten pints of beer on the night of Middlestad's murder. Sim told police he could recall nothing between leaving the bar and sitting on the woman's prone body in the alleyway behind the beer parlour.[57]

Rather than attempt a defence that would require expert testimony, Sim's court-appointed lawyer, Lorne Dawson, tried to convince the jury that some other man had raped and killed Mrs. Middlestad.[58] However, he implied an insanity defence through his cross-examination of Crown witnesses. The killer had left the victim's clothes pushed up around the waist, and jurors were shown photos of her semi-nude body, with bruises and blood in the genital area and her face severely beaten. After Dr. Lola McLatchie (one of the country's first female forensic pathologists) testified for the Crown concerning the cause of death, Dawson posed a question more appropriate for a psychiatric expert: "Would you not say that it is probable that the person inflicting those injuries … was mentally deranged?"[59] The pathologist demurred, as this was not her field of expertise, and Justice J. Boyd McBride warned the jury to reject the defence's madman speculation. In crimes that "shock and mystify the average person," the judge stated in his charge, jurors were tempted to assume "the man must have been insane to do a thing like that. Only an insane person or a crazy person would do that." McBride further advised the jury they had no basis on which to deliver a verdict of not guilty by reason of insanity. This was a feature of sound legal doctrine. If any juror was inclined to say, "Oh, well … this man acted on an uncontrollable impulse," he must recall that in Canada this defence had been "flatly rejected."[60]

The role that alcohol played in unleashing homicidal violent impulses during blackouts was a contentious matter in the defence of accused murderers. To admit a defendant had committed homicide and argue that he could not be held accountable was a risky ploy in a capital case. It required convincing the jury that the killer was insane or intoxicated to the point where he could not form the requisite intent. After Sim's conviction, leaders of the Calgary bar rallied to the condemned man's defence and filed an appeal, convinced that his counsel had failed to introduce evidence of Sim's inability to control his sexually violent impulses after drinking. Samuel J. Helman, KC, the lead counsel on the appeal, found several prominent psychiatrists prepared to contradict the Crown's psychiatric expert, who had stated Sim was intoxicated but sane.[61] Dr. Kenneth George Gray was one of them, a lecturer in medical jurisprudence at the University of Toronto and chief of the Forensic Clinic at the Toronto Psychiatric Hospital since 1949.[62] Gray signed an affidavit that stated he discovered Sim had attacked and sexually assaulted three other women over the past few years, always when drunk. This record indicated he had a "pathological" reaction to alcohol.[63] Although the prisoner was normal mentally, he likely suffered from alcoholic amnesia at the time of offence and was, therefore, unable to form criminal intent.[64] Helman also contacted Dr. T.C. Michie, the medical superintendent of the provincial psychiatric hospital, who had examined Sim prior to the trial and pronounced him "not psychotic."[65]

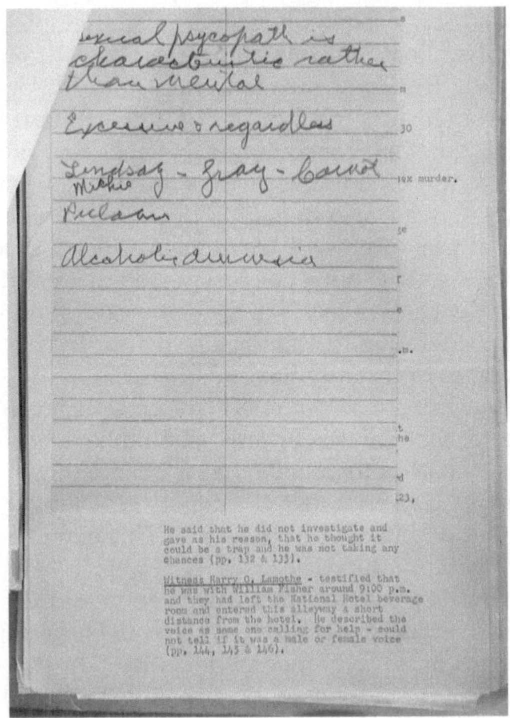

sexual psycopath is characteristic rather than mental

Lindsay - Gray - Michie

Alcoholic amnesia

He said that he did not investigate and gave as his reason, that he thought it could be a trap and he was not taking any chances (pp. 132 & 133).

Witness Harry O. Lamothe - testified that he was with William Fisher around 9:00 p.m. and they had left the National Hotel beverage room and entered this alleyway a short distance from the hotel. He described the voice as some one calling for help - could not tell if it was a male or female voice (pp. 144, 145 & 146).

Image 5.4 A Criminal Law Division clerk's notes in Robert Sim's case file record the various explanations for his rape and murder of Gharda Middlestad. Although some psychiatrists thought alcohol had a pathological effect on Sim, the government psychiatrist affirmed he was sane under the law. LAC, Sim, Volume 1752, volume 1, part 1.

After the trial, Michie agreed it was probable that Sim "tends to react in a pathological manner to alcohol."[66] However, the Appellate Division of the Supreme Court of Alberta considered this new evidence insufficient to indicate that the jury would have decided differently had it been presented at trial; furthermore, there was "no evidence of insanity or drunkenness." The ruling concluded that "no substantial wrong or miscarriage of justice actually occurred."[67] Calgarians could breathe a sigh of relief when the Supreme Court refused to hear a subsequent appeal, but the executive was not bound to take either court's ruling into account.[68]

While Robert Sim's legal representatives attempted, unsuccessfully, to appeal against his conviction, the Special Joint Committee of the House and Senate began its inquiry into the death penalty's operation. In March 1954, the minister of justice, Stuart Garson, gave evidence again, this time concerning the disposition of capital cases. His support staff provided historic data, but Garson favoured anecdotal accounts. It was customary for the counsel who represented the defendant at trial to present "reasons in support of an exercise of clemency by the Crown;" however, he stressed that petitions were not required, since "each case receives the same careful and painstaking perusal and consideration."[69] Garson also reaffirmed it was not necessary that a defence of insanity be argued at trial in order to trigger a psychiatric review of a condemned offender. Whenever the "suggestion is made after the trial that insanity should have been raised, or at the least, there is reason to believe that the condemned person is not mentally normal," Garson stated, the department sought the advice of an "independent psychiatrist of repute."[70] This expert's job included determining whether supposed insanity was just "a sham and pretence." Nevertheless, the cabinet always commuted death sentences if psychiatrists found a condemned person was "suffering from one of a variety of forms or types of mental deviation." In short, the cabinet approached every capitally convicted offender with an open mind, "no matter how friendless or terrible a rogue a man may be."[71] Garson's May 1954 testimony gave every assurance that a man in Sim's position could place his hope in the procedures and principles that underpinned executive discretion.

In the review of Sim's possible eligibility for clemency, the protocol the minister of justice recounted in his evidence was followed to the bare minimum. The government turned, as usual by the 1950s, to Dr. Cathcart. The psychiatrist "of repute" began by telephoning the local expert who had testified for the Crown during Sim's trial, Dr. Morris Carnat. Cathcart also reviewed Gray's and Michie's post-trial statements, which he dismissed as "untested." However, Dr. Carnat told his Ottawa colleague that he had changed his mind since the trial. Now, he considered Sim a sexual psychopath, who displayed "aggressive sexual assaultive behaviour [as] part of a sadistic pattern." Despite the doctor's reversal, Cathcart rejected all claims that Sim was not responsible, and for this reason he reported he did not "think it necessary … to visit and examine the prisoner"[72] The CLD agreed, and no further inquiries were made. Although MacLeod politely acknowledged Helman's final appeals for mercy, they made no impression on the division head or the cabinet, which decided that the law should take its course.[73]

Plumbing the Depths of Outrage: The "Butcher D'Youville"

The 1950s was the first decade when MPs opposed to the death penalty, starting with Ross Thatcher, introduced one private member's bill after another, convinced that their efforts would drum up support for their cause even if abolition remained a far-off goal. The St. Laurent government's overhaul of the criminal law buoyed their hopes, since the inquiries it sparked lifted the lid on the apparatus of capital case reviews. "I do not see how we can intelligently set about to change the law unless we know first of all how it works," Stuart Garson confidently declared when he appeared before the Joint Committee.[74] Similarly, Supreme Court Justice Gérald Fauteux requested and received reports from the Remission Branch, which documented in finer detail than ever before the administration of capital cases back to 1920. Yet, his committee was more focused on the future and the prospect of establishing a national parole system. It did not recommend any changes concerning the disposition of death sentence reviews. Reassured by Garson and his staff in the Department of Justice, the Fauteux Report concluded sketchily that "the senior officers of the Service follow conscientiously the principles and procedure."[75] But the government's own data revealed inequity in capital punishment's discretionary administration. Opponents of the death penalty seized on the evidence in these reports and spied it through a more suspicious lens.

In 1956, when the Special Joint Committee tabled its final report on the handling of capital cases, it offered faint praise: "On the whole, no serious criticism was offered against present remission procedures and policies."[76] The report used stronger words to criticize Canada's restrictive approach to appeals for defendants sentenced to death. Because the current law set a short period of time within which appeals could be lodged, "technical slips" could lead to delays.[77] To avoid the possibility of "injustice and embarrassment," the committee recommended that appeals before provincial appellate courts be allowed automatically. It further recommended that "every person subject to a capital sentence" should have an opportunity, by right, to be heard in the Supreme Court, the "court of last resort." However, after more than two years of intense study, the committee failed to confirm any "instance where an accused may have suffered because of an inadequate defence."[78] Anodyne statements of this sort provided targets for abolitionists with first-hand knowledge of capital trials and post-trial deliberations, and the government's own pronouncements on the integrity of capital justice became performance indicators that critics pounced on.

Most capitally convicted defendants in the mid-1950s were represented by members of the bar who were prepared to file an appeal, irrespective of the slim chance of success. This custom made the conviction of Lucien Picard in 1954 unusual. The lawyer whom the court appointed, Paul Aubut, had practised for just five years, but he had already racked up an impressive record of defending men charged with murder (four clients, none of whom was executed). Yet, when he was asked to defend Picard, he did so reluctantly, he informed the press. The crime (which involved the dismemberment of a Montreal boy, Raymond Trudeau) was "brutal and sadistic," which meant the case was one he normally "wouldn't care to handle." Aubut wished to reassure the public that he "sympathize[d] greatly with the grieved parents in their loss of an innocent son in such a brutal manner."[79] At the same time, he stressed the right of the accused to a fair trial, although he was unwilling to appeal Picard's conviction.

Montreal's newly launched scandal sheet, *Allô Police*, made a fair trial for Picard all but impossible.[80] Its founders declared they were on a mission to inform the public about crime and the risks all around them posed by sex maniacs and killers.[81] Under the guise of exposing "la verité absolue," *Allô Police* published images of the six-year-old victim's body parts, including his face. The revolting pictures illustrated the story that recounted the discovery early in August 1954 of human remains in rubbish piles in Montreal's Place D'Youville. Further body parts were discovered in the room Picard rented in a nearby boarding house, and this ghoulish evidence plus clothes helped identify the boy's identity. The images, likely leaked by the police or morgue attendants, led *Allô Police* to speculate that the butchery was the work of a homosexual pervert.[82] Once the police traced the roomer, who had left town as soon as the boy went missing, mainstream newspapers joined *Allô Police* in covering the sensational crime and the criminal's capture. Picard was a diminutive forty-four-year-old machinist, who worked as a hotel cleaner in the city's main passenger rail terminal, Windsor Station, and the police claimed he confessed he had enticed the boy to his rooms and suffocated him when the child resisted his advances. In a panic, he had dismembered the body.

MONTREAL, FRIDAY, AUGUST 6, 1954 FINAL PRICE FIVE CENTS

Crowd Threatens Picard's Life

ACCUSED SLAYER LUCIEN PICARD IS HEAVILY GUARDED

Commuters' Train Fares Will Double

Ottawa, Aug. 5 – (CP) – Higher commuter fares for Canadian railroads generally were indicated today in a Board of Transport Commissioners judgment allowing a big boost in the Toronto area.

The board, in saying Toronto district rates can be increased about 100 per cent during the next 14 months, laid down the principle that the railways should be permitted to charge enough so that commuter trains pay their way.

For many years, it has been a complaint of the companies that commutation services do not meet even the "out-of-pocket" expense of running the trains.

The board met that complaint partly in 1950 by granting a portion of a railway-requested increase. Today, it gave the railways the amount they asked for the Toronto area, though spreading its full effect over a longer time than the companies had sought.

The board's new pay-its-way principle for commuter services

Murder Charge Laid

Judge Marechal Nantel warned spectators in Arraignment Court yesterday afternoon he would not tolerate threats of violence as Lucien Picard was brought before him.

Minutes later, Picard was charged with murder.

Hundreds of spectators jammed narrow St. Vincent street outside the Coroner's Court in the morning when Picard was brought to that court and taken away from it under heavy police guard.

"Kill him," they shouted. "Lynch him," "throw him in the river," "hack him up alive."

The six-man coroner's jury found Picard, 45-year-old father of two, criminally responsible in the slaying of Raymond Trudeau. In Arraignment Court, he was

Image 5.5 Unlike the sensational *Allô Police*, the Montreal *Gazette* did not publish morgue photos of Raymond Trudeau's dismembered body. However, this front-page image shows that Montrealers poured into the streets to express their anger at Lucien Picard, the captured suspect. Montreal *Gazette*, 6 August 1954.

The arrest of Picard unleashed public fury and demands for his death. For Montrealers, this murder stirred memories of John Benson, killed by "a sadistic slayer" on Montreal's mountain less than a decade earlier.[83] News of another boy, murdered by a merciless killer, induced Benson's parents to visit the Trudeau family to offer the boy's parents their condolences.[84] Roland Chassé, the man convicted for Benson's murder, was executed in 1946, and Mrs. Trudeau told the press that she wanted Picard to hang as well for his horrible crime, "to suffer as my son did."[85] All of Montreal, it seemed, shared the mother's wrath. An estimated 2,000 onlookers jammed the street where Picard emerged from a police car, protected by a cordon of police as he entered the coroner's court: "Une foule révoltée a menacé Lucien Picard," *Le Devoir* reported.[86]

Paul Aubut performed his professional obligation to defend Picard, fully aware of this hostile atmosphere. The finding of the coroner's inquest that his client was responsible for Raymond Trudeau's death led Aubut to request that Picard be examined at the Bordeaux Hospital for the Insane. The superintendent, Dr. J.A. Huard, was one of the psychiatrists who had recently appeared before the McRuer Commission on the insanity defence, where he expressed his discomfort with the law's definition of insanity.[87] He supported the view that the M'Naghten test was "inadequate and perhaps too severe," and as a member of the Quebec Psychiatric Association, he supported its submission that the criteria should be "softened, because they may lead to the finding of a mentally ill person as guilty."[88] But when he examined Picard, Huard was confident the man was fit to stand trial.

The conviction juggernaut stalled briefly, due to a bold decision by Irénée Lagarde, a Montreal magistrate who kept a close watch on civil liberties. In the course of presiding over Picard's preliminary hearing, he ruled the police must gather further evidence before the man could be indicted for murder.[89] The province's premier and attorney general, Maurice Duplessis, was enraged. Using his legal powers, he preferred an indictment, and this unorthodox intervention allowed prosecutors to fast-track the case.[90] After a two-day trial in November 1954, brief by the standards of the day, the jury took less than twenty minutes to find Picard guilty, unconvinced by Aubut's claims that no sane man could commit such a revolting crime. Three years earlier, following the conviction of another client, Alcide Martin (for the murder of his grandparents and a neighbour), Aubut had appealed against the verdict and lobbied the executive for clemency. In Picard's trial, he detached himself from the case as soon as the jury delivered its verdict.[91] The only information the cabinet considered beyond the transcript and judge's report was a further letter on the condemned man's mental state, submitted by Dr. Huard, which merely restated his earlier opinion.[92] Perhaps the clearest evidence of Picard's sanity was the statement he made when he was arraigned: "I am guilty of murder and I wish to be hanged as soon as possible being convinced that I will obtain justice only on the other side."[93]

The Double-Edged Sword of Appeals

Of the seven appeals defence lawyers filed against convictions in sex murder cases between 1953 and the fall of the Liberal government in 1957, provincial appeal courts granted new trials to three men. Arguments against conviction were based on the same grounds raised in earlier appeals: the admission of confessions under aggressive police questioning, insufficient proof of intent to rape, and inadequate instruction on intoxication as a defence or on manslaughter as a possible verdict.[94] When courts granted appeals, they typically ordered new trials, which raised the possibility that convicted sex killers might be acquitted, convicted of manslaughter, or found to be not criminally responsible. However, subsequent trials that ended in convictions for murder and those that ended in further unsuccessful appeals took on great weight when the cabinet considered clemency. Justice Minister Garson obscured this practice when he told the Special Joint Committee "that in exercising the royal prerogative [the cabinet members] do not set themselves up as a final court of appeal." It was important for the "due administration of justice" that the prerogative of mercy operate independently. "No such rules of procedure or evidence apply or should apply," Garson proclaimed. The minister was prepared to admit that the youth of a condemned offender usually influenced the cabinet toward clemency, and he also disclosed four other mitigating factors the executive customarily took into consideration: "insanity, drunkenness, provocation and reasonable doubt."[95] Yet, when courts of appeal dismissed defence arguments that raised these matters in sex murder cases, the informal court of executive discretion did not compensate for legal rules, as Garson indicated. In fact, unsuccessful appeals propped up the decision to withhold clemency.

Although convictions of men for sex murders often hinged on circumstantial evidence and confessions, prosecutors could count on a more potent element in their favour: public outrage over violent "perverts." Townsfolk in smaller centres could be just as hostile toward suspects as urban Canadians, especially if arrestees were drifters or locals ostracized in their own communities. Lawrence Bryan Vincent, also known as Corky, fit that profile. In 1954, he was convicted on circumstantial evidence for the murder of twelve-year-old Donna Corbett, killed while she was out on an evening of carefree pleasure. Vincent was a shooting gallery operator in a travelling show that rolled into the victim's hometown of Quesnel, British Columbia, on 12 September 1953. The densely forested land of the Dakelh people provided many places to hide a body, but the girl's remains were found the day after she disappeared, her leggings torn down past her knees and her face bearing the signs of a beating. The police constructed their case based on the theory that Vincent had met her on the show grounds. Having lured the girl away, he had "tried to have intercourse with her and when she struggled he brutally beat her unconscious." Fearing she might report the assault, he strangled her.[96] The jury found the case against him credible, and Vincent was convicted and sentenced to death on 24 June 1954.[97]

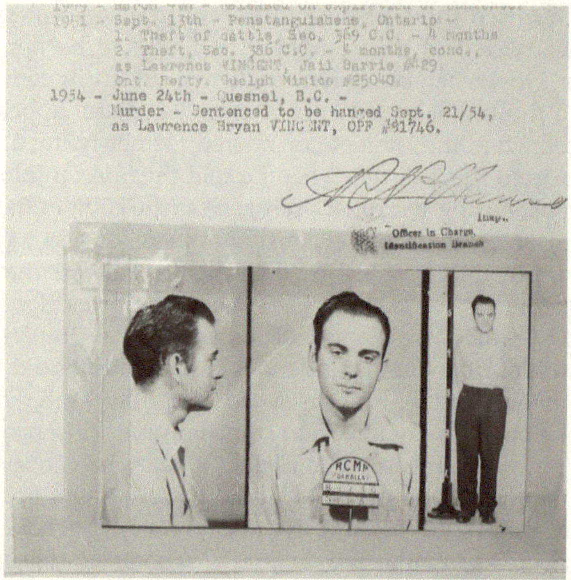

Image 5.6 Lawrence Vincent had a long criminal record prior to his conviction for the sex murder of twelve-year-old Donna Corbett in 1953. The Oakalla Prison physician, a qualified psychiatrist, informed Ottawa that the prisoner was "violently sadistic" but "not psychotic." LAC, R.G. 13, Volume 1727, volume 1, part 1, 30 July 1954.

As a man of meagre means, Vincent was fortunate to be represented by a court-appointed lawyer who appealed the verdict. Consistent with most murder appeals, R.J. Hughes argued that the confession was not voluntary and that the judge's instructions were disfavourable to the defence's theory that the police had failed to find the right man. The British Columbia Court of Appeal agreed that the trial judge's instructions on reasonable doubt were insufficient, and it ordered a retrial. Justice O'Halloran, who delivered the ruling, thought the circumstantial evidence against Vincent should have been treated with extreme caution:

> In an Assize town where a child has been brutally murdered under highly circumstantial conditions of proof, and public opinion may easily become

> inflamed to the point that mere suspicion may be confused with legitimate inference, it is, in my opinion, highly desirable that the learned Judge's charge should contain an unmistakable warning to the jury regarding the dangers of allowing suspicion to dominate their minds.[98]

Unlike Paul Aubut, R.J. Hughes stuck with his client. In the second trial, the jury could not reach a verdict; then, after the third trial ended in a conviction, Hughes followed with a second appeal and several petitions for reprieves. In his final clemency bid, Vincent's lawyer reiterated that some other person could have committed the murder on that night when townspeople and locals had mingled.[99]

The determination of the Department of the Attorney General to put Vincent on trial three times (the final one in February 1955) signalled the importance the province placed on his conviction for a tragic sex murder. Hughes complained to Ottawa that he had been forced to defend Vincent against British Columbia's newspapers and radio stations: "This case received much more publicity in the New Westminster and Vancouver press than one would expect." On that basis, Hughes claimed that the third jury "may have had preconceived notions as to the innocence or guilt of the accused."[100] In the provincial attorney general's opinion, any doubt over Vincent's guilt evaporated after the Court of Appeal dismissed the second appeal, and the CLD head agreed. A.J. MacLeod conceded "there may be some doubt" over the identification of the culprit, but he also knew from the RCMP's Criminal Investigation Branch that Vincent's record included a previous conviction and penitentiary term for rape. MacLeod duly advised the minister of justice that there were no grounds on which to interfere with the law. The itinerant roustabout disagreed. While awaiting execution he attempted to poison himself, but he went to the gallows "kicking and swearing." "Vincent Resists to the Last," one paper reported.[101]

The director of public prosecutions in Ontario went to even greater lengths in 1956 to ensure the conviction of a sex killer.[102] In 1938, in the case of John Comba, leading Crown attorneys working for the Ministry of the Attorney General had appealed to the Supreme Court against the provincial Court of Appeal's acquittal of the convicted murderer.[103] In that instance, the Crown had lost, but William B. Common, who headed Ontario's public prosecutions, worked hard to avoid a similar outcome in the case of Robert Fitton in 1956.[104] The timing and location of the crime (Toronto) turned the death of thirteen-year-old Linda Lampkin into a high-profile sex murder case, since it

$7,000 REWARD FOR KILLER

Toronto Girl, 13, Strangled

23-Year-Old Father of Two Being Questioned

LINDA LAMPKIN
Found Strangled on Toronto Street

SHIRLEY McDOUGALL, 10
Missing in Toronto

ALL PARENTS WARNED KEEP CHILDREN INDOORS

Hunters Deny Threat To Shoot Gloucester Farmer

Tenley Albright Gashes Her Leg

TENLEY ALBRIGHT

Farmer Fined $75 for Shooting Deer Illegally

Drew Queries PM on Sale Of Artillery

Quebec Vote This Year

SIMONDS CHARGES

Politicians Ignoring Manpower Problems

Image 5.7 The sex murder of Linda Lampkin in 1956 occurred after a spate of abductions and unsolved sex slayings of girls in the Toronto area. In the subsequent trial of Robert Fitton, the defence alleged the victim was "boy crazy" and that she had provoked the man. (Fitton's age in the above article was incorrect; he was twenty-two at the time of his execution.) Ottawa *Journal*, 19 January 1956.

occurred at the very moment when the Toronto *Daily Star* launched a campaign against sex offences. The home base of the Parents' Action League (PAL), Toronto was the epicentre of citizen-led campaigns to police and prosecute sex offences systematically as serious crimes and to draw greater attention to the dangers posed by "perverts" and "deviates."[105] The *Star* gave saturation coverage to sex crimes. In January 1956, the paper published stories on the death of a five-year-old girl, sexually assaulted and left to die in London, Ontario.[106] This heart-rending unsolved case prompted local women to seek support from PAL members in Toronto, and they responded by encouraging the *Star* to organize a public meeting on "sexual deviancy." In the midst of their negotiations over the event, Linda Lampkin's body was found on a lonely lakefront strip on 18 January 1956, bearing signs she had been sexually assaulted.[107] "Young Girl Brutally Murdered by Sex Fiend," the paper reported.[108]

News of an arrest broke six days before the *Daily Star* had planned to hold a "Citizens' Forum on Sex Offenders," featuring experts who were asked to update the public on the latest findings in the field.[109] Offences of this kind were "horrifying crimes," the *Star*'s editor acknowledged, but "this is no time for hysteria – nor for complacency, either."[110] As the suspect, Robert Fitton, sat in the Don Jail awaiting trial, 2,000 Torontonians gathered downtown in Massey Hall, eager to hear from learned men. One of the experts was Dr. Kenneth Gray, who had provided an affidavit in the Sim case in Calgary. An authority regularly consulted by both the Crown and defence in capital cases, Gray agreed in 1955 to serve as PAL's chief consultant. He told the audience that, in his expert opinion, "not all sex deviates are criminals and … not all sex deviates are dangerous people."[111] The men who served on the jury in Fitton's trial may have agreed with the doctor, as they found the defendant guilty of murder but added a recommendation to mercy. Their sentiments were backed by the trial judge, R.W. Treleaven, who supported the recommendation when he came to write his report to Ottawa. He also used the occasion to draw the executive's attention to the victim's attractive looks and provocative demeanour: "There was some evidence [the girl] was a bit 'boy crazy' and may have had an infatuation for the accused man … She apparently willingly got into his truck on the night in question."[112]

Fitton's lawyer, an up-and-coming barrister, was not put off by the verdict. In his appearance before the Court of Appeal, David Humphreys successfully argued that the trial judge had improperly admitted the young man's confession into evidence.[113] The ruling in favour of the defence set aside the verdict and ordered a new trial. But rather than prepare for a second prosecution, William B. Common exercised the Crown's right to appeal the ruling before the Supreme Court. When the Special Joint Committee on the death penalty sought out experts on the prosecution of murder cases at the start of their deliberations in 1954, they began with Common.[114] One of Canada's foremost prosecutors, he appealed the lower court's decision that set aside Fitton's guilty verdict. In this appearance before the Supreme Court, Common was successful. Since a majority of the country's highest court agreed with the Crown that the jury's verdict must be restored, this ruling left Fitton with no further legal means to alter his fate.[115] "Odds are the execution will never be carried out," the *Daily Star* predicted, since "legal experts" had informed the paper that very few persons convicted of murder in the past twenty years had ended up on the gallows if jurors had considered them worthy of clemency.[116] It certainly helped that the man convicted of Lampkin's murder was an Anglo-Celtic twenty-two-year-old, a married father of two. This man was no "dark" stranger or low-life drifter, just an ordinary, working-class Torontonian.

Common's legal triumph left Louis Saint Laurent's cabinet with a difficult choice: to allow the law to take its course in the face of the jury's recommendation, supported by the trial judge, or to take their cue from the country's highest court.[117] One of the justices who concurred with the decision to restore the verdict in Fitton's case was Gérald Fauteux, who had recently completed his inquiry into the Remission Branch before returning to the Supreme Court bench. Fitton's claim – that he had grabbed Lampkin's scarf and accidentally strangled her after she started to annoy him by "kibitzing" with him – was far-fetched and distasteful in Fauteux's opinion.[118] "The evidence with respect to the condition both of the body of the victim and of her clothing is violently inconsistent with any suggestion of consent on her part," he wrote.[119] Many Torontonians had their doubts. Those who pleaded for clemency favoured the defence's line of argument, which smeared the murdered girl's character. "The victim appears to have asked for trouble by her behaviour – and then to have resisted the attentions of a stupid and inflamed man," a group of west-end Torontonians wrote. Fitton's lawyer managed to find a juror who was prepared to sign an affidavit, stating he believed the young man had merely "lost his head in the heat of passion." The defence had also suggested there was an element of provocation in the encounter, and clemency supporters agreed: "The deceased contributed to and aggravated the circumstances by flirting, enticing and encouraging Fitton."[120]

In the end, the cabinet decided to rely on the Supreme Court, "which had confirmed the verdict of guilty."[121] The Toronto *Daily Star*'s prediction turned out to be incorrect. The announcement that Fitton would, indeed, pay for his crime with his life perplexed people who thought Lampkin's death was the result of a tryst with an ordinary man, not the crime of a sex fiend. "Everyone believed it unthinkable that you would override the stated wishes of this jury," one man protested to the minister of justice on the day that followed Robert Fitton's execution on 21 November. "Has Fitton's death brought us any nearer to the complex medical and social problems of which his crime was a symptom?"[122]

Ambivalent Nation: The Death Penalty in the Mid-1950s

Two of the three major inquiries into criminal justice policy reported to Parliament in 1956, and neither of them recommended significant changes to the administration of capital justice. Canada's Special Joint Committee was as "cautious and conservative" as Britain's Royal Commission on Capital Punishment. The Canadian report endorsed the retention of the death penalty, and it also rejected the prospect that murder be divided into degrees of culpability.[123] However, it did advise that no convicted murderer under the age of eighteen should face the death penalty.[124] The inquiry into the CLD made more far-reaching recommendations, foremost the establishment of a new federal parole system.[125] The Fauteux Report, which recommended the transition, set two ambitious goals for parole's administration: "a concentration of effort on treatment by way of training, rather than the mere imposition of punishment;" and a "willingness to make full-scale experiments in all phases of the correctional system."[126] The government's implicit endorsement of the principles behind this recommendation, while it maintained that the death penalty was a necessary deterrent, sounded a policy discord. The Joint Committee and the Insanity Defence Commission attempted to resolve it by intoning the royal prerogative of mercy. Likewise, Fauteux's committee accepted the testimony of Justice Minister Garson and A.J. MacLeod, who painted capital case reviews as judicious and fair-minded.[127]

Despite the maintenance of the status quo in the death penalty's administration, the defeat of the Liberals in the election of 1957 created the prospect that the new government might more enthusiastically and fully embrace the ideals expounded in the Fauteux Report.[128] Surely the Progressive Conservatives, headed by a former defence lawyer in capital cases, might handle discretionary justice in a more merciful manner. Canadians watched more closely than ever before, as the incoming government undertook death penalty reviews. Would Diefenbaker, the most forthright supporter of the CSP amendment in 1948, head a cabinet prepared to consider mental impairment and uncontrollable impulses as criteria for clemency?

The Conservatives had barely formed government when Diefenbaker's newly sworn cabinet confronted its first capital case review, Gerald Eaton's death sentence for the sex murder of a girl. The offence occurred in the spring of 1956 in Langley, British Columbia. Eaton was convicted at his first trial, but the British Columbia Court of Appeal had set aside the verdict. After his second conviction, the court dismissed Eaton's appeal, and this decision set 19 July 1957 as the date of his execution – just five weeks after the federal election.[129] The lawyer who had represented the defendant through his trials and appeals, Norman D. Mullins, was unsure whom to address to appeal for clemency. In April 1957, after another one of his clients (Joseph Carey) was convicted for his part in the shooting death of a police officer, Mullins convinced the Liberal cabinet to grant clemency.[130] But Eaton was a sex killer, convicted for sexually molesting and bludgeoning to death eight-year-old Carolynne Moore. A married man fifty-one years of age, Eaton had one prior offence (for "seduction"), and he was under investigation for having sexually abused a foster child. With neither youth nor a clean record in his favour, Eaton made a poor candidate for clemency.

The superintendent in charge of the Criminal Investigation Bureau's BC branch had nothing good to say about Eaton, a man "completely devoid of all moral principles." His attempt to sexually assault the Moore girl confirmed he was "a most despicable person." The superintendent was also anxious for the CLD to know that the citizens of Langley expected the death penalty to be carried out: "The community was outraged at the discovery of the child's body, and a great deal of public interest was shown at the trial. It is considered public opinion as a whole would be definitely adverse to the consideration of clemency in this case."[131] The RCMP officer's barely disguised recommendation that Eaton be hanged sat like a time bomb in the capital case file, ticking as Diefenbaker's new cabinet met to decide whether to defuse it or let fire.

The parents of the victim proclaimed their wish that the culprit be executed, and they also contacted federal officials directly. The child's father, Lawrence Moore, worked as a civil servant for the Department of Veterans Affairs. Fearful that Eaton might be spared, he telegrammed MacLeod to beg that the government hang the culprit: "ON OUR KNEES MY WIFE AND I MAKE OUR PLEA WITH ALL OUR HEART AND SOUL." Moore urged the new government to consider his request in light of its duty "TO CAROLYNNE HER PARENTS AND OTHER DEFENCELESS CHILDREN LIVING IN FEAR OF A FIEND." If the death sentence were commuted, Mr. Moore warned, he would hold the government "DIRECTLY RESPONSIBLE," because he feared his wife would likely end up in an "INSTITUTION" if Eaton were not hanged.[132] MacLeod considered the father's approach distasteful; since it was "vengeful" and emotional, he advised the cabinet to ignore it. Yet, the CLD made no move to order a psychiatric examination of Eaton,

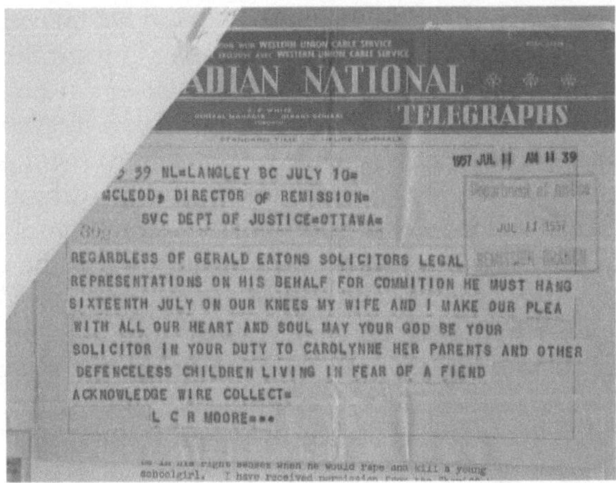

ADIAN NATIONAL
TELEGRAPHS

1957 JUL 11 AM 11 39

59 NL=LANGLEY BC JULY 10=
MCLEOD, DIRECTOR OF REMISSION=
SVC DEPT OF JUSTICE=OTTAWA=

REGARDLESS OF GERALD EATONS SOLICITORS LEGAL
REPRESENTATIONS ON HIS BEHALF FOR COMMITION HE MUST HANG
SIXTEENTH JULY ON OUR KNEES MY WIFE AND I MAKE OUR PLEA
WITH ALL OUR HEART AND SOUL MAY YOUR GOD BE YOUR
SOLICITOR IN YOUR DUTY TO CAROLYNNE HER PARENTS AND OTHER
DEFENCELESS CHILDREN LIVING IN FEAR OF A FIEND
ACKNOWLEDGE WIRE COLLECT=
L C R MOORE===

Image 5.8 Just before the new Conservative cabinet met to consider Gerald Eaton's fate, the father of Carolynne Moore telegrammed to demand that Eaton be hanged for his daughter's murder. LAC, R.G. 13, Volume 1759, volume 1, part 1, 29 June 1957.

even after the warden of Oakalla Prison wrote to catalogue the man's sexual abnormalities. "There is not the slightest shred of evidence that Eaton suffers in any way from mental impairment or mental abnormality," MacLeod concluded in his report for the new solicitor general.[133]

Disapproval of revenge in the administration of criminal justice followed the doctrine of correctionalism, which the Fauteux inquiry embraced. "In a modern correctional system there is no place for punishment which is based on nothing more than retribution," the final report proclaimed.[134] Yet, every recommendation that the law take its course clashed with correctionalism's key precept: "Persons who violate the criminal law are persons who have been 'damaged' in the life process of growing up."[135] Over the mid-1950s, the trend toward penal welfarism picked up steam. As Norman Mullins awaited word on his second Eaton appeal in the spring of 1957, the Canadian Corrections Association's First Congress took place in Montreal in May of that year. Mullins tapped into the spirit of that meeting in his plea for clemency. Eaton was a redeemable character, who had counselled Mullins's younger client – Carey – to "undertake a course of studies by correspondence to prepare himself for the time when he might eventually be released from prison." Had the fatherly Eaton not taken interest "ex gratia," Mullins stated, Carey "might well have given up the desire to work for his eventual return to society in the distant future."[136] When MacLeod read this clemency pitch, he drew a large question mark on Mullins's letter at the point where the writer claimed Eaton's execution would deprive the prison of a beneficial influence.[137] Although the CLD head condemned vengeance on the part of the victim's family, he had no hesitation in advising the cabinet that clemency would be unjust. The decision that Eaton's sentence be carried out met with broad approval. As one BC paper put it, his hanging ensured that "no other little girl will be clubbed to death by the man who dropped through the gallows trap."[138] The victim's father, one of twenty-three witnesses whom authorities allowed to watch the execution on 16 July 1957, looked on as the executioner granted his wish.[139]

Clemency on the Flip of a Coin

While the government's inquiries into the administration of justice failed to induce Canada to abolish capital punishment, they dredged up questions and doubts over the death penalty and its administration. The members of the Special Joint Committee (which tabled its final report on 12 July 1956) were divided, but the inquiry's terms of reference did not permit the submission of a minority report. The five members of the Royal Commission on the Law of Insanity as a Defence in Criminal Cases had that option, and two of McRuer's fellow commissioners submitted a formal "note of reservation." Judge Helen Kinnear and Nova Scotia psychiatrist Robert O. Jones were uncomfortable with the Insanity Commission's final report, which recommended that Canada reject the incorporation of diminished responsibility or irresistible impulse as criminal defences. The two minority members decided that Canadian courts should acknowledge "degrees of mental deficiency or mental illness not sufficient to absolve persons from all responsibility for criminal offences but sufficient nevertheless to make such persons not fully accountable for their actions."[140] In Mullins's plea for clemency he described Eaton in these terms (the man was unable to comprehend his "urges"). Claims of this nature became standard in clemency petitions for sex killers by the late 1950s, based on the theory that many forms of mental illness and abnormalities, not amounting to psychosis or organic disease, could provoke sexually aggressive behaviour.[141] The Insanity Commission's minority report lent credence to that notion.

To Harold Winch, one of the committed abolitionists on the Special Joint Committee, the royal prerogative of mercy provided an unreliable safety net for convicted killers whose minds did not fit the legal definition of insanity. The Eaton case made this clear. Writing to urge clemency for the condemned man, Winch told MacLeod it was hard to "believe that a man could be in his right mind and kill a young schoolgirl."[142] After he completed his service on the committee, the CCF member for Vancouver East broke ranks and disclosed that he had read and re-read the justice minister's testimony on executive discretion in capital cases. Yet, Winch still failed to understand why

> a person with a bad psychological background who is known as a brutal man and kicks a man to death in a fit of drunken brutality urged on by people around him hangs whereas others ... who commit murder in the course of premeditated robbery are given a life sentence.

After he undertook his own research on capital cases, unconvinced by the testimony before the committee, Winch concluded he could not "help but wonder whether executive clemency is not based on the flip of a coin; heads you die and tails you live."[143]

Deliberating over Death

In the chambers where the cabinet met, it was not a coin toss that determined Eaton's fate but the outcome of a tense debate between ministers for and against the death penalty. In the mid-1950s, Saint Laurent's cabinet deliberations over the death penalty were often protracted, particularly in cases embroiled in provincial politics. The conviction of Wilbert Coffin in 1954 for the murder of an American tourist dragged through failed appeals, the referral of the conviction to the Supreme Court, and accusations (by Quebec Premier Maurice Duplessis) of federal interference before the government finally decided in 1956 that Coffin must hang.[144] However, records of ministerial discussions in capital case reviews were not maintained consistently until Diefenbaker's Conservatives formed government. Although summary in nature, these accounts (officially called "Cabinet Conclusions") were prepared by the clerk of the Privy Council, who sometimes noted the names of ministers who took up positions for or against clemency.[145] As regards Eaton's case, the Conclusions indicate that cabinet required two meetings to hammer out a decision.

The solicitor general, Léon Balcer, was the minister responsible for capital case reviews in Diefenbaker's first cabinet.[146] A lawyer by training and a member of Parliament since 1949, his portfolio made him responsible for the CLD. However, the date of Balcer's ministerial appointment on 21 June 1957 required MacLeod and his team to steer the new minister through his responsibilities as a matter of urgency, since Eaton's scheduled execution was looming. A special memo briefed Balcer on standard procedures, and MacLeod's staff quickly prepared a list of recent capital case decisions "where a sexual attack was the motive."[147] Balcer learned that, from 1940, ten of eleven men convicted of murders similar to Eaton's had been executed.[148] But that was the past, and Eaton's capital case file included Winch's letter and messages from other Canadians who objected to his execution. One Vancouver resident wrote to condemn the former Liberal government for failing to do away with "legal murder" and to urge the "new vital government" to change course by granting Eaton clemency.[149]

Every cabinet member could see that their decision in this case would be viewed as a test for the new government. For the solicitor general, it was also a personal test, since Balcer did not support the death penalty.[150] In their first meeting, the cabinet failed to reach a consensus; when they met again, five days before Eaton's scheduled execution, the ministers resolved to let the law take its course.[151] Both Balcer and another unnamed minister (undoubtedly Diefenbaker) argued in favour of commutation, drawing on points Eaton's lawyer conveyed in his last desperate clemency bid. In the discussion that followed, most members interpreted the second provincial Court of Appeal's dismissal of Mullins's appeal as sufficient grounds for Eaton to suffer his sentence. The opposing minister cautioned: "Whenever there was the slightest doubt as to the innocence of a committed person," the government must take its "very grave responsibility to consider every possible aspect of the case." To prove his point, he referred to a case in 1930, in which an "entirely innocent" man had been convicted and executed.[152] That was the year when Diefenbaker's client, Alex Wysochan, was hanged for a murder he believed another man (the chief Crown witness) had committed.[153] But neither the prime minister nor Balcer could persuade the cabinet to recommend that Eaton be granted clemency.

Although the majority of Canadians continued to support capital punishment, vocal supporters of abolition were dismayed by the government's decision, which did not befit the values of a civilized country. One Montrealer, who described Eaton's execution as a "profound disgrace to the People of Canada," condemned the man's execution. In response,

Balcer offered the writer a lukewarm defence of the cabinet's final decision: "Capital punishment is provided for by law primarily as a deterrent. Its value as such would be destroyed if, for improper reasons, the Executive mitigated the punishment that the law directs should be imposed upon persons convicted of murder."[154] The solicitor general did not explain what "proper" reasons might constitute. As far as Canadians could judge as 1957 drew to a close, the Conservative government did not take the four factors Stuart Garson had mentioned into account as prompts for clemency. Despite the prime minister's and Balcer's misgivings over capital punishment, the Eaton decision suggested that sex killers, most notably men who murdered children, must face the penalty set by the law under the Conservative government. The cabinet reinforced that impression in December 1957, when it decided that another man convicted for the sex murder of a girl, this time in New Brunswick, would share Eaton's fate.

"Not a Single Letter" on Behalf of the Condemned

The Special Joint Committee heard from numerous witnesses who complained about the variable quality of the defence available to indigent persons who faced the death penalty if convicted. Eaton's lawyer, Mullins, was exceptionally tenacious and hard-working, but Canada lacked a national legal aid system, which made most capitally charged defendants reliant on junior members of the bar or overworked and overstressed barristers.[155] By the 1950s, some provinces provided standard fees for the defence of accused murderers, and the Criminal Code empowered courts of appeal to appoint lawyers willing to appeal guilty verdicts; however, there was no statutory amount set for their fees. After the Law Society of Upper Canada launched its profession-operated legal aid scheme for criminal cases in 1951, the New Brunswick Legislature went further, passing a Poor Prisoners Defence Act in 1952, modelled after Britain's act, first passed in 1903.[156] Fortunately for Joseph-Pierre Richard, the act's passage ensured that the lawyer who represented him was paid out of the provincial treasury (the appeal was not covered).[157] Yet, even the best lawyers found it impossible to neutralize the rage and repulsion that the sexual violation and murder of children stirred in their home communities, coupled with the strong wish that the death sentence be carried out. And when they petitioned for clemency after conviction, they discovered that the executive shared those sentiments.

Richard was arrested in February 1957, after the snow-covered body of thirteen-year-old Mary Katherine de la Perrelle was discovered

– beaten, strangled, and sexually assaulted – in the village of Charlo Station, New Brunswick. A critical account of legal aid published in *The Canadian Bar Review* in 1951 observed that, in small centres such as this, "members of the profession will undertake the defence of their poorer brother townsmen out of a sense of public duty." Most likely it was this impulse, and the possibility of making a name for himself, rather than the promise of a government cheque that prompted J.H.W. Sénéchal, a recent law graduate, to appear on Richard's behalf.[158] A decorated war hero from Campbellton, New Brunswick, he presented no evidence for the defence in the two trials of Joseph-Pierre Richard, but he fought hard for the man after his conviction, despite receiving death threats from locals who considered Richard a menace.[159] Sénéchal successfully argued that the police had failed to caution his client properly. The New Brunswick Court of Appeal ruled that the trial judge, Justice J.E. Michaud, had erred in admitting Richard's confession, and it ordered a second trial. However, in the fall of 1957, a second jury convicted Richard, and Sénéchal's attempt to file a second appeal was rejected. The only hope left was executive clemency.

The judge in the second trial admitted in his report to Ottawa that community prejudice against the accused was a factor in his conviction. Although Justice C.J. Jones pronounced the verdict proper, he hinted that the jury may have made up their minds before the trial began: "I also feel that if [Richard] had been a man of previous good reputation a conviction on the same evidence would have been more unlikely … [P]ublic sentiment was very strongly against the accused."[160] Richard's lawyer was more assertive in a desperate telegram: "QUESTION LAW APPLY WHEN PREJUDICE. ACCUSED HANGING DECEMBER 11TH. URGENTLY REPLY COLLECT ASK OPINION SUPREME COURT. DISCRETION YOURS. ADVISE IMMEDIATELY."[161] A.J. MacLeod advised the solicitor general that this "rape-murder of the victim was a notorious case" and that coverage in the Saint John *Telegraph* had stirred up strong feelings against the accused. Yet, he also advised Balcer to reject Sénéchal's final request that the minister of justice use his power to order a new trial under section 596 of the Criminal Code. MacLeod also claimed he had searched for possible reasons ("youth, age, intoxication, provocation etc.") to support clemency, but he thought none of them applied to this condemned man.[162]

There was little in Richard's capital case file to support the possible commutation of his sentence, aside from a last-minute telegram from Sénéchal claiming another man had committed the crime.[163]

Post-conviction police reports revealed that Richard had earlier served a sentence for attempted murder.[164] Because locals knew this, Balcer believed, "this grim crime had aroused the indignation of the New Brunswick population and everyone thought him guilty after they had read the evidence in the press." Some of his cabinet colleagues agreed with him that "society would not suffer too much if the convicted man were given a chance to live." But the majority sided with the New Brunswickers who thought Richard deserved his punishment. Even the solicitor general had to admit that "not a single letter had been received by his office on behalf of Richard."[165] After a bitter debate, the cabinet concluded that this twice-convicted killer's execution would cause no suffering to Canadian society.[166]

"A Practice of Long Standing:" Youth and Clemency in the Late 1950s

When Stuart Garson appeared before the criminal justice inquiries he had authorized in the mid-1950s, he referred repeatedly to youth as a mitigating factor the executive took into consideration. Had Eaton been one of the young prisoners he reportedly mentored in Oakalla Prison, he might have lived out his days behind bars. In 1954, the case of a nineteen-year-old youth convicted of a robbery murder came before the Liberal cabinet, and he was spared.[167] Balcer referred to that decision in an effort to set up clemency for another youth convicted of a sex murder in 1958. It was "a practice of long standing in Canada not to allow convicted murderers to be hanged unless they were 18 years of age," the solicitor general informed his colleagues.[168] Nevertheless, when Diefenbaker's ministers met in February 1959 to decide whether or not to recommend clemency for John J. Vollman, convicted of the sex murder of a sixteen-year-old girl, a "serious division of opinion" split the cabinet. For some, the thought of granting clemency solely on the basis of his age (nineteen) was troublesome: "It would be inadvisable to accept as a principle that convicted murderers under the age of 21 should not be hanged."[169]

In the late 1950s, the government, like the Canadian public, was "deeply and almost evenly divided" over the death penalty, and Parliament had resisted exempting youth from the ultimate penalty.[170] The facts of this homicide resembled those in the case of Robert Fitton, who admitted he had unintentionally caused Linda Lampkin's death after consensual petting. The girl Vollman had killed, teenaged Gaetane

Bouchard, was acquainted with the suspect, and she accepted a car ride from him after attending a dance in May 1958. When her body was discovered in a gravel pit on the outskirts of Edmunston, New Brunswick, there were signs she had been stabbed. The post-mortem did not confirm that a sexual assault had occurred (or, as the Crown attorney, former Conservative MP Albany M. Robichaud put it, she had not "lost her greatest treasure, her virginity"); however, the prosecution suggested that the defendant's thwarted sexual advances had angered him, leading him to kill the girl.[171] Joseph A. Pichette, QC, defended the young man under New Brunswick's criminal defence statute, and he relied on the tactic Toronto's David Humphrey had used to defend Fitton: accuse the victim of sexual provocation to encourage the jury to convict on the lesser charge of manslaughter.[172] "You did not rape Gaetane Bouchard?" Pichette asked the defendant, whom he put on the stand. "No," Vollman responded.[173] Despite the use of this defence, the Crown's framing of the crime, coupled with the judge's report, led the cabinet to treat the offence as a sex murder.

Vollman, a US citizen from a border town in Maine, claimed he had blacked out after the schoolgirl tried to fight him off. "I was at a point in a heat of passion where I don't quite remember exactly what happened." Although Justice Arthur I. Anglin believed the defendant was guilty, his report referred to the defence's theory that the victim had possibly provoked the unstable young man's uncontrollable rage. "It may have been an immoral or teasing act for the girl to refuse advances," he conceded.[174] But Anglin had disallowed Pichette's request to introduce Vollman's psychiatric record from his time in the US Air Force. The Crown's expert, New Brunswick psychiatrist Dr. Gregory, who had examined Vollman prior to the trial, testified that the prisoner had told him that, for some years, he had been "subject to overpowering sexual desires when with women."[175] This behaviour did not amount to psychosis, however. The Acadian jury followed the local psychiatrist's opinion and found the defendant guilty. Yet, the defence's version of the fatal encounter may have encouraged them to add a recommendation to mercy.

Pichette had two legal grounds on which he could have appealed against the verdict: Justice Anglin's decision to include Vollman's confession (he testified that the police had confused him); and the judge's exclusion of the defendant's psychiatric history into evidence.[176] Instead, Pichette went straight to the executive, which allowed him to dilate on his client's pattern of impulsive, uncontrollable sexual aggression. This

Justice Story

The body of Maria Gaetane Bouchard was found in this gravel pit, a lovers' trysting place.

John Jacob Vollman Jr.

She Was 16½—and Dead in the Gravel Pit

Youth Accused of Slaying Vivacious Sophomore

By RUTH REYNOLDS

Image 5.9 The fate of American John Jacob Vollman, sentenced to death after being found guilty of the murder of New Brunswick teenager Gaetane Bouchard, divided the Canadian cabinet. Some ministers considered him a heartless killer who deserved the death sentence; others, who focused on his youth, ultimately swayed the cabinet to commute his sentence on 14 February 1959. New York *Daily News*, 22 March 1959.

case was one of the first to be decided after Justice McRuer submitted his long-awaited report on the definition and sentencing of criminal sexual psychopaths, which called for a broader identification of, and more effective restraints on, sex criminals.[177] Dr. Cathcart, who was directly involved with the McRuer Commission, was the expert Ottawa assigned to assess whether Vollman's mental state might provide a justification for clemency. And it was Cathcart whose opinion shaped Vollman into a candidate for clemency.

As one of many expert witnesses who testified in McRuer's Commission on the criminal sexual psychopath law, Cathcart considered the term unhelpful, so he had no reason to take seriously the reports from Vollman's army service that American psychiatrists had diagnosed him as a psychopath. Although Cathcart did not use that term, he reported that the prisoner's blackout claim was credible. The government's expert also thought it important to note that the young man had sought "medical and psychiatric" therapy to curb the "compulsive-neurotic aspect to [his] sexual problem," but without effect.[178] When the solicitor general spoke in cabinet to support the commutation of Vollman's sentence, he picked up Cathcart's reference to the young man's concern over his urges. Surely this defendant's unsuccessful search for help was a mitigating factor, as science and "society" had failed him.[179] Because the majority of ministers feared that Vollman would be released to kill again in ten or fifteen years, the solicitor general contacted the new National Parole Board, which assured him that proper screening would be followed. After three days of debate, the cabinet finally resolved to accept Balcer's assurance (backed by the minister of justice, E. Davie Fulton) and recommended that Vollman's death sentence be commuted to life. When US papers reported the news ("Canada's Chief Commutes Death Term of Yank"), they highlighted the vice regal's formal role in granting mercy, but Canadian news editors knew that the real decision-makers were the cabinet ministers. And they also kept count: the Vollman decision marked the eighteenth commutation out of twenty-two death sentences reviewed since Diefenbaker had become prime minister in 1957.[180]

A "Good Boy" and a Divided Government

After its initial commitment to the death penalty, Diefenbaker's cabinet showed it was not just ambivalent toward the sentence but increasingly uneasy over seeing it enforced. However, executive privilege and the principle of cabinet secrecy meant that observers had no way of knowing how ministers reached their decisions. The Cabinet Conclusions confirm that they struggled, fought, and compromised. When Vollman's file appeared on the agenda in 1959, those who favoured commutation were deadlocked with their opponents over this "difficult case," since many ministers considered the murder of Gaetane Bouchard "as clear a case for execution as one could find."[181] No matter how it was reached, each recommendation to commute a death sentence gave the impression of attempting, "in effect, to change the law by executive action." As one minister commented sourly, "the government was already being accused of doing this."[182]

Abolitionists were also displeased with the government's reliance on executive discretion, and they began to voice their criticism through Parliament and professional associations. From 1957, private members repeatedly introduced bills to abolish capital punishment. A young Conservative backbencher, Frank McGee, who had served as a juror in two murder trials, was beginning to take over from Ross Thatcher and Harold Winch in carrying the torch for cross-party support. Another abolitionist, defence lawyer turned Conservative MP, Arthur Maloney, maintained his Toronto practice after he entered Parliament in 1957.[183] In his appearance before the Special Joint Committee in 1954, he testified as the chairman of the Committee on Criminal Justice of the Canadian Bar Association's Ontario branch. By that point, he had defended eleven accused murderers, four of whom were executed. He believed that "the whole sordid appearance" of hanging was "incompatible with any normal conception of what a civilized society is or ought to be." Judges differed in their "outlook, personality and temperament," which led to "inequality in the administration of justice," with fatal consequences in capital cases.[184] In Maloney's experience at the criminal bar, the majority of offenders were indigent and dependent on young, inexperienced, and, occasionally, incompetent defence counsel, few of them up to his own standards. Consequently, condemned offenders had to pin their hopes on executive clemency. His own experience in capital cases – eight requests for commutation with just two spared – convinced him that "executive clemency is extremely difficult to obtain." Maloney also observed that cabinets usually allowed the law to take its course "in cases where all appeals have been denied." On top of this, the executive rarely took medical and psychiatric evidence of impairment into account, and he illustrated his point by referring to Mervyn Hutson, hanged for a sex murder, despite evidence he suffered from epilepsy.[185] But after 1957, Maloney became a government member. Although he was a backbencher, he had a close-up view of the cabinet's drift toward clemency, and he was not above using it to save a man sentenced to death for a sex murder in 1959.

With a champion of Maloney's acumen – a brilliant campaigner in favour of the rights of the accused and a committed abolitionist – as his defence lawyer, John Bell had the best representation an accused sex killer could hope for. The Toronto police charged the eighteen-year-old with the murder of a "blue-eyed good-looking blonde" in 1959.[186] Maloney rejected the usual defence tactic of impugning the victim's reputation. Stephanie Lysyk was a thirty-year-old bookkeeper, a "quiet, refined girl supporting her widowed mother," not a "boy-crazy" teenager.[187] And Bell gave no impression of being a maniacal sex killer. Maloney stressed he was a "good boy" from a poor home and a member of Toronto's Irish Regiment, whose members had convinced the lawyer, a fellow Irishman, to represent him pro bono.[188] The amount of alcohol Bell had consumed on the night of the crime convinced Maloney to present a defence of drunkenness. In his closing address, he milked the jury's sympathy by dwelling on his client's impoverished upbringing in a "broken home": "Manslaughter is all we ask. Then he will be sent to a warmer home than he has ever known – a prison."[189] As in Vollman's case, the jury delivered a guilty verdict with a strong recommendation to mercy. This wish, endorsed by the judge, Wishart F. Spence, armed Maloney with powerful ammunition when he went to battle for Bell, not in a court of appeal but in Ottawa, where he hoped to find allies among his Conservative Party colleagues.

Maloney took on Bell's case having considerable experience in legal appeals in capital sex trials and appeals (including Sears's, Rivers's, and Chambers's cases), but by 1959 he could sign House of Commons stationery when he petitioned for clemency.[190] Prior to the trial, Maloney had hired a psychiatric expert (the ubiquitous Dr. Kenneth Gray) to examine Bell, but all the doctor could say was that the teenager was mentally dull (with an IQ the equivalent of a fourteen-year-old). However, the psychiatrist was more helpful to Bell after his conviction. Gray informed the solicitor general that the jury appeared to have underestimated the effects of alcohol on a "boy" unused to drinking. Justice Spence's report was also favourable. He concluded that a commuted sentence of less than life imprisonment would be appropriate for Bell. Even the prosecutor, Henry H. Bull, QC, wrote to urge clemency, "particularly in view of [Bell's] youth and lack of experience with alcohol." As a fellow Toronto lawyer, Bull may have granted Maloney a favour by adding he would "not have been surprised" if the jury had found Bell "guilty of manslaughter."[191]

Only The Cabinet Can Now Decide On:

THE LIFE OF JOHN BELL

By PHYLLIS GRIFFITHS
Telegram Staff Reporter

"Manslaughter is all we ask. Then he will be sent to a warmer, richer, grander life than he has ever known — a prison."—Counsel for the Defense.

John Edward Charles Bell was born on Feb. 5, 1941, in Toronto's Grace Hospital.

He was the first—and only—child of Leonard Bell and Viola Bloom.

Both parents were Toronto-born, the father of United Empire Loyalist and Irish forebears, the mother of French-Irish descent.

The Views Of Two Mothers

HIS OWN ... ... AND ANOTHER

Image 5.10 The self-confessed sex killer John Bell attracted many defenders in white working-class Toronto. This story framed the murder as a tragedy that struck two families – the victim's and the perpetrator's. This clipping from the Toronto *Telegram* (19 May 1959) appeared in Bell's case file. LAC, R.G. 13, Volume 1778, volume 1, part 1.

Unlike Bell's other supporters, Maloney could play a party trump card to drive home the message that the government ought to recommend mercy. Writing to Balcer, he concluded:

> In view of the above facts and my knowledge of the practice over the year concerning commutation in such cases, I think I am right in saying that even under the policy applied by your predecessors in office, this would definitely be a case for commutation and you would, therefore, not be setting any precedent whatever if commutation were granted in this case.[192]

Maloney may also have leaked inside information on the executive's management of the death penalty to the pro-Tory Toronto *Telegram*. Accompanying a sentimental tale of Bell's troubled upbringing and a request for readers to petition for clemency ("Only the Cabinet Can Now Decide on THE LIFE OF JOHN BELL"), the *Telegram* reported that, since taking office in June 1957, the cabinet had followed every jury recommendation to mercy, and out of the twenty-eight capital cases the executive considered by mid-1959, only six murderers had been hanged.[193] Yet, the government was unwilling to sponsor an abolition bill, and Frank McGee's private member's bill of 1959 did not reach second reading. But in the cabinet meeting held to determine Bell's fate, Balcer recited the factors Maloney had presented in support of mercy ("youth, intoxication, particularly when coupled with inexperience with alcohol, the lack of premeditation for murder, and the recommendation for mercy"). With no record of ministerial division, John Bell's death sentence was commuted to life imprisonment.[194]

Tilting toward Abolition

Flushed with the ambition of modern state building, the federal government committed unprecedented resources to conduct expert inquiries into criminal justice policy and procedures in the mid-1950s. The Liberal government's royal commissions and committees, appointed in the last years of its twenty-two-year reign over national affairs, advised no substantive change of course; aside from the introduction of a federal parole system in 1959, recommended by the Fauteux Committee, the modifications advised in the reports on the death penalty, the insanity defence, and the sentencing of criminal sexual psychopaths were minor, and few were adopted. Nevertheless, proponents of penal welfarism urged their fellow Canadians to endorse abolition and embrace a correctional approach to criminal justice, even for convicted sex murderers. And abolitionists asserted that Canada's claim to be a standard-bearer for democracy and a foe of authoritarianism required doing away with the death penalty.

Although the Conservative government tended toward clemency, case by case, it remained sensitive to the views of Canadians who were convinced that capital punishment was the only penalty appropriate for murderers. In the glow of correctional optimism, the Fauteux Report enthused that "public opinion has never been more understanding than it is at present. The people of Canada are beginning to realize that the penal reforms of the past decade in this country have been worthwhile."[195] The Special Joint Committee was more closely tuned to the tenor of the times: public support for the death penalty remained strong, which meant "it would be unwise for the Canadian Parliament to abolish capital punishment contrary to the wishes of a majority of Canadian citizens."[196] After her daughter was raped and murdered, Stephanie Lysyk's mother, like

Carolynne Moore's father, expressed her grief and anger, which most shared: "I will search for [Bell] and find him out. I will get to him even if I am 70. I'll do the same to him if I'm still around, I swear it."[197]

Retentionists who feared overhauling the Criminal Code in 1954 and reconsidering the defence of insanity and the identification of criminal sexual psychopaths would have been reassured by the record of executive clemency in sex murder cases. Aside from Vollman and Bell, both aged under twenty-one, every man convicted of a sexually motivated murder between 1953 and 1958 was executed. The age of their victims was equally significant, with Gharda Middlestad's murder in 1953 the only case in which a man was hanged for murdering an adult. The victimization of children remained the most shocking to the public, and parents and community groups mobilized over the 1950s against the threat sex "perverts" posed to children and women. When the Toronto *Telegram* reported Bell's commutation, it noted that "sex murders of young children are believed to be the type of killing least likely to win cabinet reprieve for the perpetrators."[198] For all but the most committed abolitionists, this state of affairs was the way it should be. At the Canadian Bar Association's 1954 meetings, a justice of Ontario's Court of Appeal commented: "It may be that the penalty of death be retained only for murders most foul, such as fatal attacks on small girls and defenceless women, which are often committed in terrible, unutterable circumstances."[199]

The Conservative victory in 1957 failed to produce a sudden shift in penal policy, as retentionists had feared and abolitionists decried. Yet, public support for capital punishment was on the wane as the decade came to a close.[200] Outspoken MPs and legal experts demanded that the government do away with the death penalty, and journalists played a significant role in shifting public opinion, as they built up evidence that wrongful convictions had occurred in capital cases, not just in England but in Canada. The Toronto *Daily Star* reporter John Edward Belliveau and investigative journalist Jacques Hébert, an opponent of Quebec Premier Duplessis and a defender of civil liberties, both alleged that political pressure, not sound evidence, had led to the conviction and execution of Wilbert Coffin in 1956. Interest in "l'affaire Coffin" lingered and expanded as Canadians across the country began to question whether they could count on police, prosecutors, the courts, and the executive to prevent miscarriages of justice. However, a new set of anxieties threatened to derail the abolition movement as the 1960s opened: the power of the National Parole Board to parole convicted sex killers serving commuted sentences.

6

Sex Murder in the Sixties and the Demise of the Death Penalty

Although anxiety over sex murders and concerns about the death penalty and its administration intersected periodically from Confederation, the two issues became entangled live wires as Canada approached its centenary. In Parliament, in debating societies, churches, synagogues, and social clubs, Canadians took sides over the punishment of sex killers: could the death penalty really deter their crimes, or was hanging simply a barbaric response to outrage and detestation?[1] The cabinet's decision to spare eight of the nine men convicted for sexually motivated murders between 1960 and 1967, combined with the government's stutter steps toward a trial period of partial abolition, provoked unprecedented criticism of executive discretion.[2] Supporters of the death penalty denounced the government's aversion to capital punishment, while abolitionists urged the government to replace ad hoc commutations with legislation to remove the death penalty from the Criminal Code.[3] The governing Conservatives tried to mollify disapproval by dividing murder into two categories in 1961.[4] Thereafter, only planned and deliberate homicides were subject to the mandatory penalty of death, plus homicides perpetrated in the course of committing other crimes (including rape). Thanks to the powerful police lobby, killings of guards and law officers were also defined as capital murder.[5] But the number of executions continued to dwindle, and no person sentenced to death was executed after 1962.

As life imprisonment became the standard punishment imposed on persons sentenced to death for murder, the administration of parole was thrust into the political spotlight. Public alarm over the future release of sex murderers on parole led the government to retreat from its investment in penal reform and to shore up assurance that it took public safety seriously. When the National Parole Board, one of the crowning achievements of correctionalism, replaced the former ticket-of-leave system in 1959, the board was granted full authority to fulfil its mandate: to rehabilitate prisoners and prepare them for freedom.[6] Then came the shock announcement in 1960 that Ronald McCorquodale's death sentence had been commuted after his conviction for the sex murder of a ten-year-old Calgary girl.[7] News that the Parole Board could authorize his release after he served a minimum of ten years (despite his long criminal record, including the sexual abuse of minors) enraged many Canadians, with Albertans in the lead.[8] Feeling the heat, the government imposed new guidelines in 1961 that required the Parole Board to seek cabinet approval prior to the release of any offender originally sentenced to death. In the same year, Parliament amended the sentencing provisions concerning "criminal sexual psychopaths" by introducing a new definition of the "dangerous sexual offender" and facilitating the indefinite detention of sex criminals.[9]

The cabinet's decision to deny clemency in the case of Louis Fisher, the last convicted sex murderer to be hanged, was another signal that the government of the day was prepared to prioritize public safety. One of the last executions in Canadian history, the 27 June 1961 hanging of Fisher at Toronto's Don Jail, proved that John Diefenbaker's cabinet was not lily-livered over capital punishment. Although the decision set up the expectation that other "sex fiends" would suffer the same fate, each of the five men subsequently convicted of a capital sex murder, all of their murders involving child victims, was spared, principally on the basis of psychiatric diagnoses. The official endorsement of correctionalism as the polestar of the criminal justice system became a garbled message by the early sixties: just what was the government's policy on sex murderers and capital punishment?[10]

The outcome of each death sentence review demanded an answer to that question, as journalists began to tally the number of commutations. But there was one commuted sentence, granted to a convicted sex killer, which ultimately drove the government to experiment with abolition in 1967.[11] Seven years earlier, cabinet's decision to commute fourteen-year-old Steven Truscott's death sentence for the rape-murder of twelve-year-old Lynne Harper shunted the case from news headlines. Other controversial sex murders – particularly Kenneth Meeker's slaying of a girl in British Columbia and Léopold Dion's murder of four boys in Quebec – loomed larger over the early 1960s. But Truscott's name shot back into the news in 1966, when journalist Isabel LeBourdais identified his conviction as a gross miscarriage of justice.[12] Her best-selling book on the case convinced many Canadians that the justice system was fallible, and it led Lester B. Pearson's Liberal government to refer Truscott's conviction to the Supreme Court.[13] Although the decision went against the defence, and despite the defeat of a cross-party resolution to abolish the death penalty in 1966, Truscott's case attracted converts to the cause of abolition. With support and guidance from leading lawyers involved in the abolition movement, a majority of parliamentarians imposed a five-year restriction on the death penalty as Canada celebrated its centenary.[14]

Clemency, Parole, and Provincial Alienation

The split between federal and provincial responsibilities in the realm of criminal justice, established in 1867, became a source of growing friction in the 1960s. A range of issues, including Indigenous affairs, natural resource development, and taxation, created tension between Ottawa and the provinces, and the federal executive's handling of capital case reviews added to it.[15] High-profile sex murders in the western provinces and Quebec were especially contentious, enough so that they derailed the federal government's commitment to parole in the federal penitentiary system. In Alberta, the murder of ten-year-old Lynn Lefurgey in November 1959 provoked an outpouring of grief. Her body, mutilated and partially disrobed, was found in a Calgary church basement lavatory. Reports of the girl's horrid death left locals anxious to see the killer caught and punished. Five years earlier, some Calgarians had doubted the respectability of Mrs. Gharda Middlestad, the middle-aged victim of a sex murder, but in that case the man convicted for the crime, Robert Sim, was executed. When Lefurgey's murder was reported, local media emphasized the respectability of the child's Anglo-Celtic family and gave ample coverage to their loss. News that the Calgary police were conducting a "roundup of known sex deviates" gave Mrs. Muriel Lefurgey, the girl's mother, hope that they would arrest the killer "before he does the same thing to another child ... [T]hey can't let it happen again."[16]

Just prior to Christmas 1959, Calgary police announced that Ronald H. McCorquodale was charged with the Lynne Lefurgey's murder. Relief at the suspect's capture was threatened by substantial evidence that the man was insane. At his May 1960 trial, a trio of lawyers represented McCorquodale, and they dug into records that proved he had previously been confined in mental hospitals. Two psychiatrists testified for the defence, and both considered the young man was a "sexual pervert" who was incapable of controlling his impulses. But the jury – just six men, as allowed under Alberta law – found McCorquodale guilty without adding a recommendation to mercy.[17] After the conviction, Calgary's chief of police provided a post-trial report to the Criminal Law Division, which showed that McCorquodale had been questioned in relation to the murder because he had recently served a short sentence for the sexual assault of two young girls in another Calgary church. The detective who investigated the case gave his opinion that McCorquodale was mentally unbalanced and "an admitted sexual deviate," but not insane according to the legal definition. He added a personal observation as a Calgarian: "This crime raised a great deal of feeling among the public of this City, both in relation to the brutality of the crime and the question of restraint for sex deviates."[18] The Calgary police offered a final piece of advice for the cabinet's consideration: McCorquodale "could quite conceivably commit a similar offence with absolutely no provocation ... [H]e should not be released to take a normal place in society without very serious consideration."[19]

In 1960, Albertans had good reason to anticipate that the convicted sex murderer would be hanged, as Sim was. Since the Conservatives had formed government in 1957, nine men had been executed, most recently an Indigenous man, who was executed in Kenora in June 1959 for the murder of three neighbours, his father, and a police officer.[20] There was only one victim in the McCorquodale case, but she was a defenceless girl, sexually assaulted and bashed to death by a man with a record of sexual offending. The judge who presided in the case, Chief Justice Colin Campbell McLaurin, made his feelings clear: "There is to my mind nothing that can be said in extenuation of this brutal and cowardly murder." Moreover, McLaurin (also the judge in Sim's trial) reported that the Crown's "thoroughly reliable" expert (Dr. R. Kenneth Thompson) had effectively rebutted the insanity defence. Although Thompson considered McCorquodale was a maladjusted psychopath with "sexual deviation" and a history of predation and violence, he did not think the man was psychotic.[21] And the jury had agreed:

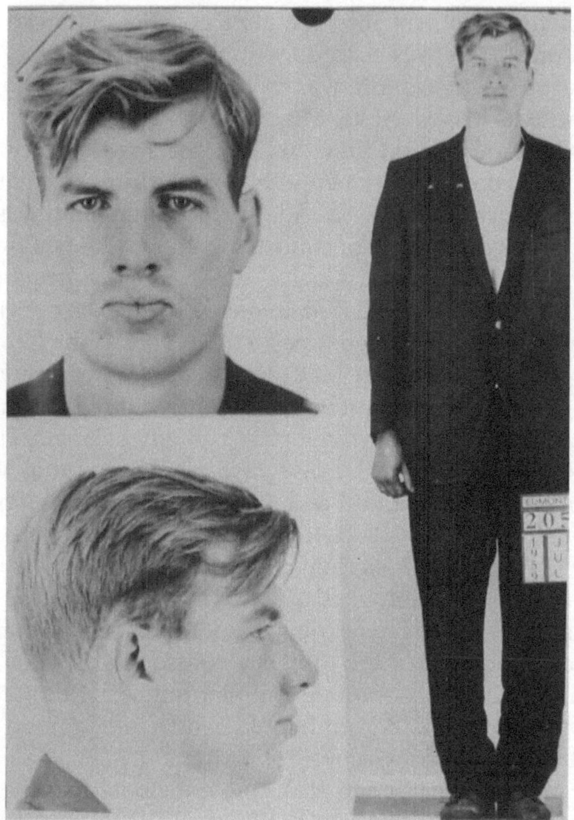

Image 6.1 Like the majority of defendants convicted of sex murder, Ronald McCorquodale was an Anglo-Celtic man. His outward appearance gave no indication of abnormality, but the government's psychiatric expert determined he was schizophrenic and psychotic, and the Diefenbaker government commuted the prisoner's death sentence. LAC, R.G. 13, McCorquodale, Volume 1833, volume 1.

McCorquodale could appreciate the nature and consequences of his acts, and he deserved no special consideration.

The assignment of psychiatrists in reviews of capital cases, whether or not the defence of insanity had been argued at trial, became standard by the 1960s, so it was business as usual when the Department of Justice turned to its most reliable expert, Dr. J.P.S. Cathcart.[22] One month prior to the date Justice McLaurin set for McCorquodale's execution,

Cathcart examined the prisoner and reached a surprising diagnosis: the man was psychotic and schizophrenic with strong compulsions toward "sex deviations." As a veteran analyst of capitally convicted offenders, Cathcart had not suddenly become soft on sex killers; yet, he reported that McCorquodale's mind was in "the most advanced psychotic state that I have seen in connection with the crime of murder."[23] The government expert's diagnosis, which contradicted the Crown's, left the government in a quandary. In their first cabinet meeting on the case, some ministers emphasized that "a strong public demand had developed for the execution of this man." The solicitor general, Léon Balcer, acknowledged that "the case has caused vigorous public revulsion in Calgary," but he stood behind Cathcart's "emphatic statement."[24] In Balcer's view, the government could not violate the "longstanding practice in Canada that insane persons are not hanged."[25] On 17 August, the government stunned the country, foremost Albertans, by announcing the commutation of McCorquodale's death sentence to life in prison.[26]

In keeping with the traditions of executive privilege, the government did not, as a rule, divulge the reasons why persons condemned to death were executed or spared. The prerogative of mercy was both a burden and a privilege. However, fury over McCorquodale's commuted death sentence led the solicitor general to break precedent. In a press release, he admitted that the prisoner's "longstanding" insanity, confirmed by an independent psychiatrist, was the reason why the government recommended that McCorquodale be spared.[27] Balcer's attempt to reassure the public backfired, however. Journalists informed the public that the Parole Board had jurisdiction over the release of prisoners, and a prominent Calgary criminal lawyer disclosed that, under the board's rules, McCorquodale could be paroled after he had served just ten years of his life sentence.[28] The lawyer, Edward J. McCormick, QC, also accused the cabinet of abusing executive power by turning to a "mysterious psychiatrist," whose diagnosis could not be cross-examined. Who was this mystery man, and what were his "private views on capital punishment?" McCormick was only too ready to express his own views on the subject of sex killers: "Persons who commit crimes of anger seldom murder again, because the circumstances of the crime are unlikely to re-occur. But sex murders are another thing." Since the federal cabinet was so cavalier about the safety of Albertans, McCormick proposed that "reprieved sex murderers should be required to live in Ottawa and work as gardeners for the people who released them." The victim's mother had greater moral authority than the sarcastic lawyer when she

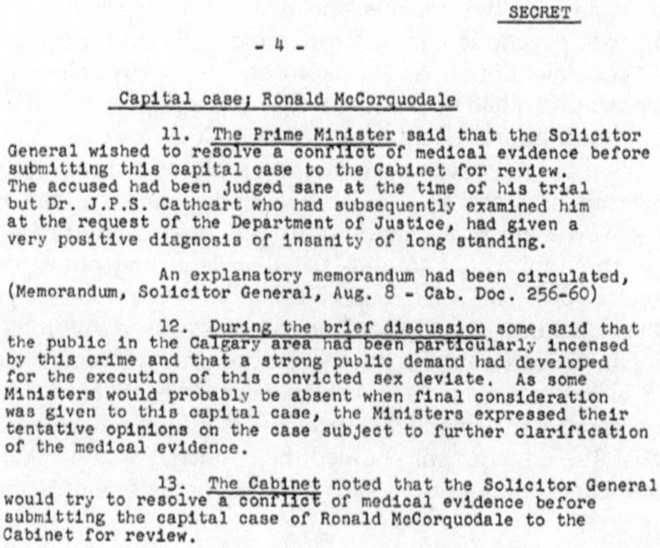

SECRET

- 4 -

Capital case; Ronald McCorquodale

11. The Prime Minister said that the Solicitor General wished to resolve a conflict of medical evidence before submitting this capital case to the Cabinet for review. The accused had been judged sane at the time of his trial but Dr. J.P.S. Cathcart who had subsequently examined him at the request of the Department of Justice, had given a very positive diagnosis of insanity of long standing.

An explanatory memorandum had been circulated, (Memorandum, Solicitor General, Aug. 8 - Cab. Doc. 256-60)

12. During the brief discussion some said that the public in the Calgary area had been particularly incensed by this crime and that a strong public demand had developed for the execution of this convicted sex deviate. As some Ministers would probably be absent when final consideration was given to this capital case, the Ministers expressed their tentative opinions on the case subject to further clarification of the medical evidence.

13. The Cabinet noted that the Solicitor General would try to resolve a conflict of medical evidence before submitting the capital case of Ronald McCorquodale to the Cabinet for review.

Image 6.2 In Ronald McCorquodale's case, cabinet ministers recognized that outraged Calgarians expected the "sex deviate" who murdered Lynne Lefurgey to hang. LAC, R.G. 2, Privy Council Office, Series A-5-a, Volume 2747, item 20076, 12 August 1960, 4.

expressed outrage over the Parole Board's powers: "You mean he may be free again in 10 years? … He murdered my little girl."[29]

Bureaucrats in the Department of Justice and the staff of the Secretary of State had advised the solicitor general to preserve cabinet secrecy, but Balcer chose to ignore their advice, which botched his attempt to manage public opinion. Clerks in the CLD knew that Prime Minister Diefenbaker had approved the attempt at transparency, but they warned that it set a dangerous precedent. One official dryly observed: "Apparently the Government is quite prepared to live with that."[30] But no one anticipated that a scandal would erupt over the timing of the cabinet's recommendation to mercy. Immediately following Balcer's announcement came the "farcical revelation" that the Alberta Court of Appeal had agreed to consider an appeal against McCorquodale's conviction. Accordingly, the commutation was premature.[31] The fault lay with the local sheriff, whose duty it was to inform Ottawa of any lodged appeals, but it left the federal government looking incompetent for failing to check. Whoever was to blame, this "bureaucratic bungling," on top of the parole controversy, left the credibility of clemency review procedures in tatters.[32]

The "public uproar" in Alberta set the government scrambling to save face by trying to reassure the public that it took the threat of a sex murderer's possible release seriously.[33] Balcer decided he could boost confidence in Ottawa's handling of the case by providing more, not less information. In this spirit, he identified Dr. Cathcart by name, and he also publicized details from McCorquodale's psychiatric records to prove he was insane.[34] In a press interview, the solicitor general acknowledged that "the people out there are up in arms."[35] He hoped Canadians would be comforted by the news that he had sought assurance from the Parole Board that it would not authorize McCorquodale's release. Yet, when reporters asked if he had the authority to issue a directive of this nature, Balcer had to admit that it amounted, at most, to a recommendation.[36] Albertans were unimpressed, as a reporter for the Lethbridge *Herald* observed: "Playing politics with the life of a man, be he saint or murderer, sane or insane, does no credit to the federal cabinet."[37]

The McCorquodale case convinced many Canadians, not just Albertans, that Diefenbaker's government was undermining the integrity of the criminal justice system every time it spared a killer from execution. Although nine men, two of them convicted for sex killings, were executed after the Conservatives took office, the cabinet recommended commutations for thirty-five convicted murderers (Steven Truscott and John Bell among them). The Calgary *Herald*, which considered the executive prerogative of mercy an important element of criminal justice, nevertheless denounced its abuse and overuse by the current government:

> This is obviously not the intention of the statutory provision for commutations. It was intended for very special cases but now it surely amounts to a policy which has not been approved by the people or Parliament. No matter how Mr. Balcer befogs the issue … commutations are being used in such a way that the function of the courts is being usurped. In one case a commutation might cause no alarm. In thirty-five it does.[38]

The sole Albertan in the federal cabinet, Minister of Agriculture D.S. Harkness, did his best to assure his provincial counterparts that Balcer's parole directive would hold, but the Alberta premier, Ernest Manning,

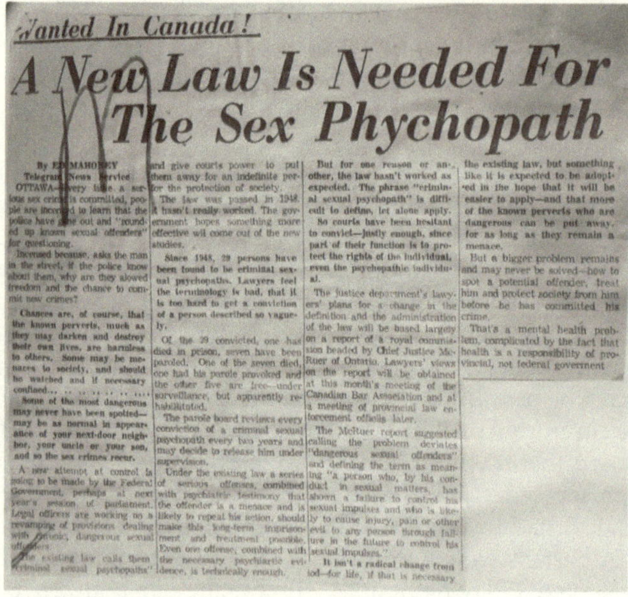

Wanted In Canada!

A New Law Is Needed For The Sex Phychopath

By ED MAHONEY
Telegram News Service

OTTAWA—Every time a serious sex crime is committed, people are incensed to learn that the police have gone out and "rounded up known sexual offenders" for questioning.

Incensed because, asks the man in the street, if the police know about them, why are they alowed freedom and the chance to commit new crimes?

Chances are, of course, that the known perverts, much as they may darken and destroy their own lives, are harmless to others. Some may be menaces to society, and should be watched and if necessary confined..

Some of the most dangerous may never have been spotted—may be as normal in appearance of your next-door neighbor, your uncle or your son, and so the sex crimes recur.

A new attempt at control is going to be made by the Federal Government, perhaps at next year's session of parliament. Legal officers are working on a revamping of provisions dealing with chronic, dangerous sexual offenders.

The existing law calls them "criminal sexual psychopaths" and give courts power to put them away for an indefinite per- for the protection of society.

The law was passed in 1948. It hasn't really worked. The government hopes something more effective wil come out of the new studies.

Since 1948, 29 persons have been found to be criminal sexual psychopaths. Lawyers feel the terminology is bad, that it is too hard to get a conviction of a person described so vaguely.

Of the 29 convicted, one has died in prison, seven have been paroled. One of the seven died, one had his parole provoked and the other five are free—under surveillance, but apparently rehabilitated.

The parole board reviews every conviction of a criminal sexual psychopath every two years and may decide to release him under supervision.

Under the existing law a series of serious offenses, combined with psychiatric testimony that the offender is a menace and is likely to repeat his action, should make this long-term imprisonment and treatment possible. Even one offense, combined with the necessary psychiartic evidence, is technically enough.

But for one reason or another, the law hasn't worked as expected. The phrase "criminal sexual psychopath" is difficult to define, let alone apply.

So courts have been hesitant to convict—justly enough, since part of their function is to protect the rights of the individual, even the psychopathic individual.

The justice department's lawyers' plans for a change in the definition and the administration of the law will be based largely on a report of a royal commission headed by Chief Justice McRuer of Ontario. Lawyers' views on the report will be obtained at this month's meeting of the Canadian Bar Association and at a meeting of provincial law enforcement offcils later.

The McRuer report suggested calling the problem deviates "dangerous sexual offenders" and defining the term as meaning "a person who, by his conduct in sexual matters, has shown a failure to control his sexual impulses and who is likely to cause injury, pain or other evil to any person through failure in the future to control his sexual impulses."

It isn't a radical change from

iod—for life, if that is necessary

the existing law, but something like it is expected to be adopted in the hope that it will be easier to apply—and that more of the known perverts who are dangerous can be put away, for as long as they remain a menace.

But a bigger problem remains and may never be solved—how to spot a potential offender, treat him and protect society from him before he has committed his crime.

That's a mental health problem, complicated by the fact that health is a responsibility of provincial, not federal government

Image 6.3 The need for stronger measures to keep Canadians safe from sexual psychopaths (despite the spelling error) received nationwide coverage after the controversial commutation of Ronald McCorquodale's death sentence. St. John's *Evening Telegram*, 30 August 1960.

refused to play along. The solicitor general's instruction to the Parole Board was "meaningless," since McCorquodale's anticipated transfer to a mental institution would allow psychiatrists to release him if they wished.[39] In Manning's eyes, the minister's behaviour was stark evidence of federal incompetence and high handedness. More fundamentally, he complained, "I think the policy of wholesale commutations is utterly indefensible and makes a mockery of our courts and the whole administration of justice."[40]

Desperate to salvage credibility after the "panicky politics" of Balcer's parole instructions, the Conservative government took the *Report of the Royal Commission on the Criminal Law Relating to Criminal Sexual Psychopaths* off the shelf and reviewed its recommendations on sentencing.[41] The commissioners had shown that offenders with records such as McCorquodale's were seldom imprisoned indefinitely. To chart a new way forward to prevent tragedies such as Lynne Lefurgey's murder, the government reached out to its critics. In September 1960, it held a conference between federal and provincial law officers to consider making changes to the sexual psychopath and parole statutes, and the federal government pledged to introduce a bill to amend the Criminal Code accordingly in the next session of Parliament.[42] In the meantime, the odour over the cabinet's decision lingered, even after McCorquodale committed suicide in prison five months into his life sentence.[43] The party faithful, not just the Conservatives' critics, numbered among those who demanded that the government clarify its policy on capital punishment. At the Progressive Conservatives' convention in March 1961, members demanded to know if the cabinet had made commutations "automatic." The minister of justice, E. Davie Fulton, admitted that the decision in McCorquodale's case (made while he was away from Ottawa on summer vacation) had "led to a flood of complaints from Calgary."[44] But he turned to the script his predecessors had followed since Confederation: each case was considered "on its merits."

Capital Murder, Dangerous Sex Offenders, and the Problem of Public Safety

Despite Fulton's bland assurance, the ructions over the McCorquodale case led the government to make good on its promise. By July 1961, two amendments to the Criminal Code were adopted into law: the division of culpable homicide into capital and non-capital murder and a new definition of the dangerous sexual offender. In most respects, these changes were in line with the aspirations that inspired Diefenbaker's government to enact the Canadian Bill of Rights, two weeks prior to announcing the commutation of McCorquodale's death sentence.[45] In addition to distinguishing degrees of murder, the revised Criminal Code required judges in capital trials to inform the jury of their right to recommend mercy if they found a defendant guilty; furthermore, persons sentenced to death acquired the automatic right to appeal to the Court of Appeal and the Supreme Court on matters of law, fact, or mixed matters. The informal practice of sparing young offenders from execution also became policy: as of 1961, no person under the age of eighteen at the time of the offence could be sentenced to death. Yet, the Code's amendment also gave teeth to the solicitor general's limp attack on the Parole Board's authority over the release of prisoners serving life sentences. From 1961, any person serving a commuted death sentence was "not to be released during

Image 6.4 Edmund Davie Fulton spearheaded the parliamentary campaign to ban crime comics in Canada in the late 1940s. From 1957 to 1962, he served as federal minister of justice, during which time cabinet deliberated over eight sex murderers sentenced to death. LAC, MIKAN 3215869.

his life or such term, as the case may be, without the prior approval of the Governor in Council."[46] Similarly, the revision to the CSP statute expressed the government's preparedness to enhance public security. Under the new law, a person who showed a "failure to control his sexual impulses" and was "likely" to fail to control them in the future could be subjected to "preventive detention."[47] Had these criteria of dangerousness been in place two years earlier, when McCorquodale pleaded guilty to assaulting two prepubescent girls in Calgary, prosecutors could more easily have applied for the court to impose an indefinite sentence. The government would not have had to issue a "panicky" parole directive, and Lynn Lefurgey would have turned eleven years old. Most commentators approved of the changes, hoping that revised legislative charts would lead to a steadier hand on the tiller of penal policy.

While the government struggled to patch up public confidence and repair party unity in the spring of 1961, the case of a Toronto man, found guilty of murdering a woman in the course of a sexual assault, made its way through the provincial Court of Appeal. The timing of Louis Fisher's final appeal against his conviction before the Supreme Court presented a dilemma as well as an opportunity for the government as it introduced revisions to capital justice and parole. During second reading of the bill to amend the Criminal Code midway through May 1961, a Liberal backbencher, Hubert Badani (Fort William), complained that the minister of justice proposed to

> set himself up as the arbiter in deciding how many years will be chopped off the life sentence. This is one of the worst features of this legislation. The fact that anyone could be kept in prison, at the pleasure – if you please – of any government, would too greatly resemble the power of a dictatorship.[48]

When Fulton replied, he made no reference to McCorquodale by name, instead referring to a hypothetical case in which "the mental condition of the individual – perhaps the very condition which justifies the commutation – also brings about a situation where the greatest care must be exercised before allowing him to be at large again."[49] The government's legislation was drafted to navigate the choppy waters between the majority of Canadians, who continued to support capital punishment, and those, Fulton acknowledged, who had "the feeling that it is not appropriate that the death penalty should be applicable automatically to every case of murder."[50] As the Conservatives marshalled support for Bill C-92 over May and June, the revised date of Fisher's execution forced the cabinet to confirm his fate before the final parliamentary vote.

The decision that Louis Fisher should hang for the murder of Toronto woman Mrs. Margaret Bennett was surprising in light of the cabinet's drift away from capital punishment. The last time a convicted sex murderer died on the gallows was 1957, when Joseph-Pierre Richard was executed in New Brunswick. John Vollman, also convicted in New Brunswick, was granted a commuted sentence in 1959, as was Steven Truscott in 1960.[51] Although two other murderers were executed after McCorquodale was sentenced to life, both men had committed multiple homicides. By June of 1961, the commutation score was in Fisher's favour: forty-one commuted sentences for persons convicted of murder versus eleven men executed since the Conservative Party had formed government. Supporters of capital punishment, however, could take heart that the tally of the executed might grow. On 27 June 1961, Fisher became the twelfth man to hang under the Conservative government.

The father of four from an Anglo-Celtic working-class neighbourhood in Toronto's east end admitted he had consorted with thirty-six-year-old "Peggy" Bennett, a woman whose family described her as a troubled alcoholic, recently separated from her husband.[52] Fisher confessed he was involved in her death, but claimed the killing was neither planned nor deliberate. On 9 June 1960, he met the woman in an east-end Toronto bar, and he picked her up. After they left for a drive, Fisher stated, she provoked him by stimulating his genitals, and when the woman threatened to inform Fisher's wife, they began to struggle. The next morning Bennett's body was found in a parking lot with her face bludgeoned. She had suffered multiple stab wounds, and her slashed clothing was raised above her waist. Fisher admitted he pushed the woman out of his car, but he denied he had raped or murdered Peggy Bennett.[53]

Although the police doubted the crime was "the work of a sex maniac," the Crown prosecuted the case as a murder committed in the course of a thwarted sexual encounter, a theory supported by evidence of sperm in the victim's remains.[54] The defence contested the theory by stressing the absence of genital bruising and by dragging Mrs. Bennett's drinking and past sexual conduct before the jury. Defence Attorney Joseph Pomerant, called to the bar just six months prior to the trial, told the jurors (all men) that this victim could have possibly engaged in sexual intercourse with any number of men in the hours before the fatal encounter. Fisher had merely snapped after the woman taunted him, Pomerant argued, and the judge lent credibility to the theory. Justice E.G. Thompson charged the jury that they could consider the defence of provocation. Although the murder was a "sadistic slaying," this victim (unlike Lynne Harper or Lynn Lefurgey) bore some responsibility for her fate.[55] The Crown's case was led by A.O. Klein, one of Ontario's most experienced trial lawyers and the same man who had prosecuted Robert Fitton in 1956.[56] The difference from that case and Fisher's was that neither the jury nor the judge had recommended mercy after Fitton was found guilty. More significantly, the legal and political context had shifted. The Supreme Court's dismissal of Pomerant's appeal on 27 June 1961 meant that the cabinet determined Fisher's fate at the very point when the government had revised the definition of murder and required that mercy be considered in court.

In the course of preparing Fisher's case file, the CLD assessed four psychiatric reports conducted before, during, and after his trial; however, the opinion of the police ultimately carried greater weight. Dr. Cathcart's post-conviction examination followed the line he took in almost every sex murder case: Fisher showed no sign of suffering from insanity. Two other psychiatrists, the man who testified for the defence and the expert the Attorney General's Office had assigned to determine Fisher's fitness to plead, reached a different conclusion: the man had a "pathological personality."[57] A fourth expert, a clinical psychologist, reported that Fisher had strong feelings of inadequacy, "derogation of the female figure," and a propensity "for exploding into aggressive action."[58] But none of these experts pointed the government toward a clear choice. Joseph Pomerant gave his all to save Fisher by using less clinical language in his clemency pitch. Addressing the minister of justice, he wrote that Fisher was a good worker and a faithful provider for his wife and children. Then he went after the victim, whom he described as a "woman of the loosest moral character." Furthermore, Fisher was a good-looking fellow, who "would not have had to use any force if he had wished to commit sexual intercourse."[59]

The Metropolitan Toronto Police had evidence, not presented at trial, that cast doubt on Fisher's alleged capacity to charm women into sex, and the cabinet took this more seriously than medical specialists' diagnoses. In their post-conviction report, detectives revealed that a woman had reported Fisher had abducted and attempted to rape her several months before Bennett was murdered. She managed to escape, but she ultimately declined to press charges.[60] Senior members of the Toronto police were so concerned that the death sentence be carried out that they travelled to Ottawa on 19 June 1961. Fisher was no lady's man but a brute, they advised, and the granting of clemency would be unacceptable.[61] Considering the government's record in recent times, the police were likely surprised to learn that the cabinet agreed.

Aware that retentionist ministers outnumbered men who objected to the death penalty, the prime minister was prepared to make concessions in order to hold his cabinet together.[62] Prior to discussing the disposition of Fisher's case, Diefenbaker informed his ministers that he planned, once the capital murder bill was passed, to set up a cabinet committee to review the files of persons sentenced to death and provide recommendations. He came up with this idea because he knew that men (like him) who had "personal experience in defending an innocent man who had gone to the gallows" would invariably favour clemency except in the "clearest cases of capital murder." At the same time, he found it unfair that this inclination "should oblige the majority to accept a course contrary to their convictions."[63] William Browne, the new solicitor general (appointed after Balcer was demoted in October 1960), had charge of Fisher's case, which he presented to the cabinet. The ministers argued vigorously until they agreed that the police evidence of the man's earlier attempted rape (untested in court) should be the deciding factor.[64] Browne was new to the portfolio, but he was fully aware of the case's timing.[65] He informed his colleagues that had Fisher been prosecuted after, not prior, to the Criminal Code's amendment, "there was room for doubt whether the conviction in this case would have been for capital murder."[66] Pomerant had made the same point, since he knew the revised Code would soon be in effect. But readers of the morning papers on 23 June 1961 saw an unexpected announcement. From the press gallery in Ottawa, the news went out via the Canadian Press and United Press International services: Fisher's death sentence would be carried out because he had "attacked the deceased with a knife inflicting sixteen wounds; he then pushed the deceased's body out of the car and fled from the scene." In addition, "there was no recommendation of mercy by the jury."[67]

Compared with the decision to commute McCorquodale's sentence, the cost to the government of recommending that a "sadistic" killer be shown no mercy was minimal.[68] As the hour of Fisher's execution drew near, a crowd of more than 100 assembled outside Toronto's Don Jail. The local press reported that the group included "teenage couples, young husbands and wives, and many youths." Most were "just passing or lived in the neighbourhood and dropped around to see what was going on." A lone man paced with a sandwich board that condemned "court officials and the Government for permitting the execution."[69] The guards inside the jail and the police who cordoned off the entrance likely felt more favourably disposed toward the government, which had responded to the demands of police lobbyists, not just in regard to Fisher but also with the amendment that split murder into two degrees. As of July 1961, all killings of police and guards fell within the new category of capital murder.

The revised law of murder became a test for the legitimacy of capital justice in the eyes of the death penalty's defenders and critics. Unlike homicides of law enforcers, murders involving sexual violence, committed or attempted, were not automatically defined as capital offences, but they could still be prosecuted as such. If the cabinet considered Fisher's execution warranted – notwithstanding inconclusive evidence of a sexual assault, the victim's drunken state and possible sexual encounters earlier on the day of her murder, plus the opinion of several experts, who diagnosed the killer as a psychopath – surely the government could not justify commuting the death sentence of any sex murderer who killed a child, let alone several children.

The National and Provincial Politics of Commutations after the Capital Murder Bill

Like all compromises devised to appease warring camps, the Criminal Code amendments of 1961 appeased neither side in the brewing debate on capital punishment. For abolitionists, the capital murder law was flawed: it merely restricted the categories of murder subject to the death penalty, and it left capitally convicted killers at the mercy of the executive. On the day following Fisher's execution, criminal lawyer G. Arthur Martin and several other legal authorities appeared before a committee of the Senate that was examining the capital murder bill. Citing his experience in "defending 40 murder cases," Martin told the senators that the draft definition of intentional murder (covering acts a reasonable person ought to know would likely cause death) was "too broad and severe." Law professor Allan W. Mewett thought that "horrible, cold-blooded or barbarous" murders were the only homicides that should be subject to the death penalty.[70] Supporters of capital punishment also voiced their displeasure after the new law on murder came into effect. Law enforcement organizations, led by the Canadian Association of Chiefs of Police, were already wary about the dilution of capital punishment's deterrent capacity, and their fears were borne out.

When capitally convicted murderer's death sentences were reviewed after 1961, cabinet continued to recommend clemency, including in cases involving murders of law enforcement agents. In December 1962, the execution of police killer Ronald Turpin and African American Arthur Lucas, convicted of a drug-related murder, gave the pro-death penalty lobby hope.[71] But the election of the Liberals in 1963 dashed them. When he was the opposition leader, Lester B. Pearson criticized the Conservatives for their administrative mishandling and their undeclared policy on executive clemency. Once in power, however, Pearson's Liberals granted clemency in every capital murder case. This violated the spirit, if not the letter of the capital murder bill, and it discredited the movement to abolish the death penalty through legislation.

Over 1964 and early 1965, four high-profile capital cases – two BC sex murders involving child victims, the murder of two Quebec police officers, and Léopold Dion's sex slayings of four boys – made Ottawa the target of provincial hostility as well as retentionists' ire. These controversial cases also posed a strategic challenge for abolitionists. To meet that challenge, leading figures in the movement established the Canadian Society for the Abolition of the Death Penalty (CSADP) in 1964. Veteran defence lawyer and former MP Arthur Maloney became its first president, who set out to elevate principles and statistics over outpourings of anger, especially intense in sex murders of children.[72]

"I Suppose I am a Psychopathic Killer"

Some of the foremost critics of executive clemency in the 1960s were abolitionists, who recognized that setting life imprisonment as the punishment for sex murderers failed to inspire confidence that the government took public safety seriously. Long-time abolitionist Harold Winch reaffirmed his opposition to capital punishment when he supported Frank McGee's 1960 abolition bill.[73] But in 1964, Winch was more concerned about the government's capacity to detain sex killers after a BC man, freed after the provincial Court of Appeal quashed his capital murder conviction, subsequently confessed that he was, in fact, guilty. As Charles Heathman revealed, he had sodomized and murdered eleven-year-old Donald Ottley.[74] The Vancouver *Sun* published the man's chilling recitation of the assault: "I enjoyed killing him. Prolonged it as long as I could and when he was dead I threw him away like a rag doll … I suppose I am a psychopathic killer, a man with a killer's instinct, a menace to society. You see, I get these urges to kill."[75] Although Heathman could have pulled these lines from a B-movie or a tawdry paperback, the publication was sensational, and it created pressure to find some way to detain him. Since the double jeopardy principle prevented placing him on trial again, provincial authorities came up with the solution of issuing a psychiatric warrant to apprehend the man under the Mental Health Act.[76] The admission in Heathman's published confession – that he experienced uncontrollable urges – allowed the province to order his treatment at British Columbia's Essondale Hospital.[77] Yet, public anxiety and frustration were reignited with the news that medical staff had pronounced Heathman cured after just two years. The man

The Sunday Sun

HEATHMAN TELLS ALL

Twice-Freed Killer Confesses Slaying

CONFESSION UNIQUE IN LEGAL HISTORY

'Got the Urge To Kill Somebody'

Algiers Terrorist Boss Salan Nabbed

Tipoff Leads to Hideout; Faces Quick Trial, Death

Murdered in 1960

Space-Age Fair Open for All Who Can Stand Sore Feet

THE ANSWER'S IN THE TREES

Greed Kills Road Victim

Barry MATHER

Russia Hints Walkout

Ex-Judge Says He Can

3 'Sons' Arrested On Terror Charges

'I Get These Urges'

Queen 36 Today

FRANCK REPORT ON PAGE 6

HEATHMAN TELLS SUN REPORTERS

'The Booze Made Me Do It'

CITY HOME OWNERS WILL HAVE TO PAY MORE

Image 6.5 The Vancouver *Sun*'s decision to pay Charles Heathman $500 for his confession to the sex slaying of Donald Ottley (after the BC Court of Appeal set aside his conviction) angered Justice Alexander M. Manson, who thought Heathman should be retried. Heathman's statement resembled fictional portrayals of sexual psychopaths. Vancouver *Sun*, 21 April 1962.

had now slipped out of sight.[78] Harold Winch, a Vancouver MP in touch with local sentiment, agreed with capital punishment's supporters that the federal government had failed to create facilities and programs to "handle criminal psychopaths."[79] Although he did not think Heathman should be executed, the disturbing twists and turns the case had taken prompted the outspoken MP to demand that Pearson's recently appointed minister of justice, Guy Favreau, introduce measures to "prevent the release from mental hospitals of potential killers and rabid sexual psychopaths."[80]

Since the BC Court of Appeal had quashed Heathman's conviction, Pearson's government could not interfere with the case. However, the federal cabinet had a direct hand in another BC sex murder case that sharpened provincial criticism over Ottawa's preparedness to grant mercy to sex killers. In June 1963, Alice Mathers, a "blonde blue-eyed" twelve-year-old girl, was walking along the highway near Mission, British Columbia, on an errand for her mother, when Kenneth Meeker and his older brother, James, snatched her, drove her to a gravel pit, raped her, and smashed her skull.[81] The Crown decided to prosecute just the younger man for murder.[82] The prosecution, led by J. McGarch and J.G. Gates, showed the jury gruesome images of the injuries she had suffered, and the court also allowed the Crown to play a taped recording of Kenneth Meeker's confession to the police. Many, including the court stenographer, sobbed as they listened to his horrifying account.[83] Fifteen minutes was all it took for the jury to return a guilty verdict with no recommendation to mercy.[84]

Like Heathman, Meeker was defended by a lawyer paid by the province's legal aid scheme, which allotted twenty-five dollars per day for criminal cases. Malvern J. Hughes represented the thirty-year-old Anglo-Celtic man on this token allowance at trial and in the Court of Appeal.[85] After the first appeal was dismissed, a more prominent member of the bar represented the defence in the Supreme Court. Gordon Henderson, QC, argued that the Crown had failed to prove that Meeker was guilty of capital murder and that the trial judge had provided insufficient instruction on the defence of drunkenness.[86] When the Supreme Court dismissed the appeal without reasons, anticipation grew in British Columbia that Alice Mathers's murderer would be hanged, despite the spell of almost two years since Canada had executed a criminal. News that the federal government decided Kenneth Meeker should serve a life sentence, with the possibility of parole in ten years, touched off a firestorm of protest that began in British Columbia and spread across the country.[87] Once again, the government stated that the prisoner would not be released without executive approval, as the revised Criminal Code confirmed. Yet, it was clear by the end of 1964 that confidence in the criminal justice system had reached a nadir, and not just in British Columbia.[88]

The public response to the commutation announcement led to overtime shifts in the Department of Justice. The staff in the CLD collected and filed sheaves of impassioned letters and newspaper stories, almost all of them critical of the government. "I think they should have put him at the end of a rope and hired me for the hangman," Alice Mathers's father vowed. "I thought this thing was over with. It didn't occur to me that they might reprieve him." Another man who wrote the solicitor general volunteered to execute Meeker, "as a veteran," and he promised "his dying would be lengthy."[89] The New Democratic Party (NDP) leader, Tommy Douglas, used more parliamentary language to question the prime minister about the matter on 6 November 1964, two days after the commutation announcement. Like his fellow party members, he opposed the death penalty, but Alice Mathers's murder was a "particularly heinous crime." Could not the commutation order make it "impossible for this man to be released unless there were adequate assurances he would no longer be a menace to the public safety?" Douglas queried. The prime minister replied that the government was considering such a measure.[90] In the meantime, Donald H. Christie, the latest head of the CLD, struggled to keep up with letters of protest over the commutation of Meeker's death sentence, mailed overwhelmingly from British Columbia, his own home province.[91] On 13 November, Christie provided the solicitor general a summary of the sentiments expressed in these letters and telegrams, adding that the majority were sent by women:

> The correspondence is full of words and phrases like: "sickening shock and mockery of justice," "strongly protest," "gross miscarriage of justice," "shocked by Cabinet's senseless leniency," "inexcusable," "horrified," "bitterness should be felt," "appalled," "cannot understand," "astounded," "heart-sick and choked up," "sickened," "irresponsible," etc.

As a counterweight to these vehement responses, Christie offered his manly professional judgment. Having supervised the preparation of capital case files since 1960, he stated that the public's reaction to Meeker's commutation "far outstrip[ped] the reaction in any other case." Christie took the trouble to check with his predecessor, Allen J. MacLeod (now commissioner of penitentiaries), who stated he knew of no other case that had caused such a furor during his headship of the CLD from 1953 to 1960.[92] A handful of Canadians wrote to support the government's decision, but they muted their approval with anxiety. One woman, writing on behalf of a Mission City United Church group, thought it necessary for "the life sentence to mean just that … We do not want there to be any chance that [Meeker] will ever repeat such a brutal crime."[93]

Although the revised Criminal Code of 1961 explicitly stated that the parole of any person imprisoned for life following the commutation of a sentence of death required executive approval, Prime Minister Pearson announced a further measure to constrain the Parole Board's authority. Moving away from the correctional ethos, the government introduced new regulations under the Parole Act to ensure that the cabinet would vet every recommendation. The Conservative MP for the Calgary riding of Bow River, who had weathered heavy criticism from his constituents over the McCorquodale commutation in 1960, asked a sensitive question during the discussion of the amendment: "Does the Prime Minister not think that he is putting a heavy responsibility directly on the executive?"[94] The question was prophetic, as one month after they recommended Meeker's commutation, the cabinet deliberated over the sentence of a man convicted of capital murder as defined by the revised Code: George Marcotte, notorious bandit and police killer.

Law, Disorder, and Disgruntlement in Quebec

A botched burglary of a suburban Montreal bank in 1962, in which two officers were gunned down with a semi-automatic rifle, led to the arrest of three thieves. The man identified as the ring leader, Marcotte, was tried and convicted of capital murder. Two years of legal appeals ended on 5 November 1964, when the Supreme Court upheld the verdict.[95] Although the executive extended the time of his execution date in order to deliberate over Marcotte's fate, the federal government was aware that law enforcement organizations and the Quebec government expected the bandit to be hanged. Finally, after protracted debate in the cabinet and several shifts of opinion on either side of the question, the government recommended clemency on 5 December 1964. When he made the announcement, Guy Favreau, the minister of justice, stated that an executive order had been issued to ensure that Marcotte and every other prisoner thereafter serving such a sentence "shall serve the entire term of the sentence of imprisonment unless, upon the recommendation of the board, the governor in council otherwise directs."[96] But the minister also threw a bone to the abolitionists: the Liberal government would allow a free vote on the death penalty in the next session of Parliament in 1965.[97]

Despite this pledge, the commutation of Meeker's and Marcotte's sentences damaged the abolitionists' cause. The publication of the National Parole Board's annual reports posed a further problem, since they confirmed the allegations of the pro-death penalty lobby. The board's records showed that, under the former ticket-of-leave regime, prisoners serving commuted death sentences were incarcerated for longer terms. In 1953, for instance, the average period life-sentenced prisoners served behind bars was sixteen years and one month; in 1964, five years after the Parole Board's takeover, that average had dropped to ten years and two months.[98] Abolitionists were also discouraged by the findings of Quebec's Brossard Commission, which investigated journalist Jacques Hébert's claim that political interference by the Quebec government and Ottawa had led to Wilbert Coffin's wrongful conviction in 1956. The commissioner firmly dismissed Hébert's accusations, announcing his findings on the same day the national press published angry responses to Marcotte's commutation, particularly bitter in Quebec.[99]

The most acerbic critic of the federal cabinet was Claude Wagner, Quebec's attorney general, a former Crown prosecutor and a law-and-order zealot. Buoyed by Justice Brossard's vindication of Coffin's execution, Wagner slammed the federal government's refusal to allow the law to take its course in Marcotte's case. "Why should justice be ridiculed?" he demanded. Furthermore, the government's intention to allow a vote on the death penalty showed it misread the mood of his province and the entire nation: "The only people ready for abolition are the criminals."[100] Law enforcement lobbyists were equally incensed over Marcotte's commutation, and their scornful attacks left the CSADP in a defensive posture. The announcement of the cabinet's recommendation occurred just hours before G. Arthur Martin's scheduled presentation on the society's mission. He may have made some last-minute edits to his speech, since he told his audience of fellow lawyers that "some murderers are so dangerous they should never go free."[101] But were some killers so dangerous that they should be executed?

According to several members of the Liberal cabinet and the majority of Quebeckers, Léopold Dion fit that profile. In his first appearance in

Quebec City's coroner's court in July 1963, and later, at his preliminary trial, he had no legal representation.[102] He was fully prepared to answer questions and testified at length about his crimes. Over more than two hours, he told the coroner's jury he had lured four boys to their deaths by posing as a magazine photographer. Prowling the public thoroughfares of Quebec City in the spring of 1963, he pursued his quarry ("pour me satisfaire").[103] When the boys resisted his sexual advances and fought back, he strangled them and hid their bodies by burying them. Before he killed one of them, he testified, he allowed him time to pray, then he "squeezed as hard as possible so he wouldn't suffer." Another died "like a little angel," reciting a Hail Mary after Dion told him he was about to die. And one had "the heart of a lion," he recalled. If only they had "consented" to his desires, they might not have died.[104] Sobs erupted in the coroner's court, where twenty provincial police officers stood guard over the suspect. Outside, a further forty lawmen were staged to prevent members of the public from attacking the accused killer after the jury took two minutes to name Dion as the culprit. To defend a man whom so many wished to see dead was to invite death threats, as Dion's lawyer, twenty-five-year-old Guy Bertrand, discovered.[105] But the committed opponent of capital punishment took the risk on principle: "C'était une bataille contre la peine de mort."[106] Although suspicions that the man was insane lasted from his arrest to the final cabinet review, no one, including his lawyer and the families of the murdered boys, doubted that the Parole Board had effectively aided and abetted Dion's crimes.

The Perils of Parole

Not one of the four boys would have died at the hands of Dion in the spring of 1963 if parole authorities had refused to allow the man's release in 1962. This fatal decision troubled the nation's abolitionists as much as it enraged Quebeckers and supporters of capital punishment.[107] When Harold Winch spoke in Parliament in 1964 about the need to fix the secure incarceration of sexual psychopaths, he also recounted the chain of events that had led to the boys' murders. In 1940, when Dion was twenty years old, he was sentenced to life for the rape of a female teacher on the outskirts of Pont-Rouge, his home town. The judge in that trial used his discretion to add ten stripes of the lash to Dion's sentence, and he recommended that Dion never be freed.[108] Yet, in 1956, the federal Remission Branch granted the prisoner a ticket of leave. Once

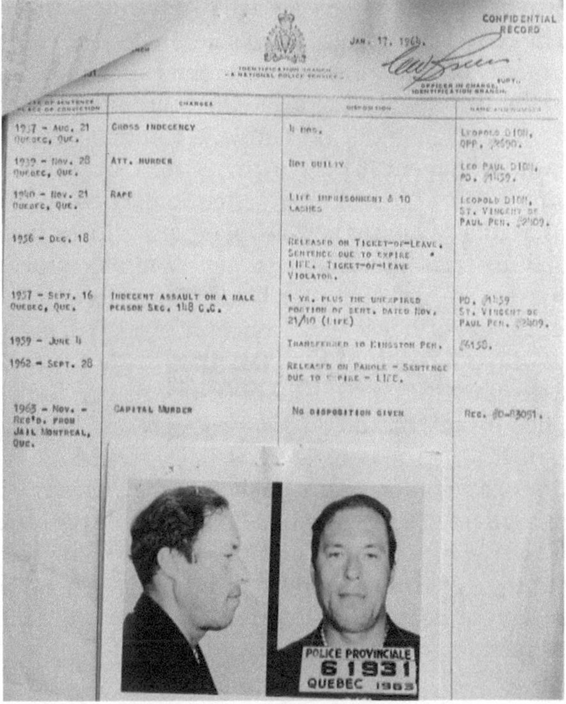

CONFIDENTIAL RECORD

JAN. 17, 1964.

OFFICER IN CHARGE, IDENTIFICATION BRANCH.

SUPT.

	CHARGES	DISPOSITION	
1937 – Aug. 21 Quebec, Que.	Gross Indecency	4 mos.	Leopold Dion, QPP, #2690.
1939 – Nov. 28 Quebec, Que.	Att. Murder	Not guilty	Leo Paul Dion, PD. #4459.
1940 – Nov. 21 Quebec, Que.	Rape	Life imprisonment & 10 lashes	Leopold Dion, St. Vincent de Paul Pen. #2409.
1956 – Dec. 18		Released on Ticket-of-Leave. Sentence due to expire • Life. Ticket-of-Leave Violator.	
1957 – Sept. 16 Quebec, Que.	Indecent assault on a male person Sec. 148 C.C.	1 yr. plus the unexpired portion of sent. dated Nov. 21/40 (Life)	PD. #4459 St. Vincent de Paul Pen. #2409.
1959 – June 4		Transferred to Kingston Pen.	#6150.
1962 – Sept. 28		Released on Parole – Sentence due to expire – Life.	
1963 – Nov. – Rec'd. from Jail Montreal, Que.	Capital Murder	No disposition given	Rec. #D-83051.

Image 6.6 In 1963, Léopold Dion was arrested for the murder of four boys when he was out on parole. As this RCMP report indicates, he had a long track record of violent sexual offences. LAC, R.G. 13, Volume 1804, volume 1, part 1.

freed, Dion began to reoffend, and a conviction (for a "homosexual act with a young boy") sent him back to prison. Despite this offence profile, Dion was not designated a criminal sexual psychopath, and the Parole Board approved his release in September 1962 on the basis that he had served the minimum period of his sentence for this latest crime. Apparently, Winch observed with bitterness, the board had judged a man who repeatedly victimized women and boys "as harmless, not dangerous to anybody."[109]

In Quebec, the failure of federal parole authorities to keep Dion locked up energized the movement for greater independence. Quebec's assistant solicitor general, Charles Cantin, accused the federal agency of having disregarded the Quebec judge's sentencing directive in 1956, and he was livid over the Parole Board's failure to warn the province or local police that Dion was allowed out in the fall of 1962. As Dion later admitted, in the months leading up to the murder he had "corrupted" twenty-five youths while out on parole.[110] Cantin's complaints made their way into Parliament via the member for Quebec–Montmorency, Guy Marcoux, party whip of the pro-retentionist Social Credit Party.[111] On 24 July 1963, the day of the coroner's inquest into the boys' murders, he demanded answers to four questions: Who recommended Dion's parole? Why was he paroled after his sentence to life? Why was he paroled after the gross indecency conviction? And, will the government undertake an investigation of the National Parole Board?[112] The parliamentary secretary to the minister of justice responded by the book: Dion's case had been "considered painstakingly and in complete objectivity by the board."[113] The minister of justice, Lionel Chevrier, affirmed that "a minute examination was made before the prisoner was set free"; nevertheless, he agreed to request that Dion's parole file be reviewed by a lawyer and a psychiatrist to determine whether "too great a risk was taken."[114] But the government's refusal to hold a general inquiry into the National Parole Board provided further grist to the mill of sovereigntist sentiment in Quebec.

"Le Monstre Que Nous Avons Créé"

The original date for Dion's execution, 10 April 1964, came and went, because his lawyer stood by his client to the end. In the trial, Guy Bertrand argued an insanity defence. The key witness for the defence was Dr. Camille Laurin, professor of psychiatry at l'Université de Montréal, who agreed the accused was not insane in legal terms but said he was utterly incapable of controlling his violent sexual compulsions. Dr. Laurin described the accused in layperson's terms. Dion was "un monstre sexuel, à figure humaine ... Toutes ses actions sont orientées vers la satisfaction de son instinct sexuel." Although he was not mentally subnormal, Dion's capacity for reason had been "subordonné à l'animalité."[115] The jury, out for seventeen minutes after the trial of sixteen days, found the defendant guilty. The Crown, Jean Bienvenue, had made a convincing case of murder by emphasizing the elaborate planning behind Dion's crimes, as well as the stealthy way he had hidden the bodies.[116] Behaviour of this nature indicated the killer could tell right from wrong, and a man of Dion's intelligence could understand the criminal nature of his acts, the Crown's psychiatrist asserted.[117]

Bertrand appealed the verdict before the Quebec Court of Appeal and the Supreme Court of Canada, but he failed to win his client a new trial.[118] As an opponent of capital punishment, he remained committed to saving Dion from the gallows. Bertrand never denied his client had killed the boys, and he expressed great sympathy for their families; yet, he insisted that "society" was responsible for Dion's crimes, not the man himself. This killer had grown up unloved, sent to an orphanage where he was sexually abused by a priest. Although he had lived the majority of his life in prison, Dion had never received psychiatric treatment, Bertrand stressed. If the state were to kill "Le Monstre que nous avons Créé ... et développé," it would do society no good. But if Dion could be sent to a secure psychiatric facility, experts could study this man and learn how to prevent future tragedies.[119]

The Supreme Court's dismissal of Bertrand's appeal, which reset Dion's execution date to 29 October 1965, required the executive to consider his case as the Liberals fought to return to government. To hostile outsiders, it appeared that the cabinet's failure to act immediately after the court's decision showed it was dodging a "contentious issue" prior to the election scheduled for 8 November.[120] But the solicitor general of the caretaker government, Lawrence Pennell, advised his colleagues on 18 October that "this difficult case" required more time for the "fullest consideration" of further psychiatric evidence. He was under no illusion that clemency would be unpopular in this case: "The revolting nature of the Dion crimes had precipitated great public indignation, especially in and around Quebec City, and the jury did not recommend mercy."[121] With the Liberals out on the hustings, hoping to return to government, cabinet postponed a decision until 26 November. At that meeting, Lucien Cardin, who had replaced Guy Favreau as minister of justice prior to the election, opposed clemency.[122] Dion was "a dangerous psychopathic killer, and because of his intelligence was capable of killing guards or escaping and committing further killings." Other ministers stressed the importance of showing Canadians that "the protection of society" was a matter of "high priority" for the government. Pearson admitted he feared that Dion would likely kill again if given a chance, making it "impossible to provide foolproof security." That worry, plus the government's plan to introduce an abolition bill, led the cabinet to buy more time. Dion's execution date was extended further to 3 December.[123]

"If Ever a Case for Execution, This Is It"

The day prior to the 26 November 1965 cabinet meeting, Jean Bienvenue, the Crown prosecutor, travelled to Ottawa to argue against the commutation of Dion's sentence. Prior to this, he had written to D.H. Christie of the CLD to emphasize that the execution should not be put off any longer: "All these events and children's murders make me feel that the execution of Dion would be very timely."[124] When Bienvenue met with the solicitor general (starting off by showing him the morgue photos of the murdered boys), he warned the federal minister that the population of Quebec would erupt in anger and riot if Dion were granted clemency. As the minutes of the meeting indicate, he also suggested that Quebeckers found Dion's murders more reprehensible than the infamous police killer's: "Marcotte furor would be nothing compared with Dion case." The government must see what Bienvenue saw: "If ever a case for execution, this is it."[125] At first, the cabinet appeared to agree, as six of the ten ministers who attended thought the "monstrous" killer should be hanged. The unsettled cabinet decided to reconvene three days later, and although it remained divided, the ministers resolved to commute. Again, special caveats accompanied the commutation recommendation. The re-elected solicitor general sought and received the Parole Board's assurance that it would not release Dion before he had served fifteen years. Cabinet also ordered that Dion be committed to a maximum security psychiatric prison or an institution for the criminally insane and that he never be "given the benefit of parole."[126] These bespoke arrangements highlighted the need for tighter parole guidelines if Canada were to abolish the death penalty. The ministers agreed that "supplementary legislation" was required to determine the "general conditions under which parole could be granted or denied."[127]

The federal government's assurances failed to pacify Quebeckers, already disgruntled over the province's place in Confederation. By the mid-1960s, Premier Jean Lesage's government was caught between suppressing radical separatists, who were turning to violence in their call for a socialist revolution, and standing up for francophone rights and self-determination. The reaction to Ottawa's decision took on greater ramifications in this testy atmosphere.[128] Justice Minister Wagner was infuriated that Dion would not be executed. Sensing that the majority of Canadians shared his disgust over the commutation, he called for a national referendum on the death penalty. Premier Lesage backed his minister, and he chimed in to condemn the federal government's

Bonner's View Of Wagner . . .

VANCOUVER — (CP) — Attorney-General Robert Bonner of British Columbia said yesterday his opposite number in Quebec "may well be Canada's answer to Batman."

Mr. Bonner made the remark in taking exception to comments by Quebec's Justice Minister Claude Wagner after the federal - provincial crime conference last week.

Mr. Wagner said his provincial police force had done more to fight crime in one year than the RCMP had done since 1951.

"Mr. Wagner can make a career of fighting crime if he goes nowhere but his own province," said Mr. Bonner.

"He may very well be the Canadian answer to Batman."

"But his post-conference remarks and his attitude at the conference are inconsistent."

Mr. Bonner said Mr. Wagner had no basis for criticizing the anti-crime efforts of the others who attended the conference.

"I'm sure he knows nothing of conditions in B.C., he said.

(Cartoon by Susan Brainerd)

BATMAN

Image 6.7 This cartoon satirized law-and-order crusader Claude Wagner, Quebec's justice minister. In the mid-1960s, he became a leading critic of parole and correctionalism, and he strongly supported the death penalty as a deterrent to murder. Montreal *Gazette*, 18 January 1966.

unjust clemency: "As long as we have practically automatic commutations for the most horrible crimes then we will continue to have horrible crimes."[129]

An Innocent Boy?

The event that boosted the fortunes of abolitionists in 1966 was not a referendum or a parliamentary vote but the publication of a book: *The Trial of Steven Truscott*. Unlike Jacques Hébert's swinging attack on Quebec's government and judicial system in the Coffin case, journalist

Isabel LeBourdais's book outlined the cascade of factors that had contributed to Truscott's conviction: the readiness of the police to arrest the last-known witness; the prejudicial publicity of the preliminary trial; the Crown's reliance on child witnesses; the judge's embellishment of the Crown's case; the impact of questionable forensic evidence; and the magistrate's decision that a boy be tried as an adult. Canadians who believed that trial verdicts, upheld by appeal courts, were beyond question dismissed LeBourdais as an "angry woman" and an "emotional mother," out to seek notoriety by stirring up sympathy.[130] Publisher after publisher turned the woman down, until she wrote a draft, assisted by the former leader of Ontario's CCF, that a Canadian publisher was prepared to support.[131] The book's release in March 1966 occurred just as Pearson's government belatedly made good on its promise to hold a free vote on the death penalty. Good timing and clever marketing maximized the book's impact in Parliament and across the country.

In January 1960, one week after the Conservative cabinet commuted Truscott's sentence, the government had pussyfooted its way around the larger issue of capital punishment. The party scuttled Frank McGee's private member's abolition bill to avoid exposing divisions of opinion.[132] Arthur Maloney was a fellow Conservative MP in 1960, and he supported McGee in principle, but he advised it was best at that juncture to abandon the bill since it "would have been 'quite badly defeated' if it had come to a vote."[133] However, the political landscape had shifted by the mid-1960s. The British Parliament passed legislation in 1965 to suspend the application of the death penalty for five years, and in Canada no person convicted of murder had been executed since 1962.[134] Bookstores struggled to keep copies of *The Trial of Steven Truscott* in stock by the time a cross-party abolition resolution was debated in Parliament on 23 March 1966. Some eighty MPs wished to speak, with roughly half in favour of the death penalty, according to some estimates.[135]

A targeted publicity campaign to promote LeBourdais's book included sending a free copy to every MP early in March 1966.[136] If some MPs tossed the book into their office bins, satisfied that the justices of the Ontario Court of Appeal and the Supreme Court of Canada were more reliable authorities than a female journalist, many politicians, including former prime minister John Diefenbaker, considered *The Trial of Steven Truscott* a game-changer in the debate over capital punishment.[137] This compelling account of a miscarriage of justice in a sex murder case had the potential to convince Canadians to follow Britain's lead and begin their own experiment with abolition.

As much as the government wished to brush aside claims that Truscott had been wrongly convicted, it could not muzzle the opposition, the media, or its own backbenchers.[138] Members of the NDP stoutly supported LeBourdais's efforts, despite sensing that some of her allegations were unfair. As the debate opened, Andrew Brewin, KC, a Toronto member and party co-founder, commended the journalist for persuading Canadians that the miscarriage of capital justice was not just a problem in other countries.[139] Now, "closer to home," the government must revisit Truscott's conviction:

> Many members in this house will have read Mrs. LeBourdais' detailed and thoughtful analysis of this case and of the trial. Some of the members of the house have even visited Steven Truscott and have talked with him. Even at this moment the government and the Solicitor General (Mr. Pennell) have undertaken a review of this case to determine whether, as the book requests, a royal commission should be arranged to inquire into it.[140]

Brewin thought the book went too far by describing Truscott's prosecution as either "corrupt, inefficient, or callous." That aside, his experience as a barrister had taught him that justice is "fallible and that mistakes can be made, particularly in the atmosphere created by the commission of horrible and detestable crimes."[141] A Liberal member from British Columbia, James Byrne, attracted nationwide media coverage by demanding that his own government investigate the case, and he vowed to stake his seat in Parliament on the outcome.[142] John Diefenbaker, now leader of the opposition, joined this chorus "in the interests of justice and so that justice not only may be done but may be seen to have been done."[143] Pearson had little choice but to respond to mounting pressure to review Truscott's conviction, but he did so by punting it to the courts, assisted by the government of Ontario.[144]

Having recently suffered stinging disapproval over the cabinet's commutations of Marcotte's and Dion's death sentences, plus outrage over federal parole decision-making, the federal government was wary about stepping on sensitive toes in Ontario, where the province's Court of Appeal had upheld Truscott's guilty verdict. Ontario's attorney general, Arthur A. Wishart, was the chief law officer in the Conservative government, but he knew more than most about capital punishment.

Representing the Crown, he had prosecuted two sex murder cases that ended in convictions: after failed appeals, Edgar Simons was hanged in 1947, and Richard Rivers was executed in 1948.[145] Wishart declined to order a new trial of Truscott in Ontario for the simple reason that the Criminal Code assigned the power to direct a new trial to the federal minister of justice.[146] In a series of private exchanges between Lawrence Pennell, the federal solicitor general, and the provincial attorney general, Wishart took the lead. Six weeks after LeBourdais's book was published, he told the press he thought the federal cabinet should request a legal review of the case, since the 1961 capital murder statute now permitted appeals by right to the Supreme Court of Canada on matters of fact as well as law.[147] The solicitor general and his cabinet colleagues decided they had their solution.[148] Using an executive order to refer the case to the Supreme Court, the government asked the justices to determine what disposition it would have made on Truscott's appeal (had it not dismissed it in 1960) "on a consideration of the existing record and such further evidence as the court, in its discretion, may receive and consider."[149] This solution was far short of the royal commission that LeBourdais and her supporters had called for; however, it did empower the Supreme Court to consider new evidence, including testimony from Truscott himself.

"The Upholding of the Death Penalty"

The referral of Truscott's case took place shortly after the retentionists prevailed in the vote on the death penalty's abolition on 5 April 1966.[150] The debate kicked off in March with a joint party resolution to test the waters for support. Representatives from the Liberal, Conservative, and New Democratic parties proposed that the mandatory sentence of life replace the death penalty for all offences to which it then applied, providing that no person so sentenced "shall be released from imprisonment without the prior approval of the Governor in Council."[151] The last clause was meant to ward off anxiety over the parole of convicted murderers, which persisted in spite of the amendment to the regulations.[152] For the majority of MPs in 1966, it was safer to rely on the traditions of punishment than to bet on social and medical science. "Sociology, criminology, and psychiatry" had failed to prevent, predict, detect, and cure criminality. Consequently, the death penalty must be retained: "Only the rope can put the fear of the Lord in these parasites and deter them."[153]

Most of the MPs who voted against abolition in 1966 represented Quebec ridings. Many told Parliament that their constituents were angry over Ottawa's decision to commute the death sentences imposed on Quebec murderers, especially Dion's. Prior to the death penalty debates, Liberal Auguste Choquette proposed an amendment to the Criminal Code, which would have assigned the executive review of death sentences to provincial authorities. He explained that his bill was prompted by the "shocking" commutation of Dion's sentence and by the "tremendous new outbreak of criminality" in the province of Quebec, including gangland and political violence. "I strongly support the Minister of Justice in the province of Quebec," Choquette declared, "when he advocates the upholding of the death penalty."[154] Réal Caouette repeated this proposal when he accused abolitionists of supporting "revolutionaries," who were "getting ready to overthrow the rule of law and order by resorting to murder, assassination and bombings."[155] The province's police also lobbied strongly against abolition.[156] The MP for Sainte-Marie, Georges Valade, referred to a telegram he had received from the Quebec Federation of Municipal Policemen (representing over 6,000 officers), which called for the government to retain capital punishment and to "institute a special compensation fund to help the dependents of murder victims."[157] Retentionists of all political stripes agreed it was safest to stick with tradition – legal and moral – and the common-sense conviction that death was the most potent deterrent against murder.

Licking their wounds after the abolition bill's defeat, abolitionists decided that the Liberal government needed to be clearer about its policy on the punishment of murderers if the death penalty were to be abolished.[158] And it was most important to convince federal MPs from Quebec.[159] Claude Wagner gloried in the bill's resounding defeat, and he used the occasion to announce the Quebec government's decision to put Léopold Dion on trial for the murder of his three other victims.[160] When Quebec provincial police escorted the prisoner into court before Chief Justice Dorion in April 1966, Dion shouted, "Hang me right now and get the business over with once and for all."[161] That spring, abolitionists could take heart in the fact that a much younger convicted sex murderer was about to have another day in court, represented by G. Arthur Martin.[162] One of the top criminal law specialists in the country, funded by the government of Ontario, Martin and his team prepared to expose the weaknesses of the Crown's case against Steven Truscott and argue the wrongfulness of his conviction.[163]

"Boy's Trial May Relax Hanging Law"

The sittings of the Supreme Court opened in Ottawa in October 1966, by which point Truscott was twenty-one years old. He never wavered over his innocence, despite efforts by the police who arrested him and the psychiatrists who examined and drugged him to induce him to confess. Before the full panel of the Supreme Court, he stated he did not rape or kill Lynne Harper.[164] In his 1959 murder trial, Truscott's lawyer, Frank Donnelly, did not call the boy to testify, a decision that led some to question the tactic. There were also allegations that Donnelly (who was elevated to the Supreme Court of Ontario immediately after the trial) kept Truscott off the witness stand because he knew the boy was guilty.[165] By contrast, G. Arthur Martin decided it was important that the Supreme Court of Canada hear from the young man, and Truscott and his parents agreed he should testify. This decision meant that the Crown and the justices could ask the convicted murderer intrusive personal questions, similar to the interrogations rape complainants faced.[166] Martin knew he would have to tackle head-on the most sensitive piece of medical evidence that had helped turn Truscott into the prime suspect: the "injuries" police had observed on the boy's penis. In the trial, the prosecution claimed these had been caused by the attack.[167] For the first time in a sex murder case, the condition of the perpetrator's genitals became pivotal, and reporters craned their necks in the red chamber to hear what a teenaged boy had been "too embarrassed" to discuss with his parents in 1959.[168]

A parade of experts in various fields of forensic science appeared in the referred case over the course of five days in October 1966, after which the Supreme Court held further hearings in January 1967, when the defence and Crown presented opposing arguments. Ted Jolliffe, the politician who had helped LeBourdais with her book, appeared with G. Arthur Martin, which gave the proceedings and the coverage it attracted the flavour of a justice campaign.[169] Although the formidable William B. Common argued on behalf of the Crown, the defence did not lose heart. Since the Liberal government appeared ready to revisit the prospect of abolition after the defeat of April 1966, opponents of capital punishment knew that a finding favourable to Truscott's defenders would boost support.[170] "Boy's trial may relax hanging law," the Manchester *Guardian* projected.[171] Yet, the ruling, announced on 4 May 1967, went against Truscott. The court stated it would have dismissed the original appeal, irrespective of the fresh evidence.[172]

wa, Friday, May 5, 1967 Phone 236-7511 METRO FINAL Forty-Eight Pages

Cabinet Action Unlikely

'I'm Not Going To Quit Now' —Truscott's Dad

DEJECTED PARENTS

Mr. and Mrs. Dan Truscott sit dejected after the announcement that the Supreme Court of Canada ruled in an 8-to-1 decision that Steven Truscott's 1959 conviction for the rape slaying of Lynne Harper, 12, should stand. The court said there was no miscarriage of justice in Truscott's conviction when he was 14.

(CP-Journal Wirephoto)

By RICHARD JACKSON of The Journal

The steel gates at Kingston's Collins Bay Penitentiary have clanged shut on Steven Truscott for what today—from all the evidence—appears to be at least another two years.

Justice was done, ruled the Supreme Court of Canada in an overwhelming 8-1 majority decision that seems to wall off solidly any further appeal.

AGITATION CONTINUES

But still the agitation to free the 22-year-old convicted killer—or at least give him still another hearing—refuses to die down.

The federal cabinet, which ordered the Supreme Court review of the hotly-controversial case, is not expected either to intervene with a recommendation of parole or to direct any further investigation such as a suggested Royal Commission inquiry.

And so, Steven Truscott whose sentence of death was commuted by the cabinet to life imprisonment, will serve out at least his minimum time, with parole possible in another two and a half years.

But the fight to free Steven is to go on, "until," as his father Dan Truscott says, "the boy's innocence is established beyond any doubt."

Mr. Truscott, a former RCAF Warrant Officer released only last week from the service, swore he would go "clean across the country collecting signatures on a petition for a new trial.

'NOT GOING TO QUIT'

Image 6.8. Steven Truscott's family received sympathetic press coverage, thanks in large part to Isabel LeBourdais's exposé of his conviction at the age of fourteen for the sex murder of Lynne Harper. Her book was instrumental in raising doubt over the infallibility of Canadian criminal justice. Ottawa *Journal*, 5 May 1967.

Although the ruling upheld the verdict, striking a blow to Truscott and his family, his supporters considered the decision a stain on Canada's hidebound judiciary, so different from the progressive interventionist US Supreme Court.[173] The minority opinion of Justice Emmett Hall, the one judge (out of nine) who considered Truscott's trial unfair and unjust, provided support for critics of the death penalty, and abolitionists capitalized on it. There were many "grave errors" in the boy's trial, Justice Hall believed, including the Crown's "conscious and deliberate" drawing out of "prejudicial" witness evidence, the trial judge's allowance of evidence adverse to the prisoner (including one doctor's statement that the penis sores "indicated a very inexpert attempt at penetration"), and the judge's redirection concerning the plausibility of Truscott's fatal encounter with Harper, which came "wholly out of thin air."[174] From a strictly legal standpoint, however, the only decision that counted was that of the majority, which concluded "no substantial wrong or miscarriage of justice" had occurred. The court's unfavourable decision, a blow to abolitionists, nevertheless underscored the importance of abolishing the death penalty to avoid future miscarriages of justice.[175]

Contending with Retentionists

When retentionists, such as the irascible Claude Wagner, pointed to the defeat of the 1966 abolition bill, they rightly claimed that the parliamentary vote reflected and respected the will of the people. Gallup polls held that year indicated that 53 per cent of Canadians supported the death penalty, with only 37 per cent in favour of abolition and the remainder undecided.[176] Abolitionists concentrated on promoting ideals and enlightening the public: no civilized state executed its citizens, and the government had a duty to lead the people in this regard. Yet, the value of pragmatism was not lost on the CSADP's president, Arthur Maloney. After scanning the edges of the polarized debate in Parliament, he became convinced that a majority of MPs would support restricting the scope of the death penalty over a trial period, even if they were not prepared to abolish it. In May 1966, Maloney informed Pearson that 17 of the 143 members who had voted against outright abolition had stated they would agree to switch their vote if a compromise bill were introduced. On behalf of the CSADP, Maloney urged the prime minister to authorize "a Government measure to abolish capital punishment for cases of capital murder except those that involved the murder of prison

Some are hanged because they're so poor: lawyer

By DAVID LEE
Tribune Staff Writer

A prominent Canadian lawyer complained here Monday that a poor person facing a murder charge has more chance of being convicted than a person with money or influence.

Arthur Maloney, of Toronto, rated one of Canada's top criminal lawyers and president of the Canadian Society for the Abolition of the Death Penalty, also complained that many persons who are charged with a crime, including murder, are forced to face an "incompetent" judge and are represented by a lawyer just out of school.

Mr. Maloney was in Winnipeg Monday night to address a dinner sponsored by the Young Progressive Conservative Association of Greater Winnipeg.

"That a man's right to live out his life in prison or to die on the gallows should hinge on human variables such as these is absolutely unthinkable," said the 47-year-old lawyer.

He said the most frequent persons to be sentenced to the gallows are those who are too poor to afford the services of a skilled lawyer and are unable to pay for an investigation that could turn up evidence to help their case.

Mr. Maloney said this proved "inequality" in the application of the death penalty.

The lawyer outlined the CSADP'S organization, objectives, and progress to the 65 lawyers, government officials and Young Conservatives attending the dinner.

He said the organization began in 1963 when a young Ontario law student approached businessmen in Toronto and united them with the view that the death penalty should be abolished. He said the new group held several meetings before finally receiving a federal charter in June, 1964.

The objective of the society was to form an organization coast to coast and set up chapters in many municipalities to foster a public opinion in favor of abolition of the death penalty. He said the society has about 25,000 members across the country.

However, recently the board of directors decided their efforts would have to be directed at the

ARTHUR MALONEY
. . . 'unthinkable'

Members of Parliament and the Senate, he said. So far, 35 MP's and 15 senators have joined the ranks of the organization.

Mr. Maloney said he personally wished to see the death of capital punishment because "it is a drastic punishment."

He said the matter would come before Parliament during the coming session but added he could not forecast what might happen then.

The federal government has commuted all sentences of death to life imprisonment for the past three years pending action on the abolition bill, he said.

Mr. Maloney said the only alternative to the abolition of the death penalty was to hand down life imprisonment sentences. He said the convicted person should not have to stay in prison for life, however, but there should be safeguards taken to make sure he was ready for society before allowed parole.

The experience of the countries that have done away with the death penalty is a safeguard, said the lawyer," and this is definitely one area where we are behind the times."

Mr. Maloney said that if the abolition is defeated in Parliament, his organization will once again begin an extensive campaign with the residents of Canada to get them to back up their demands.

"We find ourselves handicapped by a feeling of apathy among many people whom we know are abolitionists. Their apathy stems from the perfectly mistaken assumption that the outcome of the free vote in Parliament is a foregone conclusion and that the death penalty will be abolished in a matter of months," said the 47-year-old lawyer.

He said there was always the other people "who incline to the view that a program of strict, severe punishment is the only answer.

". . . but the arrest, the trial, the conviction — the humiliation to the offenders' family, the loss of the companionship of his friends and of the respect of his fellow men are all punishment of the most severe kind."

Mr. Maloney said by hanging murderers, "we are doing away with the raw material that should be studied in the prisons to find out the motivation and possibly prevent a re-occurrance."

He also said there is always the other reason for not hanging a person. "He may some day be proven not guilty."

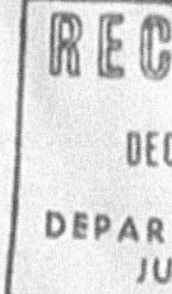

Image 6.9 Defence lawyer, former Conservative MP, and leading abolitionist lobbyist Arthur Maloney used his experience in defending indigent defendants accused of murder to argue that killers should be studied, not executed. This clipping appeared in Léopold Dion's capital case file. LAC, R.G. 13, Volume 1804, volume 3, part 6.

guards, police officers, and second murders." He also advised (likely with the Marcotte and Dion commutations in mind) that no prisoner currently sentenced to death should be executed, considering that "persons convicted of some of the most brutal crimes conceivable" had been granted clemency since December 1964.[177]

Arthur Maloney was never a cabinet member, but he made the most of his privileged access to the executive as a former MP and the country's most authoritative spokesman on the death penalty. He took pains to distinguish himself from LeBourdais, a "layman" whom he accused of the same "biased, emotional" approach she criticized in retentionists.[178] Maloney based opposition to capital punishment on his study of international penal trends and academic research, as well as his first-hand experience of defending accused murderers, most recently in 1962. In the trial of nineteen-year-old Gary McCorkell, the prosecution set out to prove that the defendant had sexually assaulted and smothered two male toddlers whom he abducted from a laneway in Toronto's west end.[179] Maloney argued for the defence that the crime should not be prosecuted as a capital murder, but the judge, Justice G.A. Gale, supported the indictment.[180] Because the prosecution, led by veteran Crown attorney A.O. Klein, called the psychiatrist who had examined the defendant at the court's request, Maloney turned his evidence into a resource for the defence.[181] Dr. Norman L. Eastman diagnosed McCorkell as a "homosexual paedophile" who "heard voices" and had a "deep psychological problem," for which he had been treated (unsuccessfully) for two years.[182] The Crown witness stopped short of determining that the prisoner was insane, but Maloney drew on his testimony to persuade the jury that his client was ill and that his mental problems were compounded by his upbringing in a "broken home" (a point he had also made in his defence of John Bell). The jury appeared to respond to this sympathetic portrayal of a young child slayer. Although they convicted McCorkell, they added a recommendation to mercy "in the strongest terms."[183] After the Ontario Court of Appeal dismissed Maloney's appeal, he waived his right to lodge a further one, pitching a clemency bid instead.[184] Because he knew that Justice Gale's report supported the jury's recommendation, Maloney's plea reiterated what he had said during the trial: that McCorkell suffered from an "abnormal appetite he neither wants nor sought."[185] Diefenbaker's cabinet responded to their colleague, and they acted on the prime minister's pledge: no convicted murderer, whom a jury had recommended to mercy, would be hanged.[186]

From Bible Class To

This is the story of a life in the balance.

A jury's recommendation for mercy is expected to tip it from death on the gallows to life imprisonment.

Garry McCorkell was 19 when he molested and then murdered two little boys in a New Toronto warehouse last April.

Wh[illegible]ened in his 19 years?

Wh[illegible]d Garry McCork[illegible] to [illegible]th cell?

By P[illegible]YLLIS [illegible]RIFFITHS
Telegram Staff Reporter

THE seven-pound 10-ounce baby born in Ottawa Civic Hospital Jan. 18, 194[illegible], was christened Garry Alexander McCorkell—proud names in families of Scottish heritage.

His mother, only 18 when she was married 13 months before, didn't have her husband's comfort. He was away in the army—a conscript.

At three Garry nearly died of nephritis, a kidney ailment, and from then on was a chronic bed-wetter.

Out of the army, Garry's father didn't pay much attention to him, "maybe because he was away when Garry was a baby," Mrs. McCorkell recalls.

MARRIAGE FAILS

Midway through 1946 the marriage broke up. Harassed by lack of money for food and resentful of her husband's frequent absences, Mrs. McCorkell brought the children to Toronto where her mother had moved.

Years on welfare followed. A court order for support got nowhere. The younger boy had become an epileptic. His seizures caused his mother to [illegible]

Garry McCorkell ... at 2½ ... at 4 ... at 9 ... and at 18

court. It was an "accident"—he had covered the boys' mouths with his hand to keep them quiet.

'NOT INSANE'

He was charged with capital murder. Medical evidence showed he was not insane but sexually abnormal.

Should mercy — recommended by the jury "in strongest terms"—be given Garry Alexander McCorkell?

Psychiatrist Dr. Lewis Easton of the Ontario Hospital at New Toronto says: "Nobody can say just how or why Garry became a pedophile.

"Keep him away from juveniles and he should be a productive citizen. He has no criminal traits—only an abnormal urge that should fade out by the time he is 30. Studies show that it does."

Garry's mother, hard-working, religious, stalwart in her love (she has never missed a week visiting him in prison), can only hope with him that mercy will save him from the gallows.

"Put him behind bars—please God not with hardened criminals—for as long as necessary," she says. "Release him only when he will harm nobody and can live a useful and good life, what there is left of it."

Ask Life Sentence In 'Clemency' Cases

HIS LORDSHIP: Do you wish to make any recommendation as to whether or not he should be granted clemency?

THE FOREMAN: We are in favor of clemency in the strongest terms.

Because of this recommendation, everybody concluded that the death sentence Mr. Justice G. A. Gale then pronounced on Garry Alexander McCorkell, 19 [illegible]

preparing a brief seeking a change in the law.

Arthur Maloney, QC, will ask the next Parliament to REQUIRE the trial judge to impose life imprisonment in capital murder cases when the jury, in finding the accused guilty, recommends clemency.

Under the present law the judge MUST sentence the accused, as he did Garry McCorkell, to be "hanged by [illegible] until you are dead."

Image 6.10 By the 1960s, sympathetic accounts of young white sex murderers began to appear in the mainstream press. This story reinforced defence lawyer Arthur Maloney's argument that Gary McCorkell was the product of a "broken home" and "abnormal," not evil. Toronto *Telegram*, 18 February 1963.

Despite his effectiveness in defending McCorkell and pleading that his death sentence be commuted, one of many such cases in his career as a defence lawyer, Maloney was anxious to distinguish himself from sob sisters. When he spoke in 1966 on behalf of the CSADP at a service club meeting in Brockville, Ontario, he told his audience that individuals convicted of capital murder "should not be released in six or seven years for good behaviour;" rather, they must serve a life sentence to "enable scientists to study the murderer and come up with an answer regarding the reason for such a murder to occur."[187] Consequently, he urged the government to come up with an abolition bill that could reassure wavering retentionists that murderers would not be released unless they reformed or were cured.

The Categorical Narrowing of Capital Murder

Political fallout from the Marcotte commutation in 1964 continued to undermine the Liberal government's confidence that it could experiment with abolition. The police had the upper hand when the bill to suspend the death penalty, Bill C-168, was introduced on 19 October 1967.[188] The Canadian Association of Chiefs of Police regularly reported the number of murders in Canada, and they attributed the rise (from 118 in 1960 to 231 in 1963) to the narrowing of the death penalty in 1961 to planned and deliberate murders.[189] Although the CSADP contested their methodology and reasoning, the national association and the provincial police force of Quebec had sufficient sway over ambivalent MPs to sink the proposed legislation.[190] When the bill reached second reading, the prime minister nervously projected that "if [this bill] failed abolition would have to be sought by another government."[191]

But retentionists and abolitionists alike questioned the logic of a law that used a victim's profession, rather than the gravity of the crime, to determine the punishment of murder. The Social Credit MP for Red Deer, R.N. Thompson, complained that if the government proposed to retain the death penalty exclusively

> to protect the lives of policemen, wardens and prison guards ... it automatically follows that it is necessary also to protect girls killed in sex murders. What is the difference between a policeman who is murdered in a bank robbery and a girl who is raped and murdered by a sex maniac? I cannot see the differentiation which this bill automatically makes.[192]

Solicitor General Lawrence Pennell, one of the cabinet members who believed that capital punishment ought to be abolished outright, conceded that the bill set aside logic to placate law-and-order lobbyists.[193] Personally, he doubted the penalty of death would deter any person inclined to kill a law enforcer; yet, "at least it provides a peace of mind and moral support to that very small group in our society who, at great risk to themselves, permit us to live our lives in the security to which we are entitled."[194]

Outside the House of Commons, Pennell addressed the Alberta MP's concern about the punishment of sex murderers in a legal article, in which he described such killers as "so dangerous that it would be unsafe to let them ever go free." It was wrong to execute them, however. To do so would be of no benefit to "society." Pennell argued that it was better to invest faith in "present developments in the scientific study of the human mind," which would lead, one day, to an understanding of "the psychopath."[195] Like Maloney and the CSADP, Pennell knew that law enforcement lobbyists' dramatic accounts were more compelling than the abstract aspirations of modern correctionalism. This awareness led the government to discriminate between victims as a first step toward their ultimate goal. On 30 November 1967, Parliament passed the "compromise bill" by a vote of 105 to 70.[196] For a five-year period, most persons convicted of murder, including sex killers, would not face the death penalty.

In the mid-1960s, as the government negotiated its way toward a partial moratorium on the death penalty, a considerable number of capital cases made slow progress through courts of appeal. Appeals to the Supreme Court against convictions in capital cases grew substantially after 1961, which lengthened the turn-around time between convictions and final judgments from months to years. This time lag meant that when the amended Criminal Code came into effect on 27 December 1967, sixteen men still faced execution.[197] The government required a quick solution to deal with these condemned men in legal limbo, one of whom still faced execution for the sex murder of a teenaged girl.

Defeated retentionists, especially Quebec MPs, thought that none of these convicted murderers should be spared, especially Marcel Bernier. A Ralliement créditiste MP, Gérard Laprise, informed Parliament that the cemetery worker had used a false advertisement for a babysitter to lure sixteen-year-old Denise Therrien. Like Dion's victims, she struggled when he forced himself on her, and he subdued her by clubbing her on the head with a pipe.[198] Convicted of the girl's murder in February 1966 (and charged with murdering another woman to cover up Therrien's murder), this man's crime was surely no less tragic than the shooting of any police officer. During the debates, Laprise stated, "I am thinking particularly about the parents of the teen-ager who was raped and murdered in Shawinigan by the gravedigger, Marcel Bernier and about the anxiety they must have felt throughout the search for their young daughter and the trial of the murderer."[199] After the jury delivered its verdict and declined to recommend mercy, the trial judge had recommended that "the law must take its course," since this murder was "un des plus odieux que l'on retrace dans nos annales criminelles."[200] But because Bernier's victim was just a girl, not a law enforcement agent, his name appeared on the list of the sixteen men spared through a "mass commutation" authorized in January under executive order 1968–49.[201]

Abolition and "the Outrage of Society"

The centenary of Confederation was an occasion for celebration and reflection over the nation's identity. Expo 67 brought Canadians together in Montreal, but other events and movements, most dramatic in Quebec, exposed disunity. One of the most divisive issues of the decade was the death penalty, which pollsters tracked during the parliamentary debates on abolition. Differences between the provinces (Alberta and Quebec most favouring retention), between French and English speakers, among people of Protestant, Catholic, and Jewish faith, people with distinct levels of education, urban and rural Canadians, men and women, and supporters of each of the major political parties found expression in the legislation that partially and temporarily suspended the death penalty in 1967.[202] Conflicting visions of the nation's character also emerged in debates over the role of the executive in a modern liberal democracy, and they grew sharper in the 1960s. To most Canadians, the federal cabinet's gratuitous use of its prerogative to grant mercy looked like an abuse of executive power. Were the government's ministers not dictatorial, and contemptuous of the majority of Canadians, every time cabinet commuted a death sentence to life imprisonment with the possibility of parole? Retentionists in Parliament claimed they were the true representatives of the people, whereas MPs who supported abolition considered it their rightful duty to lead, rather than follow opinion on contentious issues. They were supported by academic researchers, who churned out reams of tables and charts that raised doubt over the death penalty's deterrent effect. But no one needed a statistician to prove that hanging a killer eliminated the risk he would reoffend.[203]

The 1967 amendment to the Criminal Code formally suspended the death penalty's application to most murders, but it made no changes to the administration of parole for persons originally sentenced to death.[204] The government had already constrained the Parole Board's independence earlier in the decade. One of the convicted sex murderers who applied for parole after the moratorium began was Steven Truscott, quietly released in 1969, a decade after his trial. Pearson's cabinet flirted with the prospect of authorizing his parole at an earlier date, but they decided to avoid a repeat of the Dion disaster – a sex offender convicted of rape in his youth and paroled, only to murder four young boys. However, "le monstre" made no further parole applications because a fellow prisoner, serving a life sentence for a sex murder after a non-capital conviction, killed Dion. The coroner who investigated this homicide, committed in Archambault Penitentiary, criticized the maximum security institution. It was "inexcusable" that a federal prison had no secure psychiatric wing and that just one psychiatrist made twice-monthly visits.[205] Insufficient staffing and inadequate expertise in the penal system left Canadians rightly perturbed over the capacity of scientists to reform or cure aggressive sex offenders and murderers.

Optimistic abolitionists anticipated that capital punishment would lose its appeal as its use petered out.[206] Canadians need not be fearful. After all, the removal of the death penalty as a sentencing option for rape in 1955 had not led to an upsurge in sexual assaults; similarly, Canadians would discover that subjecting murderers, including sex slayers, to life imprisonment would render the nation more civilized, not more dangerous.[207] The only woman in Pearson's cabinet, lawyer Judy LaMarsh, disagreed. In her opinion, there was one category of murder for which the death penalty was the only punishment that matched the "heinousness" of the crime: the rape and murder of small children. "The outrage of society follows, not because one wants to form a lynch party and destroy the person."[208] Leading abolitionists Arthur Maloney and G. Arthur Martin anticipated that people like LaMarsh would change their minds once the penal welfare system treated "the aggressive psychopath whose abnormality has led to murder" as a social resource. The partial moratorium Parliament had set would allow the "scientific study of the mind" to uncover the "physical and psychological" causes of such murders.[209] The abolitionists could celebrate a triumph. "Solid Majority – Noose Ban Gets Approval," the Ottawa *Journal* reported.[210] But the 1967 victory was undercut by the knowledge that the majority of Canadians remained in the retentionist camp.[211]

Epilogue

The Problem of Sex Murder in the Shadow of Abolition

When Parliament imposed a five-year moratorium on the death penalty in 1967, the prospect of abolition remained uncertain. After a second moratorium was imposed in 1972, the government's decision to abolish the death penalty in 1976 was an act of political will, not a response to popular demand, as opinion polls confirmed.[1] On the eve of the historic parliamentary vote, 79 per cent of Canadians supported the death penalty for persons who killed active duty police or guards, and 69 per cent believed that capital punishment was the appropriate penalty for persons found guilty of murdering "an innocent person."[2] Because opinion surveys did not define this victim category, it was left up to respondents to construe.[3] Canadian criminal law never specified the punishment of murder according to the victim's "innocence," with the exception of the crime of infanticide. Nevertheless, the history of sex murder convictions from Confederation to abolition shows that jurors, judges, cabinet ministers, and the bureaucrats who served them found murders of children that involved sexual assault especially heinous. Elderly, middle-aged, and young adult women – all of them white – also numbered among the victims of sex killers put to death. However, white male decision-makers' sympathy toward victims was never the sole trigger for severity. Animosity toward defendants factored into the conviction and punishment of sex killers, particularly men marginalized in the white Dominion. Yet, all men sentenced to death for sex murders, not just Indigenous and black defendants, faced a greater likelihood of execution than did those convicted of other forms of murder.

After abolition, sex murders continued to challenge Canada's policy-makers, and they tested politicians' resolve to do away with the death penalty.[4] As abolitionists celebrated the first anniversary of their victorious campaign, Emanuel Jaques, a boy who shone shoes in downtown Toronto, went missing.[5] The discovery of his body in quarters above a body rub parlour revealed he had died a horrible death. The murder site, on Yonge Street's "sin strip," fanned the flames of public anger as it did when John Benson's body turned up in Montreal's "jungle" in 1945.[6] Tips from members of the city's gay community helped lead police to arrest and charge four male suspects with first-degree murder.[7] The local press, led by the Toronto *Sun*, an anglophone heir to *Allô Police*, published graphic accounts of the boy's torture and murder, which encouraged demands that the culprits be executed. Politicians responded. In August 1977, Toronto MP Otto Jelinek, supported by fellow Conservative Eldon Woolliams (the Calgary MP directly involved in the controversial commutation of Ronald McCorquodale's death sentence), based their demand for reinstatement on "the horrendous episode in Toronto involving an innocent 12-year-old boy who became a victim of a sexual orgy." Speaking on behalf of their angry constituents, they called on the minister of justice to "introduce legislation which would make sexually related murders punishable by death."[8] The case remained a touchstone for retentionist resentment four years later, when Conservative MP John Albert Gamble tabled a non-confidence motion on the matter of capital punishment – abolished against the wishes of Canadians. He reminded his fellow MPs of the men who had "raped, drugged, strangled and then drowned a certain Emanuel Jaques." As one of the sex killers had reportedly stated, "in the event there had been capital punishment, he might well not have committed the offence."[9]

Not just one boy but many innocent victims died at the hands of the "Beast of BC," Clifford Olson, who was sentenced to life in prison in 1982 for eleven child sex murders. As had happened in other sex murder cases earlier in Canada's history, many found the man so reprehensible that they demanded he be put to death. However, the response to Olson's crimes also gave rise to groups representing victims and their families.[10] Police associations and guards' unions continued to demand restoration, but new victims' rights organizations joined them in the 1980s, most of them supporting the return of capital punishment. One of the organizations was founded by Gary Rosenfeldt,

Journal CP

'Bring back the rope'

Screams of 'bring back the rope' and 'kill them' filled the air Monday afternoon at Queen's Park as hundreds of Toronto area Portuguese rallied to protest the sex-slaying of 12-year-old Emanuel Jacques last week. The young Portuguese shoe-shine boy was lured to a sex shop on the Yonge Street strip and sexually abused before being drowned in a sink. Another mass demonstration calling for the death penalty for child slayers was being planned for Parliament Hill tonight.

Image E.1 "DEATH TO ALL SEX CRIMINALS" was the message protestors delivered to Parliament after the sex murder of Emanuel Jaques, aged twelve, in 1977. Anger over the case led some MPs to call for the death penalty's restoration. Ottawa *Journal*, 9 August 1977.

whose sixteen-year-old stepson, Daryn, was murdered by Olson. Victims of Violence in Alberta, Rosenfeldt's group, called for a return to the death penalty, which he predicted would discourage the potential for vigilantism. At the 1987 meeting of the Canadian Congress on Criminal Justice, he admitted: "I inquired at one point about getting a gun, and I was going to go to the courtroom and kill the man." If Olson were ever released, Rosenfeldt knew he'd want to "kill the son of a bitch."[11] Speaking for the Toronto chapter of Victims of Violence, Carol Cameron (whose son Mark was murdered in another case) estimated that 98 per cent of families who had lost loved ones to murder supported capital punishment. Another parent, Val Daniels, established Citizens for Capital Punishment in 1984, not because Olson had murdered her child but because she "thought about how those parents would feel, and I decided I favoured capital punishment and should do something about it."[12] The Conservatives' thumping win in the 1984 election opened up the possibility that criminals like Olson might face execution. In 1987, Prime Minister Brian Mulroney made good on his promise to allow a free vote on the death penalty.[13] Despite the bill's failure to win majority support in Parliament, it was not a defeat for the broader victims' rights movement, which continued to funnel fear and anger into support for capital punishment's return.[14]

Olson and his crimes resurfaced in 1997 because he exercised his right to apply for a judicial review of his parole eligibility.[15] The statute that replaced the death penalty with life imprisonment in 1976 included a clause (section 745.6 of the Criminal Code) that granted prisoners the "faint hope" of release after serving fifteen years of the mandatory twenty-five-year minimum term of imprisonment.[16] The prospect that Olson could re-traumatize his victims' families by conducting a parole hearing shocked and disgusted victims' rights groups, but they now had a powerful parliamentary ally in the right-wing populist Reform Party.[17] Led by Preston Manning, son of the Alberta premier who blasted the federal executive in 1960 for commuting McCorquodale's death sentence, Reformers and other law-and-order MPs demonstrated their parliamentary power by persuading the government to tighten parole regulations. The revised criteria for parole, passed in December 1996, denied multiple murderers' eligibility to apply for parole prior to serving their mandatory minimum term of punishment.[18] But the amendments were not retroactive, which meant Olson could indulge his faint hope of release. On 10 March 1997, a Reform MP moved that the House "urge the Liberal government to formally apologize" to the families of Olson's victims "for repeatedly refusing to repeal section 745 of the Criminal Code." Olson, and any other creatures like him, deserved no hope of release: "He is a predatory vulture, a slime bag, a scum bag of the lowest order."[19]

While Olson sat in prison concocting his parole application, the crimes of another sex murderer, Paul Bernardo, sent shockwaves across the country. Convicted in 1995 of two counts of murder – the sex torture and murder of teenagers Leslie Mahaffy and Kristen French, committed in league with his wife, Karla Homolka – Bernardo's long history of rape, abduction, and murder heightened fear and anger over sexual predators. Although this case did not initiate the move toward public safety as the key purpose of criminal justice, it added weight to it.[20] In 1977, immediately after the death penalty's abolition, the Criminal Code was revised to create a new definition of the "dangerous offender," and Bernardo became the 146th person sentenced as such to an indefinite term of imprisonment on top of his two life sentences for murder.[21] Despite the deletion of the term "sexual" from the definition of dangerousness in 1977, the vast majority of offenders designated as dangerous offenders after that point were persons sentenced for committing sexual offences.[22] As the Crown psychiatrist stated at the opening of Bernardo's dangerous offender hearing, "sexual sadism ... is extremely difficult to treat. I would think in the present state of knowledge, his conditions are irremediable."[23] When the Toronto *Star* reported the outcome of the 1995 hearing ("BERNARDO: JAILED FOREVER"), it made the 1950s, when the Favreau Report projected a new era of penal reform, look like a time of rosy optimism.

In the shadow of the death penalty's abolition, the principles of risk minimization and community protection effectively replaced the resort to capital punishment for sex killers.[24] By the time Paul Bernardo had served twenty-five years in prison, the faint hope clause had disappeared, removed from the Criminal Code by the Conservative government in 2011.[25] And the Parole Board was not about to veer from the course of risk minimization when Bernardo appeared before it in 2018 to assert that he was no longer dangerous. Officially, the board based its decision to deny Bernardo parole on the consensus that he is a psychopath and, consequently, unamenable to correction.[26] Evidently, the fields of psychiatry, psychology, and neurobiology, which originated in the late nineteenth century, had come no further in treating or curing sexual aggression, as the mid-twentieth-century abolitionists had envisioned. One of the psychiatrists who examined Bernardo prior to his trial, Dr. John Bradford, stated that the physical abnormalities in Bernardo's brain had led this outwardly normal man to commit his cruel and dehumanizing crimes: "He's not just evil ... People who have this problem have had their temporal lobe damaged in some way. There's something that's gone wrong."[27] Another Canadian expert on psychopathy had a different view of the prisoner, who exhibited a long history of sexual violence. According to psychology professor Dr. Robert D. Hare, "Bernardo was a cold-blooded predator

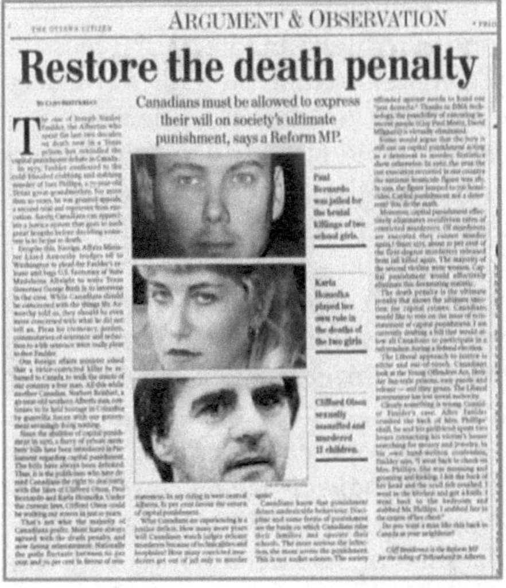

ARGUMENT & OBSERVATION

Restore the death penalty

Canadians must be allowed to express their will on society's ultimate punishment, says a Reform MP.

Paul Bernardo was jailed for the brutal killings of two school girls.

Karla Homolka played her own role in the deaths of the two girls.

Clifford Olson sexually assaulted and murdered 11 children.

Image E.2 Outrage over the sex murders of Clifford Olson, Paul Bernardo, and his co-accused, Karla Homolka, led to demands that Parliament respond to the will of the people, overwhelmingly supportive of capital punishment. Ottawa *Citizen*, 11 Dec 1998.

lacking in remorse. He is a perfect example of a psychopath."[28] Ironically, Bernardo did not fit Hare's widely used psychometric test for psychopathy, but the Parole Board was satisfied that he fit the criteria set by the Diagnostic and Statistical Manual of Mental Disorders (DSM).[29] Debates between experts over the motivations of sex killers are not new, nor is the ongoing tension between moral ("evil," "predator") and scientific explanations for homicidal sexual violence. Experts in the criminal mind have criss-crossed and clashed since the time of Confederation. Medical science continues to search for a definitive way to detect, treat, and cure violent sexual behaviour, and new diagnostic tools may yet lead to a breakthrough. But no matter what the outcome of this research, questions concerning individual will and criminal responsibility will continue to demand answers that scientists cannot provide.[30]

While proponents of capital punishment have often used revolting sex murders to support the death penalty's reinstatement, opponents have pointed to the dangers of wrongful convictions for sex murder when passions run high. In the mid-1960s, Isabel LeBourdais convinced many Canadians that the police, prosecutors, and courts exposed an innocent boy to public condemnation and severe sanctions, partly because Lynne Harper's murder was so disturbing and tragic. Since then, journalists, lawyers, and advocates for the poor have uncovered further miscarriages of justice in murder cases, many of them involving sex killings. In the lead-up to the parliamentary vote to restore the death penalty, one of the most effective lobby groups against the proposition was the Coalition Against the Return of the Death Penalty, an organization established by the Canadian Council of Churches and led by Reverend James Scott. One of its key strategies was to publicize cases of innocent people wrongly accused, tried, and punished. Journalist Michael Harris aided the cause in 1986 with the publication of *Justice Denied*, which exposed how a Mi'kmaq youth, Donald Marshall Jr., had been wrongfully convicted of murder in 1971 and incarcerated for eleven years.[31] One senator, struck by the book, commented: "That poor bugger would have been dead if there had been capital punishment."[32] Restorationists pointed out that Marshall was no sex slayer; besides, the courts had set him free. High-profile defence lawyer Edward "Eddie" Greenspan, a leading critic of the death penalty, interpreted Marshall's case differently: "Make no mistake about it. If you bring back the death penalty, there's no way you're only going to kill a Clifford Olson. Someday you're going to kill a Donald Marshall."[33]

In the 1980s and 1990s, campaigns for the exoneration of David Milgaard and Guy Paul Morin, both convicted of sex murders, added more faces to the concept of wrongful convictions by showing how easily police and prosecutors could turn innocent suspects into despised killers.[34] The legal team that took on Morin's case, successfully using DNA evidence to acquit him, transformed into an organization in 1996 called the Association in Defence of the Wrongfully Convicted (later Innocence Canada).[35] Among its subsequent causes was the successful campaign to overturn the 1990 conviction of Robert Baltovitch, the man convicted for the abduction and murder of Elizabeth Bain, allegedly one of Paul Bernardo's victims.[36] And publicity and legal advocacy on Steven Truscott's behalf finally paid off after numerous books and investigative exposés finally led his conviction to be overturned. In 2007, the Ontario Court of Appeal set aside his guilty verdict and pronounced it a "miscarriage of justice."[37]

COVER

A VOCAL OPPONENT

COVER

AN ARDENT ADVOCATE

Image E.3 On the eve of the parliamentary vote on the death penalty's reinstatement in 1987, Edward Greenspan depicted proponents of capital punishment as vindictive and ill-informed. Ontario Conservative MP Bill Domm countered that most Canadians considered the death penalty just and that releasing murderers on parole was riskier than the possibility of a wrongful conviction. *Maclean's*, 11 March 1987, 10–11.

Perpetrators, Victims, and the Imperative of History

When Canada looked close to restoring the death penalty in 1987, Greenspan reminded the public about the time when the country's convicted murderers had faced execution. From Confederation to the partial moratorium of 1967, a condemned person's likelihood of dying on the gallows was "a freakish lottery," albeit not random. The odds were skewed, Greenspan said, by "the temper of the judge, the skill of the defence counsel, the emotional climate, whether you're up against a tough prosecutor."[38] To this list, he could have added disagreements over psychological diagnoses and the gulf between legal and medical interpretations of criminal responsibility, especially significant in the executive's review of sex murderers' sentences. Underlying all of those factors were the substructures of white supremacy and class divisions, and the distrust of outsiders in a nation dominated by people of Anglo-Celtic heritage. As Greenspan observed, most persons executed in Canada were "minorities, the friendless and the defenceless."[39] When white jurors, judges, and prosecutors looked at defendants whose heritage differed from their own, they saw men whom they considered suspect by nature, and defence lawyers also deployed racist stereotypes to defend and seek mercy for their clients. The hobo, the drifter, the travelling show man, the rootless ex-soldier – these were the personae who tempted communities to take the law into their own hands, especially if they considered white victims of sex murders wholly innocent. Bureaucrats and politicians who reviewed capital cases also relied on typecasting to guide the cabinet toward or away from mercy. The explicitly moral language in prosecutors' and judges' statements, in press coverage of capital sex crime trials, and in bureaucrats' recommendations that the law take its course tapped deep emotions that led thirty-nine men to the gallows.

Steven Truscott escaped that fate thanks to executive clemency, criminal appeals, dedicated lawyers, and political pressure, not forensic evidence. He was also saved by his age. In 1966, former prime minister Diefenbaker admitted that if Truscott had been twenty years old at the time of his trial, "he would have been executed. We did not give reprieves for that type of offence."[40] How many more accused sex killers would have been found innocent, or guilty of manslaughter, or not criminally responsible if their cases had received a fraction of the attention that Truscott's attracted? And how many men, executed for sex murders, were wrongfully convicted? Almost every man found guilty was poor and poorly defended. Occasionally, indigent and stigmatized defendants benefitted from the services of skilled and diligent counsel, who stood behind their clients in trials and in appeals, working either pro bono or for skimpy recompense. Conservative leaders of the Canadian bar and ministers of justice insisted that every defendant, no matter how poor or friendless, was represented before the courts, and numerous lawyers did sacrifice a great deal, putting their health, safety, and reputations at risk to defend men despised for committing sex murders.[41] But even the most dedicated defenders had to pick and choose which defendants to represent at trial or in appeal. Canada's cherished ideals of equality before the law and the right to representation in criminal proceedings fail if tested against the shameful historical evidence that three men, hanged for committing sex murders, faced trial without a lawyer to defend them.

Since the 1950s, when Canada conducted its first major inquiry into the prospect of abolishing the death penalty, the issue has divided critics of capital punishment (who tar retentionists as bloodthirsty and vengeful) from supporters of the death penalty (who sling mud at abolitionists for caring more about criminals than victims).[42] Bob Ringma, the MP who introduced a restoration bill in 1996, proclaimed that "executing a murderer like Olson … is not half as repugnant as was the raping and clubbing to death of young boys and girls."[43] The Reform member had a point. One of the shortcomings of the movement that led to the death penalty's abolition was its elite leaders' reluctance to acknowledge the traumatic impact of murder on families and the communities who shared in their loss. Social scientists dismissed supporters of capital punishment as ignorant and driven by "primitive" emotions. Criminologist Thorsten Sellin, the most prominent debunker of the death penalty's deterrent value (and an expert whom Canadian officials consulted from the 1950s to the 1980s), stated that support for capital punishment was based on "tradition, and the fact that it is an emotional problem so heavily tinged with the primitive desire for vengeance and retribution that it is difficult to think about it rationally."[44] The founder of Citizens for Capital Punishment and many restorationists countered statistics with a moral declaration: "Vengeance is not a nasty word."[45]

One progressive outcome of Canada's drift away from offender-oriented correctionalism is the government's growing acknowledgment of the harm suffered by victims of crime. Policies have taken numerous forms, from sentencing and healing circles to financial compensation, including payments to the families of murdered individuals. Enacted in 2015, the federal Act for the Recognition of Victims' Rights recognized that "victims of crime and their families deserve to be treated with courtesy, compassion and respect, including respect for their dignity" and that "consideration of the rights of victims of crime is in the interest of the proper administration of justice."[46] One of its most notable spin-offs has been the recognition of victims of historic crimes through apologies, inquiries, and memorialization. In 2015, the newly elected Liberal government established a National Inquiry into Missing and Murdered Indigenous Women and Girls.[47] Initial work by the Native Women's Association of Canada through its Sisters in Spirit Initiative documented 600 cases of missing and/or murdered Indigenous women and girls from the mid-1970s to 2010, and subsequent research has uncovered far more.[48] The inquiry's final report concluded in 2019 that "thousands of women's deaths or disappearances have likely gone unrecorded over the decades."[49] Three of those women appear in the chapters of this book, along with other victims – women, girls, boys, and men – whose horrid deaths have, in most instances, faded from national memory. Some, such as Anglo-Celtic teenagers Jessie Keith in Ontario and Annie Kempton in Nova Scotia, have been remembered through monuments that depict them as innocent victims who died protecting their honour. Controversies over the memorialization of Robert Pickton's murder victims – scores of girls and women, the majority of them Indigenous, abducted from Vancouver's Downtown Eastside – demonstrate the challenges of respectfully acknowledging the suffering and loss of so many victims of sexually related homicides.[50] Despite these difficulties, ongoing civic engagement and dialogue, anchored in knowledge of the past, can achieve what monuments and government policies cannot accomplish. No victim deserves to be forgotten, irrespective of their status or those who grieve their loss.[51] But supporting the return of capital punishment is not the only way to remember, honour, and pay respect.[52]

Reflection on Sources and Methods

The collection of capital case files, held by the Library and Archives Canada (LAC), is the chief primary source for this study of the death penalty's administration in response to convictions for sex murders. A remarkably rich and complete body of records, it allows historians to trace the outcome of prosecuted cases in which persons were sentenced to death from Confederation to abolition.[1] In the early 1990s, archivists prepared a finding aid that catalogued several factors in individual cases, one of which was the "motive" of the murder. To determine motive, they read the judge's post-trial report and the Remission Branch's file summary, and the results of their review turned up forty-one cases of murderers motivated by rape or sexual assault.[2] Because they did not list a motive for every case, I looked for every murder in which the victim was a child unrelated to the perpetrator and every case in which a male was convicted of an unrelated female's murder. I excluded cases of men found guilty of murdering their wives because contemporaries did not view these cases as sex killings, even if victims suffered sexual trauma; furthermore, the criminal law exempted husbands from criminal liability for sexual violation in the period when the death penalty was still in effect.[3] After checking newspaper coverage of all the non-spousal cases, I found a further twenty sex murders, bringing the total to sixty-one.

Researchers' access to the contents of capital case files is subject to review under the Access to Information Act and the Privacy Act (ATIP).[4] There are few restrictions on documents and images in files produced prior to the mid-twentieth century, and trial transcripts are open for the entire period.[5] My accounts of cases in this book abide by ATIP restrictions and protocols. Although some historians anonymize the identity of perpetrators and victims, I have used the real names of all parties involved in capital cases cleared for research – officials (judges, lawyers, bureaucrats, politicians), defendants, victims, and members of the public. The names of persons sentenced to death for murder and their victims are published in the LAC's finding aid, now available online.[6] Even if their names were anonymized, the locations of murders and the dates of their arrests, trials, commutations, and executions would make their names, and those of their victims, accessible. The notoriety of murder, particularly cases that end in convictions and executions, leaves unerasable traces: reported cases, news stories, popular crime accounts, scholarly articles, and popular books. The digitization of primary sources, family history websites, and "true crime" online sources make it easier than ever before to trace the history of murder. It is impossible at this point to reel back the threads of evidence already in the public domain. No defendant convicted of murder and no victim in a prosecuted case was, is, or will be anonymous. Nevertheless, ethical considerations on the use of capital case files must be born in mind. I have refrained from disclosing information about family members of victims or perpetrators unless it appears in online sources or was pertinent to appeals. And there are no crime scene or morgue photos or images in this book. However, we cannot forget that jurors, lawyers, judges, bureaucrats, and cabinet ministers had no choice but to look at this disturbing evidence, which undoubtedly deepened their disgust toward the men found responsible for these crimes.

Although we can never state with certainty why some convicted murderers were executed while others were spared, the "conclusions" of cabinet meetings provide the strongest clues available to historians. Starting in 1944, these summary minutes and agendas provide extraordinary insight into the federal cabinet's business. Until the late 1950s, when Prime Minister John G. Diefenbaker's Conservatives formed government, the executive's consideration of capital cases was not recorded, and his unease over capital punishment and concern about possible wrongful convictions possibly prompted the shift. Thereafter, the Cabinet Conclusions document ministerial machinations over individual cases and their disputes over how they should exercise their executive powers. Archivist Michel Dufresne underscores the unique value of these records, originally stamped "SECRET." Their public disclosure has "democratic significance for the insight and transparency

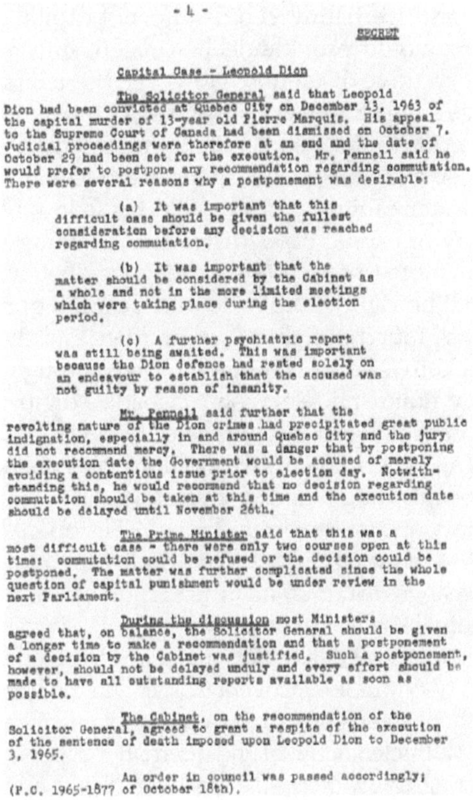

- 4 -

SECRET

Capital Case - Leopold Dion

The Solicitor General said that Leopold Dion had been convicted at Quebec City on December 13, 1963 of the capital murder of 13-year old Pierre Marquis. His appeal to the Supreme Court of Canada had been dismissed on October 7. Judicial proceedings were therefore at an end and the date of October 29 had been set for the execution. Mr. Pennell said he would prefer to postpone any recommendation regarding commutation. There were several reasons why a postponement was desirable:

(a) It was important that this difficult case should be given the fullest consideration before any decision was reached regarding commutation.

(b) It was important that the matter should be considered by the Cabinet as a whole and not in the more limited meetings which were taking place during the election period.

(c) A further psychiatric report was still being awaited. This was important because the Dion defence had rested solely on an endeavour to establish that the accused was not guilty by reason of insanity.

Mr. Pennell said further that the revolting nature of the Dion crimes had precipitated great public indignation, especially in and around Quebec City and the jury did not recommend mercy. There was a danger that by postponing the execution date the Government would be accused of merely avoiding a contentious issue prior to election day. Notwithstanding this, he would recommend that no decision regarding commutation should be taken at this time and the execution date should be delayed until November 26th.

The Prime Minister said that this was a most difficult case - there were only two courses open at this time: commutation could be refused or the decision could be postponed. The matter was further complicated since the whole question of capital punishment would be under review in the next Parliament.

During the discussion most Ministers agreed that, on balance, the Solicitor General should be given a longer time to make a recommendation and that a postponement of a decision by the Cabinet was justified. Such a postponement, however, should not be delayed unduly and every effort should be made to have all outstanding reports available as soon as possible.

The Cabinet, on the recommendation of the Solicitor General, agreed to grant a respite of the execution of the sentence of death imposed upon Leopold Dion to December 3, 1965.

An order in council was passed accordingly; (P.C. 1965-1877 of October 18th).

Image R.1 The cabinet postponed consideration of the "revolting" sex killer Léopold Dion's sentence because they anticipated a negative response to the prospect of commutation and because they planned soon to abolish the death penalty. LAC, R.G. 2, Privy Council Office, series A-5-a, Volume 6271, item 26999, 18 October 1965.

they make possible … [The conclusions] provide a revealing window into the workings of our democratic state."[7] Although the government began in the 1960s to tell the Canadian public the reasons behind their capital case decisions, official press releases never spelled out the opinions of various ministers or the tussles between them.[8] Previously hidden from public view, these minutes detail the final steps taken as the executive decided who lived and who died on the gallows.

In an ideal world, verbatim records of every capital case discussion since 1 July 1867 would provide deeper insight into the personalities and politics of executive discretion. However, these later summaries of cabinet meetings suggest that earlier ministers must also have differed over clemency prior to the 1950s. When parliamentarians first considered a private member's bill to abolish the death penalty in 1914, George P. Graham, a former cabinet minister, told his fellow MPs that he had found the review of capital cases distressful. Looking back, he felt he could have done more to convert his colleagues, "believing in my heart that the State had no right, morally, to inflict capital punishment."[9]

Most Canadians found out about sex murders and the trial and punishment of men convicted of committing them through the press, later supplemented by radio and television.[10] Canada's digitization of historic newspapers has been sluggish, but commercial services, academic subscriptions, provincial and county archival collections, plus online news archives provide an ever-expanding range of sources available to enrich the social and cultural history of crime and punishment.[11] Historians have long relied on newspapers to analyse representations of individual criminal cases; however, long-term changes in crime and justice reportage can also be discerned through longitudinal analysis of media accounts.[12] Using keyword searches (starting with victims' and defendants' names), I traced newspaper stories on each of the sixty-one cases.[13] Coverage is lean in the late nineteenth century; yet, even then, some sex murder cases (notably Chattelle's, the suspected "Ripper") attracted national and international press. In that case, the alleged murderer narrowly escaped a lynching. Newspapers did not document the lynching of any sex murderer, but several suspects, whites as well as blacks, came close to dying at the hands of white vigilantes.[14]

Official correspondence in the files of men who were not Anglo-Celtic is stained by ethnic and racial prejudice, and newspaper coverage of their murder cases shows that many strains of bigotry were pervasive in Canadian culture. Throughout the period when the death penalty was in effect, the mainstream press was unreservedly sexist, racist, xenophobic, classist, and homophobic. Lawyers who defended accused sex killers frequently claimed that pre-trial press coverage made it impossible for their clients to receive a fair trial, but most were ready to invoke racist stereotypes in an effort to win sympathy from jurors and the executive in clemency campaigns. Disparaging portrayals of suspects' psychological abnormalities also appeared in reportage of accused sex killers, and defenders as well as prosecutors appealed to popular understandings of madness. Sympathetic accounts that presented these criminals as afflicted and in need of treatment began to appear in the 1950s, primarily in cases involving young white defendants. However, across the century that followed Confederation, the "sex maniac" was a persistent figure of fear, anger, and revulsion. The presence of press clippings in many sex murder capital case files indicates that decision-makers considered the public's impression of sex murderers as they contemplated whether these men should live or die.

Quantitative and Qualitative Analysis

Although I have not discussed every sex murder in the text, the book draws on quantitative analysis of key characteristics in each of the sixty-one cases (the age, sex, race, and ethnicity of both offenders and victims). Connecting those data to case outcomes makes it possible to pose questions that cannot be asked of a single case.[15] To test the hypothesis that sex killers were judged more harshly than other capital offenders, I compared their execution rate with that of male murderers whose crimes involved robbery or burglary. I chose this cohort because they faced a high likelihood of execution. In 1954, future minister of justice E. Davie Fulton spoke in favour of whipping as a sentencing option for robbery and armed burglary, because those crimes (along with incest, rape, and indecent assault) had "some element of horribleness, something about [them] which is disgusting or particularly reprehensible."[16] In his testimony before the Joint Committee on Corporal and Capital Punishment, the sitting minister of justice, Stuart Garson, agreed. Since these offences were "planned and premeditated," it was appropriate that "such types of murder will deserve a lower rate of commutation generally." Like sex killers, armed burglars who killed for gain were public menaces.[17] Yet, aside from the late 1940s and early 1950s, sex murderers were executed at a higher rate, and this severity gap was statistically significant.[18]

Statistical analysis also confirms that youth – principally the age of the offender – was a significant factor in sex murder case outcomes. Because the data set is small, Fisher's exact test, rather than Pearson chi-square tests, was conducted with cross-tabulations of offenders' age categories. The outcome of murder cases (adult/youth) was statistically significant, confirming that men twenty-one years of age and over were more likely than youth to be executed for sex murders.[19] This result confirms that uneasiness over the execution of young persons worked in favour of persons sentenced to death as teenagers from the late nineteenth century onward, despite significant changes in understandings of psychosocial development.[20] The same test involving victims (child/not child) determined, surprisingly, that men convicted of murders of adults were more likely to be executed than child sex killers; however, this finding must be considered in light of the higher proportion of adult victims in the earlier decades, when commutations and successful appeals were less frequent. It is also the case that many of the males convicted of child murders were themselves youths. And finally, no matter what the statistics reveal, they can never capture the impact of a sex murder case on loved ones, communities, courts, or the decision-makers who reviewed capital case files in their Ottawa quarters.

The deep reading of each case file, down to the marginalia on transcripts and letters, confirms that sex murder cases generated strong emotions as they brought together a distinctive cluster of individuals in traumatic circumstances. Official and unofficial actors contributed to case outcomes, operating within the contours of religion, morality, politics, law, and culture. These sixty-one cases, read together, reveal themes that cannot be analysed quantitatively: the characterization of victims and offenders; the quality of defence counsel at trial and after conviction; the degree and nature of violence perpetrated; the prosecutorial and judicial construction of defendants' culpability; the impact of psychiatric expertise; the terms in which outsiders were identified; the influence of top clerks in cueing cabinet decisions; the shifting provisions for legal appeal; and the changing politics of the death penalty.

Every homicide involving sexual motives or abuse put a unique spin on the larger challenge of criminal justice: how to ensure public safety and hold offenders to account, while protecting the rights of the accused and continuing to seek effective means to deter and treat violent sexual offending. A handful of judges and lawyers appeared in more than one sex murder case, and many officers of the law found them hard to forget. On his retirement, the judge who sentenced Léopold Dion to death recalled he had wept in court over "toutes les horreurs" the defendant had committed, his "sadisme," and most of all, the "souffrances et .... l'angoisse des enfants."[21] By contrast, accomplished Crown attorney William B. Common boasted that one of his signal accomplishments was to convince the Supreme Court to restore the conviction of Robert Fitton for the sex murder of Linda Lampkin.[22] Public opinion sometimes swayed in a convicted man's favour; however, across the nineteenth and twentieth centuries, most Canadians felt as Common did: the death penalty was the appropriate punishment for murder. Commutations of convicted sex killers frequently provoked protest, but no execution did.

Notes

1. The Politics of the Death Penalty and the Problem of Sex Murder

1 Canada followed the common law's determination of seven years as the age of criminal responsibility, and it was not raised (to twelve) until 1984. Anthony N. Doob and Michael Tonry, "Varieties of Youth Justice," *Crime and Justice: A Review of Research* 31 (2004): 1–20, 6. Common law doctrine also determined that people unable to understand the nature of criminal charges against them or to participate in their defence could not be tried. Trial judges could also assess the mental competence of defendants during the course of criminal proceedings. Paul S. Lindsay, "Fitness to Stand Trial in Canada: An Overview in Light of the Recommendations of the Law Reform Commission of Canada," *Criminal Law Quarterly* 19, no. 3–4 (September 1977): 303–48, 326.

2 The five-year trial of abolition limited the death penalty to the murder of peace on-duty police and prison, parole, and probation officers. C.H.S. Jayewardene, "The Canadian Movement against the Death Penalty," *Canadian Journal of Criminology and Corrections* 14, no. 4 (1972): 366–90, 337. Jayewardene described the amendment as a "compromise between the strong retentionist and abolitionist emotions" (373).

3 The Library and Archives Canada (LAC) lists 1,533 capital case files. Lorraine Gadoury and Antonio Lechasseur, *Persons Sentenced to Death in Canada, 1867–1976: An Inventory of Case Files in the Fonds of the Department*

of Justice (Ottawa: National Archives of Canada, 1994). Ken Leyton-Brown found that one case involved a man executed prior to Confederation; another one (coincidentally the first man executed for sex murder) appears in two separate files. Because several rape cases are missing, the total is possibly as high as 1,540, of whom 704 were executed. Leyton-Brown, *The Practice of Execution in Canada* (Vancouver: UBC Press, 2010), 163n51.

4 This number was determined with the aid of the LAC's guide to capital cases. It was supplemented by searches of primary and secondary sources. See the Reflection on Sources for a full explanation of case criteria and selections.

5 Michael Petrunik, "The Hare and the Tortoise: Dangerousness and Sex Offender Policy in the United States and Canada," *Canadian Journal of Criminology and Criminal Justice* 45, no. 1 (2003): 43–72; Monica K. Miller, Timothy Griffin, Samantha S. Clinkinbeard, and Rebecca M. Thomas, "The Psychology of AMBER Alert: Unresolved Issues and Implications," *The Social Science Journal* 46, no. 1 (2009): 111–23; Julian V. Roberts, "Listening to the Crime Victim: Evaluating Victim Input at Sentencing and Parole," *Crime and Justice* 38, no. 1 (2009): 347–412.

6 Since the abolition of the death penalty, polling has consistently shown highest support for capital punishment's reintroduction for sex murderers, child murderers, serial killers, and terrorists. Andrew S. Thompson, "Uneasy Abolitionists: Canada, the Death Penalty, and the Importance of International Norms, 1962–2005," *Journal of Canadian Studies* 42, no. 3 (Fall 2008): 172–92. This view is not exclusive to Canada. See Lizzie Seal, *Capital Punishment in Twentieth Century Britain: Audience, Justice, Memory* (London: Routledge, 2014), 148–9.

7 In 2016, an Abacus poll found that 59 per cent of Americans and 58 per cent of Canadians supported the death penalty. Bruce Anderson and David Coletto, "Canadians' Moral Compass Set Differently from That of Our Neighbours to the South," Abacus Data, 9 July 2016, https://abacusdata.ca/canadians-moral-compass-set-differently-from-that-of-our-neighbours-to-the-south/.

8 David F. Greenberg and Valerie West, "Siting the Death Penalty Internationally," *Law and Social Inquiry* 33, no. 2 (Spring 1998): 295–348; Robert M. Bohm, *The Death Penalty Today* (London: Routledge, 2017); Austin Sarat and Christian Boulanger, *The Cultural Lives of Capital Punishment: Comparative Perspectives* (Stanford, CA: Stanford University Press, 2005).

9 Douglas Hay, "Writing about the Death Penalty," *Legal History* 10, no. 1–2 (2010): 35–51, 51.

10 Stuart Banner, *The Death Penalty: An American History* (Cambridge, MA: Harvard University Press, 2002), 267–75. For a robust critique of the 1976 ruling, see David Garland, *Peculiar Institution: America's Death Penalty in an Age of Abolition* (Cambridge, MA: Harvard University Press, 2010), 263–6. As of June 2020, 1,518 individuals had been put to death since 1977, although the annual rate has declined since the turn of the century. Death Penalty Information Centre, accessed 11 July 2019, https://deathpenaltyinfo.org/executions/execution-database.

11 Jennifer Carter, "Capital Punishment: A Struggle to Satisfy Evolving Standards of Decency – Reviewing the Debate in the United States and Canada," *Southwestern Journal of International Law* 17, no. 2 (2011): 237–58.

12 Ezzat A. Fattah, "Canada's Successful Experience with the Abolition of the Death Penalty," *Canadian Journal of Criminology* 25, no. 4 (October 1983): 421–32. Fattah's review of the arguments leading to abolition included no reference to race.

13 Jayewardene, "The Canadian Movement against the Death Penalty"; Carolyn Strange, "The Lottery of Death: Capital Punishment, 1867–1976," *Manitoba Law Journal* 23 (1995): 594–619, 617–18.

14 Economist Kenneth L. Avio was the first to use statistical analysis to prove the racial, ethnic, and class biases of capital justice. Avio, "The Quality of Mercy: Exercise of the Royal Prerogative in Canada," *Canadian Public Policy/Analyse de Politiques* 13, no. 3 (September 1987): 366–79, 369–70. See also Avio, "Capital Punishment in Canada: Statistical Evidence and Constitutional Issues," *Canadian Journal of Criminology* 30, no. 4 (October 1988): 331–50.

15 Canada, "An Act to Amend the Criminal Code," *Statutes of Canada*, 1948, c. 39. On the gender specificity of the perpetrator in this statute and the capital definition it amended, see Emma Cunliffe, "Infanticide: Legislative History and Current Questions," *Criminal Law Quarterly* 55, no. 1–2 (2009): 94–119.

16 John M. Beattie stressed the significance of condemned men's characters (as presented and appraised) in determining the exercise of mercy. Beattie, *Crime and the Courts in England, 1660–1800* (Princeton, NJ: Princeton University Press, 1986), 440–2.

17 Avio, "The Quality of Mercy," 369. The proportion of convicted sex murderers executed (63.9 per cent), compared to the proportion of males convicted of robbery and burglary murders (54.3 per cent), was substantial, though not statistically significant. Pearson's chi-square test determined a difference in proportions of .079 (p=.169).

18 On the centrality of the criminal law to white supremacy in Canada, see Barrington Walker, ed., *The History of Immigration and Racism in Canada: Essential Readings* (Toronto: Canadian Scholars, 2008) and Constance Backhouse, *Colour Coded: A Legal History of Racism in Canada, 1900–50* (Toronto: University of Toronto Press for the Osgoode Society for Canadian Legal History, 1999). More recent studies connect Canadian white nationalism to transnational histories of imperialism and colonization. See Laura Madokoro, Francine McKenzie, and David Meren, eds., *Dominion of Race: Rethinking Canada's International History* (Vancouver: UBC Press, 2017).

19 Lawrence Lessig, "Social Meaning and Social Norms," *University of Pennsylvania Law Review* 144, no. 5 (May 1996): 2181–90. For a full explanation of the selection of murder cases based on these broad criteria, see the Reflection on Sources and Methods.

20 In the 1970s, feminist rape law reformers campaigned against the strict statutory definition of penetration and criticized judges' tendency to emphasize the need for physical evidence of resistance. Canadian law moved toward a broader definition of sexual assault of males and females over the 1970s and 1980s. Constance Backhouse, *Carnal Crimes: Sexual Assault Law in Canada, 1900–1975* (Toronto: Irwin Law, 2008), 5.

21 Canada, "An Act to Amend the Criminal Code," *Statutes of Canada*, 1948, c. 39, s. 1054A. On the factors leading to the passage of the criminal sexual psychopath amendment, see Patrick Brode, "'Perverts a Menace': The Development of the Criminal Sexual Psychopath Offence, 1948," in *Essays in the History of Canadian Law, Volume X: A Tribute to Peter N. Oliver*, ed. Jim Phillips, R. Roy McMurtry, and John T. Saywell (Toronto: University of Toronto Press for the Osgoode Society for Canadian Legal History, 2008), 107–28.

22 On the punitive consequences of moral revulsion, see John Douard, "Sex Offender as Scapegoat: The Monstrous Other Within," *New York Law School Law Review* 53 (2008): 31–52, 36–7.

23 Canada, *Report of a Committee Appointed to Inquire into the Principles and Procedures Followed in the Remission Service of the Department of Justice of Canada* (Ottawa: Queen's Printer, 1956), 28.

24 An Act for the Union of Canada, Nova Scotia, and New Brunswick, and the Government Thereof; and for Purposes Connected Therewith, 1867, 30–1 Vict., c. 3 (UK). On the tensions between the federal and provincial governments over the pardon power, see M. Keith Evans, "The Prerogative of Pardon in Canada, Its Development 1864–1894" (master's thesis, Carleton University, 1971).

25 Barbara J. Messamore, "'The Line Over Which He Must Not Pass': Defining the Office of Governor General, 1878," *Canadian Historical Review* 86, no. 3 (2005): 453–83; Marcella Firmini and Jennifer Smith, "The Crown in Canada," in *The Oxford Handbook of the Canadian Constitution*, ed. Peter Oliver, Patrick Macklem, and Nathalie Des Rosiers (New York: Oxford University Press, 2017), 129–50, 137; Norman Mclean Rogers, "Cabinet Government in Canada," *The Canadian Bar Review* 11, no. 1 (1933): 1–17, 5.
26 Jonathan Swainger, *The Canadian Department of Justice and the Completion of Confederation, 1867–78* (Vancouver: UBC Press, 2000), 56–78.
27 Swainger, *The Canadian Department of Justice*, 39.
28 This observation has been made by other historians who have examined capital cases. See, for instance, Robert J. Sharpe, *The Lazier Murder: Prince Edward County, 1884* (Toronto: University of Toronto Press for the Osgoode Society for Canadian Legal History, 2011).
29 The memo referred to the rape and strangulation murder of two sisters, Eliza and Mary McMonagle (aged twelve and thirteen), in L'Orignal, ON. Power to Minister of Justice, 21 May 1891. Larocque, Volume 1427, file 249A. Narcisse Larocque was executed for the crime on 4 June 1891.
30 Like Power, Côté was a legal officer, second in command until Power retired in 1912. Clarke was appointed the remission registrar in 1911, after serving as the minister of justice's private secretary; he was appointed chief of the Remission Service in 1918, after Côté's death. LAC, R.G. 2, Privy Council Office, Series A-1-a, items 403, 806.
31 Gallagher began in the Department of Justice in 1915 at the age of twenty-nine as a clerk. He became a legal officer in the branch in 1918, serving under Clarke. Canada, Secretary of State, *The Civil Service List of Canada, 1918* (Ottawa: King's Printer, 1919), 191.
32 Joseph Henri Armand Proulx, convicted of the murder of Barbara Smith in 1945, was seventeen years old at the time of the crime; Francis Sykes, also seventeen, was spared after his conviction for the murder of Laura Grant in 1950.
33 Rob Canton, "Crime, Punishment and the Moral Emotions: Righteous Minds and the Attitudes toward Punishment," *Punishment and Society* 17, no. 1 (2015): 54–72. According to Canton, anger, indignation, and resentment over serious harms produce the moral imperative to censure.
34 On the connection between dehumanization and punitiveness, see Milica Vasiljevic and G. Tendayi Viki, "Dehumanization, Moral Disengagement, and Public Attitudes to Crime and Punishment," in *Humanness and Dehumanization*, ed. Paul G. Bain, Jeroen Vaes, and Jacques-Philippe Leyens (New York: Psychology Press, 2014), 137–54.

35 Most established churches upheld the death penalty's legitimacy, but those involved in prison chaplaincy were more likely to favour abolition from the nineteenth century. Harry Potter, *Hanging in Judgment: Religion and the Death Penalty in England from the Bloody Code to Abolition* (London: SCM Press, 1993). For an analysis that places greater weight on non-conformists (especially Quakers), Jews, and individual believers, see Hugh McLeod, "God and the Gallows: Christianity and Capital Punishment in the Nineteenth and Twentieth Centuries," *Studies in Church History* 40 (2004): 330–56.

36 Carolyn Strange, "The Undercurrents of Penal Culture Punishment of the Body in Mid-Twentieth-Century Canada," *Law and History Review* 19, no. 2 (Summer 2001): 343–85, 375–6. On greater support for the death penalty among Catholics by the mid-twentieth century, see Ezzat A. Fattah, *The Canadian Public and the Death Penalty: A Study of a Social Attitude* (Burnaby, BC: Department of Criminology, Simon Fraser University, 1976), 11–13, 27–9. On the broader history of Catholic attitudes toward capital punishment, see Cardinal Avery Dulles, "Catholicism and Capital Punishment," in *Moral Issues and Christian Responses*, 8th ed., ed. Patricia Beattie Jung and L. Shannon Jung (Minneapolis, MN: Fortress Press, 2012), 410–15.

37 Although the first parliamentary campaigner against the death penalty, Robert Bickerdike, was a Liberal, the Co-operative Commonwealth Federation and its successor, the New Democratic Party, both left of centre, opposed the death penalty from the 1930s. On party politics and the death penalty, see David B. Chandler, *Capital Punishment in Canada: A Sociological Study of a Repressive Law* (Ottawa: Carleton University Institute of Canadian Studies, 1976).

38 The phrase first appeared in Michel Foucault's *Discipline and Punish: The Birth of the Prison*, trans. Alan Sheridan (New York: Vintage Books, 1977). Most histories of the death penalty focus only on executions. Frank W. Anderson, *A Concise History of Capital Punishment in Canada* (Calgary: Frontier Publishing, 1973); Chandler, *Capital Punishment in Canada*; Alan Hustak, *They Were Hanged* (Toronto: Lorimer, 1987); Frank W. Anderson, *A Dance with Death: Canadian Women at the Gallows, 1754 to 1954* (Saskatoon: Fifth House, 1996); Robert J. Hoshowsky, *The Last to Die: Ronald Turpin, Arthur Lucas, and the End of Capital Punishment* (Toronto: Dundurn Press, 2007); Jeffrey Pfeifer and Kenneth Leyton-Brown, *Death by Rope: An Anthology of Canadian Executions* (Regina: Centax Books, 2007); Leyton-Brown, *The Practice of Execution*; Lorna Poplak, *Drop Dead: A Horrible History of Hanging in Canada* (Toronto: Dundurn Press, 2017); Donald

Fyson, "The Spectacle of State Violence: Executions in Quebec, 1759–1872," in *Violence, Order, and Unrest: A History of British North America, 1749–1876*, ed. Elizabeth Mancke, Jerry Bannister, Denis McKim, and Scott W. See (Toronto: University of Toronto Press, 2019), 383–407.

39 See, especially, Dimitri Anastakis, *Death in the Peaceable Kingdom: Canadian History since 1867 through Murder, Execution, Assassination, and Suicide* (Toronto: University of Toronto Press, 2010); and Mancke et al. *Violence, Order, and Unrest*.

40 Works that focus on discretion and clemency include Carolyn Strange, ed., *Qualities of Mercy: Justice, Punishment and Discretion* (Vancouver: UBC Press, 1996); Avio, "The Quality of Mercy," 366–79. Works that incorporate the analysis of mercy include F. Murray Greenwood and Beverley Boissery, *Uncertain Justice: Canadian Women and Capital Punishment, 1754–1953* (Toronto: Dundurn Press for the Osgoode Society for Canadian Legal History, 2000); Kimberley White, *Negotiating Responsibility: Law, Murder, and States of Mind* (Vancouver: UBC Press, 2007); Lesley Erickson, *Westward Bound: Sex, Violence, and the Law, and the Making of a Settler Society* (Vancouver: UBC Press for the Osgoode Society for Canadian Legal History, 2011); Barrington Walker, *Race on Trial: Black Defendants in Ontario's Criminal Courts, 1858–1958* (Toronto: University of Toronto Press for the Osgoode Society for Canadian Legal History, 2010); and Teresa Iacobelli, *Death or Deliverance: Canadian Courts Martial in the Great War* (Vancouver: UBC Press, 2013).

41 For influential studies of royal mercy, see Natalie Zemon Davis, *Fiction in the Archives: Pardon Tales and Their Tellers in Sixteenth-Century France* (Stanford, CA: Stanford University Press, 1987) and V.A.C. Gatrell, *The Hanging Tree: Execution and the English People* (Oxford: Oxford University Press, 1994), 543–65.

42 In modern criminal justice systems, displays of emotion were "held in check and retracted," not eliminated. John Pratt, "Emotive and Ostentatious Punishment: Its Decline and Resurgence in Modern Society," *Punishment and Society* 2, no. 4 (2000): 417–39, 418. Pratt draws on sociologist Norbert Elias's concept of the "civilizing process." On the limits of civilization in conquering punitiveness, see Robert Van Krieken, "The Barbarism of Civilization: Cultural Genocide and the 'Stolen Generations,'" *British Journal of Sociology* 50, no. 2 (1999): 297–315. For a critique of the delayed attention to emotions in criminological research, see Willem de Haan and Ian Loader, "On the Emotions of Crime, Punishment and Social Control," *Theoretical Criminology* 6, no. 3 (2002): 234–53.

43 David Garland, *Punishment and Welfare: A History of Penal Strategies* (Aldershot, UK: Gower, 1985). Garland's *Punishment and Modern Society: A Study of Social Theory* (Chicago: University of Chicago Press, 1990) has one index entry for capital punishment: "abolition of." John Pratt traces the abolition of public executions and the end of hangings, but emphasizes the "civilization" of punishment in his *Punishment and Civilization: Penal Tolerance and Intolerance in Modern Society* (London: Sage, 2002).

44 In Canada, this concern prompted an inquiry in 1937 on the prospect of replacing hanging by more efficient and less painful means of execution. Strange, "The Undercurrents of Penal Culture," 345–50.

45 Canada, House of Commons, *Debates*, 11 April 1924, 1285.

46 De Haan and Loader, "On the Emotions of Crime," 244; Ian Loader, "Playing with Fire? Democracy and the Emotions of Crime and Punishment," in *Emotions, Crime and Justice*, ed. Susanne Karstedt, Ian Loader, and Heather Strang (Oxford, UK: Hart Publishing, 2011), 347–62, 351.

47 Susan Bandes, "Repellent Crimes and Rational Deliberation: Emotion and the Death Penalty," *Vermont Law Review* 33, no. 3 (Spring 2009): 488–518. David Garland underlines that each capital murder case "begins with an atrocious crime that ignites community anger and demands a retributive response." Garland, *Peculiar Institution*, 287.

48 Canton, "Crime, Punishment and the Moral Emotions," 61.

49 Chandler, *Capital Punishment in Canada*, 17–19.

50 Much of this literature emerged out of the anti-psychiatry movement of the 1960s and 1970s. See, for instance, Garland, *Punishment and Welfare*; David J. Rothman, *Conscience and Convenience: The Asylum and Its Alternatives in Progressive America* (Boston: Little, Brown, 1980); Dorothy E. Chunn, John McLaren, and Robert J. Menzies, eds., *Regulating Lives: Historical Essays on the State, Society, the Individual, and the Law* (Vancouver: UBC Press, 2002).

51 Don Peacock, "What Makes a Man Kill?" *Maclean's* 73, no. 4 (13 February 1960): 13–15, 53–6, 54. At that point in his career, Cathcart had provided his expert opinion in thirty cases of men condemned to death.

52 Fattah, "Canada's Successful Experience with the Abolition of the Death Penalty," 429–30, 432.

53 Canada, "An Act Respecting Procedure in Criminal Cases, and Other Matters Relating to Criminal Law," *Statues of Canada*, 1869, section 107. This section also permitted the judge (or another judge of the same court) to reprieve the sentence of death in any case to allow "the consideration of the case by the Crown." The provision of the transcript was not

statutory but an expected part of the package. Jonathan Swainger, "A Distant Edge of Authority: Capital Punishment and the Prerogative of Mercy in British Columbia, 1872–1880," in *Essays in the History of Canadian Law, Volume VI: British Columbia and the Yukon*, ed. Hamar Foster and John McLaren (Toronto: University of Toronto Press for the Osgoode Society for Canadian Legal History, 1995), 204–42, 209.

54 LAC, R.G. 13, Auger, Volume 1411, file 72a. Auger's name also appears in the file as Osier and Ozier. Hereafter, references to capital case files will appear with convict's last name and volume and file numbers.

55 Justice Alan Manson to Secretary of State, 23 March 1950, in Ducharme, Volume 1688, part 1.

56 Jenkins, Volume 1454, part 2. Chief Justice Gordon Hunter applied for a new trial, contending that the verdict had gone against the weight of evidence, but the application was denied. The court's decision appears in Jenkins's file. On criticism of Hunter's conduct in the trial, see Hamar Foster and John McLaren, "For the Better Administration of Justice: The Court of Appeal for British Columbia, 1910–2010," *BC Studies* 162 (Summer 2009): 5–24, 13–14.

57 Pierre M. Côté to Minister of Justice, 9 January 1914, in Taylor, Volume 1484, file 500a. Côté, Augustus Power's immediate successor, was the clerk responsible for summarizing Taylor's file.

58 The first tests to distinguish animal from human blood were conducted in 1901. Toronto established a fingerprint division in 1911, just after the Dominion Police established a Criminal Identification Bureau. Marjorie Freeman Campbell, *A Century of Crime: The Development of Crime Detection Methods in Canada* (Toronto: McClelland & Stewart, 1970), 138–9, 189; Greg Marquis, *Policing Canada's Century: A History of the Canadian Association of Chiefs of Police* (Toronto: University of Toronto Press for the Osgoode Society for Canadian Legal History, 1993), 71.

59 The first forensic laboratory in North America (Laboratoire provincial de recherches médico-légales) was set up in Montreal by the government of Quebec in 1914, led by Dr. Wilfrid Derome. Ontario followed in 1932. Jacques Côté, *Wilfrid Derome, expert en homicides: récit biographique* (Montreal: Boréal, 2003).

60 This literature is extensive. For an excellent feminist resource that tracks historical and contemporary data concerning sexual violence and homicide, see Canadian Femicide Observatory for Justice and Accountability, https://femicideincanada.ca/.

61 Government of Canada, National Inquiry into Missing and Murdered Indigenous Women and Girls, *Reclaiming Power and Place: The Final Report*

of the National Inquiry into Missing and Murdered Indigenous Women and Girls, vols. 1a and 1b (Ottawa: Queen's Printer, 2019).

62 Marc Riedel, "Stranger Violence: Perspectives, Issues, and Problems," *The Journal of Criminal Law and Criminology* 78, no. 2 (1987): 223–58, 231; Wendy C. Regoeczi, Leslie W. Kennedy, and Robert A. Silverman, "Uncleared Homicides: A Canada/United States Comparison," *Homicide Studies* 4, no. 2 (May 2000): 135–61, 137; Thomas S. Alexander and Charles F. Wellford, "Solving Homicides Trends, Causes, and Ways to Improve," in *The Handbook of Homicide*, ed. Fiona Brookman, Edward R. Maguire, and Mike Maguire (Chichester, UK: Wiley & Sons, 2017), 533–47, 541.

63 In eleven of the thirty-six child cases, victims were males. In the case of Ronald Sears, ultimately convicted of manslaughter after a successful appeal, the victims were adult males. On the role of homophobia in the Sears case, see Patrick Brode, *The Slasher Killings: A Canadian Sex-Crime Panic, 1945–1946* (Detroit, MI: Wayne State University Press, 2009).

64 On the familial power relations that discouraged the exposure of father-daughter incest in rural Quebec, see Marie-Aimée Cliche, "Un secret bien gardé: l'inceste dans la société traditionelle québécoise, 1858–1938," *Revue d'histoire de l'Amérique française* 50, no. 2 (1996): 201–26. On the association of rural locales with incest in Ontario, see Joan Sangster, "Masking and Unmasking the Sexual Abuse of Children: Perceptions of Violence against Children in 'the Badlands' of Ontario, 1916–1930," *Journal of Family History* 25, no. 4 (October 2000): 504–26.

65 On homophobia in Canadian history, see Thomas E. Warner, *Never Going Back: A History of Queer Activism in Canada* (Toronto: University of Toronto Press, 2002), 3–16; Patrice Corriveau, *Judging Homosexuals: A History of Gay Persecution in Quebec and France*, trans. Käthe Roth (Vancouver: UBC Press, 2011); Paul Jackson, *One of the Boys: Homosexuality in the Military During World War II* (Montreal: McGill-Queen's University Press, 2004), 110–46; Gary Kinsman and Patricia Gentile, *The Canadian War on Queers: National Sexuality as Sexual Regulation* (Vancouver: UBC Press, 2010); Steven Maynard, "On the Case of the Case: The Emergence of the Homosexual as a Case History in the Early Twentieth Century," in *On the Case Explorations in Social History*, ed. Franca Iacovetta and Wendy Mitchinson (Toronto: University of Toronto Press 1998), 65–87.

66 The LAC's database of capital case files confirms that Ontario courts produced more convictions for capital crime than any other from Confederation to abolition. Quebec's execution rate exceeded that of Ontario's in the 1920s and 1930s, but only one of the prisoners hanged in those decades (Alexandre Lavallée, 1927) was executed for a sex murder.

On execution rate comparisons, see Donald Fyson, "Penal Justice and State Violence in Quebec, 1760–1960" (unpublished paper, April 2016). I am grateful for Don's permission to refer to his research in progress.

67 The Ontario Provincial Police force was established in 1909, and by 1922 it employed 195 officers, working in nine divisions across the province. Dahn D. Higley, *O.P.P.: The History of the Ontario Provincial Police Force* (Toronto: Queen's Printer, 1984). William B. Common and James C. McRuer, both of whom prosecuted in high-profile Ontario sex murder cases, were nation-leading authorities on criminal prosecution. Christopher Moore, *The Law Society of Upper Canada and Ontario's Lawyers, 1797–1997* (Toronto: University of Toronto Press for the Osgoode Society for Canadian Legal History, 1997), 274–5, 283–7.

68 Elise Chenier, *Strangers in Our Midst: Sexual Deviancy in Postwar Ontario* (Toronto: University of Toronto Press, 2008), 28–34.

69 Successful appeals saved four men convicted of child murders, and commutations spared five youths sentenced to death for child murders perpetrated when they were under the age of twenty-one.

70 News coverage of sex murder cases came mainly from the government's clippings services, but also from members of the public. Clerks may also have cut clippings from their own copies of newspapers.

71 Many early radio stations were owned by newspapers. William J. Buxton and Catherine McKercher, "Newspapers, Magazines and Journalism in Canada: Toward a Critical Historiography," *Acadiensis* 28, no. 1 (Autumn 1998): 103–26, 110. On the rise of crime news content in the twentieth century, see Gene Allen, *Making National News: A History of Canadian Press* (Toronto: University of Toronto Press, 2013), 260. On radio and television, see Canadian Communications Foundation: History of Canadian Broadcasting (website), https://www.broadcasting-history.ca.

72 Jane Caputi claims that the "Ripper" murders inspired subsequent sex killers. Caputi, *The Age of Sex Crime* (Bowling Green, OH: Bowling Green State University Press, 1987). However, she discounts the growing capacity to detect stranger homicides. On the centrality of the "Ripper" in building the concept of sexual sadism, see Angus McLaren, *Trials of Masculinity: Policing Sexual Boundaries, 1870–1930* (Chicago: University of Chicago Press, 1997), 170–1.

73 Toronto *Globe*, 4 July 1896.

74 Toronto *Daily Star*, 9 August 1920.

75 The paper regularly published macabre photographs of victims and details of crimes. André Beaulieu and Jean Hamelin, *La presse québécoise: des origines à nos jours*, tome 8, *1945–1954* (Québec: Presses de l'Université

Laval, 1987), 238. A spicy tabloid, *Le Petit Journal*, published murder stories from 1926, but not in as explicit detail as *Allô Police*. For a detailed analysis of the paper's origins and impact, see Mathieu-Olivier Côté, "La représentation du crime dans la press écrite québécoise: Le cas d'*Allô-Police*" (master's thesis, University of Laval, 2002).

76 The first to expose the Truscott conviction as a miscarriage of justice was Isabel LeBourdais, *The Trial of Steven Truscott* (Toronto: McClelland & Stewart, 1966). Since then, the Truscott case has inspired hundreds of articles, numerous books, documentaries, and works of fiction.

77 In 2008, the government of Ontario subsequently granted Truscott $6.5 million in compensation for suffering a miscarriage of justice. Sydney L. Robins, QC, authored the report that led to the award, which included the recommendation that Mrs. Marlene Truscott be granted $100,000 to compensate her for her efforts to clear her husband's name.

78 Compassion toward the condemned was more openly expressed when executions were public. See Gatrell, *The Hanging Tree*, 325–33. On demonstrations of compassion toward capital offenders in modern Britain, see Lizzie Seal, *Capital Punishment in Twentieth-Century Britain* (Abingdon, UK: Routledge, 2014), 33–53.

79 Ken Leyton-Brown covers most of the men hanged for sex murders in his general history of executions in Canada. Several cases are studied in Lesley Erickson's *Westward Bound* and in Karen Dubinsky's *Improper Advances: Rape and Heterosexual Conflict in Ontario, 1880–1929* (Chicago: University of Chicago Press, 1993). Cases from the mid-twentieth century appear in Carolyn Strange and Tina Loo, *True Crime, True North: The Golden Age of Canadian Pulp Magazines* (Vancouver, BC: Raincoast Books, 2004). Kim Casey includes the case of Arthur Bliss in *Thunder Bay City's True Murder Investigations, 1882 to 2017* (Sault Ste Marie, ON: Ahneen Publishing, 2017); Christopher Dummit studies the case of Frederick Ducharme in *The Manly Modern: Masculinity in Postwar Canada* (Vancouver: UBC Press, 2007); Frank Anderson covers the case of Earl Nelson in *The Dark Strangler: A Study in Strange Behaviour* (Calgary: Frontier Publishing, 1974); the case of Albert Nogaret appears in Dollard Dansereau's *Causes célèbres du Québec: les grands procès de l'histoire du Québec* (Montreal: Leméac, 1974) and in Jacques Côté's *Wilfrid Derome, expert en homicides*; Patrick Brode examines the case of Ronald Sears in *The Slasher Killings;* the case of Peter Wheeler is the focus of Debra Komar's book, *The Lynching of Peter Wheeler* (Fredericton, NB: Good Lane Editions, 2014).

80 Carolyn Strange, "Determining the Punishment of Sex Criminals in Confederation-Era Canada: A Matter of National Policy," *Canadian Historical Review* 99, no. 4 (Winter 2018): 541–62. The penalty for rape changed in 1877 with the passage of the Act to Amend the Act Respecting Offences against the Person, 1873, chapter 50. Until 1954, the penalty of death could be imposed at the judge's discretion, but only one offender received this sentence, in 1927. An earlier amendment to the act (chapter 28, section 2) in 1875 reduced the penalty for carnal knowledge to imprisonment, ranging from five years to life.

81 Angus McLaren, *Trials of Masculinity: Policing Sexual Boundaries, 1870–1930* (Chicago: University of Chicago Press, 1997), 133–58.

82 James E. Moran argues that "the endurance of legal custom, as inherited from English legal precedent in the form of the M'Naghten Rules, in many instances held more power than the Canadian law of insanity encoded into the Criminal Code itself." Moran, "Mental Disorder and Criminality in Canada," *International Journal of Law and Psychiatry* 37, no. 1 (2014): 109–16, 110.

83 On the concept of "lower" and "lesser" races and hierarchical racial thinking in Canadian history, see Barrington Walker, "Finding Jim Crow in Canada, 1789–1967," in *A History of Human Rights in Canada: Essential Issues*, ed. Janet Miron (Toronto: Canadian Scholars, 2009), 81–98, 87–90. On the disproportionately severe treatment of Indigenous capitally accused offenders in the twentieth century, see Jacqueline Briggs, "Exemplary Punishment: T.R.L. MacInnes, the Department of Indian Affairs, and Indigenous Executions, 1936–52," *Canadian Historical Review* 100, no. 3 (September 2019): 398–438.

84 The Criminal Code of 1892 did allow the defence or Crown, if refused a reserved question of law, to appeal to the attorney general for special leave to appeal. Vincent M. Del Buono, "Right to Appeal in Indictable Cases: A Legislative History," *Alberta Law Review* 16, no. 3 (1978): 446–69, 452.

85 The most famous in nineteenth-century Canada was John Wilson Murray, who was involved in the apprehension of Almeda Chattelle, a "tramp," who was executed in 1895 for the sex murder and mutilation of Jesse Keith, aged thirteen. See Murray's *Memoirs of a Great Detective: Incidents in the Life of John Wilson Murray*, ed. Victor Speer (New York: The Baker and Taylor Company, 1905), 385–9.

86 In 1943, 73 per cent of Canadians were in favour of capital punishment; ten years later, the percentage slipped only slightly to 71 per cent. Chandler, *Capital Punishment in Canada*, 41.

87 T.R.L. MacInnes, the senior bureaucrat in the Department of Indian Affairs, regularly advised Gallagher on capital cases that involved Indigenous convicts, almost invariably advising against clemency. Briggs, "Exemplary Punishment."

88 Strange, "The Undercurrents of Penal Culture," 351–3, 356.

89 Carter, "Capital Punishment," 249–51; Avio, "The Quality of Mercy," 270–1; Chandler, *Capital Punishment in Canada*, 18.

90 Garrett Wilson and Kevin Charles Wilson, *Diefenbaker for the Defence* (Saskatoon: Avoca Publishing, 1988).

91 This resource of formerly secret records (from 1944 to 1979) is fully searchable online through the LAC's web portal: Cabinet Conclusions, http://www.bac-lac.gc.ca/eng/discover/politics-government/cabinet-conclusions/Pages/cabinet-conclusions.aspx.

92 The death penalty continued to apply to offences committed by military personnel, prosecuted under the National Defence Act. It was abolished in 1998. This two-step process occurred in numerous countries in the late twentieth century. Roger Hood and Carolyn Hoyle, "Abolishing the Death Penalty Worldwide: The Impact of a 'New Dynamic,'" *Crime and Justice* 38, no. 1 (2009): 1–63, 8–9.

2. Sex Fiends and the Death Penalty at the Turn of Canada's Century

1 Gordon Darroch, ed., *The Dawn of Canada's Century: Hidden Histories* (Montreal: McGill-Queen's University Press, 2014); Ninette Kelley and Michael J. Trebilcock, *The Making of the Mosaic: A History of Canadian Immigration Policy* (Toronto: University of Toronto Press, 1998), 111–63.

2 In 1885, the Chinese Immigration Act introduced a "race"-specific head tax, which Prime Minister Laurier raised in 1900 and in 1903. Restrictions on black immigrants from the United States were informal and unaccountable, often imposed by border agents. Kelley and Trebilcock, *The Making of the Mosaic*, 151–6. Section 38 (c) of the Immigration Act, 1910, prohibited the entry of "immigrants belonging to any race deemed unsuited to the climate or requirements of Canada."

3 Sarah Carter, *Aboriginal People and Colonizers of Western Canada to 1900* (Toronto: University of Toronto Press, 1999); Sidney L. Harring, *White Man's Law: Native People in Nineteenth Century Jurisprudence* (Toronto: University of Toronto Press, 1998), 217–38.

4 Blair Stonechild and William A. Waiser, *Loyal till Death: Indians and the North-West Rebellion* (Calgary: Fifth House, 1997); Bob Beal and Rod Macleod, *Prairie Fire: The 1885 North-West Rebellion* (Toronto: McClelland & Stewart, 1994); John L. Tobias, "Canada's Subjugation of the Plains Cree, 1879–1885," *Canadian Historical Review* 64, no. 4 (1983): 519–48.

5 Ted McCoy, "Legal Ideology in the Aftermath of Rebellion: The Convicted First Nations Participants," *Histoire sociale/Social History* 42, no. 83 (2009): 175–201; Sandra Estlin Bingaman, "The Trials of Poundmaker and Big Bear, 1885," *Saskatchewan History* 28, no. 3 (1975): 81–94; Cyril Greenland, "The Last Public Execution in Canada: Eight Skeletons in the Closet of the Canadian Criminal Justice System," *Criminal Law Quarterly* 29, no. 4 (September 1987): 415–20.

6 The rate of execution for this subset of males convicted of other sorts of murder was statistically significant in this period. Eleven of the thirteen sex murder offenders were hanged (84.6 per cent), and 222 (51.2 per cent) were executed for other murders. The difference in proportions was .334 (p=.017).

7 James S. Woodworth, *Strangers within Our Gates, or Coming Canadians* (Toronto: The Missionary Society of the Methodist Church). One of Woodsworth's chapters, "The Negro and the Indian," referred to non-immigrant groups as racially distinct and at a lower stage of development. See also Valerie Knowles, *Strangers at Our Gates: Canadian Immigration and Immigration Policy, 1540 to 2015*, 4th ed. (Toronto: Dundurn Press, 2016), 124–36.

8 Norbert Elias argues that insiders (established power holders) "attribute to its outsider group as a whole the 'bad' characteristics of that group's 'worst' section." Elias, "Introduction: A Theoretical Essay on Established and Outsider Relations," in *The Established and the Outsiders: A Sociological Enquiry into Community Problems*, by Norbert Elias and John L. Scotson (London: Sage, 1994 [1976]), xv–lii.

9 In 1892, the Criminal Code formally adapted the British House of Lords' decision in the M'Naghten case of 1843. J. Arboleda-Florez, "The Insanity Defence in Canada," *Canadian Psychiatric Association Journal* 23, no. 1 (1978): 23–8, 24.

10 In 1888, German psychiatrist J.L.L. Koch introduced the concept of psychopathy. The internationally influential Richard Von Krafft-Ebing coined the term "sadism" and regarded sexual psychopathy as incurable. Bruce A. Arrigo and Stacey Shipley, "The Confusion over Psychopathy

(1): Historical Considerations," *International Journal of Offender Therapy and Comparative Criminology* 45, no. 3 (2001): 325–44. In Quebec, French degeneracy theory exerted greater influence over the development of psychiatry in the late nineteenth century. Peter Keating, *La Science du mal: l'institution de la psychiatrie au Québec, 1800–1914* (Montreal: Éditions du Boréal, 1993).

11 The Criminal Code, 1892, *S.C.*, 55–6 Victoria, c. 29, sections 747 and 748. Section 748 applied in the course of "any application of the mercy of the Crown on behalf of a person convicted of an indictable offence." Under s. 743, subsection 2, trial judges could reserve any question of law for the opinion of the court of appeal.

12 On the distinction between "status" and "non-status" "Indians," see Larry Gilbert, *Entitlement to Indian Status and Membership Codes in Canada* (Scarborough, ON: Carswell, 1996). The 1901 Census identified the mother tongue of Joseph Bennett's mother as Mohawk and his father's as Tuscarora. Fourth Census of Canada, 1901, District 46, Tuscarora Township, 1, http://data2.collectionscanada.ca/1901/z/z002/jpg/z000052538.jpg. On the erosion of Indigenous peoples' sovereignty in Ontario, see Robin Jarvis Brownlie, *A Fatherly Eye: Indian Agents, Government Power, and Aboriginal Resistance in Ontario, 1918–1939* (Don Mills, ON: Oxford University Press, 2003), 9–28.

13 On common sense versus scientific knowledge, see Clifford Geertz, "Common Sense as a Cultural System," in *Local Knowledge – Further Essays in Interpretative Anthropology*, 3rd ed. (New York: Basic Books, 2000), 84. I am grateful to Jonathan Swainger for this reference.

14 Psychiatrists rarely appeared in trials prior to the 1920s; however, they earned substantial fees for providing pre-trial and post-conviction sanity reviews. Alison Kirk-Montgomery, "'Loaded Revolvers': Ontario's First Forensic Psychiatrists," in *Mental Health and Canadian Society: Historical Perspectives*, ed. Janet Moran and David Wright (McGill-Queen's University Press, Montreal 2006), 117–48, 120–1.

15 Paul Rutherford, *A Victorian Authority: The Daily Press in Late Nineteenth-Century Canada* (Toronto: University of Toronto Press, 1982), 52–7. Rutherford tracked a significant rise from the 1870s to 1900 in the percentage of columns devoted to crime, scandals, and disasters in many of Canada's big-city papers. See also Minko Sotiron, *From Politics to Profit: The Commercialization of Canadian Daily Newspapers, 1890–1920* (Montreal: McGill-Queen's University Press, 1997).

16 Karen Dubinsky, *Improper Advances: Rape and Sexual Conflict in Ontario, 1880–1929* (Chicago: University of Chicago Press, 1993), 95–6, 103–4.

17 Edwin C. Guillet, *The Mutilation of Jessie Keith: A Study of the Evidence in The Queen versus Almeda Chattelle, 1894–1895*, vol. 28 of *Famous Canadian Trials* (Toronto: s.n., 1945), 18.

18 Jonathan Swainger, *The Canadian Department of Justice and the Completion of Confederation 1867–78* (Vancouver: UBC Press, 2000), 11–12. Bernard was Macdonald's personal secretary from 1857 and his brother-in-law as of February 1867, when his sister, Agnes, married Macdonald. Peter B. Waite, "Hewitt Bernard," in *Canadian Dictionary of Biography*, vol. 12, *1891 to 1900*, ed. Frances G. Halpenny (Toronto: University of Toronto Press, 1997 [1990]), 98.

19 Augustus Power, born in Quebec City in 1847, was the son of Lower Canadian Superior Court Justice William Power. He earned a bachelor of civil law degree from McGill in 1868 and joined the Department of Justice in 1874 as a first-class clerk. The position of chief clerk was established in 1879. Mélanie Brunet, *Out of the Shadows: The Civil Law Tradition in the Department of Justice Canada, 1868–2000* (Ottawa: Queen's Printer, 2000), 17–18.

20 An Act to Provide for the Conditional Liberation of Penitentiary Convicts, S.C., 1899, c. 49, ss.1 and 2. This act was informally known as the Ticket of Leave Act. On the development of supervised release, see A. Keith Bottomley, "Parole in Transition: A Comparative Study of Origins, Developments and Prospects in the 1990s," *Crime and Justice: A Review of Research* 12 (1990): 319–74, 323.

21 Section three of the act identified the Dominion Police as the agency responsible for issuing warrants for arrest and delivering paroled inmates to court for recommitment to penal servitude.

22 *The Civil Service of Canada*, special issue of *The Civilian* (Ottawa: 1914), 33–7.

23 Carolyn Strange, "The Lottery of Death: Capital Punishment, 1867–1976," *Manitoba Law Journal* 23, no. 3 (1995): 594–619, 599.

24 Barrington Walker, *The History of Immigration and Racism in Canada* (Toronto: Canadian Scholars, 2008); Constance Backhouse, *Colour-Coded: A Legal History of Racism in Canada, 1900–1950* (Toronto: University of Toronto Press for the Osgoode Society for Canadian Legal History, 1999); James W. St. G. Walker, *"Race," Rights and the Law in the Supreme Court of Canada: Historical Case Studies* (Waterloo, ON: Wilfrid Laurier University Press for the Osgoode Society for Canadian Legal History, 1997).

25 Byron Moffatt Britton, QC, had just completed a term as mayor of Kingston before he represented the Crown in this case.

26 The criminal law defined death, resulting from any act or omission of a perpetrator committed "feloniously, wilfully, of his malice aforethought" within one year of the act, as culpable homicide. Henri Elzéar Taschereau, *The Criminal Law Consolidation and Amendment Acts of 1869, 32–33 Vict., for the Dominion of Canada*, vol. 1 (Montreal: Lovell Printing and Publishing, 1874), 163–3.

27 LAC, R.G. 13, Burk, Volume 1416, file 120a, transcript of evidence (hereafter, references to capital case files will appear with convict's last name and volume and file numbers). McPherson was tried with Burk (file 121a), but they have separate files.

28 Robert A. Harrison, chief justice, to Secretary of State, 4 May 1878, in Burk, Volume 1416, file 121a. Harrison came to the bench with significant experience as a defence lawyer in criminal trials. Peter Oliver, ed., *The Conventional Man: The Diaries of Ontario Chief Justice Robert A. Harrison, 1856–1878* (Toronto: University of Toronto Press for the Osgoode Society for Canadian Legal History, 2003), 71–2.

29 David A. Wilson, *Thomas D'Arcy McGee: The Extreme Moderate, 1857–1868* (Kingston, ON: McGill-Queen's University Press, 2011), 355–8. The lead defence counsel was John Hillyard Cameron (no relation).

30 Carolyn Strange, "Determining the Punishment of Sex Criminals in Confederation-Era Canada: A Matter of National Policy," *Canadian Historical Review* 99, no. 4 (2018): 541–62; Constance Backhouse, "Nineteenth-Century Canadian Rape Law, 1800–92," in *Essays in the History of Canadian Law: Volume II*, ed. David H. Flaherty (Toronto: University of Toronto Press for the Osgoode Society for Canadian Legal History, 1983), 200–47.

31 Although Lash was a Liberal and Cameron a Conservative, the two were prominent Toronto bar members, and Lash lectured in commercial and criminal law at Osgoode Hall. Lash served as deputy minister from 1876 to 1879. Swainger, *The Canadian Department of Justice*, 39–40.

32 The consolidated criminal statutes of 1869 abolished "the convict's right to seek review and the appeal courts' power to order new trials in criminal matters." Christopher Moore, *The Court of Appeal for Ontario: Defining the Right of Appeal, 1792–2013* (Toronto: University of Toronto Press for the Osgoode Society for Canadian Legal History, 2014), 26. In 1888, appeals to the Judicial Committee of the Privy Council were prohibited. John T. Saywell, *The Lawmakers: Judicial Power and the Shaping of Canadian Federalism* (Toronto: University of Toronto Press for the Osgoode Society for Canadian Legal History, 2002), 199.

33 Harrison, in Oliver, *A Conventional Man*, 609.

34 Justice Harrison to Secretary of State, 18 May 1878, in Burk, Volume 1416, file 121A.

35 The Court of Queen's Bench, the precursor to the High Court, had jurisdiction over civil and criminal matters in Ontario. Margaret A. Banks, "The Evolution of the Ontario Courts, 1788–1981," in *Essays in the History of Canadian Law: Volume II*, ed. David H. Flaherty (Toronto: University of Toronto Press for the Osgoode Society for Canadian Legal History, 1983), 492–57, 517–20. Judges of these courts were also ex officio judges of the Court of Error and Appeal.

36 Cameron to James McDonald, minister of justice, 17 November 1880, in McPherson, Volume 1416, file 120a. In the original clemency petition Cameron drew up on 3 May 1878, he referred to the men under sentence of death for the "alleged rape and murder" of Mrs. Bennett.

37 James McDonald to the Secretary of State, 23 March 1881 (strikeout in original), in McPherson, Volume 1416, file 120a. The heading of his report, "In the matter of convicts Burk and McPherson," lent a further legalistic gloss to his recommendation. McDonald resigned from Parliament later in 1881 after his appointment as chief justice of Nova Scotia.

38 Both men were released. "Return of Convicts who have been Pardoned out of the Kingston Penitentiary during the Year ending 30th June, 1881, giving Crime and Place where Convicted," Canada, *Sessional Papers*, vol. 7, no. 12 (1882), 9.

39 Joseph Osier or Auger, executed in 1873 (francophone, tried in Pembroke, ON); Narcisse Larocque, executed in 1891 (francophone, tried in L'Orignal, ON); Almeda Chattelle, executed in 1894 (francophone, tried in Stratford, ON); Peter Wheeler, executed in 1896 (Mauritian, tried in Digby, NS); Joseph Bennett, executed in 1905 (Indigenous, tried in Brantford, ON); Lawrence Gowland, executed in 1907 (Anglo-Celtic, tried in Morden, MB); James Jenkins, executed in 1908 (African American, executed in New Westminster, BC); Frank Roughmond, executed in 1909 (black, tried in Stratford, ON); Edward Jardine, executed in 1911 (Anglo-Celtic, tried in Goderich, ON); James Taylor, executed in 1914 (Anglo-Celtic, tried in Brantford, ON); and Gustav Brauer, executed in 1914 (German Silesian, tried in Sydney, NS).

40 Annie Lukovitz, the woman murdered by Auger, was eighty years old; Mary Peake, murdered by Frank Roughmond in 1909, was sixty-six; Betsey Jacobs, murdered by Joseph Bennett in 1905, was middle-aged and physically disabled. In eight of the cases, the victims were under the age of eighteen.

41 Joseph Auger, aged twenty-four, was executed on 27 December 1873. An itinerant worker, he died claiming that a "shantyman" had committed the crime. "Shocking Murder in Brudenell," Renfrew *Mercury*, 12 July 1872.

42 On the rise of the tramp problem in industrializing societies, see James M. Pitsula, "The Treatment of Tramps in Late Nineteenth Century Toronto," *Historical Papers* 15, no. 1 (1980): 116–32; David Bright, "'Loafers Are Not Going to Subsist upon Public Credulence': Vagrancy and the Law in Calgary, 1900–1914," *Labour/ Le travail* 36 (Fall 1995): 37–58; Jim Phillips, "Poverty, Unemployment and the Administration of the Criminal Law: Vagrancy Laws in Halifax, 1864–1890," in *Essays in the History of Canadian Law, Volume III: Nova Scotia*, ed. Philip Girard and Jim Phillips (Toronto: University of Toronto Press for the Osgoode Society for Canadian Legal History, 1990), 128–60; Lisa Helps, "Bodies Public, City Spaces: Becoming Modern in Victoria, British Columbia, 1871–1901" (master's thesis, Department of History, University of Victoria, 2002).

43 The punishment of recidivist public order offenders was less harsh in Canada than in the United States or Britain, but it was prompted by similar "social anxieties and fiscal concerns." Helen Boritch, "The Criminal Class Revisited: Recidivism and Punishment in Ontario, 1871–1920," *Social Science History* 29, no. 1 (Spring 2005): 137–70, 165.

44 Donald Fyson, *Magistrates, Police and People: Everyday Criminal Justice in Quebec and Lower Canada, 1784–1837* (Toronto: University of Toronto Press, 2006); Alan Greer, "The Birth of the Police in Canada," in *Colonial Leviathan: State Formation in Mid-Nineteenth-Century Canada*, ed. Alan Greer and Ian Radforth (Toronto: University of Toronto Press, 1992), 17–49; Greg Marquis, "The 'Irish Model' and Nineteenth-Century Canadian Policing," *The Journal of Imperial and Commonwealth History* 25, no. 2 (1997): 193–218; Jeffrey Ian Ross, "The Historical Treatment of Urban Policing in Canada: A Review of the Literature," *Urban History Review/ Revue d'histoire urbaine* 24, no. 1 (October 1995): 36–41.

45 The Ontario government established a provincial police force in 1909, but John Wilson Murray was appointed the first full-time provincial police official in 1875. Provincial constables were employed shortly after, and Murray was officially appointed as a detective, along with Joseph E. Rogers and William D. Greer in the mid-1880s. Jim Phillips and Joel Fortune, "MURRAY, JOHN WILSON," in *Dictionary of Canadian Biography*, vol. 13, University of Toronto/Université Laval, 2003–, http://www.biographi.ca/en/bio/murray_john_wilson_13E.html; Dahn D. Higley,

O.P.P.: The History of the Ontario Provincial Police Force (Ottawa: Queen's Printer, 1984).

46 Toronto *Daily Mail*, 22 October 1894. Chattelle's name was spelled various ways in the French and English press. Official correspondence refers to him primarily as "Almeda Chattelle," and I have used that spelling for the sake of consistency except for primary quotations.

47 Dean Robinson, "A Dark Blot on the Fair Record of Perth County," Stratford *Beacon Herald*, 1 August 1974. This article condemns the reportage of the case for inciting racist community outrage.

48 This wording appeared in many reports, framing clemency as a departure from the course laid out by the law.

49 The majority of press reports were published in 1888. At least forty-two Canadian newspapers across the country published and republished stories of the murders and theories about the culprit's identity and motive. See the website maintained by Stephen P. Ryder, "Casebook: Jack the Ripper," https://www.casebook.org/press_reports.

50 On the enduring impact of the "Ripper" in defining the sex murderer, see Judith R. Walkowitz, "Jack the Ripper and the Myth of Male Violence," *Feminist Studies* 8, no. 3 (1982): 547–72. On the myth's impact in this case, see Dubinsky, *Improper Advances*, 100–2.

51 Speculation that Chattelle might have committed the Whitechapel murders was not exclusive to English Canada. "EST-CE JACQUES L'EVENTREUR?" was the title of an article about the case, published in *Le Courrier du Canada*, 31 October 1894.

52 "BRUTAL MURDER, The Listowel Tragedy the Work of a Fiend," Toronto *Daily Mail*, 22 October 1894. On press coverage of crime, see Paul Rutherford, *A Victorian Authority: The Daily Press in Late Nineteenth-Century Canada* (Toronto: Toronto University Press, 1982), 139. The *Daily Mail* as well as the Toronto *World* and *Empire* sent their own reporters to cover the inquest and trial.

53 "POOR JESSIE! The Fiendish Act which Deprived a Child of Life. A JACK THE RIPPER CRIME. Her Body Horribly Mutilated by Her Slayer and Hidden Away Under Leaves. SEARCHING FOR A SUSPECTED TRAMP," *Toronto News*, 24 October 1894.

54 "Chatelle est-il le meurtrier de Jessie Keith?," *L'Électeur* (Quebec), 25 October 1894. The conflation of beggars (gueux) and vagabonds (with an inference of worthlessness as well as itineracy) indicates that French Canadians made associations similar to English Canadians.

55 "Almeda Chattelle, the Hairy Man," in *Memoirs of a Great Detective: Incidents in the Life of John Wilson Murray*, ed. Victor Speer (London:

Heinemann, 1904), 360–5. Although the veracity of Murray's account is doubtful, cross references to newspaper reports on the Chattelle case suggest his own version was accurate, albeit highly opinionated. Phillips and Fortune, "MURRAY, JOHN WILSON."

56 "THE LISTOWEL TRAGEDY," Toronto *Daily Mail*, 23 October 1894.

57 Barrington Walker, *Race on Trial: Black Defendants in Ontario's Criminal Courts, 1858–1958* (Toronto: University of Toronto Press for the Osgoode Society for Canadian Legal History, 2010), 129–30.

58 For a review of critical approaches to the notion of fairness as a hallmark of Canadian law, see Lori Chambers, "Exposing the Myth of the Peaceable Kingdom: Trends and Themes in Recent Canadian Legal History," *Acadiensis* 41, no. 1 (January 2012): 247–56.

59 "THE AUTHORITIES POSITIVE THEY HAVE THE ASSASSIN," Toronto *Daily Mail*, 25 October 1894.

60 The population of Listowel in 1891 was 2,587. Canada, Department of Agriculture, *Census of Canada*, bulletin 1 (August 1891), 9.

61 "PLEADS GUILTY. Chattelle Acknowledges Having Killed Jessie Keith. SENSATION IN THE COURT. Overwhelming Evidence of the Prisoner's Guilt," Toronto *Daily Mail*, 27 October 1894.

62 Ibid.

63 In Murray's account, he pushed Chattelle into a rail car (which the crowd tried to uncouple) and told him to crouch on the floor. He then guarded the door until the train pulled out. Speer, *Memoirs of a Great Detective*, 364.

64 When Gustav Brauer, a German immigrant, was apprehended for the murder and "ravishment" of six-year-old Elizabeth Kozial in Sydney, Nova Scotia, a near lynching took place as "hundreds crowded around the [jail] yard and even forced their way into the jail itself." Sydney *Post*, 20 May 1914.

65 "THE FIEND YET AT LARGE. THE WORK OF A HUMAN BRUTE," Aylmer *Express*, 25 October 1894.

66 Cyril Greenland, "The Life and Death of Louis Riel: Surrender, Trial, Appeal and Execution," *Canadian Psychiatric Association Journal* 10 (1965): 253–9.

67 Richard J. Gwyn, *Nation Maker: Sir John A. Macdonald: His Life, Our Times* (Toronto: Random House, 2011), 463. Although it was still possible for criminal convicts to appeal to the Judicial Committee of the Privy Council, it refused to hear Riel's appeal.

68 The local press in St. Hyacinthe disavowed any connection with the accused murderer after local parish records were checked to find

a reference to his birth. "Chatel accusé de meurtre," *Courrier de St-Hyacinthe*, 27 October 1894.

69 Armour was chief justice of the Queen's Bench division of the High Court of Ontario.

70 Armour to Secretary of State, 15 April 1895, in Chattelle, Volume 1832, file 273a. Armour stated that he had informed Chattelle of his right to testify through a private communication with the sheriff.

71 The report of the medical examiner on the victim's genitals was not disclosed at the inquest because it was completed on 28 October 1894, the day after. Archives of Ontario, Criminal Indictment file, RG 22, Series 392, Chattelle, 1894.

72 Harry Oosterhuis, *Stepchildren of Nature: Richard von Krafft-Ebing, Psychiatry, and the Making of Sexual Identity* (Chicago: University of Chicago Press, 2000).

73 Toronto *Evening Star*, 28 March 1895. Richard Von Krafft-Ebing, *Psychopathia Sexualis, with Special Reference to Contrary Sexual Instinct: A Medico-Legal Study*, trans. Charles Gilbert Chaddock (Philadelphia: F.A. Advis Company, 1894), 56.

74 Krafft-Ebing, *Psychopathia Sexualis*, 380–1. East wrote the minister of justice on 9 May and referred him to pages of the text that corresponded to this edition. He did not refer to page 62, where Krafft-Ebing described "lust murder." Chattelle, Volume 1832, file 273a.

75 The Toronto *World* connected the Chattelle case to the case of Clara Ford. When detectives arrested her for murder in November 1894, they discovered men's clothing, allegedly worn to disguise herself. In both cases, cross dressing was associated with sexual perversion. Patrick Brode, *Death in the Queen City: Clara Ford on Trial, 1895* (Toronto: Dundurn Press, 2005), 60.

76 Dr. Albert Roberts Pyne, affidavit, 9 April 1895, in Chattelle, Volume 1832, file 273a.

77 Power to Minister of Justice, 18 May 1895, in Chattelle, Volume 1832, file 273a. Martin L. Friedland also notes Power's dismissive attitude to psychiatrists who challenged the legal definition of criminal insanity. Friedland, *The Case of Valentine Shortis: A True Story of Crime and Politics in Canada* (Toronto: University of Toronto Press, 1986), 39–41, 149–51.

78 Criminal Code, chapter 29, s. 11.

79 Criminal Code, chapter 29, s. 748. The section applied to any mercy plea after a conviction for indictable offences in which the relevant minister "entertains a doubt whether such person ought to have been convicted."

80 Power to Minister of Justice, 18 May 1895, in Chattelle, Volume 1832, file 273a (strikeout in original).

81 *Le Monde*, 2 April 1895, in Chattelle, Volume 1832, file 273a. The article further stated that clemency would constitute an attack on the jury, which acted "avec conscience de leur devoir envers société."

82 In Anglo-Protestant representations of race in the nineteenth century, the French (along with the Irish and most southern Europeans) were frequently considered not white. Corrie Scott, "How French Canadians Became White Folks, or Doing Things with Race in Quebec," *Ethnic and Racial Studies* 39, no. 7 (2016): 1280–97.

83 Speer, *Memoirs of a Great Detective*, 386.

84 In Canada, the association of darkness with innate savagery and criminality also occurred in criminal cases involving Indigenous peoples, Asians, and southern Europeans. Backhouse, *Colour-Coded*, 63–50. On the connections between racism, hereditarian thinking, and criminology, see Nicole Hahn Rafter, *Creating Born Criminals* (Urbana: University of Illinois Press, 1997).

85 Michael J. Pfeifer, *The Roots of Rough Justice: Origins of American Lynching* (Urbana: University of Illinois Press, 2011).

86 The sex murder of Annie Kempton, aged fourteen, in Bear River, Nova Scotia, was also interpreted as a defence of her honour. Peter Wheeler, a former sailor from Mauritius, was convicted of the murder and executed on 8 September 1896. For an analysis that criticizes the outcome as a judicial murder (on the basis of current-day appraisals of the forensic evidence), see Debra Komar, *The Lynching of Peter Wheeler* (Fredericton, NB: Goose Lane Editions, 2014).

87 The Nanaimo *Daily News* ("A Woman Outraged and Murdered") reported on 10 June 1908 that a posse of men was scouring the border district for "a tramp, a young white man." The Vancouver *Daily World* ("FIENDISH MURDER NEAR HAZELMERE") reported the suspect as "dark complexioned" (12 June 1908). When he was indicted for murder on 26 June 1908, the Victoria *Daily Colonist* described Jenkins as a "half-breed negro" ("JENKINS ARRAIGNED ON MURDER CHARGE"). "HAZELMERE MURDER SUSPECT ARRESTED" recounted the arrest and release of a "mulatto" and "octoroon" who matched the suspect's description (Victoria *Daily Colonist*, 13 June 1908).

88 "MURDERER IS STILL AT LARGE," Winnipeg *Tribune*, 11 June 1908. The New Westminster *Daily News* accused the local chief of preferring his "feather bed" to tracking down the murderer. "CAPTURE OF JENKINS REFLECTS NO CREDIT ON CHIEF SPAIN," 26 June 1908.

89 Victoria *Daily Colonist*, 24 June 1908. The Webster–Ashburton Treaty of 1842, negotiated through Britain and the United States, included murder as an extraditable offence, and Canada exercised oversight of extradition from 1883. Bradley Miller, *Borderline Crime: Fugitive Criminals and the Challenge of the Border, 1819–1914* (Toronto: Toronto University Press for the Osgoode Society for Canadian Legal History, 2016), 200.
90 "HAZLEMERE MURDERER MUST EXPIATE CRIME ON GALLOWS," New Westminster *Daily News*, 26 October 1908.
91 "Closing Scenes of Murder Trial," Vancouver *Daily World*, 26 October 1908. The paper described McQuarrie's defence as a "brilliant appeal for an acquittal."
92 "LITTLE MARY MORRISON SPRINGS SENSATION IN COURT," New Westminster *Daily News*, 24 October 1908.
93 After 1897, the Supreme Court of British Columbia considered cases on appeal by sitting en banc. However, the separate Court of Appeal was not established until November 1909. Hamar Foster and John McLaren, "For the Better Administration of Justice: The Court of Appeal for British Columbia, 1910–2010," *BC Studies* 162 (Summer 2009): 5–24, 8.
94 This point, for a new trial, was argued under section 1021 of the Criminal Code. Hunter also applied for a reserved case under section 1014, which covered his charge to the jury on the deficiency of the circumstantial evidence.
95 "Rex v. Jenkins," *The British Columbia Reports, Being Reports of Cases Determined in the Supreme and County Courts and in Admiralty, Volume 13* (Victoria: The Colonist Printing and Publishing Company, 1908), 61–75, 65. Cassidy was a Liberal and in 1919 appeared for the defence in the trial of the Winnipeg general strike leaders. Tom Mitchell, "'Repressive Measures': A.J. Andrews, the Committee of 1000 and the Campaign against Radicalism after the Winnipeg General Strike," *Left History* 3, no. 2 (Fall 1995): 133–67, 159.
96 "Rex v. Jenkins," 72. In 1899, a manhunt in the United States led to the capture of Marion Brown, an African American "tramp," who was convicted and executed in London, Ontario, for the murder of a police officer. Walker, *Race on Trial*, 74–86.
97 "Rex v. Jenkins," 71.
98 In 1908, Hunter also clashed with a rival judge on the Supreme Court, Archer Martin, who resented Hunter's appointment as chief justice in 1902. Hunter took to drinking excessively. Christopher Moore, *The British Columbia Court of Appeal: The First Hundred Years* (Vancouver: UBC Press, 2010), 15–18.

99 Attorney General of British Columbia to Minister of Justice, 13 November 1908, in Jenkins, Volume 1454. Bowser also alleged that Hunter had appeared on the bench "in a state of intoxication" on several occasions. He added that the Vancouver *World* called for Hunter's resignation on 20 June 1908 and that the Bellingham (Washington) *Herald* claimed British justice had "Slipped a Cog" as a result of delays caused by Hunter's drunkenness.

100 Power to Minister of Justice, 2 December 1908, in Jenkins, Volume 1454, file 39a.

101 The other two men executed were Lee Chung and Jack Petrella.

102 Backhouse, *Colour-Coded*, 5.

103 "IS A FOUNTAIN OF CRIME: DISEASE PHYSICAL AND MENTAL, SAYS SURGEON," Toronto *Globe*, 21 August 1909.

104 Ibid.

105 Although Ellis is best known for his work on sexual identities and behaviours, his first major work was *The Criminal* (1890). David Garland, "British Criminology before 1935," *The British Journal of Criminology* 28, no. 2 (Spring 1988): 1–17, 5–6; Matthew Levay, *Violent Minds: Modernism and the Criminal* (Cambridge: Cambridge University Press, 2019), 2–6.

106 Mary Gibson, *Born to Crime: Cesare Lombroso and the Origins of Biological Criminology* (Westport, CT: Praeger, 2002), 97–126.

107 Daniel Pick, *Faces of Degeneration: A European Disorder, circa 1848–circa 1918* (Cambridge: Cambridge University Press, 1989); Peter D'Agostino, "Craniums, Criminals, and the 'Cursed Race': Italian Anthropology in American Racial Thought, 1861–1924," *Comparative Studies in Society and History* 44, no. 2 (2002): 319–43; Neil Davie, "A 'Criminal Type' in All but Name: British Prison Medical Officers and the 'Anthropological' Approach to the Study of Crime (c. 1865–1895)," *Victorian Review* 29, no. 1 (2003): 1–30.

108 In 1909, groups of African American farmers from Oklahoma began to migrate to Canada, and resistance to their settlement exposed latent racism. R. Bruce Shepard, "The Origins of the Oklahoma Black Migration to the Canadian Plains," *Canadian Journal of History* 23, no. 1 (1988): 1–24. From 1896 to 1911, fewer than 1,000 of the more than one million American immigrants to Canada were African Americans. Harold Troper, *Only Farmers Need Apply: Official Canadian Government Encouragement of Immigration from the United States, 1896–1911* (Toronto: Griffin House, 1972), 121–2.

109 "FARMER'S WIFE MURDERED. FOUND BY HER SON IN CELLAR OF HOME. NEGRO DRUNK BESIDE HER," Toronto *World*, 1 October

1908. The paper further identified the subject as "Frank Roughmond. A Vagrant."

110 "THE MURDER SITUATION," Stratford *Herald*, 3 October 1908.

111 Walker, *Race on Trial*, 127–9. Riddell (1852–1945) considered himself to be a progressive on racial relations, and he published eleven pamphlets on the history of slavery. For a critical appraisal of his time on the bench, see Backhouse, *Colour-Coded*, 123–31.

112 Transcript of evidence, 84. Roughmond, Volume 1455, file 412A. The postmortem revealed that Mrs. Peake suffered from heart disease, which Coughlin emphasized.

113 Dr. R.W. Bruce Smith, provincial inspector of the Prisons and Public Charities for Ontario, frequently assessed the sanity of condemned criminals. He also espoused eugenic theories of inherited criminal tendencies. Angus McLaren, *Our Own Master Race: Eugenics in Canada, 1885–1945* (Toronto: McClelland & Steward, 1990), 38–42. Charles Kirk Clarke was one of the most influential "alienists" in the country in 1909 and dean of the Faculty of Medicine at the University of Toronto. He expressed his strong eugenicist views in his demands that the government deport "defective" immigrants. Ian Dowbiggin, *Keeping America Sane: Psychiatry and Eugenics* (Ithaca, NY: Cornell University Press, 1997), 133–90.

114 The doctors co-signed a letter after their first visit. One month prior to the date set for Roughmond's execution, they reported again, jointly, to Justice Riddell. Roughmond, Volume 1455, file 412A. On the development of forensic psychiatry, see John P.M. Court, Alexander I.F. Simpson, and Christopher D. Webster, "Contesting Mad versus Bad: The Evolution of Forensic Mental Health Services and Law at Toronto," *Psychiatry, Psychology and Law* 21, no. 6 (2014): 918–36, 924–5.

115 Power to Minister of Justice, 10 June 1909. Roughmond, Volume 1455, file 412A.

116 "The prisoner has been skillfully and ably defended by the young gentleman, Mr. Coughlin, whom I asked yesterday to take that position." Transcript of evidence, 88, in Roughmond, Volume 1455, file 412A. Coughlin was thirty-eight at the time of the trial. Roughmond spent seven months in prison prior to the trial's opening in May 1909.

117 Power to Minister of Justice, 10 June 1909, in Roughmond, Volume 1455, file 412A. The defendant claimed that he was born in the Gaspé Peninsula and that he had lived in Halifax, where he had married and had two children.

118 The Department of Indian Affairs was established in 1880, putting into effect the Indian Act of 1876. In the Prairies, only a "fortunate few" had legal representation in capital cases as late as 1905. Shelley Gavigan, *Hunger, Horses, and Government Men: Criminal Law on the Aboriginal Plains, 1870–1905* (Vancouver: UBC Press for the Osgoode Society for Canadian Legal History, 2012), 86.

119 On the strategic use of mercy in cases of wendigo murders in the late nineteenth century, see Catherine L. Evans, "Heart of Ice: Indigenous Defendants and Colonial Law in the Canadian North-West," *Law and History Review* 36, no. 2 (2018): 199–234, 225.

120 "VERDICT AGAINST BENNETT," Brantford *Courier*, 18 July 1905.

121 E.D. Cameron to Deputy Superintendent General of Indian Affairs, 28 July 1905. LAC, R.G. 10, Volume 7466, file 19032–7 Pt. 1. Four chiefs participated in the coroner's jury, and they may have demanded the superintendent's assistance. See Edmund Jefferson Danziger, *Great Lakes Indian Accommodation and Resistance during the Early Reservation Years, 1850–1900* (Ann Arbor: University of Michigan Press, 2009). See also Sidney L. Harring, "The Liberal Treatment of Indians: Native People in Nineteenth Century Ontario Law," *Saskatchewan Law Review* 56, no. 2 (1992): 297–371.

122 The Brantford law firm of Heyd and Heyd was paid $771.38 for expenses related to Rex v. Bennett. The expenditure was listed under "legal expenses." Canada, "Annual Report of the Indian Affairs Department for the Year ending 30 June 1906," *Sessional Papers*, vol. 1 (Ottawa: King's Printer, 1907), 3.

123 The press identified Bennett as the likely culprit from the earliest reports on the crime: "He Has the Name of Being a Bad Indian," Wingham *Advance*, 13 July 1905.

124 Brantford *Courier*, 29 September 1905. The closing address of the defence ran for over two hours after Heyd opened with these remarks. He focused on the inconsistencies in the Crown evidence and on Bennett's alibi.

125 Brant County spent $1,200 to prosecute the case, and it appealed for federal compensation on the basis that Bennett was "an Indian and a Ward of the Government." The minister of the interior agreed that the county "should not have to bear the cost of administering justice to the Indians." Toronto *Globe*, 30 March and 28 May 1906.

126 The filing of such requests was permissible under section 744 of the Criminal Code.

127 "COURT DECLINES TO GRANT NEW TRIAL FOR JOS. BENNETT," Toronto *Daily Star*, 4 December 1905.

128 At the same Assizes, Felix Doyle, a white man, was convicted for the murder of his mother. The Toronto *Globe* anticipated (correctly) that his death sentence would be commuted because of "the apparent weak mindedness of the accused," and his lawyer pleaded for mercy on the basis of Doyle's "mental state." "BRANT MURDER CASES," 28 September 1905.

129 Power to Minister of Justice, 21 November 1905, in Bennett, Volume 1450, file 373A. Bennett was executed 15 December 1905. He was not buried in the jail yard but on the Grand River reservation. The funeral was held in his mother's house. "MURDERER BENNETT. REV. MR. HARVEY GIVES OUT HIS WARNING TO YOUNG PEOPLE," Wingham *Advance*, 28 December 1905.

130 Charles Joseph Doherty (born 1855) served as a justice of the Quebec Superior Court from 1891 to 1906. He fought the Métis as a lieutenant in a Montreal battalion. First elected as a Conservative to federal Parliament in 1908, he became minister of justice in 1911 and served in that capacity until 1921.

131 Tina Loo, "Savage Mercy: Native Culture and the Modification of Capital Punishment in Nineteenth-Century British Columbia," in *Qualities of Mercy: Justice, Punishment and Discretion*, ed. Carolyn Strange (Vancouver: UBC Press, 1996), 104–29. Crimes committed within Indigenous communities were the least likely to be prosecuted. Robert C. Macleod and Heather Rollason, "'Restrain the Lawless Savages': Native Defendants in the Criminal Court of the North West Territories, 1878–1885," *Journal of Historical Sociology* 10 (1997): 157–83.

132 For a typical example, see Andrew Baldwin, Laura Cameron, and Audrey Kobayashi, eds., *Rethinking the Great White North: Race, Nature, and the Historical Geographies of Whiteness in Canada* (Vancouver: UBC Press, 2011). For a critique that focuses on British immigrants, see Janice Cavell, "The Imperial Race and the Immigration Sieve: The Canadian Debate on Assisted British Migration and Empire Settlement, 1900–30," *The Journal of Imperial and Commonwealth History* 34, no. 3 (2006): 345–67.

133 C.K. Clarke, "Defective and Insane Immigration," *Bulletin of the Ontario Hospitals for the Insane* 2 (1908): 3–22. On psychiatric diagnoses as rationales for deportation, see Dowbiggin, *Keeping America Sane*, 142–4; Robert Menzies, "Governing Mentalities: The Deportation of 'Insane' and 'Feebleminded' Immigrants Out of British Columbia from Confederation

to World War II," *Canadian Journal of Law and Society* 13, no. 2 (1998): 136–73.

134 Hilda Blake, one of only two women executed between 1873 and 1914, was a British immigrant brought out to work in service through an English orphan charity. She pleaded guilty to shooting her mistress dead, but initially she blamed the shooting on a tramp with a foreign accent. Blake was hanged in Brandon, Manitoba, on 27 December 1899. Reinhold Kramer and Tom Mitchell, *Walk towards the Gallows: The Tragedy of Hilda Blake, Hanged 1899* (New York: Oxford University Press, 2002), 110–32.

135 W.J.C. Cherwinski, "Wooden Horses and Rubber Cows: Training British Agricultural Labour for the Canadian Prairies, 1890–1930," *Historical Papers of the Canadian Historical Association* 15, no. 1 (1980): 133–54.

136 Lesley Erickson, *Westward Bound: Sex, Violence, the Law, and the Making of a Settler Society* (Vancouver: UBC Press for the Osgoode Society for Canadian Legal History, 2011), 115–17. Erickson notes that approximately 70,000 British children and youths were given assistance to migrate to Canada between 1870 and 1920 and that commentators, such as Woodsworth, considered most to be morally undesirable.

137 Gowland, Volume 1452, file 389A, 7 November 1907.

138 R. v. Gowland, transcript of evidence, 1, in Gowland, Volume 1452, file 389A.

139 Morden became the seat for the Southern Judicial District of Manitoba in 1904, and its courthouse opened in 1906. *Milestones: Themes and Events in Morden's History* (Morden, MB: City of Morden, 2017).

140 Ibid.

141 Phippen's failure to recall the execution of Hilda Blake, only eight years earlier, after a trial without counsel, suggests the matter of criminal defence was not high in his mind.

142 R. v. Gowland, transcript of evidence, 1.

143 Phippen to Secretary of State, 5 November 1907 in Gowland, Volume 1452, file 389A. Phippen was a bencher of the Law Society of Manitoba and served on the provincial Court of Appeal as of 1906. Gordon Goldsborough, "Memorable Manitobans: Frank Hedley Phippen (1863–1932)," Manitoba Historical Society, http://www.mhs.mb.ca/docs/people/phippen_fh.shtml.

144 Finch to Minister of Justice, 30 October 1907; Wiley to Minister of Justice, 3 November 1907, in Gowland, Volume 1452, file 389A.

145 R. v. Gowland, transcript of evidence, 30, in Gowland, Volume 1452, file 389A.

146 Phippen to Secretary of State, 5 Nov 1907 in Gowland, Volume 1452, file 389A.

147 Power to Minister of Justice, 26 November 1907, in Gowland, Volume 1452, file 389A. Gowland was executed 13 December 1907.

148 Finch to Minister of Justice, 30 October 1907, in Gowland, Volume 1452, file 389A.

149 Power to C.W. Finch, 4 November, 1907, in Gowland, Volume 1452, file 389A.

150 R. v. Gowland, sentencing statement, transcript of evidence, 47, in Gowland, Volume 1452, file 389A.

151 Power studied at the Jesuit seminary at St. Mary's College. He died in Vancouver on 4 September 1912. At his retirement, he earned an annual salary of $3,700. Brunet, *Out of the Shadows*, 18.

152 Côté, born in 1861, was the son of a former clerk of the Privy Council. He replaced Power on 1 April 1911 at a lower salary. Both were Roman Catholics, but Côté was the only francophone among the department's senior civil servants until 1909. He was made King's Counsel in 1915. J.D. Clarke, who served as the secretary to four ministers of justice, was Côté's second in command, and he took over after Côté died suddenly in 1918. Brunet, *Out of the Shadows*, 19, 21.

153 "The Civil Service of Canada," special issue, *The Civilian: A Fortnightly Journal Devoted to the Interests of the Civil Service of Canada* (1914), 37.

154 Falconbridge to Aylesworth, 16 April 1911, in Jardine, Volume 1459, file 441a, part 1 (underlining in original). The judge became a justice of the High Court, Queen's Bench division, in 1900 and was knighted in 1908. One testimonial commented that Falconbridge represented "all the old traditions, literary, scholastic, social, professional and judicial, which have lent honour and dignity to the British Bench and Bar." Jamie Benidickson, "FALCONBRIDGE, Sir WILLIAM GLENHOLME," in *Dictionary of Canadian Biography*, vol. 14, University of Toronto/Université Laval, 2003–, http://www.biographi.ca/en/bio/falconbridge_william_glenholme_14E.html.

155 "GIRL MURDERED AT GODERICH: Lizzie Anderson Found with Her Throat Cut," Toronto *Globe*, 27 September 1910.

156 Dancey was fifty-one years old at the time of the Jardine trial and a barrister of long standing in Huron County.

157 "JARDINE TO BE TRIED FOR MURDER," Toronto *Globe*, 12 April 1911. The *Globe* also reported that Justice Falconbridge "practically instructed the Grand Jury to find a true bill, and ordered them not to reduce the charge to manslaughter."

158 "JARDINE SENTENCED TO BE HANGED," Toronto *Globe*, 15 April 1911. The jury deliberated for just over one hour.
159 Côté to Minister of Justice, 1 June 1911, in Jardine, Volume 1459, file 441a, part 1. He referred to one doctor for the defence, who claimed that sexual perverts could acquire sexual satisfaction only through "onanism or sodomy or the violation of a corpse, and other such unnatural acts."
160 Dr. Daniel Clark, superintendent of the Asylum for the Insane in Toronto from 1875 to 1905, published a text on masturbation and insanity. Clark, *Self Abuse* (Toronto: s.n., 1878).
161 Evan H. Hare, "Masturbatory Insanity: The History of an Idea," *Journal of Mental Science* 108, no. 452 (1962): 1–25. By the early twentieth century, eugenicists associated the habit of masturbation with degeneracy. Thomas W. Laqueur, *Solitary Sex: A Cultural History of Masturbation* (London: Zone Books, 2004), 50–1.
162 "JARDINE SENTENCED TO BE HANGED ON JUNE 16," Toronto *Globe*, 15 April 1911. Blackstock, the son of a Methodist minister, acted frequently in criminal trials, usually representing the Crown. The case that brought him to national prominence was the Blenheim murder, in which he defended Reginald Birchall (unsuccessfully). Gordon K. Murphy, "Birchall and Benwell: Murder in a Canadian Swamp," *American Journal of Forensic Medicine and Pathology* 9, no. 3 (1988): 255–7.
163 German immigrant Gustav Brauer was executed on 11 November 1911. Most of his family was in Germany, and Côté noted his family was "too poor to procure the services of an expert on insanity." Côté to Minister of Justice, 7 November 1914, in Brauer, Volume 1466, file 516a.
164 R. v. Roughmond, transcript of evidence, 90, 102, in Roughmond, Volume 1455, file 412a.
165 Peter Becker and Richard F. Wetzell, eds., *Criminals and Their Scientists: The History of Criminology in International Perspective* (Cambridge: Cambridge University Press, 2006).
166 In Ontario alone, forensic psychiatrists testified in thirty homicide trials between 1870 and 1900. Kirk-Montgomery, "'Loaded Revolvers': Ontario's First Forensic Psychiatrists," 117–48.

3. Contesting Convictions and Questioning Culpability between the Wars

1 Robert Bickerdike introduced abolition bills in 1914, 1915, 1916, and 1917. After he made a fortune in the meat packing industry, he devoted himself to social justice issues. "Robert Bickerdike," in *The Storied Province*

of Quebec Past and Present, ed. William Charles Henry Wood (Toronto: Dominion Publishing, 1931); Jack Jedwab, "BICKERDIKE, ROBERT," in *Dictionary of Canadian Biography*, vol. 15, University of Toronto/Université Laval, 2003–, http://www.biographi.ca/en/bio/bickerdike_robert_15E.html. William Irvine, the Labour MP for Calgary East, introduced a private member's abolition bill in 1924. A former Unitarian minister, he opposed capital punishment throughout his seventeen-year service as an MP, later with the CCF. In 1947, he served as a member of the Special Joint Committee on Human Rights and Fundamental Freedoms. See "William Irvine," Library of Parliament, Historical Information (Parlinfo), Parliamentarians, https://lop.parl.ca/sites/ParlInfo/default/en_CA/People/Profile?personId=12115.

2 Canada, House of Commons, *Debates*, 14 January 1914, 483–4 (hereafter *Debates*).

3 Approximately 55 per cent of condemned offenders were executed in Canada between 1880 and 1920. The rate rose to 75 per cent in the 1930s, dipping slight to 62.2 per cent in the 1940s. Carolyn Strange, "The Lottery of Death: Capital Punishment, 1867–1976," *Manitoba Law Journal* 23 (1995): 594–619, 613n54.

4 The home provinces of the twelve men were Ontario (six), New Brunswick (three), Quebec (two), and Manitoba (one).

5 Based on research conducted among prisoners in New York State, psychiatrist Bernard Glueck found that 19 per cent of the inmates were psychopaths and 12 per cent had committed sexual offences. Glueck, "A Study of 608 Admissions to Sing Sing Prison," *Mental Hygiene* 2, no. 1 (January 1918): 85–151, 92–4.

6 Elise Chenier, *Strangers in Our Midst: Sexual Deviancy in Postwar Ontario* (Toronto: University of Toronto Press, 2008), 21–2. On Toronto as a leading centre of research into sexual deviance, see Edward Shorter, ed., *TPH: History and Memory of the Toronto Psychiatric Hospital, 1925–1966* (Toronto: Wall & Emmerson, 1996).

7 On the diagnosis of war trauma in this period, see Mark Humphries, "War's Long Shadow: Masculinity, Medicine, and the Gendered Politics of Trauma, 1914–1939," *Canadian Historical Review* 91, no. 3 (September 2010): 503–31; Tracey Loughran, "Shell Shock, Trauma, and the First World War: The Making of a Diagnosis and Its Histories," *Journal of the History of Medicine and Allied Sciences* 67, no. 1 (January 2012): 94–119.

8 The periodization in this chapter slightly exceeds the interwar period in order to follow the clustering of sex murder cases from 1921 to 1942.

9 Quebec sponsored the first forensic laboratory in North America, established in Montreal in 1914. In 1932, Ontario developed a similar lab as a branch of the Office of the Attorney General. The federal laboratory, run by the RCMP, was established in 1937. Marjorie Freeman Campbell, *A Century of Crime: The Development of Crime Detection Methods in Canada* (Toronto: McClelland & Stewart, 1970), 192–6.

10 Pierre M. Côté died in office in 1918, and J.D. Clarke, who replaced him, headed the Remission Branch from 1918 to 1924. Mélanie Brunet, *Out of the Shadows: The Civil Law Tradition in the Department of Justice Canada, 1868–2000* (Ottawa: Queen's Printer, 2000), 19–20.

11 LAC, R.G. 32, Volume 103, M.F. Gallagher, "Classification Card," 26 July 1923. Gallagher was appointed to the first division of departmental clerks in 1919. "Report of the Auditor General for the Year Ended 31st March, 1919," *Sessional Papers of the Dominion of Canada* 54, no. 1 (1919), L3. In 1922, his promotion came with the expectation that he reduce the number of tickets of leave (parole approvals), which he halved by 1927. Correctional Service of Canada, "Backgrounder: A History of Conditional Release in Canada" (Ottawa: Media and Public Services, 1989), 3, https://www.publicsafety.gc.ca/lbrr/archives/cnsgc00035143-89-1-eng.pdf.

12 On racism and ethnocentrism in the criminal and civil legal systems of Canada, see Constance Backhouse, *Colour-Coded: A Legal History of Racism in Canada, 1900–1950* (Toronto: University of Toronto Press for the Osgoode Society for Canadian Legal History, 1999); James W. St. G. Walker, *"Race," Rights and the Law in the Supreme Court of Canada: Historical Case Studies* (Waterloo, ON: Wilfrid Laurier University Press for the Osgoode Society for Canadian Legal History, 1997).

13 Carolyn Strange, "Comment: Capital Case Procedure Manual," *Criminal Law Quarterly* 41 (1998): 184–97, 190–1.

14 Lucy Bland and Laura Doan, eds., *Sexology Uncensored: The Documents of Sexual Science* (Chicago: University of Chicago Press, 1998); Nicholas Matte, "International Sexual Reform and Sexology in Europe, 1897–1933," *Canadian Bulletin of the History of Medicine* 22, no. 1 (Fall 2005): 253–70.

15 Simon N. Verdun-Jones and Russell Smandych, "Catch-22 in the Nineteenth-Century: The Evolution of Therapeutic Confinement for the Criminally Insane in Canada," *Criminal Justice History: An International Annual* 2 (1981): 85–108; Dominique Bourget and Gary Chaimowitz, "Forensic Psychiatry in Canada: A Journey on the Road to Specialty," *Journal of the American Academy of Psychiatry and the Law* 38, no. 2 (June 2010): 158–62.

16 The murder occurred on 7 August 1920. Davis was not apprehended until he turned up at New York's Auburn prison in 1921. "To Face Murder Trial Here," Toronto *Daily Star*, 14 November 1921. The two-day trial opened on 21 January 1922.
17 On the Roughmond case, see chapter two.
18 LAC, R.G. 13, Davis, Volume 1517, part 1 (hereafter, references to capital case files will appear with convict's last name and volume and file numbers).
19 William Renwick Riddell, "A Case of Supposed Sadism," *Journal of the American Institute of Criminal Law and Criminology* 32, no. 1 (May 1924): 32–41.
20 "WILD PURSUIT OF FOREIGNER ENDS TAMELY. Mistaken for Murderer, He Evades Capture then Reports to Police," Toronto *Globe*, 11 August 1920. On the settlement of Jews in Toronto, see Gerald Tulchinsky, *Taking Root: The Origins of the Canadian Jewish Community* (Toronto: University of Toronto Press, 1992); Stephen A. Speisman, *The Jews of Toronto to 1937* (Toronto: McClelland & Stewart, 1979).
21 City of Toronto, *Annual Report of the Chief Constable of the City of Toronto for the Year 1920* (Toronto: Carswell, 1921), 5. Steven Maynard does not refer to this murder, but he observes that juries often considered pubescent working-class males as partners in crime in cases involving older men. Maynard, "'Horrible Temptations': Sex, Men, and Working-Class Male Youth in Urban Ontario, 1890–1935," *Canadian Historical Review* 78, no. 2 (June 1997): 191–235.
22 Mrs. Goldberg's business may have been profitable, as she put up a $500 reward herself after her son's body was found. "Mother Puts Price on Murderer's Head," Toronto *Globe*, 17 August 1920. At the inquest, the police revealed that she covered up evidence that might have led to the killer's capture. "AVERS SILENCE OF MOTHER LET SLAYER ESCAPE," Toronto *Globe*, 18 September 1920.
23 "MUST NOW FACE TRIAL ON CHARGE OF MURDER," Toronto *Daily Star*, 14 November 1921. Davis was arrested in Rochester, New York, and was imprisoned at Auburn State Penitentiary.
24 "MURDER OF BOY, PHILIP GOLDBERG, LEADS TO ARREST," Toronto *Daily Star*, 24 June 1921.
25 Some newspapers speculated that Taylor was a "half-breed," but Chief G.W. Hill of the Six Nations Council wrote to confirm that the man, a resident of Brantford, was not related to anyone on the reservation. He had "not one drop of Indian blood." "TAYLOR NOT INDIAN," Brantford *Courier*, 13 September 1913.

26 Harley to Minister of Justice, 15 January 1914, in Taylor, Volume 1464, file 500A. Harley stated that he had represented Taylor "to the best of my ability," considering the "short notice" he was given before the trial began.

27 W.F. Cockshutt to Minister of Justice, 15 January 1914. Cockshutt was a pro-conscription Conservative MP who did not favour the commutation. F. Douglas Reville, *History of the County of Brant* (Brantford, ON: The Hurley Printing Company, 1920), 374–6.

28 On Smith's interpretation of homosexual desire as a pathological condition, for which "asexualization" was a cure, see Steven Maynard, "On the Case of the Case: The Emergence of the Homosexual as a Case History in Early-Twentieth-Century Ontario," in *Queerly Canadian: An Introductory Reader in Sexuality Studies*, ed. Maureen FitzGerald and Scott Rayter (Toronto: Canadian Scholars, 2012), 153–70, 161.

29 Côté to Minister of Justice, 19 January 1914, in Taylor, Volume 1464.

30 R.E. Watkins, *An Historical Review of the Role and Practice of Psychology in the Field of Corrections* (Ottawa: Research and Statistics Branch, Correctional Service of Canada, 1992). By 1918, psychological illnesses were recorded in 2.5 per cent of the Canadian Expeditionary Force, approximately 15,000 men. Humphries, "War's Long Shadow," 513.

31 R. v. Davis, transcript of evidence, 16, in Davis, Volume 1517.

32 Gallagher may have been covering for Chief Remission Officer J.D. Clarke. Two decades later, Minister of Justice Ernest Lapointe confirmed Gallagher's practice of marking up documents when he was asked to explain the review of capital cases. The chief, he said, "underlines all the parts which ought to be called to the attention of the minister." *Debates*, 27 February 1941, 1091.

33 Riddell to Minister of Justice, 9 February 1922, in Davis, Volume 1517. Gordon Bates, "Health League of Canada," *Canadian Journal of Public Health* 61, no. 1 (January/February 1970): 60–2.

34 Gallagher to Deputy Minister of Justice, 18 April 1922, in Davis, Volume 1517.

35 Essery was a partner in his father's downtown Toronto law firm, Essery and Roebuck. He lived in the upscale Annex district and was a member of the Toronto Club.

36 Essery to Minister of Justice, 4 May 1922, in Davis, Volume 1517, part 1.

37 Ibid. David Harri's sentence was commuted on 1 May 1922. Later in his career, Essery was disbarred for unprofessional conduct involving the misallocation of client funds. Discipline Committee, Law Society of Ontario, Minutes of Convocation, 15 March 1945, 477. I am grateful

to Paul Leatherdale for this reference and for all other references to members of the bar of Ontario.

38 Minister of Justice to Essery, 6 May 1922, in Davis, Volume 1517, part 1.

39 In reply to a letter from a J.E. Dobbs, who claimed to represent the Toronto Society for the Abolition of Capital Punishment, Gallagher explained why David Harri's sentence was commuted but Davis's was not: "Latter case was revolting." Gallagher to J.E. Dobbs, 8 May 1922, in Davis, Volume 1517, part 1.

40 Peter Barnham, *Forgotten Lunatics of the Great War* (New Haven, CT: Yale University Press, 2004), 236–45.

41 Dr. Daniel Phelan to Gallagher, 15 March 1925, in Harry D. Williams, Volumes 1533 and 1534, part 1, volume 1. Phelan noted that the minister of justice had requested that he evaluate whether Williams was "impaired at present, and if so to what degree" and also determine whether at the time of the offence his "mentality was then impaired, and to what degree, if any."

42 Williams, known previously as Darius Thornton, was tried only for the murder of the elder of the two girls he killed.

43 LeBlanc, a prominent Acadian lawyer admitted to the bar of New Brunswick in 1906, had just been appointed to the bench in 1924, and the Williams case was tried in January 1925. He was also a devout Catholic, on whom Pope Pius XI conferred a Papal Knighthood. Moncton *Times-Transcript*, 11 January 1957.

44 "Doctors Swear Prisoner Suffering from Dementia and Confusional Insanity," Fredericton *Daily Gleaner*, 26 January 1925. Dr. Anglin, of the St. John Hospital, likely learned about this diagnosis through the treatment of men with shell shock. See, for instance, W. Johnson, "The Acute Confusional States in the Psychoneurosis," *Journal of Neurological Psychopathology* 1, no. 1 (1920): 131–41.

45 Hughes was called to the bar in 1902 and made a KC in 1923. He was noted for his "meticulous preparation of cases and masterful courtroom presentations." He was elevated to the provincial Supreme Court bench in 1945. Fredericton *Daily Gleaner*, 15 October 1959.

46 "WILLIAMS WIFE HOLDS NO MALICE: Mrs. Ada Thornton Convinced Her Former Husband Is Insane," Fredericton Daily *Gleaner*, 2 December 1924.

47 "ARRIVES AT VERDICT 43 MINUTES AFTER LEGAL BATTLE ENDS," St. John *Telegraph Journal*, 27 January 1925. The capital case file refers to the second indictment for the murder of Neacia Foster. Multiple spellings of her name appear in press accounts.

48 "Williams Changed His Name So Wife Could Not Find Him," Fredericton *Daily Gleaner*, 17 December 1924.

49 Williams to Phelan, 12 March 1925, in Williams, Volume 1533, part 1, volume 1. Phelan included this letter, along with another in which Williams claimed he had previously lived "in the Service of Satan."

50 Phelan to Gallagher, 15 March 1925. Phelan was appointed the "surgeon" at Kingston Penitentiary in 1897, where he developed his standing as an expert in criminal insanity and degeneracy. Roger Neufeld, "Cabals, Quarrels, Strikes, and Impudence: Kingston Penitentiary, 1890–1914," *Histoire sociale/Social History* 31, no. 61 (1998): 95–125. Phelan also advised the government on Davis's sanity without examining him.

51 Keirstead to Minister of Justice, 30 March 1925, in Williams, Volume 1533, part 1, volume 1. On Keirstead as a social scientific thinker, equally anchored in theology, see Daniel C. Goodwin, "The Origins and Development of Wilfred Currier Keirstead's Social and Religious Thought," *Acadiensis* 37, no. 2 (Summer/Autumn 2008): 18–38.

52 John Kidman, secretary, Canadian Prisoners' Welfare Association to Lapointe, 17 April 1925, in Williams, Volume 1533, part 1, volume 1.

53 "MOTHER OF VICTIMS SAYS SHE COULD CUT HER HALF BROTHER'S BODY IN PIECES BIT BY BIT," Fredericton *Daily Gleaner*, 29 November 1924. Williams was executed, as scheduled, on 23 April 1925.

54 According to the *Daily Gleaner*, Williams "went overseas in September, 1918, with a draft of the 4th Siege Battery. He later joined the 3rd Divisional Ammunition Column in France, but afterwards transferred to the Trench Mortars of the 3rd Division with which he served throughout the rest of the war until the armistice." Fredericton *Daily Gleaner*, 28 November 1924. His wife might have mistaken months for years.

55 The letter, dated 1 February 1925, was published in the St. John *Telegraph Journal* on 5 February 1925. I am grateful to Michael Boudreau for sharing this source.

56 Frank W. Anderson, *The Dark Strangler: A Study in Strange Behaviour* (Calgary: Frontier Publishing, 1972), 36. The Winnipeg Police Service website features the case, including the names of twenty-four other murdered women suspected of being Nelson's victims. See John Burchill, "The Strangler," Winnipeg Police Service, https://www.winnipeg.ca/police/history/story21.stm. These sources overlook the racist framing of sexual danger. See Lesley Erickson, "Murdered Women and Mythic Villains: The Criminal Case and the Imaginary Criminal in the Canadian West, 1886–1930," in *People and Place: Historical Influences on Local Culture*,

ed. Jonathan Swainger and Constance Backhouse (Vancouver: UBC Press, 2003), 95–119, 107–12.

57 Anderson, *The Dark Strangler*, 37.

58 Stitt to Ernest Lapointe, n.d. (c. December 1927) in Nelson, Volume 1545, volume 1, part 5. Stitt's "argument for reprieve" was twenty-eight typed pages long. The City of Winnipeg paid $200 for Nelson's defence, out of $15,000 spent in total to capture and prosecute him. Winnipeg *Evening Tribune*, 7 November 1927.

59 *Canadian Police Bulletin* 13, no. 7 (September 1927): 15–19, in Nelson, Volume 1545, part 7, volume 1. In Nelson's case file, Remission Branch staff pasted in thirty-five pages of news clippings on the trial, verdict, and execution. The Manitoba *Free Press* alone published over 100 articles on the Winnipeg murders (Winnipeg *Free Press* archives). Stitt claimed the news of Nelson's arrest boosted the press's circulation by fifty thousand. Stitt to Earnest Lapointe, c. December 1927, 20, in Nelson, Volume 1545, part 5, volume 1, 21.

60 Erickson, "Murdered Women," 107–12.

61 Although Stitt was thirty-six at the time of Nelson's trial, he had only recently taken up law after serving in the Great War. In 1930, he was elected as a Conservative MP for Selkirk. See "James Herbert Stitt, Q.C., M.P.," Library of Parliament, Historical Information (Parlinfo), Parliamentarians, https://lop.parl.ca/sites/ParlInfo/default/en_CA/People/Profile?personId=10921.

62 Stitt to Lapointe, c. December 1927, in Nelson, Volume 1545, part 5, volume 1, 22. Stitt claimed that every lawyer in Winnipeg had agreed.

63 Gallagher to Minister of Justice, 15 December 1927 in Nelson, Volume 1545, part 2, volume 1.

64 H.C. Hendrie and J. Varsamis, "The Winnipeg Psychopathic Hospital 1919–1969. An Experiment in Community Psychiatry," *Canadian Psychiatric Association Journal* 16, no. 2 (April 1971): 185–6. Dr. Alvin Trotter Mathews served in the Great War and directed the hospital from 1919 to 1942.

65 "DOCTOR SAYS NELSON NOT INSANE. Wife and Aunt Tell Prisoner's Life Story; Crown Calls Expert," Winnipeg *Evening Tribune*," 4 November 1927. Stitt claimed he had asked four doctors to examine Nelson for the defence, but each had offered an excuse. Stitt to Lapointe, c. December 1927, in Nelson, Volume 1545, part 5, volume 1, 21. Thomas Beattie Roberton, columnist for the *Free Press*, criticized Stitt for failing to put his client on the stand to challenge contradictions in the Crown's chain of evidence. "The Insanity Plea," Manitoba *Free Press*, 9 November 1927.

66 Stitt to Earnest Lapointe, 10 December 1927, in Nelson, Volume 1545, part 2, volume 1. Stitt sent further petitions for clemency on 30 December and 4 January 1928.

67 Cabinet reviewed seven capital cases in December 1927, which meant Nelson's fate was not finalized until a month after Gallagher's recommendation. Toronto *Globe*, 7 December 1927. "Officers of the law department" leaked the report's recommendation to the press one day before cabinet met. "SLIM CHANCE OF REPRIEVE," Winnipeg *Tribune*, 11 January 1928.

68 Rosemary Pattenden, *English Criminal Appeals, 1844–1994: Appeals against Conviction and Sentence in England and Wales* (Oxford: Oxford University Press, 1996).

69 Canada, *Statutes of Canada*, 1920, c. 43, s. 16; *Statutes of Canada*, 1921, c. 25, s. 22; and *Statutes of Canada*, 1923, c. 41, s. 9. Vincent M. Del Buono argues that these enlargements were counterbalanced by the right of the attorney general to appeal judgments that set aside convictions. Uncertainty over the Crown's right of appeal after the 1923 amendment prompted amendments in 1925 and 1927. Buono, "Right to Appeal in Indictable Cases: A Legislative History," *Alberta Law Review* 16, no. 3 (1978): 446–69, 160–1.

70 The 1923 amendment revised s. 1014 of the 1906 *Revised Statutes*. "An Act Respecting the Criminal Law," *Revised Statutes of Canada*, 1927.

71 Ibid., s. 1014 (2).

72 John Paris's conviction was set aside, and the New Brunswick Supreme Court, Appeal Division ordered a new trial in March 1922. "The King v. Paris," *New Brunswick Reports*, 49 (1922), 400–23; Albert Nogaret's conviction was set aside by the Quebec Court of King's Bench, Appeal Side, and a new trial was ordered in June 1931. "Nogaret v. R.," Carswell Quebec, Cour du Banc du Roi du Québec, 70 (1931): 51–2; the Ontario Court of Appeal quashed John Comba's conviction in 1937 and entered an acquittal, which the Supreme Court of Canada upheld. "The King v. Comba," *S.C.R.* (1938): 396–8; and in an oral judgment, the Ontario Court of Appeal set aside the conviction of Demitres Papastamatiou and ordered a new trial in May 1942. I do not discuss the Paris and Papastamatiou cases, as their relevance to the clemency review process was less significant than it was in the other two cases.

73 "An Act Respecting the Criminal Law," *Revised Statutes of Canada*, 1927, c. 39, s. 1016 (4). The length of detention of such offenders was determined at the "governor's pleasure."

74 Dr. Mathers, transcript of evidence, 307, in Nelson, Volume 1545, part 1.

75 Christopher Moore, *The Court of Appeal for Ontario: Defining the Right of Appeal, 1792–2013* (Toronto: University of Toronto Press for the Osgoode Society for Canadian Legal History, 2014), 82–3. McMeans studied law in Ontario and practised in Winnipeg from the 1880s, often acting as a Crown attorney.

76 Kimberley White, *Negotiating Responsibility: Law, Murder and States of Mind* (Vancouver: UBC Press, 2008), xv–xvii. White's study is based on sixty-six capital case files, chosen randomly from the 570 considered by cabinet between 1920 and 1950.

77 "2 Coups de couteau au coeur auraient causé la mort d'une fillette trouvée en une cave," *La Presse*, 19 September 1930. Although significant decomposition had occurred before the autopsy, Dr. Derome claimed at the trial that he had found "very distinct signs" of a "criminal assault."

78 R. v. Nogaret, transcript of evidence, in Nogaret, Volume 1568, volume 2, part 1, 63. Derome was Professor of Legal Medicine and Toxicology at l'Université de Montréal from 1910. He was principally recognized for his expertise in ballistics, and J. Edgar Hoover consulted him before establishing the FBI's laboratory. Since Derome died in November 1931, the second trial of Nogaret in September 1931 was one of the last in which he appeared for the Crown. Jacques Côté, *Wilfrid Derome: expert en homicides* (Quebec: Editions Boréal, 2003).

79 "ALBERT NOGARET A ÉTÉ DÉCLARÉ CRIMINELLEMENT RESPONSABLE DE LA MORT DE LA FILLETTE CARON," *La Presse*, 7 October 1930.

80 "WITNESS FAINTS THRICE TESTIFYING IN CHILD'S MURDER," Montreal *Gazette*, 5 March 1931.

81 "A. NOGARET TROUVE COUPABLE DE MEURTRE SERA PENDU EN JUIN," *La Patrie*, 11 March 1931.

82 The order, founded in France in 1821, focused on providing boys' education, particularly the poor. Robin S. Gendron, "Education and the Origins of Quebec's International Engagement," *American Review of Canadian Studies* 46, no. 2 (2016): 217–32, 219.

83 Abbé Adélard Delorme was charged with murdering his brother in 1922, but no jury could agree on the verdict after four trials. At the age of twenty-five, Gendron was an associate on the defence team, and Dr. Derome testified for the Crown. Jean Monet, *La soutane et la couronne. Le procès du siècle: l'affaire Delorme* (Saint-Laurent, QC: Trécarré, 1993).

84 Gendron (1890–1959) was an early specialist in criminal law. In 1928, he was appointed a KC. Provincially, he supported the Union Nationale. Conservative Prime Minister R.B. Bennett appointed Gendron to his

cabinet in 1935. He appeared numerous times before the Quebec Court of Appeal and the Supreme Court of Canada, including in several capital cases. "L'hon. Lucien Gendron célèbre juriste, décedé," *La Presse*, 6 April 1959.

85 "NOGARET TO APPEAL MURDER CONVICTION AND DEATH PENALTY," Montreal *Gazette*, 31 March 1931; "MURDERED GIRL'S RING FIGURES IN NOGARET'S APPEAL," Montreal *Gazette*, 16 May 1931.

86 Justice Galipeault quoted from section 959 of the Criminal Code, which required the judge to declare a mistrial if he considered that "such disobedience might cause injustice." However, the interference was not discovered before the verdict was delivered. "Nogaret v. R.," Carswell Quebec, Cour du Banc du Roi du Québec, 70 (1931): 51–3, 52.

87 "MURDERED GIRL'S RING FEATURES IN NOGARET'S APPEAL," Montreal *Gazette*, 16 May 1931. Gendron argued that the letter could have only come from the self-identified murderer, but the Crown claimed that Nogaret had somehow managed to send it while in custody.

88 Justice Lafontaine in "Nogaret v. R.," 52.

89 Eugène Lafontaine (1857–1935) was chief justice of Quebec from 1922 to 1932. He was a member of the Quebec Liberal Party and represented Napierville from 1886 to 1890. Wilson (1869–1936) was appointed to the Court of King's Bench in 1922. He specialized in criminal law as a Crown prosecutor before his appointment. He ran federally for the Liberal Party and represented Laval in 1902. Benjamin Sulte, C.E. Fryer, and L.O. David, *A History of Quebec, Its Resources and People*, vol. 2 (Montreal: The Canada History Company, 1908), 766.

90 Justice Galipeault, in Sulte, Fryer, and David, *A History of Quebec*, 53. *La Presse* commented that "la Cour d'appeal … ne croit devoir se prononcer sur les autres motifs d'appel." "La Cour d'appel et la sentence contre Nogaret," *La Presse*, 26 June 1931.

91 Gendron was aided by Joseph Jean and Philippe Monette.

92 In the first trial, Godon fainted several times while giving his testimony. At the second trial, Justice Aimé Marchand ordered Godon from the courtroom because of his outbursts during testimony adverse to his accounts. "GODON INTERRUPTS TRIAL IN DRAMATIC MANNER," Montreal *Gazette*, 28 September 1931.

93 "Nogaret Acquitted at Second Trial of Murdering Girl," Ottawa *Journal*, 30 September 1931. Justice Marchand's charge referred directly to the defence's contention that Godon was the real killer and placed greater

emphasis on reasonable doubt concerning the Crown's evidence. The jury delivered its not guilty verdict in less than two hours.

94 Gendron was one of the leading organizers who "prepared to do everything in their power to bring Duplessis to victory." Patricia Dirks, *Failure of L'Action Libéral Nationale* (Montreal: McGill-Queen's University Press, 1991), 76.

95 Bernard L. Vigod. *Quebec before Duplessis: The Political Career of Louis-Alexandre Taschereau* (Montreal: McGill-Queen's University Press, 1986); Antonin Dupont, *Les relations entre l'Église et L'État sous Louis-Alexandre Taschereau* (Montreal: Guérin, 1972); Alexandre Dumas, "L'Église et l'État, de Taschereau à Duplessis: mythes et constructions historiques," *Mens* 16, no. 2 (Spring 2016): 9–36. The archbishop of Quebec, Jean-Marie-Rodrigue Villeneuve, appointed in 1931, became a strong supporter of Duplessis.

96 Susan Mann Trofimenkoff, *L'Action française: French-Canadian Nationalism in the Twenties* (Toronto: University of Toronto Press, 1975); Catherine Pomeyrols, "Les intellectuels nationalistes québécois et la condamnation de l'Action française," *Vingtième Siècle. Revue d'histoire* 1, no. 73 (2002): 83–98.

97 "S'EVANOUIT EN PLEINE COURT," Sherbrooke *Tribune*, 2 December 1938. In addition, Dr. Rosario Fontaine, who conducted the autopsy, confirmed that a different knife was the weapon used to stab the victim.

98 Antoine Rivard, KC, assisted in the prosecution. He was a criminal law specialist and a Conservative Party organizer in the 1930s. Jean Trépanier, "Hon. Antoine Rivard," *La Patrie*, 12 October 1958.

99 "JUDGE HALTS TRIAL OF ANTONIO GODON, ASKS SANITY TESTS. Lazure Thinks Caron Murder Accused Is Probably Insane," Montreal *Gazette*, 26 January 1939.

100 Ibid. The defence, led by Valmore Bienvenue, KC, and Antonio Laplante, objected because they did present an insanity defence.

101 "GODON HELD INSANE, UNFIT TO BE TRIED FOR CARON MURDER. Pointe-au-Trembles Mystery Left Unsolved by Jury's Decision," Montreal *Gazette*, 31 January 1939. The headline for the story of Godon's verdict, published in newspapers across North America linked to the Associated Press, was "MAN GETS LIFE FOR CRIME OF WHICH HE ACCUSED ANOTHER."

102 "GODON HELD INSANE UNFIT TO BE TRIED FOR CARON MURDER," Montreal *Gazette*, 31 January 1939. Michel Proulx, former Quebec Court of Appeal judge, states that Godon died shortly after his incarceration in the Criminal Insane Asylum at Bordeaux Prison. Daniel Proulx, "L'affaire Nogaret: qui a tué la petite Simone Caron?," in *Les*

Grands Procès du Québec (Montreal: Les éditions internationals Alain Stanké, 1996), 111–18, 118. On the risk of life imprisonment in association with evidence of insanity, see H.B. Spaulding, "Insanity and Criminal Responsibility from the Legal Point of View," *The Ontario Journal of Neuro-Psychiatry* 2 (March 1933): 11–24, 15.

103 Casgrain was first elected in 1927. He was a member of a Quebec law firm that included Louis-Alexandre Taschereau, Liberal premier from 1920 to 1936 and attorney general at the time of Nogaret's trial. Casgrain served as attorney general from 1942 to 1944 and was appointed judge of the Superior Court in 1948. Assemblée nationale du Québec, *Dictionnaire des parlementaires du Québec de 1792 à nos jours* (Québec: Presses de l'Université du Québec, 2010), http://www.assnat.qc.ca/en/deputes/casgrain-leon-2455/biographie.html.

104 "MURDER TRIAL IS CALLED ACT OF VENGEANCE. Liberal M.L.A. Charges Political Motive behind Man Known to Be Insane," Ottawa *Journal*, 8 February 1939.

105 Abel Vineberg, "Nogaret Trial 'Persecution' by Liberals, Premier Says. Duplessis Counters Casgrain Charge That Trial of Godon for Caron Murder Was Political Vengeance," Montreal *Gazette*, 8 February 1939.

106 "INHUMAN METHODS AT NOGARET TRIAL PROBED BY QUEBEC. Legislature Approves Bill Calling for Inquiry into Murder Case," Montreal *Gazette*, 15 April 1939. Duplessis referred to the methods used by police investigators and prosecutors in Nogaret's case as "scandalous and indescribable."

107 Duplessis's bill was titled "An Act to authorize an inquiry respecting the whole arrest of Albert Nogaret and the procedure and proceedings taken against him."

108 "PROBE SOUGHT INTO MURDER PROSECUTION," Toronto *Globe and Mail*, 15 April 1939.

109 "Brother Dosithée Passes in France," Montreal *Gazette*, 16 December 1938.

110 The quotation in this section's heading is taken from the newspaper article "SUPREME COURT ACQUITS COMBA. Dismisses Crown's Appeal to Uphold Murder Conviction," Montreal *Gazette*, 24 June 1938

111 Christopher Moore found that just one Catholic – Francis Latchford – was appointed to the Court of Appeal (out of fourteen appointments) between 1913 and 1938. He was the dissenting judge in the Comba decision. Moore, *The Court of Appeal for Ontario*, 96.

112 Starting in the 1950s, the government published reports that indicated considerable variations over time in the rate of execution. In the 1930s, the rate was 75 per cent, sliding to 66.2 per cent in the 1940s. Guy Favreau,

Capital Punishment: Material Relating to Its Purpose and Value (Ottawa: Information Canada, 1965), Appendix I, 98.

113 Testimony of Dr. J.J. McCann, transcript of evidence, 509, in Comba, Volume 1621, volume 2. Tests of fluid in the vagina and rectum did not reveal evidence of sperm, but Dr. Frankish, the Crown's expert, stated that he rarely found sperm in murder victims who had been "assaulted." Frankish, transcript of evidence, 555.

114 Galligan, a Pembroke, Ontario, KC, was called to the bar in 1915, and in 1933 he defended Renfrew's chief of police (who was the principal Crown witness in the Comba trial) in a slander suit. "Chief Greer Wins His Suit Against Renfrew Resident," Ottawa *Journal*, 13 December 1033.

115 Maloney's father, Dr. Martin J. Maloney, was a Conservative MP from 1925 to 1935. J.A. Maloney was called to the bar in 1924. In 1961, he predeceased his brother, Arthur Maloney, also a Conservative MP, but better known as a defence lawyer and opponent of the death penalty. Charles Pullen, *The Life and Times of Arthur Maloney: The Last of the Tribunes* (Toronto: Dundurn Press for the Osgoode Society for Canadian Legal History, 1994).

116 "JUDGE DECIDES COMBA'S WORDS ARE EVIDENCE," Ottawa *Journal*, 20 November 1937. The inspector of the Criminal Identification Branch confirmed that, once Comba was cautioned, he refused to talk. E.E. Gurnett to Chief Inspector, 29 November 1937, in Comba, Volume 1621, volume 2.

117 "Entering Appeal from Conviction in Comba Case," Ottawa *Journal*, 30 November 1937.

118 "Rex v. Comba," *The Ontario Reports, 1938: Cases Determined in the Supreme Court of Ontario, the Court of Appeal for Ontario and the High Court of Justice for Ontario* (Toronto: The Carswell Company, 1939), 200–38, 212. Middleton also criticized the Crown for presenting "exceedingly imperfect" forensic evidence (208).

119 Canada, "An Act to Amend the Criminal Code," *Statutes of Canada*, 1930, c. 11, s. 28. The revision stated that the attorney general "shall have the right to appeal to the court of appeal against any judgment or verdict of acquittal of a trial court in respect of an indictable offence on any ground of appeal which involves a question of law alone."

120 Christopher Moore, *The Court of Appeal for Ontario*, 83. Appeals arose slowly also because of the expenses involved: "legal representation for criminal defendants' appeals often depended on charitable measures by courts or the bar" (83).

121 Chevrier's elevation to the High Court of Ontario in 1936 made him the first French Canadian to serve. "Edgar-Rodolphe-Eugène Chevrier, Q.C., M.P.," Library of Parliament, Historical Information (Parlinfo), Parliamentarians, https://lop.parl.ca/sites/ParlInfo/default/en_CA/People/Profile?personId=12535.

122 Canada, "Fraser v. the King," *S.C.R., 1936* (Ottawa: J.O. Patenaude, 1937), 1–4.

123 Quoted in Benjamin Berger, "The Rule in Hodge's Case: Rumours of Its Death Are Greatly Exaggerated," *The Canadian Bar Review* 84 (2005): 47–74, 52. The rule was "wholeheartedly embraced" in Comba, Berger contends (50).

124 The release of Comba from custody before the attorney general of Ontario appealed the acquittal decision to the Supreme Court was unprecedented. It prompted the government to pass "An Act to Amend the Criminal Code," *Statutes of Canada*, 1938, chap. 44, s. 49. Thereafter, prisoners had to remain in prison pending the outcome of an appeal by the attorney general. "Change in Law Arises from Comba Trial," Ottawa *Journal*, 28 August 1938.

125 "Rex v. Comba," 214. Middleton's quote was from Justice Rinfret's decision in "Fraser v. the King."

126 Latchford, eighty-four at the time of the Comba appeal, had a reputation among his fellow judges as an uncongenial man, whom former chief justice Mulock found to be "narrow and impulsive." Quoted in Moore, *The Court of Appeal for Ontario*, 90.

127 "SUPREME COURT ACQUITS COMBA," Montreal *Gazette*, 24 June 1938.

128 Canada, "The King v. Comba," *Canada Law Reports, 1938* (Ottawa: J.O. Patenaude, 1939), 396–8.

129 "Comba Household Is Filled with Joy at Court's Ruling. Mother Feels Highest Court in Land Has Upheld Faith She Had in Her Son's Innocence." Ottawa *Citizen*, 23 June 1938.

130 "DEEP SORROW AT FUNERAL OF RENFEW GIRL," Ottawa *Journal*, 6 August 1937; "Supreme Court Leaves John Comba Free of Murder Charge," Ottawa *Evening Citizen*, 23 June 1938.

131 Anton Kaes, *M* (London: British Film Institute, 1999), 69. The film fictionalizes the case of Fritz Haarmann, executed in 1925 for a series of sex murders of boys and men, and Peter Kürten, executed in 1931 for the sex murders of girls and women.

132 "TAYLOR KILLER ANOTHER MAN DEFENCE COUNSEL INSISTS," Toronto *Daily Star*, 8 November 1935. Regan (1885–1940) worked in civil and criminal cases, and he gained a reputation for taking on unpopular

cases and causes. However, his "antics" and abusive treatment of witnesses drew criticism from many in the legal profession. Robert Sharpe, *The Last Trial, the Last Hour: The Currie Libel Trial* (Toronto: University of Toronto Press for the Osgoode Society for Canadian Legal History, 2009 [1988]), 240–3. Justice Nicol Jeffrey admonished Regan for inappropriate outbursts at numerous points in the trial.

133 After Regan's death in 1940 at the age of fifty-six, the press referred to his defence of O'Donnell as one of his most noteworthy trials, in which he displayed his "penchant for fighting the cause of the underdog." Toronto *Globe and Mail*, 10 June 1940.

134 Several months after the O'Donnell trial, Prime Minister King appointed McRuer, a loyal Liberal and fierce critic of the penitentiary system, to be a commissioner on the Archambault Commission. J. Patrick Boyer, *A Passion for Justice: How "Vinegar Jim" McRuer became Canada's Greatest Law Reformer* (Dundurn Press for the Osgoode Society for Canadian Legal History, 2008).

135 Ontario, *Report of the Royal Commission to Inquire into and Report upon the Events and Circumstances Connected with the Arrest of Albert Dorland and William Toohey* (Toronto, 1933). Although Chief Draper was also implicated, he remained in power. Edward Butts, *Running with Dillinger: The Story of Red Hamilton and Other Forgotten Canadian Outlaws* (Toronto: Dundurn, 2008).

136 The trial, which opened on 2 February, was "likely to be the longest in city history," the *Globe* speculated on 20 January 1936 when McRuer announced the Crown would call forty-six witnesses, including six forensic science experts.

137 The Canada Evidence Act restricted the number of experts whom counsel could call to five. Justice Nicol Jeffrey allowed McRuer to call more, as "any witness can be considered an expert." O'Donnell, Volume 1602, part 1, transcript of evidence, 17.

138 "ANALYSES OF BLUE HAIR DISSENTING," Toronto *Globe*, 12 February 1936. Regan's expert in textiles and forensic chemistry, Dr. Frederick Zeidler, contended that blue fibres found on O'Donnell's clothes came from his wife's sweater, not Taylor's.

139 Douglas M. Lucas, "Professor L. Joslyn Rogers: A Tribute to a Canadian Pioneer in Forensic Science," *Canadian Society of Forensic Science Journal* 42, no. 4 (2009): 223–7. Dr. Linnaeus J. Rogers appeared in over two hundred criminal cases and specialized in chemical analysis.

140 "O'DONNELL GUILTY, TO HANG MAY 5," Toronto *Globe*, 16 February 1936.

141 Toronto mayor, Jimmie Simpson, and Max Clavir, justice of the peace, both used this term when they advocated a reward of $2,000 for the capture of the man responsible for Taylor's murder. "POLICE BOARD APPROVES PRICE ON SLAYER'S HEAD," Toronto *Daily Star*, 6 November 1935.

142 Chief Constable of Toronto, D.A. Draper, to the Commissioner of the Royal Canadian Mounted Police, 19 February 1936, in O'Donnell, Volume 1601–02, part 3. On the outpouring of sympathy for Taylor, and the panic her murder caused among working women, see Katrina Srigley, *Breadwinning Daughters: Young Working Women in a Depression-Era City, 1929–1939* (Toronto: University of Toronto Press, 2010), 69–71, 88–93.

143 The court rejected the appellant's claim that the "sight of these photographs prejudiced the jury against the accused." "R. v. O'Donnell," *Dominion Law Reports*, 2 (1936), 517–32, 517. This criminal appeal was the first to consider this ground. Rodney G.S. Carter, "'Ocular Proof': Photographs as Legal Evidence," *Archivaria* 69 (Spring 2010): 23–47, 38–9.

144 "O'DONNELL CONFESSION LISTS OTHER ATTACKS," Toronto *Daily Star*, 16 May 1936. O'Donnell used the identical tactics in the same neighbourhood to sexually assault a woman. He was convicted in 1929 of attempted rape and sentenced to three years at the Kingston Penitentiary, but he was granted a ticket of leave in 1930. W.W. Watson, Finger Print Section, RCMP, to T.S. Waldron, Remission Branch, 21 February 1936, in O'Donnell, Volume 1601, part 3.

145 Ernest Lapointe was one of the most experienced ministers of justice up to that point, having served three times in the role for a total of eight years in office by 1936. He appears to have taken a rest cure in April 1936. "Minister of Justice Leaves for Paris," Ottawa *Journal*, 3 April 1936.

146 Clare to Acting Minister of Justice, 1 May 1936, in O'Donnell, Volume 1601, part 4.

147 Ibid. Dr. Clare earned his medical degree in 1901. He was superintendent at the Ontario Hospital for the Insane from 1920 to 1925, when he became superintendent of the Homewood Sanitarium. He was also an advisor to the Hospitals Department and administrator of the Ontario Hospital in Toronto. Cheryl Krasnik Warsh, *Moments of Unreason: The Practice of Canadian Psychiatry and the Homewood Retreat, 1883–1923* (Montreal: McGill-Queen's University Press, 1989), 35–6.

148 Strange, "The Lottery of Death," 613. Thomas S. Waldron, a senior law clerk, was Gallagher's chief assistant by the 1930s. As of 1942, Gallagher's

salary was $6,440, and Waldron's was the next highest at $3,000. Canada, *Report of the Auditor General to the House of Commons (for the fiscal year ended 31 March 1942)* (Ottawa: King's Printer, 1942), 131.

149 On the historic and contemporary dimensions of this tactic, see Elizabeth Sheehy, ed., *Sexual Assault in Canada: Law, Legal Practice and Women's Activism* (Ottawa: University of Ottawa Press, 2012).

150 Canada, *Report of the Royal Commission to Investigate the Penal System of Canada, Joseph Archambault, Chairman*, vol. II (Ottawa: J.C. Patenaude, 1938), 307.

151 On the homosexual as the focus of public fear and policing in the United States, see Estelle B. Freedman, "'Uncontrolled Desires': The Response to the Sexual Psychopath, 1920–1960," *The Journal of American History* 74, no. 1 (1987): 83–106. For the impact of Hoover's "war" in Canada, see Elise Chenier, "The Criminal Sexual Psychopath in Canada: Sex, Psychiatry and the Law at Mid-Century," *Canadian Bulletin of Medical History* 20, no. 1 (2003): 75–101, 84.

152 J. Edgar Hoover, "WAR ON THE SEX CRIMINAL," Los Angeles *Times Magazine*, 26 September 1937, 2, 13. The story that followed in Hoover's series was titled "Parole and Its Abuses."

153 J. Edgar Hoover to RCMP Commissioner, 22 November 1939. Hoover closed with the following words: "Assuring you of my desire to afford you every cooperation in the exchange of criminal identifying data." Nighswander, Volume 1623, part 2. Information on Nighswander's criminal convictions and his imprisonment at the Erie County Penitentiary came from the special agent in charge at Buffalo. W.W. Watson to Chief of Remission Service, 15 November 1939, in Nighswander, Volume 1623, part 2.

154 New York State Senator Walter J. Mahoney responded to the boy's murder by proposing state legislation to "curb sex crimes such as this." He criticized the Erie County Penitentiary for releasing a man who was not treated for committing a minor moral offence, a common prelude to sex murders. "MAHONEY URGES BILL TO PREVENT NEW SEX CRIMES," Buffalo *Evening News*, 24 June 1939.

155 "'I JUST MURDERED A MAN' NURSE QUOTES NIGHSWANDER," Toronto *Daily Star*, 7 July 1939.

156 "Nighswander Was Freed to Care for Ill Mother," Buffalo *Evening News*, 23 June 1939. In New York State, a Special Joint Legislative Committee was struck in 1937 in response to sex murders of children, and in 1939 the City of New York established a Mayor's Committee on Sex Offences. Stephen Robertson, *Crimes against Children: Sexual Violence and Legal*

Culture in New York City, 1880–1960 (Chapel Hill: University of North Carolina Press, 2005), 142–2.

157 Cromarty, called to the bar in 1937, made it known in the trial that this was his first case. "Murder Method Cited," Buffalo *Evening News*, 14 October 1939.

158 Common joined the Ontario Department of the Attorney General in 1926 and was named a KC at the age of thirty-two in 1931. A profile on his retirement in 1964 noted that he had served under eleven attorneys general and "helped prosecute more rapists and murderers than almost any other lawyer in the nation." Tom Ford, "William Common: Gray Eminence of Ontario Law," Toronto *Daily Star*, 21 November 1964.

159 Frank A. Colligan, "Murder Was Methodical, Crown Prosecutor Claims," Buffalo *Evening News*, 14 October 1939.

160 "NIGHSWANDER'S LAWYER TO ASK FOR CLEMENCY," Buffalo *Courier-Express*, 17 October 1939.

161 "PSYCHIATRIST GIVES EVIDENCE IN MURDER CASE. States He Treated Man Accused in Welland for 'Unusual Tendencies,'" Toronto *Globe and Mail*, 13 October 1939. A fellow inmate in the Erie County Penitentiary testified that Nighswander had admitted to his sexual desires for boys.

162 "NIGHSWANDER HELD PSYCHOPATHIC CASE," Montreal *Gazette*, 13 October 1939.

163 Cromarty to Minister of Justice, 1 December 1939, in Nighswander, Volume 1623, part 2.

164 "BUFFALO MAN IS CONVICTED IN MURDER CASE," Toronto *Globe and Mail*, 16 October 1939.

165 Chevrier to Minister of Justice, 28 October 1939, in Nighswander, Volume 123, part 2.

166 Clare to Chief of Remission Service, 8 December 1939, in Nighswander, Volume 123, part 2. A clerk in the branch also provided a short unauthored memo giving the definitions of schizophrenia and dementia.

167 Gallagher, memorandum for the Minister of Justice, 12 December 1939, in Nighswander, Volume 123, part 2. After John Cromarty complained he could not afford to hire psychiatrists or fund an appeal, Gallagher granted him a personal visit in Ottawa on 9 December 1939. "NIGHSWANDER'S CLEMENCY PLEA BEFORE CABINET, Ruling Expected Within Day or Two; Buffalonian Doomed to Be Hanged Next Monday," Buffalo *Courier Express*, 12 December 1939.

168 *Hush*, 22 February 1936. The editorial, published just as O'Donnell's trial closed, claimed that people who criticized the paper's lurid warnings "should be more concerned with preventing a repetition of this horrible crime than in pouring over the details of a killing which shocked the whole city."

169 The association between female alcohol consumption and loose morals, prostitution, and feeble-mindedness was evident on the bench in this period as well as in the minds of male jurors. See especially Constance Backhouse, *Carnal Crimes: Sexual Assault Law in Canada, 1900–1975* (Toronto: Irwin Law for the Osgoode Society for Canadian Legal History, 2008), chapters two and three.

170 The murder of Bernice Connors in Black Harbour, New Brunswick, in 1942 also took place after she socialized with strangers (servicemen from a nearby airbase) at a dance where alcohol flowed freely. The defence claimed that Sergeant Thomas Hutchings suffered from "pathological drunkenness," but he was convicted and executed for the crime on 16 December 1942. B.J. Grant, *Six for the Hangman* (Fredericton, NB: Goose Lane Editions, Fiddlehead Poetry Books, 1983), 43–51.

171 Craig Heron, *Booze: A Distilled History* (Toronto: Between the Lines, 2003), 276. The exception was Prince Edward Island, where restrictions remained tight until 1940.

172 Quoted in Justice Nicol Jeffrey to Minister of Justice, 9 November 1936, in Bliss, Volume 1606, part 1. The judge referred to evidence in the coroner's inquest and preliminary trial.

173 The doctors were John N. Senn, medical superintendent of the Ontario Hospital at Hamilton, and George E. Hobbs, acting superintendent. Bliss, Volume 1606, part 2, 5 and 17 October 1936. In 1946, Senn sent submissions to the Royal Commission on Criminal Sexual Psychopaths, and Hobbs became president of the Canadian Psychiatric Association. On Senn's inclination to consider sex offenders criminally responsible, see Chenier, *Strangers in Our Midst*, 84–5.

174 Quoted in Chief Constable C.E. Watkins, Fort William, to Commissioner of the RCMP, 26 October 1936, in Bliss, Volume 1606, part 1.

175 When Babe died in 1963 at the age of 81, he was remembered as "one of the few lawyers in Canada to have successfully entered a plea of guilty in a murder case." His obituary referred to the "sex murder" case of the 1930s, in which he respected his client's desire to "protect his socially prominent family." "Obituary, Fred Babe," Toronto *Daily Star*, 10 June 1963.

176 Justice Jeffery to Secretary of State, 9 November, in Bliss, Volume 1606, part 1.
177 Ibid. Jeffrey referred to Section 1061 of the Criminal Code.
178 Gallagher to Minister of Justice, 16 December 1931, in Bliss, Volume 1606, part 2.
179 The chief constable emphasized that Bliss's home environment was "of an exceptionally high character" and that his parents were "exceptionally devout people."
180 Babe to Ernest Lapointe, Minister of Justice, 9 December 1936, in Bliss, Volume 1606, part 2. Gallagher's red pen scores this section of Babe's letter with the marginal comment: "Police report says [Bliss] stated he wishes to avoid publicity to save parents from further grief."
181 Gallagher to Minister of Justice, 16 December 1936, in Bliss, Volume 1606, part 2.
182 Cecil S. Snyder to Ernest Lapointe, 2 December 1936 in Bliss, Volume 1606, part 2. Snyder also informed J.W. McFadden, KC, the Crown attorney for the County of York (Toronto). He sent a draft of his article to the minister "with a hope that it may be of some use to you at this time." Snyder served as deputy attorney general of Ontario from 1938 to 1948 and prosecuted close to forty murder cases in his career. "Cecil Snyder. Lawyer Wrote Tax Decisions," Toronto *Globe and Mail*, 29 August 1974.
183 "Rex v. Bliss, annotated," *Dominion Law Reports*, vol. 1 (1936), 1–17, 3, 11, 12, 13.
184 Strange, "Comment: Capital Case Procedure Manual," 187.
185 "NO INTERFERENCE IN DEATH SENTENCE," Lethbridge *Herald*, 4 January 1937. Bliss was executed in Port Arthur, Ontario, on 5 January 1937.
186 *Debates*, 12 February 1915.
187 These developments helped save John Paris, a black Nova Scotian, from execution after he was convicted of the murder of a "crippled" white girl, Sadie McAuley. The conviction was appealed, but after three subsequent trials, no (all-white) jury could agree on a verdict. Paris, Volume 1516.
188 Cromarty to Minister of Justice, 1 December 1939, in Nighswander, Volume 1623, part 2. Cromarty was named a QC in 1954, and he was elevated to the Supreme Court of Ontario in 1971. "New Judge from Welland to Be Sworn in Dec. 17," St. Catharines *Standard*, 27 November 1971.
189 "Summary of Recommendations," in Canada, *Report of the Royal Commission to Investigate the Penal System of Canada*, 354.
190 Ibid., 149–58.

4. Sexual Psychopathy and Penal Severity in the Post-War Era

1 Carolyn Strange and Tina Loo, *True Crime, True North: The Golden Age of Canadian Pulp Magazines* (Vancouver, BC: Raincoast Books, 2004). Many covers featured alluring women in imminent danger of sexual attack. See Will Straw, "Canada: The Canadian True Crime Magazine of the 1940s and 1950s," https://willstraw.com/canada-the-canadian-true-crime-magazine-of-the-1940s-and-1950s.

2 See, for example, "Murder Wave in Canada: Takes 100 Lives in 1947; Ontario's Rate Highest," Toronto *Globe and Mail*, 14 January 1948. The story referred to several solved and unsolved "sex-slayings." See also Elise Chenier, *Strangers in Our Midst: Sexual Deviancy in Post-War Ontario* (Toronto: University of Toronto Press, 2008), 18.

3 Between 1942 and 1946, the number of arrests for murder doubled, and the number of rapes increased by 50 per cent. Dominion Bureau of Statistics, *Statistics of Criminal and Other Offences for the Year Ended September 30, 1946* (Ottawa: Edmond Clouthier, 1948), viii. The mainstream press publicized official figures. Sydney Katz, "The Truth about Sex Criminals," *Maclean's* 60 (1 July 1947): 12, 46–8.

4 On the role of homophobia in criminal justice policy in the 1940s, see Patrick Brode, "'Perverts a Menace': The Development of the Criminal Sexual Psychopath Offence, 1948," in *Essays in the History of Canadian Law, Volume X: A Tribute to Peter N. Oliver*, ed. Jim Phillips, R. Roy McMurtry, and John T. Saywell (Toronto: University of Toronto Press for the Osgoode Society for Canadian Legal History, 2008), 107–28.

5 Salter Hayden, Canada, Senate, *Debates*, 16 June 1948, 582 (hereafter Senate, *Debates*). Hayden was a Liberal, appointed by Prime Minister Mackenzie King in 1940. In 1954, he became the co-chair of the Joint Committee on Capital and Corporal Punishment and Lotteries.

6 Mary Louise Adams, *The Trouble with Normal: Postwar Youth and the Making of Heterosexuality* (Toronto: University of Toronto Press, 1997); Mona Gleason, *Normalizing the Ideal: Psychology, Schooling, and the Family in Postwar Canada* (Toronto: University of Toronto Press, 1999); Gary Kinsman, *The Regulation of Desire: Homo and Hetero Sexualities* (Toronto: Black Rose Books, 1996).

7 Correctionalism was characterized by normalizing, corrective, and segregative strategies, which represented the state in a positive light. David Garland, *Punishment and Welfare: A History of Penal Strategies* (New Orleans, LA: Quid Pro Quo Books, 2018 [1985]), 227–8.

8 These cases are analysed, with twelve other cases involving Indigenous capitally convicted offenders, in Charlène Renaud, "La peine de mort et les autochtones au Canada (1940–1960)" (master's thesis, University of Ottawa, 1998).

9 On the over-representation of Indigenous capitally convicted offenders in this period, see Jacqueline Briggs, "Exemplary Punishment: T.R.L. MacInnes, the Department of Indian Affairs, and Indigenous Executions, 1936–52," *Canadian Historical Review* 100, no. 3 (2019): 398–438. On clemency as a tool of colonization in the colonial period, see Jonathan Swainger, "A Distant Edge of Authority: Capital Punishment and the Prerogative of Mercy in British Columbia, 1872–1880," in *Essays in the History of Canadian Law, Volume VI: British Columbia and the Yukon*, ed. Hamar Foster and John McLaren (Toronto: University of Toronto Press for the Osgoode Society for Canadian Legal History, 1995), 204–41; Tina Loo, "Savage Mercy: Native Culture and the Modification of Capital Punishment in Nineteenth-Century British Columbia," in *Qualities of Mercy: Justice, Punishment, and Discretion*, ed. Carolyn Strange (Vancouver: UBC Press, 1996), 104–30.

10 On homophobic police practices in Canada in this period, see Brode, "Perverts a Menace"; for the United States, see Douglas M. Charles, *Hoover's War on Gays: Exposing the FBI's "Sex Deviates" Program* (Lawrence: University Press of Kansas, 2015), 22, 252.

11 Chenier, *Strangers in Our Midst*, 125.

12 "Prison 'Futile Gesture' for Sex Offenders," Toronto *Globe and Mail*, 22 April 1947. The title and quote were the words of James C. McRuer, chief justice of Ontario.

13 The Canadian Association of Chiefs of Police strongly supported the death penalty in this period. Greg Marquis, *Policing Canada's Century: A History of the Canadian Association of Chiefs of Police* (Toronto: University of Toronto Press for the Osgoode Society for Canadian Legal History, 1993), 218–19. The majority of Canadians also approved of the lash. A.S. Marshall, "Crime Wave," *Maclean's* (15 April 1946): 7–8, 53–5.

14 National opinion polls conducted in 1943 indicated that 73 per cent of Canadians were in favour of capital punishment; that number went down just slightly to 71 per cent by 1953. David Chandler, *Capital Punishment in Canada: A Sociological Study of a Repressive Law* (Toronto: McClelland & Stewart, 1976), 41.

15 James Ilsley, Minister of Justice, Canada, House of Commons, *Debates*, 14 June 1948, 5184 (hereafter *Debates*). In 1950, CCF MP Ross Thatcher

introduced a private member's abolition bill, which did not reach third reading.

16 On Gallagher's disinclination to mercy, see Carolyn Strange, "Comment: Capital Case Procedure Manual," *Criminal Law Quarterly* 41 (1998): 184–97, 191.

17 In 1947, section 1023 of the Criminal Code was amended to allow persons whose convictions were upheld by a provincial court of appeal to appeal against the sustaining of the conviction to the Supreme Court on any ground of appeal involving a question of law alone. An Act to Amend the Criminal Code, 1947, chapter 55.

18 In the United States, the National Association of Legal Aid Societies was established in 1911. Scott Cuthbert, "Legal Aid for the Poor," *The Canadian Bar Review* 13, no. 3 (March 1935): 152–63, 156.

19 John P. Nelligan, "Legal Aid in Canada: Existing Facilities," *The Canadian Bar Review* 29, no. 6 (June–July, 1951): 589–620, 606–7.

20 The Supreme Court of Canada granted leave to appeal in two sex murder cases in this period: Vescio v. R and Ducharme v. R. Both men were executed after the court denied their appeals.

21 G.H. Stevenson, "Report on the Formation of the Canadian Psychiatric Association," *Canadian Medical Association Journal* 65 (December 1951): 592–4, 593.

22 Federal Conservative MP Dr. H.A. Bruce tabled this report in Parliament on 18 October 1945.

23 "A Lesson to Heed," Toronto *Globe and Mail*, 22 October 1945. On anxiety concerning the restoration of manliness among men who had served, see Christopher Dummitt, *The Manly Modern: Masculinity in Postwar Canada* (Vancouver: UBC Press, 2011), 33–9.

24 Dorothy E. Chunn, *From Punishment to Doing Good: Family Courts and Socialized Justice in Ontario, 1880–1940* (Toronto: University of Toronto Press, 1992).

25 Rose Ricciardelli and Dale C. Spencer, *Violence, Sex Offenders and Corrections* (London: Routledge, 2018), 16–17; Chenier, *Strangers in Our Midst*, 6–7.

26 Katz, "The Truth about Sex Criminals," 12. The subtitle of the article summarized the problem: "We jail these men, we lash them, then turn them loose to sin again – A frank report on a hush-hush subject."

27 Tamara Rice Lave, "Only Yesterday: The Rise and Fall of Twentieth Century Sexual Psychopath Laws," *Louisiana Law Review* 69, no. 3 (April 2009): 549–91.

28 Chenier, *Strangers in Our Midst*, 28–9. A Progressive Conservative, Green was active in social justice initiatives of the United Church. Marilyn Harrison, "The Social Influence of the United Church of Canada in British Columbia, 1930 to 1948" (master's thesis, University of British Columbia, 1967), 75. First elected to Parliament in 1935, Green later served as MP for Vancouver Quadra from 1949 to 1963. "Howard Green Fonds," City of Vancouver Archives, https://searcharchives.vancouver.ca/howard-green-fonds.

29 *Debates*, 3 July 1947, 5031.

30 *Debates*, 3 July 1947, 5033–4. Finance minister during the Second World War, Ilsley took a step down by accepting the justice portfolio on 10 December 1946.

31 Warren Baldwin, "Ilsley Plans Treatment for Sex Psychopaths," Toronto *Globe and Mail*, 4 June 1948. Although the government sponsored the bill, it answered "an appeal by John G. Diefenbaker."

32 Diefenbaker developed a nationwide reputation as a defence lawyer prior to entering Parliament. He was appointed a KC in 1930 and first elected the member from Lake Centre, Saskatchewan, in 1940. Garrett Wilson and Kevin Charles Wilson, *Diefenbaker for the Defence* (Ann Arbor: University of Michigan, 1988).

33 *Debates*, 14 June 1948, 5196. In 1929, Diefenbaker argued in R. v. Olson that the trial jury had unreasonably dismissed evidence of insanity. The Court of Appeal in Saskatchewan dismissed the appeal, but the cabinet commuted the sentence of another man whom Diefenbaker described as feeble-minded. Wilson and Wilson, *Diefenbaker for the Defence*, 70–3.

34 *Debates*, 14 June 1948, 5198. Smith was a "formidable criminal trial lawyer who was nationally respected." Legal Archives Society of Alberta, "Centennial," http://www.legalarchives.ca/exhibits/LASAcentennial.pdf.

35 At approximately 11 p.m., Bill 337, An Act to Amend the Criminal Code, was read a second time, considered in Committee of the Whole, reported with amendments, and considered as amended. "By leave, the said Bill was read the third time and passed." Canada, *Journals of the House of Commons*, 14 June 1948, 574. Since no vote was taken, Chenier's claim that the vote was "unanimous" is incorrect. Chenier, *Strangers in Our Midst*, 8.

36 Brode, "Perverts a Menace," 121.

37 Pouliot specialized in municipal law. He was a populist and an anti-intellectual, who attacked the power and lack of accountability of civil servants. He was also "infamous for the volume and sharpness of his

criticisms." Robert A. Wardhaugh, *Behind the Scenes: The Life and Work of William Clifford Clark* (Toronto: University of Toronto Press, 2010), 130.

38 *Debates*, 14 June 1948, 5199.

39 *Debates*, 14 June 1948, 5199. Ilsley resigned from Parliament and returned to his law practice in October 1948. He was appointed to the Nova Scotia Supreme Court in May 1949. *Celebrating the 250th Anniversary of the Supreme Court of Nova Scotia*, https://courts.ns.ca/history_of_courts/history_noframes/chiefjustices.htm.

40 This cohort comprised one seventh of the case load in this period.

41 This text defined the criminal sexual psychopath in the final draft of the legislation. *Debates*, 14 June 1948, 5203.

42 W.W. McBride, "The Bloody Knife Points to Death," *Daring Crime Stories*, February 1947, 26–9, 38. Although the high school student was out on her own, the story did not question her sexual morals. The story's subtitle was "A YOUNG GIRL'S HARMLESS WALK ENDED IN HER HORRIBLE MURDER."

43 Interest was most intense at the preliminary hearing, when the "crowd overpacked the courtroom." Winnipeg *Tribune*, 30 August 1945. Unlike the Winnipeg *Free Press*, the *Tribune* published the police theory that "attempted criminal assault" was the motive. The *Free Press*, 17 October 1945, reported the victim's sister found her with her dress "up around her neck and her bloomers were torn off."

44 R. v. Proulx, transcript of evidence, 254, 258, in LAC, Proulx, Volume 1651, volume 1 (hereafter name, Volume).

45 Ibid., 256, 261.

46 "REPRIEVE SAVES PROULX: Death Penalty Changed to Life Imprisonment for St. Boniface Youth," Winnipeg *Free Press*, 28 December 1945.

47 On controversies over the identification of Métis people, see Chris Andersen, *"Métis": Race, Recognition, and the Struggle for Indigenous Peoplehood* (Vancouver: UBC Press, 2014).

48 Gallagher's summary, which conveyed the judge's recommendation to clemency, did not refer to the advice he had received from the Indian Affairs Branch on this case. On death penalty recommendations concerning Métis accused, see Briggs, "Exemplary Punishment," 422–9.

49 Chunn, *From Punishment to Doing Good*, 40–1; Deborah Weinstein, *The Pathological Family: Postwar America and the Rise of Family Therapy* (Ithaca, NY: Cornell University Press, 2013).

50 Andrew Knox Dysart, a Catholic, was appointed to the Manitoba Court of King's Bench in 1921. Dale Brawn, *The Court of Queen's Bench of Manitoba*,

1870–1950: A Biographical History (Toronto: University of Toronto Press for the Osgoode Society for Canadian Legal History, 2006), 268–76. See also Roy St. George Stubbs, "Mr. Justice Dysart," *The Canadian Bar Review* 32 (1954): 161–78.

51 The Winnipeg branch was established in 1933. Winnipeg *Tribune*, 24 July 1933. Brock was appointed a KC in 1941 and was active in the Kiwanis Club. See "Cadet Clifford Wallace Brock," Canadian Great War Project, http://canadiangreatwarproject.com/searches/soldierDetail.asp?ID=141309.

52 Dr. A.T. Mathers was former director of the Manitoba Psychopathic Hospital. Dr. Brian Bird, the assistant provincial psychiatrist, also testified for the defence. Brock to Minister of Justice, 10 November 1945, in Proulx, Volume 1651, volume 2, part 1.

53 Winnipeg's juvenile court was one of the first to operate under the authority of the Juvenile Delinquents Act in 1909. Winnipeg *Telegram*, 7 February 1909.

54 Dr. Mathers used this phrase in his testimony for the defence. "Proulx Statement Is Not Admissible," Lethbridge *Herald*, 18 October 1945. For the commutation, see Proulx, Volume 1651, part 1.

55 In the 1930s, seven young capital offenders were executed, and the executive commuted the sentences of an equal number. In the 1940s, seven of twenty-three capitally convicted offenders aged twenty or under were executed. Canada, Joint Committee of the House and Senate on Capital Punishment, Corporal Punishment and Lotteries, "Minutes of Proceedings and Evidence," Number 12, Table H, 517.

56 Gallagher to Minister of Justice, 7 December 1945, in Proulx, Volume 1651, part 1. Newspapers claimed that Proulx's age, and the fact that "medical authorities" found him "mentally deficient," prompted the commutation. "Death Sentence on Proulx Commuted," Medicine Hat *Daily News*, 28 December 1945.

57 Jeffrey S. Leon, "The Development of Canadian Juvenile Justice: A Background for Reform," *Osgoode Hall Law Journal* 15, no. 1 (1977): 71–106. On the broader trend toward "socialized justice," see Chunn, *From Punishment to Doing Good*.

58 "Juvenile Delinquents Act," *Statutes of Canada*, 1908, chapter 40. In 1921, the act was amended to expand the definition of "juvenile delinquent" to include youth "guilty of sexual immorality or any similar form of vice." "An Act to Amend the Juvenile Delinquents Act," *Statutes of Canada*, 1921, chapter 37, s. 1.

59 Leon, "The Development of Canadian Juvenile Justice, 71–106, 100.

60 Xiaobei Chen, *Tending the Gardens of Citizenship: Child Saving in Toronto, 1880s–1920s* (Toronto: University of Toronto Press, 2005); Tamara Meyers, *Caught: Montreal's Modern Girls and the Law, 1869–1945* (Toronto: University of Toronto Press, 2006); Michael Boudreau, "'Delinquents Often Become Criminals': Juvenile Delinquency in Halifax, 1918–1935," *Acadiensis* 39, no. 1 (January 2010): 108–32.
61 Mary Louise Adams, "Youth, Corruptibility, and English-Canadian Postwar Campaigns against Indecency, 1948–1955," *Journal of the History of Sexuality* 6, no. 1 (1995): 89–117.
62 "Youthful Criminals. Ontario Has Many Trials Involving the Charge of Murder," Branford *Expositor*, 10 January 1946. During 1945, the story stated, twenty-one male youths were charged with murder in Ontario.
63 "THIS FIEND MUST BE CAUGHT," Windsor *Star*, 20 August 1945. All five attacks occurred in Windsor's "beats" frequented by men seeking other men for sexual encounters.
64 The police later charged one of these survivors, Alexander Voligny, with gross indecency. Patrick Brode, *The Slasher Killings: A Canadian Sex-Crime Panic, 1945–1946* (Detroit, MI: Wayne State University Press, 2009), 157.
65 Sheriff of Essex County to the Secretary of State, 17 October 1946, in Sears, Volume 1659, volume 1. Sears's parents were English; he was a Canadian-born Anglican.
66 Brode, *The Slasher Killings*, 67–9.
67 "Youth Cracks when Charged as Slasher," Ottawa *Journal*, 10 July 1946.
68 Report of Justice Dalton Wells to Minister of Justice, 1 October 1946, in Sears, Volume 1659, volume 1, part 1.
69 Ibid. Wells also noted that Sears was convicted of only one of the two murders and that the three charges of attempted murder had been traversed.
70 Ibid.
71 Joseph Patrick O'Brien, the writer of the letter dated 16 November 1946, identified himself as a staff member of the Victoria Hospital in London, Ontario. Sears, Volume 1659, volume 1, part 2.
72 Brode, *The Slasher Killings*, 149. The Sears family had paid a Windsor lawyer, W.L. Clark, 100 dollars to defend their son and mortgaged their home to him. His forma pauperis filing prompted the court to appoint a lawyer to represent Sears's appeal.
73 Charles Pullen, *The Life and Times of Arthur Maloney: The Last of the Tribunes* (Toronto: Dundurn Press for the Osgoode Society for Canadian Legal History, 1994), 54. Arthur Maloney agreed to represent Sears

after the Windsor Crown attorney decided to try him subsequently for attempted murder.

74 "Slashings and Normal Life for Boy, 17, 'Absurd' – Justice," Toronto *Daily Star*, 19 November 1946.

75 Ibid.

76 "Police Third-Degree Questioning of 'Slasher' Scored by Appeal Court," Toronto *Globe and Mail*, 19 November 1946. A new civil rights magazine cited the Sears case as a violation of fundamental rights, narrowly averted by the Court of Appeal. *Civil Rights* 1, no. 4 (December 1946): 6.

77 Adams, "Youth, Corruptibility."

78 Ethel Huffman to Minister of Justice, 28 November 1946, in Sears, Volume 1659, file 2. Gallagher responded on 6 November, merely to inform her that the conviction had been set aside.

79 "TRAGEDY BRED BY LAXNESS," Montreal *Gazette*, 27 February 1945.

80 Matthieu Carron, "Modernizing Mount Royal Park: Montréal's Jungle in the 1950s" (master's thesis, Université de Montréal, 2016). On the reactionary "clean-up" campaign that followed the Benson murder and intensified over the following decade, see Mathieu Lapointe, *Nettoyer Montréal: les campagnes de moralité publique, 1940–1954* (Québec: Septentrion, 2014), 107.

81 "TRAGEDY," Montreal *Gazette*, 27 February 1945.

82 "Aux funérailles du jeune John Benson," *La Presse*, 28 February 1945. "Dead Girl's Parents," Winnipeg *Tribune*, 30 July 1945. The story included large images of Smith's step-father and mother, and her sister who found her.

83 "Une souricière tendue pendant les obsèques," *La Presse*, 28 February 1945. The police, posted at the Anglican church where the funeral was held, hoped they might trap the culprit. *Le Devoir* also covered the crime extensively and claimed that no other case had caused such revulsion in Montreal. Carron, "Modernizing Mount Royal Park," 28–9.

84 "POLICE SAY DERELICT ADMITS KILLING BOY, 9," Toronto *Daily Star*, 18 April 1945.

85 Operated by the federal Bureau of Prisons, this hospital was established to treat federal prisoners who were insane or psychopathic. Louis N. Robinson, "Institutions for Defective Delinquents," *Journal of Criminal Law and Criminology* 24, no. 2 (July–August 1933): 352–99, 373–4.

86 The detective office of the Montreal Police Department relayed this information on Chassé's background to the RCMP on 6 June 1945, shortly after the trial. Their report alleged he had told the officers "that he was a pervert, that he went in 'for sodomy,'" and that he had previously sexually attacked boys. Chassé, Volume 1650, volume 1, part 1.

87 Drapeau (1916–99) began his career in criminal law. After the Benson trial, he led clean-up campaigns that focused on the area where the boy's body was found. From 1950 to 1953, he served as a prosecutor for the Caron Commission, which investigated complaints of corruption on the Montreal police force. Magaly Brodeur, *Vice et corruption à Montréal: 1892–1970* (Québec: Presses de l'Université du Québec, 2001), chapter two.

88 "Roland C. Chassé rend témoignage," *La Presse*, 29 May 1945.

89 Cited in Michael Gallagher's report to the Minister of Justice, 6 February 1946 in Chassé, Volume 1650, volume 1, part 1. Lazure was a "quiet, ascetic-looking man with a broad knowledge of criminal law. He was stern yet not without compassion." Fred Kaufman, *Searching for Justice: An Autobiography* (Toronto: University of Toronto Press for the Osgoode Society for Canadian Legal History, 2005), 110.

90 Drapeau recounted his efforts to appeal in his final bid for clemency. Drapeau to Minister of Justice, 31 January 1946 in Chassé, Volume 1650, volume 1, part 1.

91 Gallagher to Minister of Justice, 6 February 1946, in Chassé, Volume 1650, volume 1, part 2.

92 "Derelict Charged in Benson Murder," Ottawa *Journal*, 18 April 1945.

93 "'STRANGE BROTHERS' MENACE: HUNDREDS OF SEX FIENDS AT LARGE," *Justice Weekly* 1, no. 40 (5 October 1946): 2. The article referred to the Vescio, Staley, and Sears cases, among others.

94 Winnipeg police arrested Michael Vescio for the September 1946 murder of thirteen-year-old George Smith. He was also suspected of the murder of Roy McGregor on 4 January 1946. He, too, was an ex-serviceman, found guilty of shooting his victims and attempting sodomy. He was executed on 19 November 1948. Diane Anderson, *Bloodstains: Canada's Multiple Murders* (Calgary: Detselig, 2006); Lee Mellor, *Cold North Killers: Canadian Serial Murder* (Toronto: Dundurn, 2012).

95 Staley informed police he had murdered and sexually assaulted Gary Billings on 5 July and Donnie Goss on 24 July. He was not tried for the first murder after he was capitally convicted in Alberta.

96 Quoted in Justice William R. Howson to Under Secretary of State, 8 October 1946, in Staley, Volume 1660, volume 1, part 1.

97 RCMP to Department of Justice, 11 October 1946, in Staley, Volume 1660, volume 1, part 1. On the policing of homosexuality in the Canadian forces, see Paul Jackson, *One of the Boys: Homosexuality in the Military during World War II*, 2nd ed. (Montreal: McGill-Queen's University Press, 2010). On sexual offending among Canadian troops, see Jeffrey

A. Keshen, *Saints, Sinners, and Soldiers: Canada's Second World War* (Vancouver: UBC Press, 2004), 246.

98 Staley's confession, including details of his past sexual offences, was published widely in the press after his arrest in August and again during his trial. See, for instance, "'I Killed Boy,' Staley Admits," Calgary *Herald*, 30 August 1946; "Staley on Stand Tells Court of Early Troubles," Calgary *Herald*, 3 October 1946.

99 This hospital, at Ponoka, Alberta, also functioned as an assessment centre for persons deemed to be eugenically unfit and therefore subject to sexual sterilization. See Alberta Ponoka Hospital, Eugenics Archive, http://eugenicsarchive.ca/discover/institutions/map/517da5df9786fa0a73000002.

100 "Jury Names Staley Killer," Medicine Hat *Daily News*, 23 August 1946. That report referred to the coroner's inquest. The preliminary hearing before Calgary magistrate, H.G. Jensen, elicited similar coverage: "Vancouver Detective Tells Court of Staley's Voluntary Confession," Lethbridge *Herald*, 29 August 1946.

101 "Staley's Admission of Murder Given Jury as Trial Opens," Calgary *Herald*, 30 September 1946. Blanchard worked closely with the provincial Department of the Attorney General in the 1940s.

102 Calgary *Herald*, 26 August 1946. The front-page story included a large portrait of the victim and a picture of the "distraught" family, including the victim's twin sister. The *Herald* subsequently published Staley's confession verbatim on the front page of its 29 August 1946 edition.

103 "Rex v. Kaetiler and Stolski," *Dominion Law Reports* 3 (1945): 272–86. The appeal against conviction was dismissed. Blanchard argued the Crown's case.

104 Howson served in the provincial legislature and became leader of the Liberal Party during the 1930s. In 1936, he was appointed to the Supreme Court of Alberta, and he became chief justice in 1944. Ernest G. Mardon and Austin A. Mardon, *Alberta's Judicial Leadership, a Biographical Account* (Edmonton: Golden Meteorite Press, 2011), 45–6.

105 Chief Justice Howson to Under Secretary of State, 7 October 1946 in Staley, Volume 1660, volume 1, part 1.

106 Gallagher's memo to file, on 20 Nov. 1946, in Staley, Volume 1660, volume 1, part 1. In this case, he stated that he reviewed the "essential features" of the case with the solicitor general.

107 "Staley Mental Case, Doctors Agree in Court," Winnipeg *Tribune*, 5 October 1946.

108 Miss W. Grant to Louis St. Laurent, 7 October 1946, in Staley, Volume 1660, volume 1, part 1.

109 Ibid.

110 "Prison Futile for Sex Offenders," Toronto *Globe and Mail*, 22 April 1947. McRuer described the youth's attack as "hideous" and "most revolting and serious." It indicated the prisoner had "sadistic tendencies."

111 "$1,000 Reward Posted by Police Commission for Sex Killer's Arrest," Toronto *Globe and Mail*, 24 September 1947. Playford's body was discovered in a ditch in the "long lanes" district, "the scene of bootlegging operations and illicit drinking parties," according to local authorities. "Can This Crime Breeding Situation Not Be Cleaned Up?," Owen Sound *Daily Sun Times*, 23 September 1947.

112 "Hundreds Attend Funeral of Girl Murder Victim," Toronto *Globe and Mail*, 26 September 1947. Owen Sound's population was approximately 15,000 in 1947.

113 The trope of the carnival as a site of licence and sexually charged danger is explored in Robertson Davies's 1970 novel, *The Fifth Business*, which is set in the fictional small Ontario town of Deptford.

114 "Confessed Killer of Girl Detained," Montreal *Gazette*, 27 September 1947; "Fred Bussey, Confessed Murderer of Betty Playford, Taken to Owen Sound," Montreal *Gazette*, 29 September 1947.

115 On 4 October 1947, Isaacs wrote the minister of justice to request an opportunity to have an appeal heard by a different bench of the Court of Appeal from the one that had ruled in the first appeal or to argue an appeal before the Supreme Court of Canada. On 9 October, Gallagher advised him to lodge another appeal before the Ontario Court of Appeal or "apply for commutation, or an exercise of the Royal Prerogative of Mercy." Chambers, Volume 1664, part 2. Arthur Maloney conducted the second appeal, which was dismissed, and Chambers was executed on 4 February 1948.

116 Hope worked in the Department of the Attorney General from 1938 to his death in 1947.

117 "REGINIAN HELD AS SUSPECT IN OWEN SOUND SLAYING," Saskatoon *Star Phoenix*, 26 September 1947.

118 Justice Kelley to Minister of Justice, 26 November 1947, in Bussey, Volume 1669, volume 1, part 1. Charles Simmons Tennant later testified in support of the Criminal Code's definition of criminal insanity before the Royal Commission on the Insanity Defence. "Report of Public Sessions held at Toronto and Ottawa Commencing April 12, 1955," in Minutes of Proceedings of the Commission, LAC, R.G. 33, series 130, vol. 1, 1300–1326.

On the development of forensic psychiatry, see F.C. Rhodes Chalk, C.A. Roberts, and R.E. Turner, "Forensic Psychiatry in Canada, 1945–80," *Canadian Journal of Psychiatry* 40, no. 3 (April 1995): 121–4.

119 Bussey, Volume 1669, part 2. The doctor, John M. Senn, shared Dr. Tennant's views on the legal definition of insanity. Chenier, *Strangers in our Midst*, 84.

120 "Bussey to Hang for Murder of Owen Sound Girl," Ottawa *Journal*, 18 November 1947. The paper quoted from Hope's closing statement.

121 "Newspaperman Awarded $1,000," Ottawa *Citizen*, 13 April 1948. The decision was made by the Owen Sound Police Commission.

122 Isaacs to Minister of Justice, 19 November 1948, in Bussey, Volume 1669, volume 1, part 1.

123 Bussey's father and mother both wrote letters to James Ilsley, which depicted their son as sick. Mr. and Mrs. F.O. Bussey to Minister of Justice, 6 December 1948, in Bussey, Volume 1669, volume 1, part 1.

124 The report, twelve single-spaced pages of typescript, was prepared by Miss Ruth M. Bentley of the Mental Health Clinic in Regina, and it was submitted on 5 January 1948. Bussey, Volume 1669, volume 1, part 1.

125 The letter was sent on 24 January 1948 by Ursula Henry, a "vocational social worker" for public schools in York Township, Ontario. Gallagher reviewed it on 29 January and pencilled Dr. Cathcart's opinion before writing his recommendation on 30 January.

126 Gallagher's marginalia referred to an undated in-person conversation with Cathcart, in Bussey, Volume 1669, volume 1, part 1. Cathcart (1890–1977) was a medical officer during the Great War. He was critical of shell shock as an explanation for veterans' difficulty in readjusting to civilian life. Terry Copp and Bill McAndrew, *Battle Exhaustion: Soldiers and Psychiatrists in the Canadian Army, 1939–1945* (Montreal: McGill-Queen's University Press, 1990), 13.

127 Elise Chenier, "The Criminal Sexual Psychopath in Canada: Sex, Psychiatry and the Law at Mid-Century." *Canadian Bulletin of Medical History* 20, no. 1 (April 2003): 75–101, 81.

128 James R. Miller, *Skyscrapers Hide the Heavens: A History of Native-Newcomer Relations in Canada*, 4th ed. (Toronto: University of Toronto Press, 2018 [1989]), 207–29; John F. Leslie, "Assimilation, Integration or Termination? The Development of Canadian Indian Policy, 1943–1963" (PhD diss., Carleton University, 1999); Michael Morden, "Theorizing the Resilience of the Indian Act," *Canadian Public Administration* 59, no. 1 (March 2016): 113–33.

129 Leslie, "Assimilation, Integration or Termination?," 81–2.

130 On the resilience of savagery as a concept in the legal system, see Constance Backhouse, *Colour-Coded: A Legal History of Racism in Canada* (Toronto: University of Toronto Press for the Osgoode Society for Canadian Legal History, 1999), 40–70.

131 The Special Joint Committee of the Senate and the House of Commons Appointed to Examine and Consider the Indian Act conducted their hearings from May 1946 to 1948. Under the federal Inquiries Act, the government also established a Commission on Indian Affairs, which met over 1946 and 1947. Hugh Shewell, *'Enough to Keep Them Alive': Indian Welfare in Canada, 1873–1965* (Toronto: University of Toronto Press, 2004), 200–3.

132 Mark Cronlund Anderson and Carmen L. Robertson, *Seeing Red: A History of Natives in Canadian Newspapers* (Winnipeg: University of Manitoba Press, 2011).

133 Ibid., 7.

134 On post-war class relations and worker exploitation in logging camps, see Scott Prudham, "Sustaining Sustained Yield: Class, Politics, and Post-War Forest Regulation in British Columbia," *Environment and Planning D: Society and Space* 25, no. 2 (2007): 258–83.

135 Corporal Davidson, Crime Report, 21 November 1946, in Houston, Volume 1663, volume 1, part 1.

136 Shewell, *'Enough to Keep them Alive,'* 181–2.

137 Hodgson's payment appeared under the category of "contingencies arising out of prosecutions." Province of British Columbia, *Public Accounts, Fiscal Year Ended 31st March 1948* (Victoria, BC: Kings Printer, 1948), 58.

138 Hodgson affiliated with the Reconstruction Party in the 1930s. James Naylor describes its members as "middle-class socialists." Naylor, *The Fate of Labour Socialism: The Co-operative Commonwealth Federation and the Dream of a Working-Class Future* (Toronto: University of Toronto Press, 2016), 79–80.

139 R. v. Houston, transcript of evidence, 250–1, in Houston, Volume 1663, volume 1, part 3.

140 Farris to Minister of Justice, 24 January 1947, in Houston, Volume 1663, volume 1, part 1.

141 Gallagher to Minister of Justice, 24 September 1947, in Houston, Volume 1663, volume 1, part 1. Gallagher's case summary refers almost exclusively to Justice Manson's report.

142 Hodgson to Minister of Justice, 29 September 1947, in Houston, Volume 1663, volume 1, part 1. He further claimed that his client confessed to

save his father from being recommitted to the provincial hospital at Essondale.

143 *Debates*, 14 June 1948, 5199.

144 Brendan F.R. Edwards, "'I Have Lots of Help behind Me, Lots of Books, to Convince You': Andrew Paull and the Value of Literacy in English," *BC Studies* 164 (Winter 2009/10): 7–30, 10–14.

145 Joan Brockman, "Exclusionary Tactics: The History of Women and Visible Minorities in the Legal Profession in British Columbia," in *Essays in the History of Canadian Law, Volume VI: British Columbia and the Yukon Territory*, ed. Hamar Foster and John McLaren (Toronto: University of Toronto Press for the Osgoode Society for Canadian Legal History, 1995), 508–62, 549n122.

146 Minutes of Proceedings and Evidence, Special Joint Committee, 6 May 1947, 897. Anglo-Celtic journalist Maisie Hurley may also have provided assistance in the Houston case. Eric Jamieson, *The Native Voice* (Halfmoon Bay, BC: Caitlin Press, 2016).

147 Canada, Special Joint Committee, *Minutes and Evidence*, 1947, no. 18, 899. This claim of equality was made by Major Donald M. McKay, BC's Indian commissioner. The Joint Committee's reliance on government employees to counter Indigenous witnesses' complaints made this inquiry "a tool of state propaganda." Shewell, *'Enough to Keep Them Alive'*, 206.

148 Transcript of evidence, 417, in Rivers, Volume 1672, part 2. Justice Gale quoted from s. 260 of the Criminal Code in response to a question from the foreman.

149 "Accused Unable to Recall Events of Murder Night," Toronto *Globe and Mail*, 25 September 1948. The officers were members of the Criminal Investigation Branch of the Ontario Provincial Police.

150 On the long association between Indian status and drunkenness, see Robert A. Campbell, "Making Sober Citizens: The Legacy of Indigenous Alcohol Regulation in Canada, 1777–1985," *Journal of Canadian Studies/ Revue d'études canadiennes* 42, no. 1 (2008): 105–26.

151 The Ontario public accounts records do not refer to the fiscal arrangements for Rivers's defence.

152 Only a minority of "status" Indians made this choice. Maria C. Manzano-Muguía, "Indian Policy and Legislation: Aboriginal Identity and Survival in Canada," *Studies in Ethnicity and Nationalism* 11, no. 3 (2011): 404–26, 410–11.

153 Transcript of evidence, 624–36, in Rivers, Volume 1672, part 2.

154 Ottawa *Journal*, 1 October 1948. This clipping was pasted into Rivers's capital case file by Remission Branch staff. When Munro called his client

to testify, the Toronto *Globe and Mail* reported: "Accused Indian Gives Testimony in Murder Trial," 30 September 1948.

155 Shewell, *'Enough to Keep them Alive'*, 121. Prior to 1936, the federal government had maintained a Department of Indian Affairs.

156 T.R.L. MacInnes promoted the bureau's work publicly. See his "History of Indian Administration in Canada," *The Canadian Journal of Economics and Political Science/Revue canadienne d'Economique et de Science politique* 12, no. 3 (August 1946): 387–94.

157 MacInnes stated that sixty-five Indigenous men had been prosecuted for homicide since 1928, twenty of whom had followed the "old aboriginal idea that the husband has power of life and death over his wife and can exercise it at his caprice." Cited in Kimberley White, *Negotiating Responsibility: Law, Murder and States of Mind* (Vancouver: UBC Press, 2008), 87.

158 MacInnes to Gallagher, 29 November 1948, in Rivers, Volume 1672, part 1. For an extended analysis of MacInnes's support for severity, see Briggs, "Exemplary Punishment," 129–31.

159 Michael L. Shaughnessy to Minister of Justice, 11 October 1948, in Rivers, Volume 1672, part 2.

160 The attorney general likely approached the firm of Edmonds, Maloney on the basis of Arthur Maloney's reputation for representing "the little man and woman." Pullen, *The Life and Times of Arthur Maloney*, 4.

161 The Ontario Court of Appeal dismissed Vannini's application (on the ground that one of the jurors had been separated from the others because of illness) on 24 November 1948. "Motion to Appeal Rivers' Sentence Still Being Considered," Ottawa *Journal*, 10 December 1948. The chief justice granted a reprieve to allow Vannini to lodge an application for leave to appeal to the Supreme Court of Canada, but it was denied on 11 December.

162 "Rivers' Request for Appeal Fails," Toronto *Globe and Mail*, 14 December 1948. The ninety-three–word article referred to him twice as an "Indian."

163 The Crown attorney underlined that Rivers had consumed a "considerable quantity of alcohol," and he added: "Rivers is an Indian." Wishart to Gallagher, 13 December 1948, in Rivers, Volume 1672, part 1.

164 Vannini to Governor General, 13 December 1948, in Rivers, Volume 1672, part 1.

165 Gallagher's note in Rivers, Volume 1672, part 1. The underlined portion referred to his conversation with Common when he was in Ottawa arguing against Vannini's appeal to the Supreme Court of Canada.

166 Lethbridge *Herald*, 16 December 1948. Few press accounts described the case as a sex slaying, although references to the "nearly nude" body indicated the likely motive.

167 "NO ARREST YET IN BLUDGEON DEATH PROBE BLIND RIVER MURDER THEORY," Sault *Daily Star*, 24 July 1948.

168 Sean P. Harvey, "The Unchangeable Character of the 'Indian Mind,'" in *Native Tongues: Colonialism and Race from Encounter to the Reservation* (Cambridge, MA: Harvard University Press, 2015), 145–81. On the racist character of the criminal law's "reasonable man," see Barbara Hudson, "'Beyond White Man's Justice': Race, Gender and Justice in Late Modernity," *Theoretical Criminology* 10, no. 1 (2006): 29–47.

169 Victor Bailey, "The Shadow of the Gallows: The Death Penalty and the British Labour Government, 1945–51," *Law and History Review* 18, no. 2 (2000): 305–50. The House of Lords rejected the abolition clause of the Criminal Justice Bill.

170 In the 1940s, the majority of Canadians supported this stance. Ezzat A. Fattah, *The Canadian Public and the Death Penalty: A Study of Social Attitude* (Ottawa: Solicitor General, 1976), 1, 105.

171 The two children were Dorothy (aged 10) and Ernie (aged 5). All were killed by shotgun wounds. The coroner found no sexual abuse of the children.

172 James R. Miller, *Skyscrapers Hide the Heavens: A History of Indian-White Relations in Canada*, 3rd ed. (Toronto: University of Toronto Press, 2000 [1989]), 326.

173 White, *Negotiating Responsibility*, 85; Shelagh D. Grant, *Arctic Justice: On Trial for Murder, Pond Inlet, 1923* (Montreal: McGill-Queen's University Press, 2002), 49. Prior to the 1920s, clemency was favoured as a tool of colonization in the North. See McKay Jenkins, *Bloody Falls of the Coppermine: Madness, Murder, and the Collision of Cultures in the Arctic, 1913* (New York: Random House, 2005).

174 Frank Wade, *Advocate for the North: Judge John Parker, His Life and Times* (Bloomington, IN: Trafford Publishing, 2005). Parker was the prosecutor in this case.

175 Constance Backhouse, *Carnal Crimes: Sexual Assault Law in Canada, 1900–1975* (Toronto: Irwin Law for the Osgoode Society for Canadian Legal History, 2008), 218.

176 Gibben to Secretary of State, 27 June 1951, in Beaulieu, Volume 1698, part 2.

177 Transcript of evidence, 178, 10, in Beaulieu, Volume 1698, part 3. The Remission Branch's condensed summary (n.d.) cited "sexual intercourse"

as the motive for the crime. In addition to breaches of protocol in Beaulieu's file, officials made numerous errors in dates.

178 "An Act Respecting the Criminal Law," *Revised Statutes of Canada, 1927*, chapter 36, s. 1065. In 1938, the Union Nationale government, under Maurice Duplessis, unilaterally decided to conduct all Quebec executions in Montreal's Bordeaux prison. I am grateful to Donald Fyson for this information.

179 Corporal Armstrong to Secretary of State, forwarding letter from J.A. Peacock, officer in charge of Criminal Investigation Branch of RCMP, 5 September 1951. Beaulieu, Volume 1698, part 2.

180 Gallagher to Minister of Justice, 16 November 1951, in Beaulieu, Volume 1698, part 1.

181 After the war, security concerns unleashed new and more invasive designs on the colonization of the North and its peoples. Shelagh D. Grant, *Sovereignty or Security? Government Policy in the Canadian North, 1936–1950* (Vancouver: UBC Press, 1994 [1988]).

182 Gallagher to Minister of Justice, 17 January 1952, in Beaulieu, Volume 1689, part 2. Hugh Andrew Young, a former major-general, was the commissioner, whose duties were similar to that of lieutenant-governors.

183 Canada, Royal Commission on Aboriginal Peoples, *The High Arctic Relocation: A Report on the 1953–55 Relocation* (Ottawa: Communications Canada, 1994); Frank Tester and Peter Kulchyski, *Tammarniit (Mistakes): Inuit Relocation in the Eastern Arctic, 1939–63* (Vancouver: UBC Press, 1994).

184 "$250 Reward Posted in Woman's Mystery Death," Vancouver *Sun*, 10 November 1949. Numerous newspaper clippings on the case were pasted into Ducharme's capital case file. Ducharme, Volume 1688.

185 Columnist Jack Webster, a pugnacious Vancouver *Sun* reporter, wrote extensively on the Ducharme case. Jack Webster, *Webster! An Autobiography* (Vancouver, BC: Douglas & Macintyre, 1990).

186 Christopher Dummitt argues that the case was the "most sensational trial" in post-war Vancouver's history. Dummitt, *The Manly Modern*, 116–18.

187 Constable Armstrong to the Commissioner of the RCMP, 27 July 1951, in Beaulieu, Volume 1689. Armstrong also categorized him as "of halfbreed extraction."

188 Ducharme was examined in the "mental ward" of Vancouver General Hospital. Ducharme, Volume 1688, volume 1, part 1.

189 McAlpine represented Ducharme pro bono, but received $100 from the attorney general to hire his expert witness, Dr. Dobson, from

the psychiatric unit of the Shaughnessy Hospital in Vancouver. F.W. Thompson memo, 8 July 1950, in Ducharme, Volume 1688. McAlpine was the brother of Claude Lorne McAlpine, a partner in leading law firm Farris, McAlpine, Stultz, Bull & Farris.

190 Norris was a leading member of the Vancouver bar, elected as its president in 1948. He was elevated to the bench in 1959. Although he was not a criminal law specialist, he kept a case file on the Ducharme case from 1950 to 1956.

191 Scott Kerwin, "The Janet Smith Bill of 1924 and the Language of Race and Nation in British Columbia," *BC Studies* 121 (Spring 1999): 83–114, 99. The prosecution of the murder of Janet Smith, a white nanny in a wealthy Vancouver home, was alleged to have involved police torture of the prime suspect (a Chinese servant in the house) to divert suspicion from wealthy white men.

192 The appeal was dismissed on the grounds of the judge's proper admission of evidence and his clear instructions to the jury that "the facts were for them to decide, and he was right not to instruct them to disregard the evidence of the accused as ramblings of a disorderly mind." "R. v. Ducharme," *Canadian Criminal Cases* 97 (1950), 247.

193 Manson to Secretary of State, 23 March 1950, in Ducharme, Volume 1688, volume 1, part 1.

194 Gallagher to Solicitor General, 9 June 1950, in Ducharme, Volume 1688, volume 1, part 1.

195 Cathcart to Department of Justice, 20 June 1950, in Ducharme, Volume 1688, volume 1, part 1. Cathcart had worked in the Department of Veterans Affairs since the 1920s.

196 McAlpine sought special leave to appeal to the Supreme Court on the basis that he had found witnesses who placed Ducharme away from the crime scene. McAlpine to Minister of Justice, 21 June 1950; Gallagher, memo to file, 27 June 1950, in Ducharme, Volume 1688, volume 1, part 1.

197 Gallagher to Solicitor General, 8 July 1950; Gallagher to McAlpine, 13 July 1950, in Ducharme, Volume 1688, volume 1, part 1.

198 Don Duff, "Ducharme Executed, Silent to the End," Vancouver *Daily Province*, 14 July 1950.

199 Children and Young Persons Act [England], chapter 12, 1933. On the relation between juvenile offending and welfare, see Harry D. Hendrick, *Child Welfare: England, 1872–1989* (London: Routledge, 1993).

200 Thomas H. Goode, *Debates*, 19 October 1951, 193. Goode was an English-born Liberal backbencher involved in "boys work" at the Oakalla Prison Farm in his riding. He stated he had visited Sykes in prison.

201 Manson described Sykes's testimony as "calm, cold and shameless." Manson to Secretary of State, 8 June 1951, in Sykes, Volume 1697, part 1, volume 1.

202 The Farris firm remains prominent today. See "We've Been Around Since 1903, But We're Just Getting Started," Farris (website), https://farris.com/about-us.

203 "YOUNGEST TO FACE HANGING IN B.C.," Vancouver *Sun*, 4 June 1951.

204 Manson to Secretary of State, 8 June 1951, in Sykes, Volume 1697, part 1, volume 1.

205 In 1954, Burton defended Peter Boreniuk for the murder of a woman in Alert Bay (he was executed on 29 March 1955). "Murder Victim's Estate Sued," Vancouver *Sun*, 27 February 1956. In 1955, Burton defended a twenty-four-year-old Vancouver man charged with the murder of another man. Robert Graham was executed on 22 May 1956. "Killer's Father Raps Cabinet 'Favoritism,'" Vancouver *Sun*, 25 May 1956.

206 R. v. Sykes, British Columbia Court of Appeal, transcript of oral judgment by O'Halloran, J.A., 4 October 1951, in Sykes, Volume 1697, volume 1, part 1.

207 Thatcher to Garson, 12 June 1951, in Sykes, Volume 1697, volume 1, part 1. W. Ross Thatcher, a member of the CCF, became an independent in 1955.

208 C.H.S. Jayewardene, *The Penalty of Death: The Canadian Experiment* (Lexington, MA: Lexington Books, 1977), 2.

209 Garson to Thatcher, 30 June 1951, in Sykes, Volume 1697, part 1, volume 1. The minister of justice's executive assistant wrote Gallagher on 20 June and described the MP as "an opponent of capital punishment." Hence, his inquiry was a "matter which requires the preparation of a careful reply."

210 Frances Menzies to Minister of Justice, 17 July 1951; Gallagher to Menzies, 26 July 1951, in Sykes, Volume 1697, volume 1, part 1.

211 British novelist Malcolm Lowry captured the outcry against Sykes's death sentence in his posthumously published novel, *Ferry to Gabriola* (1971). See Victor Doyen, "From Innocent Story to Charon's Boat: Reading the 'October Ferry' Manuscripts," in Sherill Grace, ed., *Swinging the Maelstrom: Perspectives on Malcolm Lowry* (Montreal: McGill-Queen's University Press, 1992), 163–208, 183–4.

212 "Cruel Delay," Vancouver *Sun*, 10 October 1951; "Sykes Case," Vancouver *Sun*, 11 October 1951.

213 Gallagher to Minister of Justice, 13 October, in Sykes, Volume 1697, part 1, volume 1.

214 "Scotty," Letter to the Editor, Vancouver *Sun*, 11 October 1951.

215 "H. Burnet," Letter to the Editor, Vancouver *Sun*, 11 October 1951.

216 Canada, "An Act Respecting the Criminal Law," *Revised Statutes of Canada*, 1927, chapter 37, section 1014 (2).

217 Senator Arthur Roebuck, in Senate of Canada, *Proceedings of the Standing Committee on Banking and Commerce*, 16 December 1952, 76. Roebuck was chairman of the Senate Special Committee on Human Rights and Fundamental Freedoms (struck in 1950), which promoted the introduction of the Canadian Bill of Rights. George Egerton, "Entering the Age of Human Rights: Religion, Politics and Canadian Liberalism, 1945–50," *Canadian Historical Review* 85, no. 3 (2004): 451–80.

218 The 1948 statute defined the sexual psychopath as someone without "power to control his sexual impulses and who as a result is likely to attack or otherwise inflict injury, loss, pain or other evil on any person." An Act to Amend the Criminal Code, 1948, c. 39, sections 43 and 8.

219 Pouliot, *Debates*, 14 June 1948, 5199.

5. Sexual Psychopathy, Insanity, and the Death Penalty under Scrutiny in the 1950s

1 The Canadian Penal Association merged with the Canadian Welfare Council's Division on Crime and Delinquency in 1956 to form the Canadian Corrections Association (a branch of the Canadian Welfare Association). Montreal hosted the first Canadian Congress on Corrections in May 1957. The first issue of the *Canadian Journal of Corrections* appeared in 1958. Matthew G. Yeager, *The First 75 Years: A History of the Canadian Criminal Justice Association, 1919 to 1994* (Ottawa: Canadian Criminal Justice Association, 1994), 9–10.

2 Canada, *Report of Royal Commission on the Revision of Criminal Code* (Ottawa: Queen's Printer, 1954). The revised Code came into effect in 1955, after the passage of the Act Respecting the Criminal Law, 1953–1954, *Statutes of Canada*, 1954, c. 51. It removed death as the maximum punishment for rape, but it left the lash as an added discretionary punishment. Constance Backhouse, *Carnal Crimes: Sexual Assault Law in Canada, 1900–1975* (Toronto: Irwin Publishing for the Osgoode Society for Canadian Legal History, 2008), 281.

3 The Canadian Psychiatric Association formed in 1951. Many of its leaders presented briefs to the commissions and inquiries of the 1950s. G.H. Stevenson, "Report on the Formation of the Canadian Psychiatric Association," *Canadian Medical and Allied Journal* 65 (December 1951):

592–4; Isabel Dickson, "The Canadian Psychiatric Association, 1951–1958," *Canadian Journal of Psychiatry* 25, no. 1 (1980): 86–97.

4 Corporal punishment and lotteries were the other two issues addressed along with capital punishment. Canada, *Report of Royal Commission on the Revision of Criminal Code*, 64.

5 A.J. MacLeod and J.C. Martin, "The Revision of the Criminal Code," *The Canadian Bar Review* 33 (1955): 3–19.

6 Patrick J. Boyer, *A Passion for Justice: How 'Vinegar Jim' McRuer Became Canada's Greatest Law Reformer* (Toronto: Dundurn Press, 2008), 41. The Presbyterian McRuer's puritanical tendencies earned him the nickname.

7 Elise Chenier, *Strangers in Our Midst: Sexual Deviancy in Postwar Ontario* (Toronto: University of Toronto Press, 2008), 9, 66.

8 The Co-operative Commonwealth Federation was the only national party that supported abolition in the 1950s. In 1953, the Canadian Penal Association also went on record against the death penalty. Carolyn Strange, "The Undercurrents of Penal Culture: Punishment of the Body in Mid-Twentieth-Century Canada," *Law and History Review* 19, no. 2 (Summer 2001): 343–85, 362–3.

9 For the wider North American context of the death penalty's critical review, see Jennifer Carter, "Capital Punishment: A Struggle to Satisfy Evolving Standards of Decency – Reviewing the Debate in the United States and Canada," *Southwestern Journal of International Law* 17, no. 2 (2011): 237–58.

10 Canada, Department of Justice, *Report of a Committee Appointed to Inquire into the Principles and Procedures Followed in the Remission Service of the Department of Justice of Canada* (Ottawa: Queen's Printer, 1956), 1 (hereafter Fauteux Report).

11 Fauteux Report, 8. Fauteux was Montreal's Crown prosecutor from 1930 to 1936. He served as the province of Quebec's chief Crown prosecutor until 1940, when he was appointed to the Supreme Court. In 1970, he became chief justice.

12 Dale C. Thomson, *Louis St. Laurent: Canadian* (Toronto: Macmillan, 1967); Jack W. Pickersgill, *My Years with Louis St. Laurent: A Political Memoir* (Toronto: University of Toronto Press, 1975).

13 Between 1953 and 1959, there were 97 robbery and burglary capital convictions, and 27 were executed, in contrast to 8 of 10 sex murderers. Using Fisher's exact test, a statistically significant difference was recorded (p=<.002).

14 MacLeod was appointed commissioner of penitentiaries in September 1960, charged with making large-scale reforms. Canada, *Report of the*

Sub-Committee on the Penitentiary System in Canada (Ottawa: Minister of Supply and Services Canada, 1977), 14.

15 MacLeod graduated from Dalhousie University Law School in 1942, served overseas, was called to the bar in 1945, and began working in the Department of Justice in 1947. In 1950, he joined the Remission Branch, becoming acting head in 1953 and permanent head in 1954. "Staffing Changes," *Federal Corrections* 1, no. 1 (1961): 6. He was directly involved in the work to revise the Criminal Code.

16 Maloney's representation of two members of the notorious Boyd Gang in 1952 led him to support abolition. Roy McMurtry, *Memoirs and Reflections* (University of Toronto Press for the Osgoode Society for Canadian Legal History, 2013), 110–11.

17 Chenier, *Strangers in Our Midst*, 77. By 1958, one third of Canadians favoured the abolition of capital punishment, 51 per cent supported it, and the remainder were undecided. David B. Chandler, *Capital Punishment in Canada: A Sociological Study of Repressive Law* (Toronto: McClelland & Stewart, 1976), 41.

18 McRuer to J.W. Pickersgill, Secretary of State, 17 November 1953, in LAC, R.G. 13, Hutson, Volume 1721, part 1, (hereafter name, Volume).

19 "Hutson to Hang on February 9," Ottawa *Journal*, 6 November 1953. The paper referred to the girl's "ravished" body but did not detail the sexual element of the crime.

20 In the 1895 trial of Valentine Shortis, the defence presented considerable evidence concerning inherited epilepsy and its alliance with insanity. Martin L. Friedland, *The Case of Valentine Shortis: A True Story of Crime and Politics in Canada* (Toronto: The University of Toronto Press for the Osgoode Society for Canadian Legal History, 1986), 49.

21 William C.J. Meredith, "Insanity as a Criminal Defence: A Conflict of Views," *The Canadian Bar Review* 25, no. 3 (March 1947): 251–9, 254, n15. Meredith was dean of the Faculty of Law at McGill University from 1950 to 1960. He wrote an authoritative treatise on the insanity defence in 1931. Fred Kaufman, *Searching for Justice: An Autobiography* (Toronto: University of Toronto Press for the Osgoode Society for Canadian Legal History, 2005), 80.

22 Dieter Hoehne, *Legal Aid in Canada* (Lewiston, NY: Edwin Mellon, 1989), 59. The Law Society Amendment Act of 1951 established the province's first statutory legal aid plan. The government of Ontario was not involved in administering the scheme until 1966.

23 Doyle's psychiatric wing at St. Michael's opened in 1953. M. Irene McDonald, *For the Least of My Brethren: A Centenary History of St. Michael's*

Hospital (Toronto: Dundurn Press, 1992), 156. During the Second World War, he reached the rank of lieutenant-colonel as a neuropsychiatric advisor concerning army personnel under sentence. William John Pratt, "Medicine and Obedience: Canadian Army Morale, Discipline, and Surveillance in the Second World War, 1939–1945" (PhD diss., University of Calgary, 2015), 93.

24 McRuer to Pickersgill, 19 November 1953, in Hutson, Volume 1721, part 1.

25 The rule's narrowness meant that "many who raised an insanity defence ... were unsuccessful and were hanged." Friedland, *The Case of Valentine Shortis*, 41.

26 McRuer to Pickersgill, 19 November 1953, in Hutson, Volume 1721, part 1.

27 Ibid.

28 The CSP sentencing provision applied only to persons convicted of rape, carnal knowledge of a girl under 14, indecent assault on a female, buggery, bestiality, indecent assault on a male with intent, and gross indecency (plus the attempt to commit any of those offences). Chenier, *Strangers in Our Midst*, 82.

29 Ibid.

30 Cathcart to MacLeod, 1 February 1954, in Hutson, Volume 1721, part 1. Cathcart advised an electroencephalograph test. On the use of this technology to detect aggressive sexual tendencies in this period, see Denis Hill and D.J. Watterson, "Electroencephalograph Studies of Psychopathic Personalities," *Journal of Neurology & Psychiatry* 5 (1942): 47–65.

31 MacLeod to Minister of Justice, 2 February 1954, in Hutson, Volume 1721, part 1.

32 "Terms of Reference and Appointment of Personnel," in Canada, *Report of the Royal Commission on the Law of Insanity as a Defence in Criminal Cases* (Hull, QC: Queen's Printer, 1956), vi (hereafter McRuer Insanity Report).

33 Sidney Katz, "The Truth about Sex Criminals," *Maclean's* 60, no. 13 (1 July 1947): 12, 46–8. Katz earned a master's degree in social work from the University of Toronto and a diploma in alcohol and drug addiction from Yale University before becoming a feature writer for *Maclean's* in the early 1950s. Sandra Martin, "Journalist Sidney Katz Dies," Toronto *Globe and Mail*, 19 September 2007.

34 Section 203 of the revised Criminal Code confirmed that culpable homicide could be reduced to manslaughter if committed in the "heat of passion." J. Arboleda-Florez, "Insanity Defence in Canada," *Canadian Psychiatric Association Journal* 23 (1978): 23–7, 26.

35 On 1 March 1954, McRuer sentenced army lieutenant Peter Balcombe to death, after he was found guilty of the stabbing murder of a CWAC

sergeant, Marie Anne Carrier, with whom he was romantically involved. He was executed in Cornwall on 25 May 1954.

36 Ezzat A. Fattah, *The Canadian Public and the Death Penalty: A Study of Social Attitude* (Burnaby, BC: Criminology Department, Simon Fraser University, 1975), 1.

37 Canada, *Report of the Royal Commission on the Criminal Law Relating to Criminal Sexual Psychopaths* (Ottawa: Queen's Printer, 1958), 15 (hereafter McRuer CSP Report).

38 Chenier, *Strangers in Our Midst*, 108–9.

39 Report of Dr. Senn to the Ontario Department of Health, 7 October 1936, in Bliss, Volume 1606, part 1.

40 McRuer CSP Report, 22.

41 Chenier, *Strangers in Our Midst*, 84–5.

42 McRuer CSP Report, 137–65.

43 Ibid., 137–8.

44 Ibid., 124. The report advised the expansion of research in the field and that "special provision be made in the penitentiary system for the custody, control and treatment of every sexual offender under preventive detention" (129).

45 Garson was a Manitoba lawyer who first became a cabinet member in 1950, serving as solicitor general.

46 McRuer Insanity Report, 2. Garson gave almost identical testimony before the Fauteux Commission on the Remission Branch.

47 McRuer Insanity Report, 2, 41. By stating the English law, the report referred to the Criminal Lunatics Act, chapter 64 (1884), s. 2(4).

48 McRuer Insanity Report, 20, and n1. The report indicated that Dr. Senn also testified before this commission, and it referred to Dr. Cathcart as "one of Canada's most experienced court psychiatrists" (55).

49 Marjorie Freeman Campbell, *A Century of Crime: The Development of Crime Detection Methods in Canada* (Toronto: McClelland & Stewart, 1970), 195–216. The Canadian Society of Forensics (later Forensic Science) was established in 1953 and had its first annual meeting in 1954.

50 When John C. Chisholm, Toronto's chief of police, testified before the CSP Commission, he stressed that these records were vital because "sex offenders are not necessarily zoot-suiters, pool-room frequenters or corner boys." McRuer CSP Report, 60.

51 The Canadian Association of Chiefs of Police strongly supported the death penalty in this period. Greg Marquis, *Policing Canada's Century: A History of the Canadian Association of Chiefs of Police* (Toronto: University of Toronto Press for the Osgoode Society for Canadian Legal History, 1993), 265–6.

52 Backhouse, *Carnal Crimes*, 97–8.

53 MacLeod later described the victim as "a respectable married woman" who did domestic work for the local YMCA. She lived with her husband, "a respectable working man," in a "modest residential district." Memorandum for Solicitor General, 23 June 1954, in Sim, Volume 1723, volume 1.

54 "Brutal Slayer Still At Large," Calgary *Herald*, 10 March 1953.

55 The reward of $5,000 was paid in July 1955, but the police did not reveal the name of the recipient. It was likely Mrs. Sim. "Father Awaiting Trial While Family in Dire Straits," Lethbridge *Herald*, 10 December 1953.

56 A Calgary *Herald* sketch artist drew a sketch of the suspect, based on a fellow drinker, who thought he was "mentally deranged." "Newspaper Sketch Sparks Search for Calgary Murderer," Medicine Hat *News*, 20 March 1953.

57 "Statements Admitted as Evidence," Lethbridge *Herald*, 5 February 1954. The dismissal of the appeals left the Calgary police feeling vindicated. "Defends Calgary Police Methods," Lethbridge *Herald*, 5 August 1954.

58 Dawson received a modest fee that the legal aid funded, supported and operated by a small group of Calgary lawyers.

59 Rex v. Sim, transcript of evidence, 1778, in Sim, Volume 1725, part 8.2. McLatchie (who also testified in the Staley case of 1946) was the only woman among the fifteen pathologists who founded the Canadian Association of Pathologists in 1949. Jagdish Butany, "A Dream Fulfilled: The Plan, the Journey and the Promises," *Canadian Journal of Pathology* 1, no. 1 (April 2009): 24–7, 26.

60 Justice McBride's charge to the jury, Rex v. Sim, transcript of evidence, 1778; 1863; 1866–67, in Sim, Volume 1725, part 8.2.

61 Helman, the son of Russian Jewish immigrants, was appointed a KC in 1930. Known for his "weakness for becoming involved with lost causes," he had a "mediocre won-lost batting average" in the cases he accepted. James H. Gray, *Talk to My Lawyer: Great Stories of Southern Alberta's Bar and Bench* (Edmonton: Hurtig, 1987), 195.

62 Dominique Bourget and Gary Chaimowitz, "Forensic Psychiatry in Canada: A Journey on the Road to Specialty," *Journal of the American Academy of Psychiatry and the Law Online* 38, no. 2 (June 2010): 158–62.

63 Michie to Helman, 14 April 1954, in Sim, Volume 1752, volume 1, part 2.

64 Dr. Kenneth Gray, affidavit, 3 May 1954, in Sim, Volume 1752, volume 1, part 2.

65 Michie to Crown prosecutor, 19 January 1954, in Sim, Volume 1752, volume 1, part 2. In his testimony before the CSP Commission hearing

in Edmonton, Michie stated: "I doubt there is such a thing as lack of power of control." "Urge Special Institutions for Sexual Psychopaths," Lethbridge *Herald*, 11 September 1954.

66 Michie to Helman, 14 April 1954, in Sim, Volume 1752, volume 1, part 2.

67 Helman's appeal raised twenty-five points. "New Sim Appeal Is Considered by Defence," Calgary *Herald*, 11 June 1954.

68 Helman also argued that the judge erred in allowing the Crown to show the jury images of the victim's face and body. Don Maclean, "Sim Goes to Gallows June 29," Lethbridge *Herald*, 24 June 1954.

69 Garson testimony, Special Joint Committee of the Senate and the House of Commons on Capital and Corporal Punishment and Lotteries, *Minutes of Proceedings and Evidence*, no. 12, 11 May 1954 (Ottawa: Queen's Printer, 1954), 477; ibid., no. 1, 2 March 1954, 39 (hereafter Joint Committee, *Minutes*).

70 Joint Committee, *Minutes*, no. 12, 11 May 1954, 479.

71 Garson, Joint Committee, *Minutes*, no. 1, 2 March 1954, 38.

72 Cathcart to MacLeod, 15 June 1954, in Sim, Volume 1752, volume 1, part 2. Dr. Carnat told Helman he would have testified that Sim suffered from alcoholic amnesia had he been questioned on the matter.

73 Helman and Milvain to MacLeod, 10 June 1954; MacLeod to Helman, 16 June 1954, in Sim, Volume 1752, volume 1, part 2.

74 Garson, Joint Committee, *Minutes*, no. 1, 2 March 1954, 30.

75 Fauteux Report, 31. The committee had access to the same data provided to the Joint Committee.

76 "Final Report on Capital Punishment," in Canada, *Reports of the Joint Committee of the Senate and House of Commons on Capital Punishment, Corporal Punishment and Lotteries* (Ottawa: Queen's Printer, 1956), 6 (hereafter Joint Committee, *Report*).

77 The Criminal Code set a maximum of thirty days within which lawyers could file a notice of appeal. "Final Report on Capital Punishment," Joint Committee *Report*, 19.

78 Ibid., 19–20.

79 Vince Row, "Lawyer Says Insanity to Be Picard Defence," Montreal *Gazette*, 11 August 1954. Paul Aubut was called to the bar of Quebec in 1949 at the age of thirty-five, after he had served in the Second World War, reaching the rank of captain. He specialized in criminal law from the start of his practice.

80 A critical retrospective showed that 42.6 per cent of *Allô Police*'s front pages concerned murder and that rapes were strongly over-represented. Its purpose was to "manipuler l'opinion publique par des articles ou des

titres faisant appel à la repression, au châtiment et à la délation, exaltant les sentiments de vengeance, montrant une police efficace, un justice sympathique, et des criminels *prêtre* à tout, sanguinaires." Paul Roy, "L'Office des droits des détenus fustige le jaunisme du *Journal de Montréal* et d'*Allô Police*," *La Presse*, 17 November 1978.

81 Mathieu-Olivier Côté, "La représentation du crime dans la press écrite québécoise: le cas d'*Allô Police*" (Memoire, MA, Département d'athrophologie, Université Laval, 2002), 33–5. The first issue of the weekly appeared on 28 February 1953, with a cover story on the attempt of convicted murderer Peter Mentenko to have Cardinal Leger plead for clemency. Mentenko was executed in Montreal on 6 March 1953.

82 *Allô Police*, 8 August 1954: 1, 3–4. Toronto's *Justice Weekly* also focused on sexual offences. André Beaulieu and Jean Hamelin, *La presse québécoise: des origines à nos jours*, tome 8, *1945–1954* (Québec: Presses de l'Université Laval, 1987), 238.

83 The 8 August 1954 edition of *Allô Police* linked Trudeau's murder to Benson's with a full-page retrospective (page 8). I am grateful to Don Fyson for this reference.

84 Dan Woodward, "Two Families United in Common Sorrow," Montreal *Gazette*, 3 August 1954. Unlike the assault on Benson, there was no physical evidence that Trudeau had been sodomized before or after death.

85 Ibid. Trudeau's funeral was held on 3 August, one day after Picard was arrested.

86 *Le Devoir*, 6 August 1954. Unlike most of the Montreal dailies, *Le Devoir* was critical of these scenes of threatened mob justice.

87 Huard also testified for the defence in the Alcide Martin murder case.

88 McRuer Insanity Report, 18. Huard was a member of the association, and he also testified along the same lines (58n7). Alexandre Klein, "Le mythe des deux solitudes. Des relations entre les psychiatres francophones et anglophones dans le Montréal des années 1950," *Canadian Bulletin of Medical History* 34, no. 2 (Fall 2017): 393–418.

89 "Le juge Lagarde réclame une prevue additionnelle contre l'accusé L. Picard," *La Presse*, 12 August 1954. Lagarde adjourned the proceedings on the basis that the Crown's evidence was purely circumstantial.

90 "Duplessis Orders Trial for Picard," Ottawa *Journal*, 18 August 1954. As attorney general, Duplessis's use of this power was within the law. Fred Kaufman, "The Role of the Private Prosecutor: A Critical Analysis of the

Complainant's Position in Criminal Cases," *McGill Law Journal* 7, no. 2 (1960–1): 102–14, 106–7.

91 The Court of Queen's Bench, Appeal Division, granted Aubut leave to appeal on 25 March 1952. The appeal was unsuccessful, but the cabinet commuted the sentence on 14 January 1953.

92 The CLD solicited Dr. Huard's opinion again, shortly before the date set for Picard's execution. He confirmed that Picard "manifests neither delusions nor psychotic symptoms." Huard to MacLeod, 24 January 1955, in Picard, Volume 1736, volume 1, part 1.

93 John Benet, "Picard Stuns Court … Admits Slaying Boy; 'I Wish to Be Hanged,'" Montreal *Gazette*, 3 November 1954. Justice Wilfrid Lazure did not accept his plea, but he referred to it when he sentenced Picard to death.

94 The revised Criminal Code, section 202, defined culpable homicide as murder where "a person causes the death of a human being while committing or attempting to commit" any one of a series of offences including rape, indecent assault, or forcible abduction. "An Act Respecting the Criminal Law," *Statutes of Canada*, 1954–1955, chapter 51.

95 Garson, Joint Committee, *Minutes*, no. 12, 11 May 1954, 478, 479, 482.

96 RCMP Criminal Investigation Branch to Department of Justice, 28 July 1954, in Vincent, Volume 1727, volume 1 part 2.

97 The Crown argued that the homicide occurred in the course of attempted rape, and the jury's verdict of murder (rather than manslaughter) confirmed their interpretation of Vincent's motive.

98 O'Halloran, JA, oral judgment in Regina vs. L.B. Vincent, 22 October 1954, in Vincent, Volume 1727, volume 1, part 2.

99 Hughes to CLD, 9 May 1955, in Vincent, Volume 1 part 2. On 29 April 1955, the British Columbia Court of Appeal unanimously dismissed Hughes's second attempt to appeal against conviction.

100 Ibid.

101 "Kicking and Swearing, Show Worker Hanged," Nanaimo *Daily News*, 14 June 1955. Vincent also cursed and spat at the hangman, calling him "You dirty yellow pig."

102 In Ontario, Crown attorneys were responsible to the director through the attorney general.

103 C.P. Hope and S.L. Snyder argued the case for the attorney general against the acquittal entered. The Comba case is discussed in chapter three.

104 As of 1954, Common supervised forty-six Crown attorneys through the Ministry of the Attorney General. William B. Common, testimony, Joint Committee, *Minutes*, no. 2, 4 March 1954, 71.

105 The murder of Susan Carter, aged eight, inspired three "housewives" to form the Parents' Action League in 1955. The girl was not sexually assaulted, but initial coverage attributed her abduction to a "sex maniac." Elise Chenier, *Strangers in Our Midst*, 43.

106 Susan Cadieux went missing on 6 January 1956. The case remains unsolved; however, suspicion has been cast on Alexander Kalichuk, the man suspected of the murder of Lynn Harper. "Murder Suspect Died 25 Years Ago," CBC News, http://www.cbc.ca/news/canada/murder-suspect-died-25-years-ago-1.234995.

107 Rex v. Fitton, transcript of evidence, 59, in Fitton, Volume 1755, volume 3, part 1. The pathologist confirmed that the victim was a virgin, and the blood and sperm he found in her vagina indicated she had been raped, then strangled (61).

108 Toronto *Daily Star*, 18 January 1956.

109 The chairman of the forum, Edson L. Haines, was past vice-president of the Canadian Bar Association. The *Daily Star*'s editor-in-chief as of 1955, Beland Honderich, organized the forum. He began to write at the *Daily Star* in 1943. Sandra Martin, "Beland Honderich, 86," Toronto *Globe and Mail*, 8 November 2005, https://www.theglobeandmail.com/news/national/beland-honderich-86/article1130520/.

110 "Aroused Public Demands Sex Crime Prevention," editorial, Toronto *Daily Star*, 19 January 1956.

111 "All Sex Deviates Not Criminals, Must Use Caution – Doctor," Toronto *Daily Star*, 27 January 1956.

112 Treleaven to Minister of Justice, 7 May 1956, in Fitton, Volume 1755, volume 1, part 1.

113 R. v. Fitton, *Ontario Reports*, 1956, 696–717. David Humphrey was called to the bar in 1950 and in 1955 devoted himself to criminal defence cases. In 1971, he established the Criminal Lawyers' Association. He represented Fitton at trial and in two appeals pro bono. Kirk Makin, "David Humphrey, 83: Lawyer, Judge, and Mean Left Foot," Toronto *Globe and Mail*, 28 May 2009.

114 Common joined the provincial Department of the Attorney General in 1926 at the age of twenty-seven and was a veteran of scores of murder trials by the time Fitton was tried.

115 Section 598 of the Criminal Code allowed the attorney general of a province to appeal to the Supreme Court of Canada "on any question of law on which a judge of the court of appeal dissents." "The Queen v. Fitton," *Supreme Court Reports* (24 October 1956), 958–91. See also Victor Del Buono, "Right to Appeal in Indictable Cases: A Legislative History," *Alberta Law Review* 16, no. 3 (1978): 446–69, 462.

116 "SEE JURY'S CLEMENCY PLEA SAVING FITTON FROM GALLOWS," Toronto *Daily Star*, 28 April 1956. The front-page story included a picture of Fitton, his mother, and his wife, who screamed and collapsed when her husband was sentenced to hang.

117 This case, the last Common argued in the Supreme Court, "buttressed what he considered an important concept," namely that confessions should be considered voluntary if there is no evidence of "beating or undue influence." Tom Ford, "William Common: Gray Eminence of Ontario Law," Toronto *Daily Star*, 21 November 1964. The story marked his retirement on the eighth anniversary of Fitton's execution.

118 In this context, the inference of the term was not chatting but giving unwanted or annoying comments.

119 "The Queen v. Fitton," 987. The autopsy revealed the girl's hymen and peritoneum were torn. With the majority, Fauteux agreed that the Court of Appeal had split over matters of law, not fact.

120 Residents of 206 Jameson Ave. to Minister of Justice, 13 November 1956; affidavit of Sidney Brice, mechanic, Newmarket, 12 November 1956, in Fitton, Volume 1755, volume 1, part 1.

121 RG2, Privy Council Office, Series A-5-a, Volume 5775, item 15434, 19 November 1956 (hereafter Cabinet Conclusions).

122 John E. Saul to Minister of Justice, 23 November 1956, in Fitton, Volume 1755, volume 1, part 1. The second quote comes from an editorial ("An Eye for an Eye"), which appeared in the Toronto *Daily Star* on 21 November 1956, condemning the execution. In recounting his turn toward abolition, Roy McMurtry refers to the execution of Fitton (whom he met at the Don Jail) for the "rape and panic murder of a teenaged girl … His youthful face haunted my dreams for many months." McMurtry, *Memoirs and Reflections*, 112.

123 "Why Not Try Abolition of Death Penalty?," editorial, Toronto *Daily Star*, 28 June 1956. The division of murder into two degrees was recommended in the English report, but the Conservative government did not act on that recommendation. Great Britain, *Report of the Royal Commission on Capital Punishment* (London: Her Majesty's Stationery Office, 1953).

124 "BY ONE VOTE: Urge Retention of Death Penalty," Ottawa *Journal*, 28 June 1956; "Canada Urged to End Hanging," *New York Times*, 28 June 1956. Strange, "The Undercurrents of Penal Culture," 343–85, 349.
125 Alan W. Mewett, "Criminal Law Revision in Canada," *Alberta Law Review* 7, no. 2 (1969): 272–80, 275–6.
126 Fauteux Report, 87.
127 Ibid., 31. The report reprinted Garson's testimony statements to the Special Joint Committee.
128 The first Canadian Congress on Corrections occurred in Montreal just before the election in May 1957. Criminology also established a foothold in Canadian universities in the 1950s. Gary Parkinson, "Recovering the Early History of Canadian Criminology: Criminology at the University of British Columbia, 1951–1959." *Canadian Journal of Criminology and Criminal Justice* 50, no. 5 (October 2008): 589–620.
129 The election occurred on 10 June 1957 and left a caretaker government in place until 21 June. The Court of Appeal dismissed the second appeal on 13 June.
130 This case involved two defendants who attempted a robbery. Mullins appealed the conviction of Carey against the principle of "carrying out of the common unlawful purpose." The British Columbia Court of Appeal allowed the appeal, which the BC attorney general appealed. The Supreme Court restored the conviction on 15 January 1957. "The Queen v. Carey," *Supreme Court Reports* (1956): 266–84. The sentence was commuted on 1 April 1957.
131 RCMP Criminal Investigation Branch Superintendent J.R.W. Bordeleau to RCMP Commissioner, 21 January 1957, in Eaton, Volume 1759, volume 1, part 1.
132 Moore to MacLeod, 11 July 1957; Moore to Howard Green, 29 June 1957, in Eaton, Volume 1759, volume 1, part 1. Green was the Progressive Conservative MP for Vancouver Quadra.
133 MacLeod to Solicitor General, 9 July 1957, in Eaton, Volume 1759, volume 1, part 1. Warden Hugh Christie reported to the Remission Branch that Eaton had confided in him "concerning sexual problems of many years duration for which he is aware he should have sought treatment many years ago." Ibid., 29 January 1957.
134 Fauteux Report, 11.
135 Ibid., 71. MacLeod's recommendation also contrasted with the sentiments he expressed in the Correctional Planning Report, which he produced with a committee in 1960.
136 Mullins to Macleod, 27 June 1957, in Eaton, Volume 1759, volume 1, part 1.

137 Ibid. MacLeod's marginal notation beside Mullins's comment about Eaton's service to Carey commented: "For this he might receive an extra helping of something or other."

138 "Justice Prevails," Victoria *Daily Colonist*, 17 July 1957.

139 "Eaton Confesses Girl's Murder," Nanaimo *Daily News*, 16 July 1957.

140 Kinnear, "Memorandum of Dissent," in McRuer Insanity Report, 49. Jones founded the Department of Psychiatry at Dalhousie University in 1949 and went on to serve as the charter president of the Canadian Psychiatry Association.

141 Eaton's diary entries were leaked to the press after his execution. "Why? Why? I don't know. It was an urge and once I started beating her I could not stop." "Eaton Confesses Girl's Murder," in Eaton, Volume 1759, volume 1, part 1.

142 Winch to MacLeod, 12 July 1957, in Eaton, Volume 1759, volume 1, part 1.

143 Canada, House of Commons, *Debates*, 13 August 1956, 7492. Winch squeezed his ersatz minority report into a debate on supply for the Department of Justice. An electrician by trade, he entered federal Parliament in 1953, after serving for twenty years in the Legislative Assembly of British Columbia. "Harold Edward Winch," Library of Parliament, Historical Information (Parlinfo), Parliamentarians, https://lop.parl.ca/sites/ParlInfo//default/en_CA/People/Profile?personId=8684.

144 Jack Little, "L'affaire Coffin/Hébert: justice, politique et liberté de presse au Québec, 1953–1966," *Bulletin d'histoire politique* 25, no. 1 (2016): 113–150, 116, 120.

145 For an explanation of the record series, see Cabinet Conclusions, Library and Archives Canada, https://www.bac-lac.gc.ca/eng/discover/politics-government/cabinet-conclusions/Pages/cabinet-conclusions.aspx.

146 Balcer, the member for Trois-Rivières, led the Quebec campaign for the party and served as Diefenbaker's Quebec lieutenant.

147 F.W. Thompson to MacLeod, 24 June 1957, in Eaton, Volume 1759, volume 1, part 1. Thompson included the 1943 case of Albert Westgate, who murdered sixteen-year-old Grace Cook who had been living with him in a hotel in Winnipeg. Since the two were sexually involved, the prosecution did not focus on rape as a motive. Westgate had already served fourteen years of a commuted life sentence after his conviction for the murder of a romantic partner in 1928.

148 F.W. Thompson to MacLeod, 3 July 1957, in Eaton, Volume 1759, volume 1, part 1.

149 Mrs. MacLeod to E. Davie Fulton, Minister of Justice, 5 July 1957, in Eaton, Volume 1759, volume 1, part 1. Simma Holt, a journalist with the Vancouver *Sun*, also wrote to protest against the execution.

150 On 17 January 1960, Quebec journalist René Lévesque interviewed Balcer and Irénée Lagarde, the magistrate in the Picard preliminary hearing, and both expressed misgivings over the death penalty. Encyclopédie sur la mort, "René Lévesque enquête sur la peine de mort," http://agora.qc.ca/thematiques/mort/dossiers/rene_levesque_enquete_sur_la_peine_de_mort.

151 In the initial meeting on 4 July, Balcer had recommended that the law take its course, but he added this resolution to flag that the decision was not final. Cabinet Conclusions, Volume 1892, item 16023, 2.

152 Cabinet Conclusions, Volume 1893, item 16055, 2–3.

153 A criminal defence specialist, Diefenbaker defended three men and one woman charged with murder in the 1930s. Denis Smith, *Rogue Tory: The Life and Legend of John G. Diefenbaker* (Toronto: Macfarlane Walter and Ross, 1995), 84. On the Wysochan case, see Garrett Wilson, *Diefenbaker for the Defence* (Toronto: James Lorimer, 1988), 110–24.

154 Balcer to Irving Todres, 13 August 1957, in Eaton, Volume 1759, volume 1, part 1.

155 In March 1964, Mullins defended Lawrence Haase for the sex murder of two girls and stuck with his indigent client up to appealing to the Supreme Court. His final clemency campaign was successful on 4 May 1965. Haase, Volume 1965.

156 This act was revised in 1930, when it provided capitally accused indigent persons certificates to qualify by right to legal aid. Albert Utton, "The British Legal Aid System," *The Yale Law Journal* 76, 2 (December 1966): 371–8.

157 In the 1950s, only Alberta and Saskatchewan provided counsel in appeal payment through statute. John P. Nelligan, "Legal Aid in Canada: Existing Facilities," *The Canadian Bar Review* 29, no. 6 (1951): 589–620, 608, 611.

158 Nelligan, "Legal Aid in Canada," 616.

159 Alan Hustack claims (without a reference) that Sénéchal said "he received numerous death threats. 'I was warned that if I got Richard off a second time, it would be me who they would hang.'" Hustack, *They Were Hanged* (Toronto: Lorimer, 1987), 75.

160 Justice C.J. Jones to Minister of Justice, 9 October 1957, in Richard, Volume 1761, volume 1, part 2.

161 Sénéchal to Minister of Justice, 6 December 1957, in Richard, Volume 1761, volume 1, part 2.
162 MacLeod to Solicitor General, 5 December 1957, in Richard, Volume 1761, volume 1, part 2. MacLeod also said the CLD always reviewed capital case files to determine if a possible miscarriage of justice had occurred.
163 Sénéchal to Solicitor General, 9 December 1957, in Richard, Volume 1761, volume 1, part 2. MacLeod had already reassured the solicitor general that there was no evidence that another person had committed the offence.
164 In that earlier case, he was accused of shooting a cab driver. Justice Michaud presided in that trial, which ended in Richard's conviction for attempted murder.
165 Cabinet Conclusions, Volume 1893, items 16587 and 16595, 5 and 6 December 1957.
166 Richard was executed on 11 December 1957, the last man executed in the province. The father of the victim pressured the sheriff to witness the hanging, and he relented. Hustack, *They Were Hanged*, 76–7.
167 Balcer referred to William Gash, convicted of a robbery murder in which the victim was bashed to death. The Liberal cabinet commuted his sentence on 16 June 1954. Cabinet Conclusions, Volume 2655, item 13652, 15 June 1954.
168 Cabinet Conclusions, Volume 2744, 12 June 1959, 2. In 1958, commutations were granted in three other cases of young men: Aubrey Blades, aged seventeen, and Robert Boudreau, aged sixteen, in June 1958; and seventeen-year-old Rodney Montgomery in July 1958.
169 Cabinet Conclusions, Volume 2744, item 1802, 14 June 1959, 3, 2.
170 Ibid., 3.
171 Rex v. Vollman, transcript of evidence, 1476, in Vollman, Volume 1773, volume 1, part 4. After the second trial, Robichaud was elevated to the bench of the Supreme Court of New Brunswick. Albany Robichaud fonds, Centre for Acadian Studies, University of Moncton, https://web.archive.org/web/20020927193207/http://www.umoncton.ca/etudeacadiennes/centre/instru005/intro210.htm.
172 Pichette was appointed to the Court of Queen's Bench in New Brunswick in October 1963. *Le Madawaska*, 10 October 1963.
173 Rex v. Vollman, transcript of evidence, 1438, in Vollman, Volume 1773, volume 1, part 4.
174 Ibid., 1421, 1535.

175 Ibid., 1397. When testifying on his own behalf, Vollman stated: "I had no control over myself with women" (1407). Gregory was the superintendent of the Provincial Hospital of New Brunswick.

176 Pichette told the jury he lacked the resources to mount an insanity defence: "I am not pleading insanity because if we were pleading insanity we would have to have some psychiatrists here." Rex v. Vollman, transcript of evidence, in Vollman, Volume 1773, volume 1, part 4.

177 McRuer CSP Report, 127. McRuer submitted his report to the minister of justice on 21 March 1958, but it was not tabled for over one year, on 16 April 1959.

178 Cathcart to CLD, 15 June 1959, in Vollman, Volume 1773, volume 2, part 1.

179 Cabinet Conclusions, Volume 2744, item 18006, 12 February 1959, 3.

180 Binghamton (New York) *Sunday Press*, 15 February 1959; "Eighteenth Sentence Commuted by Government," Ottawa *Journal*, 16 February 1959.

181 Cabinet Conclusions, Volume 2744, item 18024, 14 February 1959, 3. The other solution discussed was to require a two-thirds vote to justify letting the law take its course. The record indicates that Diefenbaker was the person who called the case "difficult."

182 Ibid., 2.

183 In 1954, Maloney lobbied the Ontario section of the Canadian Bar Association to endorse abolition. "The Abolition of Capital Punishment," *The Canadian Bar Review* 32, no. 5 (May 1954): 485–519. At the open forum held in Toronto on 5 February, his motion was defeated and the matter postponed.

184 Maloney testimony, Joint Committee, *Minutes*, 16 March 1954, 151, 154. Maloney also moved in 1954 that the Toronto chapter of the Canadian Bar Association support abolition. G. Arthur Martin seconded the motion, but it was not passed.

185 Ibid., 155, 156.

186 The Toronto *Daily Star*, 17 February 1959. The paper featured full-page stories of Lysyk's murder over three days, emphasizing her beauty while building up an impression of her respectability. Chantal Faucher, "Bad Boys and Girls, Yesterday and Today: A Century of Print Media Perspectives on Youthful Offending" (PhD diss., Simon Fraser University, 2007), 343–4.

187 "Youth Charged in City Girl's Slaying," Winnipeg *Free Press*, 9 February 1959. Lysyk's family lived in Winnipeg.

188 "'Good Boy' Faces Charge of Murder in Death of Blonde," Toronto *Daily Star*, 18 February 1959. After his conviction, the leader of the Toronto regiment continued to plead on behalf of Bell. Lieutenant-Colonel Heard to Solicitor General, 4 May 1959, in Bell, Volume 1778, volume 1.

189 Numerous papers on the Canadian Press network picked up this phrase in Maloney's seventy-minute closing address. See "Mother Collapses as Son Sentenced," Ottawa *Citizen*, 9 April 1959.

190 Maloney to Balcer, 22 May 1959, in Bell, Volume 1778, volume 1, part 1.

191 Gray to Balcer, 5 June 1959; Bull to Balcer, 16 June 1959, in Bell, Volume 1778, volume 1, part 1. Maloney's 22 May 1959 letter referred to a conversation with Justice Spence.

192 Maloney to Balcer, 22 May 1959, in Bell, Volume 1778, volume 1, part 1.

193 Toronto *Telegram*, 19 May 1959.

194 Cabinet Conclusions, Volume 2745, item 18592, 9 July 1959, 2.

195 Fauteux Report, 78.

196 Special Joint Committee, *Final Report*, 10. In this section, the report summarized the views of retentionists.

197 "Killer Gets Life, Victim's Mother Vows Revenge," Toronto *Globe and Mail*, 11 July 1959.

198 Toronto *Telegram*, 19 May 1959.

199 Justice J. Keillor Mackay, in "The Abolition of Capital Punishment," *The Canadian Bar Review* 32, no. 5 (May 1954): 485–519, 494. Mackay was appointed to Ontario's Supreme Court in 1935 and to the Court of Appeal of Ontario in 1950.

200 By 1960, 41 per cent of Canadians were opposed to capital punishment, almost double the proportion (22 per cent) in 1953. Chandler, *Capital Punishment in Canada*, 41.

6. Sex Murder in the Sixties and the Demise of the Death Penalty

1 David B. Chandler, *Capital Punishment in Canada: A Sociological Study of a Repressive Law* (Toronto: McClelland & Stewart, 1976), 99–102. On faith-based activism concerning the death penalty, see Carolyn Strange, "The Undercurrents of Penal Culture: Punishment of the Body in Mid-Twentieth-Century Canada," *Law and History Review* 19, no. 2 (Summer 2001): 343–85, 375.

2 C.H.S. Jayewardene, "The Canadian Movement against the Death Penalty," *Canadian Journal of Criminology and Corrections* 14, no. 4 (1972): 366–90, 367; C.H.S. Jayewardene, *The Penalty of Death: The Canadian*

Experiment (Framingham, MA: Lexington Books, 1977); Chandler, *Capital Punishment*, 80–1.

3 Out of ninety-seven persons sentenced to death from 1960 to 1967, five were executed. The cabinet recommended clemency in sixty-six of those cases, with legal appeal decisions accounting for the remainder.

4 "An Act to Amend the Criminal Code (Capital Murder)," *Statutes of Canada*, c. 44, 1961, section 1.

5 The revised Criminal Code defined as capital murder killings of police officers or constables, sheriffs or their delegates, plus wardens, jail instructors, keepers, and guards.

6 The enabling legislation was the "Act to Provide for the Conditional Liberation of Persons Undergoing Sentences of Imprisonment," *Statutes of Canada*, c. 38, 1958. It was proclaimed in force on 15 February 1959 (hereafter Parole Act).

7 Canada, *Report of the Royal Commission on the Criminal Law Relating to Criminal Sexual Psychopaths* (Ottawa: Queen's Printer, 1958) (hereafter McRuer CSP Report).

8 Alberta's premier, Ernest Manning, led the attack. "Sparing Slayers Mocks Courts, Manning Says," Toronto *Globe and Mail*, 26 August 1960.

9 Michael Petrunik, Lisa Murphy, and J. Paul Fedoroff, "American and Canadian Approaches to Sex Offenders: A Study of the Politics of Dangerousness," *Federal Sentencing Reporter* 21, no. 2 (December 1998): 111–23, 116; Elise Chenier, "The Criminal Sexual Psychopath in Canada: Sex, Psychiatry and the Law at Mid-Century," *Canadian Bulletin of Medical History* 20, no. 1 (June 2003): 75–101, 93.

10 The Department of Justice established a "Correctional Planning Committee" in 1960, which acted on reforms first recommended by the Archambault Committee. In 1959, the *Canadian Journal of Corrections and Criminology* published its first volume.

11 Isabel LeBourdais, *The Trial of Steven Truscott* (Toronto: McClelland & Stewart, 1966).

12 LeBourdais later reflected: "I came to the conclusion this was not a sick boy who needed treatment but a normal boy who was innocent." Bill Gladstone, "Isabel LeBourdais, 1909–2003: Her Book Said Truscott Trial Wrong," Toronto *Globe and Mail*, 14 April 2003.

13 In 1960, the Ontario Court of Appeal refused the defence's application for leave to appeal. Supreme Court of Canada, "In the Matter of a Reference Re: Steven Murray Truscott," *Canada Law Reports*, 1967, 309–412.

14 Canada, "An Act to Amend the Criminal Code," *Statutes of Canada*, c. 15, 1967.

15 Garth Stevenson, "Federal Provincial Conflict and Its Resolution," *Unfulfilled Union: Canadian Federalism and National Unity*, 5th ed. (Montreal: McGill-Queen's University Press, 2009), 210–34. Quebec separatism also arose in the 1960s. Donald V. Smiley, "Federal-Provincial Conflict in Canada," *Publius* 4, no. 3 (Summer 1974): 7–24, 9–10.

16 "Calgary Slaying," Lethbridge *Herald*, 21 November 1959. News of the murder circulated in the United States through the Associated Press network, where papers published claims that the victim had been raped.

17 "McCorquodale Appeal Likely," Calgary *Herald*, 28 May 1960. On Alberta's six-man jury system, see W.G. Morrow, "An Historical Examination of Alberta's Legal System – the First Seventy-Five Years," *Alberta Law Review* 19, no. 2 (1981): 148–70.

18 Chief L.S. Partridge to D.W.H. Henry, acting director of the Criminal Law Division, 17 June 1960, in LAC, R.G. 13, McCorquodale, Volume 1833, volume 3 (hereafter name, Volume).

19 Report of Detective-Sergeant Gordon Gilkes, 16 June 1960, in McCorquodale, Volume 1833, volume 3. Gilkes headed the investigation.

20 The deaths occurred on Christmas Eve, 1958, in Ear Falls, Ontario. Thomas Young was tried in March 1959 for the murder of OPP constable Cal Fulford, and he was hanged at the Kenora District Jail on 30 June 1959. Andrew F. Maksymchuk, *From Muskeg to Murder: Memoirs of Policing Ontario's Northwest* (Victoria, BC: Trafford Publishing, 2008), 136.

21 McLaurin to CLD, 10 June 1960; Dr. R. Kenneth Thomson to E.P. Adolphe, Crown prosecutor, 18 May 1960, in McCorquodale, Volume 1833, volume 3.

22 A report released on 25 June 1965, in anticipation of a free vote on abolition, indicated that post-conviction psychiatric reports were ordered in every case from 1958. Guy Favreau, *Capital Punishment: Material Relating to Its Purpose and Value* (Ottawa: Information Canada, 1965).

23 Cathcart to Henry, n.d., in McCorquodale, Volume 1883, volume 3. Cathcart examined McCorquodale on 29 July 1960 in the Lethbridge Provincial Jail, where most executions in southern Alberta were carried out.

24 LAC, R.G. 2, Privy Council Office, Series A-5-a, Volume 2747, item 20076, 12 August 1960, 4; ibid., item 20097, 17 August 1960, 6 (hereafter Cabinet Conclusions).

25 "Balcer Defends Action Taken in Death Sentence," Nanaimo *Daily Free Press*, 30 August 1960.

26 "Life Term Shocks City," Calgary *Herald*, 23 August 1960.

27 "Insanity Saves Girl's Slayer from Gallows," Toronto *Globe and Mail*, 20 August 1960.
28 Section five of the Parole Act stated: "The Board has exclusive jurisdiction and absolute discretion to grant, refuse to grant, or revoke parole." The regulations determined that prisoners serving life sentences, commuted from death, could expect to be paroled after serving ten years in prison. T. George Street, *Canada's Parole System* (Ottawa: National Parole Board, 1966), 25.
29 McCormick's and mother's quotes, both in "Mrs. Lefurgey Opposes Cabinet Action; Mother Is Angry over Commutation," Lethbridge *Herald*, 23 August 1960.
30 "S.S." (likely Secretary of State) to D.H.W. Henry, acting head of the CLD, 18 August 1960, in McCorquodale, Volume 1883, volume 3. Balcer asked his staff to seek a precedent for an explanatory commutation. In one previous case (involving a man whose sentence was commuted on 19 November 1959, also diagnosed as insane), the government had requested that he not be released on parole. However, no press release was issued.
31 Tom Gould, "The McCorquodale Case," Lethbridge *Herald*, 3 September 1960. The appeal was filed on 9 June, but Ottawa was not officially notified until 9 September. The Alberta Court of Appeal reprieved the death sentence on 20 June to 3 October. It further reprieved the sentence, after the commutation, to 14 December 1960. On 11 October 1960, the attorney general of Alberta ordered the appeal to be withdrawn.
32 Gould, "The McCorquodale Case."
33 Tom Gould, "DID CABINET EXCEED ITS AUTHORITY IN LATEST ORDER TO PAROLE BOARD?," Lethbridge *Herald*, 25 August 1960.
34 "Solicitor-General Defends Gov't Action Commuting McCorquodale Sentence," Lethbridge *Herald*, 30 August 1960. McCorquodale was treated earlier at the Selkirk Hospital for the Insane, where he had "accused the doctors … of having 'separated his head from his body' and then of placing it on a shelf for a period of three months," Balcer disclosed.
35 Quoted in Gould, "DID CABINET EXCEED ITS AUTHORITY?"
36 Ibid.
37 Gould, "The McCorquodale Case." This account also criticized the government for not directing that McCorquodale be sent to a high-security mental institution if he was insane.
38 "More than McCorquodale's Sanity," Calgary *Herald*, 31 August 1960.
39 "Sparing Slayers Mocks Courts, Manning Says," *The Albertan*, 25 August 1960.

40 "Manning Critical," Lethbridge *Herald*, 25 August 1960.
41 Gould, "The McCorquodale Case."
42 The meeting, called in conjunction with the 1960 annual meeting of the Canadian Bar Association, was to be held under the auspices of the Commission on Uniformity of Legislation. "Change Law on Sexual Psychopaths," Ottawa *Journal*, 26 August 1960.
43 McCorquodale was transferred to the psychiatric wing of the Prince Albert Penitentiary, where he took his own life on 26 January 1961. Lethbridge *Herald*, 2 February 1961.
44 "Automatic Commutation Not Gov't Policy – Fulton," Lethbridge *Herald*, 20 March 1961.
45 "Canadian Bill of Rights," *Statutes of Canada*, 1960, c. 44. One of the few organizations that supported prisoners' rights in the 1960s was the Ligue des droits de l'homme. Dominique Clément, *Canada's Rights Revolution: Social Movements and Social Change, 1937–82* (Vancouver: UBC Press, 2008), 97–102.
46 "An Act to Amend the Criminal Code (Capital Murder)," *Statutes of Canada*, c. 44, 1961, section 15.
47 Ibid., c. 43, section 34.
48 Badani, Canada, House of Commons, *Debates*, 23 May 1961, 5238 (hereafter *Debates*).
49 Fulton, ibid., 5320.
50 Ibid., 5224.
51 See chapter five.
52 "Charge Sex Slaying to Father of Four," Toronto *Daily Star*, 22 June 1960.
53 Toronto Deputy Police Chief to Christie, 9 November 1960, in Fisher, Volume 1785, volume 2, part 1.
54 "No Clues Yet Found in Sadistic Slaying of Toronto Woman," Toronto *Globe and Mail*, 11 June 1960. Police Inspector Charles Cook told the press the killer "must have become infuriated over something." After Fisher's capture on 22 June, the Toronto *Daily Star*'s front-page headline was "CHARGE SEX SLAYING TO FATHER OF FOUR."
55 Report of Justice E.G. Thompson to Minister of Justice, 7 November 1960. The judge stated the evidence indicated Bennett was "not morally stable." Fisher, Volume 1785, part 2.
56 Ibid. As of 1964, when Klein was appointed chief justice of Ontario, he had prosecuted over fifty people charged with murder. He was also the Crown in the prosecution of Ronald Turpin, one of the two last men to be executed on 11 December 1962.
57 Easton prepared his report on 7 July 1960 (which Klein forwarded to Ottawa on 15 November 1960). Dr. R.E. Turner examined Fisher prior to

his trial and did not find him mentally ill. He provided Pomerant a full account of his findings on 25 January 1961. Pomerant forwarded this letter to the Department of Justice. Fisher, Volume 1785, part 2.

58 Report of Dr. Harry C. Hutchison, c. August 1960, in Fisher, Volume 1785, part 2.

59 Pomerant to Minister of Justice, 2 June 1961, in Fisher, Volume 1785, part 2.

60 Deputy Chief of Toronto Police to Christie, 4 May 1961, in Fisher, Volume 1785, part 2.

61 Donald H. Christie, Memorandum to Solicitor General, 19 June 1961, in Fisher, Volume 1785, part 2.

62 Harold Greer, "Too Many Conservatives Oppose Abolition: Vote on Death Penalty Unlikely Until Next Parliament," Toronto *Globe and Mail*, 23 January 1960.

63 Cabinet Conclusions, Volume 6177, item 22610, 22 June 1961, 3.

64 Balcer broke with the Conservative Party in protest over Diefenbaker's leadership, and he announced his plan to join the Liberal Party on 6 April 1966, the same day the majority of Conservatives voted against the abolition bill. "Balcer Turns Liberal," Lethbridge *Herald*, 6 April 1966.

65 Browne, a Newfoundland KC and former colonial minister of justice, was minister without portfolio prior to his elevation in October 1960. "William Browne: Newfoundland Politician Opposed Confederation," Toronto *Globe and Mail*, 11 January 1989.

66 Cabinet Conclusions, Volume 6177, item 22610, 22 June 1961, 4.

67 Press release "Re: Louis William Baldwin Fisher," 23 June 1961, in Fisher, Volume 1785, part 2. A tally of "commuted" and "executed" offenders since 1957, plus the number of jury recommendations to mercy, appeared at the bottom of the release.

68 "Sadistic" was used to describe the murder from the time of Fisher's capture. "Charge Sex Slaying to Father of Four," Toronto *Daily Star*, 22 June 1960.

69 "Killed Woman, Fisher Hanged at Midnight," Toronto *Globe and Mail*, 27 June 1961.

70 "Make Hanging Bill Clearer – Lawyer," Toronto *Daily Star*, 28 June 1961. John Ll. J. Edwards of Dalhousie University (who later founded the Centre of Criminology at the University of Toronto in 1963) predicted the bill's lack of clarity would create "additional difficulties for the courts."

71 C.H.S. Jayewardene, "The Death Penalty and the Safety of Canadian Policemen," *Canadian Journal of Criminology and Corrections* 15, no. 4 (1973): 356–66.

72 Arthur Maloney was the MP for Parkdale between 1957 and 1962. G. Arthur Martin was also a leading spokesman, and Paul T. Matlow (later a justice of the Ontario Superior Court) helped establish the society, which received its charter in June 1964. "Society Wages War on Death Penalty," Toronto *Globe and Mail*, 28 July 1964. Léon Balcer served on the board of directors. Sherbrooke *Daily Record*, 14 November 1964. Joel Kropf, "'A Matter of Deep Personal Conscience': The Canadian Death Penalty Debate, 1957–1976" (master's thesis, Carleton University, 2007), 45–6.

73 On 18 February 1960, Winch told the House of Commons he was proud of his twenty-five-year record as an opponent of the death penalty. *Debates*, 1192.

74 The verdict in the first trial was set aside in March 1961, and a second trial occurred in May. After his second conviction, the court, in a 3 to 2 decision, quashed the verdict and directed an acquittal on 31 October 1961. "Gallows Lose to Heathman," Nanaimo *Daily Free Press*, 1 November 1961.

75 Simma Holt and Jack Brooks, "Twice-Freed Killer Confesses Slaying. Confession Unique in Legal History," Vancouver *Sun*, 21 April 1962. Three weeks earlier, the *Sun* had published a first-person account of his ordeal as an innocent man. Charles Heathman, as told to Stephen Franklin, "I Spent a Year Waiting to Be Hanged," Vancouver *Sun Weekend Magazine*, 31 March 1962.

76 The principle, with origins in English law, is that individuals should not be harassed by multiple prosecutions for the same matter. Martin L. Friedland, *Double Jeopardy* (Oxford: Clarendon Press, 1989), 3. Friedland refers to the Heathman case to observe that offenders who boast of their guilt after acquittal are "extremely rare" (5).

77 Robert Menzies, "The Making of Criminal Insanity in British Columbia: Granby Farrant and the Provincial Mental Home, Colquitz, 1919–1933," in *Essays in the History of Canadian Law, Volume VI: British Columbia and the Yukon*, ed. Hamar Foster and John McLaren (Toronto: University of Toronto Press for the Osgoode Society for Canadian Legal History, 1995), 274–312. The Fritz Lang film *M* is available at https://www.youtube.com/watch?v=jJ6Z8jn-BQQ.

78 Heathman, released on 13 February 1964, was paroled in the care of a Vancouver resident but fled Canada on 21 February. "U.S. Asked Watch, Arrest Heathman for Deportation," Nanaimo *Daily News*, 26 February 1964.

79 Alberta's Premier Ernest Manning accused the federal government of reviewing the question of parole only after the McCorquodale case "blew

up in their faces." "Manning Favours Central Federal Insane Asylum," Lethbridge *Herald*, 29 August 1960.

80 Winch, address in reply to the Speech from the Throne, *Debates*, 27 Feb 1964, 333. Another NDP MP, Reid Scott, the member for Danforth, introduced a private member's bill to abolish the death penalty for murder on 20 February 1964.

81 The description of the victim appeared in "Sex Monsters Isolated," Brandon *Sun*, 20 November 1964.

82 James Meeker, aged thirty-five, was sentenced to ten years for the carnal knowledge of Alice Mathers. He was also found guilty of indecent assault of an elderly woman, for which he was sentenced on 28 May 1964 to preventive detention as a dangerous sexual offender. Meeker, Volume 1803, volume 1, part 1.

83 In the closing and the appeals, the defence raised the "emotional impact" of the recording as a factor contributing prejudicially to the conviction. Hughes to Minister of Justice, 19 October 1964, in Meeker, Volume 1803, volume 1, part 1.

84 R. v. Meeker, transcript of evidence, 633, in Meeker, Volume 1803, volume 9.

85 Anne E. Beveridge, "History of Social Justice (Poverty) Law Services Pre-2002," unpublished memo, 30 December 2009, https://www.cbabc.org/For-the-Public/Legal-Aid-Resources/History-of-Legal-Aid. On the 1960s as a turning point in British Columbia concerning pro bono representation, see Leonard T. Doust, *Foundation for Change: Report of the Public Commission on Legal Aid in British Columbia* (Vancouver: Public Commission on Legal Aid, 2011), 39–40.

86 After the final appeal failed, Hughes's clemency plea stated he had "voluntarily accepted on a Legal-Aid basis the defence" and assisted Henderson. Meeker, Volume 1903, volume 1, part 1, 19 October 1964.

87 "Shock, Bitterness Greets News Meeker Not to Hang," Nanaimo *Daily News*, 5 November 1964.

88 "Parole Ruling for Commuted Death Penalties," Montreal *Gazette*, 11 November 1964.

89 The Canadian Press network covered the father's reaction. "B.C. Communities Alarmed. Shock, Bitterness Greet Killer's Reprieve," Brandon *Sun*, 5 November 1964; unnamed (from Terrace, BC) to Thompson, 15 November 1964, in Meeker, Volume 1903, volume 1, part 1.

90 *Debates*, 6 November 1964, 9834.

91 Christie was called to the bar of British Columbia in 1951 and practised in Langley until 1953, when he moved to the Department of Justice. In 1967,

he was promoted to assistant deputy attorney general and became the associate deputy minister of justice in 1973. For his later career, see Tax Court of Canada, "Former Chief Justices," https://www.tcc-cci.gc.ca/tcc-cci_Eng/About/Judges/Former_judges.html.

92 Memorandum, D.H. Christie to Solicitor General T.D. MacDonald, 13 November 1964, in Meeker, Volume 1803, volume 1, part 1.

93 Unnamed to Guy Favreau, Minister of Justice, 9 November 1964, in Meeker, Volume 1803, volume 1, part 1.

94 Eldon M. Woolliams, *Debates*, 10 November 1964, 9947. In 1960, when the Parole Board still had unfettered authority to parole convicted murderers after they served ten years, Woolliams stated he had "'enough faith' in any minister of justice, regardless of party, to … 'see that any parole board is staffed with men of good judgment.'" "MOTHER IS ANGRY OVER COMMUTATION," Lethbridge *Herald*, 23 August 1960.

95 This appeal challenged the Crown's reliance on testimony from the two accomplices in the hold-up. On the controversy surrounding Marcotte's commutation, see Kropf, "'A Matter of Deep Personal Conscience,'" 3–11.

96 Order in Council 1964–1827, 3 December 1964. This order amended the regulations under which the Parole Board operated. This wording replaced section 2 of the 1960 regulations with section 3.

97 Cabinet Conclusions, Volume 6265, item 25822, 3 December 1964, 2. Over 1964, the cabinet met eleven times to consider the Marcotte case. In the cabinet meeting of 26 November, ministers acknowledged that the "possible commutation of sentence for Marcotte in Quebec had political overtones." Cabinet Conclusions, Volume 6265, item 25803, 3.

98 Solicitor General of Canada, *Annual Report of the National Parole Board, 1964* (Ottawa: Information Canada, 1965), 11.

99 "Marcotte's Reprieve 'Blow to Justice'"; "Coffin Defence Claim Judge 'False, Unjust,'" Montreal *Gazette*, 5 December 1964.

100 Bill Bantey, "Wagner to Press 2nd Case," Montreal *Gazette*, 5 December 1964.

101 "Martin: Why Hangings Should End," Toronto *Daily Star*, 4 December 1964. The accompanying page one article by Richard Snell ("Now – All-Out Drive to Fire the Hangman") flagged that Dion, "sentenced to death for the sex-murder of four boys," was one of the murderers who might be spared in response to the government's projected free vote on abolition.

102 Asked if he had a lawyer, Dion replied: "I haven't got the money." Quebec Superior Court Justice Albert Dumontier indicated he would

arrange for "legal aid." Thomas Sloan, "Quebecker Unmoved by 4 Murder Counts," Toronto *Globe and Mail*, 12 September 1963.

103 Jean-Yves St. Pierre, "Mort des quatres garçonnets. Dion raconte tout," *La Presse*, 25 July 1963; Jos-L. Hardy, "Quatre accusations de meurtre qualifié contre Léopold Dion," *Le Soleil*, 25 July 1963. At the 24 July coroner's inquest, Dion was found criminally responsible for the death of Pierre Maquis, aged 13. Guy Luckenuck, Michel Morel, and Alain Carrier were between the ages of 8 and 12. Dion was charged with four counts of murder at the 13 September preliminary hearing.

104 "Confesses He Killed Four Boys," Ottawa *Journal*, 25 July 1963; "Murders of Four Boys Described," Montreal *Gazette*, 25 July 1963.

105 Guy Bertrand developed an illustrious and often controversial legal and political career, which included co-founding the Parti Québécois. He refers to his heroic defence of Dion in the first volume of his memoirs, *"Tu seras toujours un mal aimé, mon fils" – première période: 1937–1972* (Québec: Les Éditions GID, 2018).

106 "Léo-Paul Dion: Le monstre de Pont-Rouge," *Tout la Monde En Parlait*, broadcast 6 May 2014, http://ici.radio-canada.ca/emissions/tout_le_monde_en_parlait/2014/reportage.asp?idDoc=337048. I am grateful to the ombudsman of Radio Canada for supplying me with the transcript.

107 "Dion Case Sparks Parole Probe Demand," Montreal *Gazette*, 30 July 1963.

108 Jacques Rioux, "Léopold Dion fut libéré sans que le Québec soit consulté," *Le Soleil*, 26 July 1963. Justice Cannon made this request in June 1941, after Dion had been lashed. His earlier record included a conviction (at seventeen) for gross indecency and a charge of attempted murder in 1939 (tried and acquitted due to lack of proof).

109 Winch, *Debates*, 27 February 1964, 333.

110 "Accused Ingenious but Slave to Impulse: MD," Toronto *Globe and Mail*, 10 December 1963.

111 Marcoux, a medical doctor, conducted research on sexual psychopathy in relation to the Dion case. LAC, MG 32-C78, box 1 (1). The national Social Credit Party split in 1963 under the leadership of its deputy leader, Réal Caouette, who renamed the Quebec wing the Ralliement créditiste du Québec. Caouette became one of the most vocal of retentionist parliamentarians.

112 Marcoux, *Debates*, 24 July 1963, 2564.

113 Donald Macdonald, parliamentary secretary, in *Debates*, 24 July 1963, 2564.

114 Lionel Chevrier, minister of justice, *Debates*, 24 July 1963, 2606. Chevrier, a long-serving minister in the Liberal governments of Mackenzie King and Saint Laurent, preceded Favreau as Pearson's Quebec lieutenant. Mabel Tinkiss Good, *Chevrier: Politician, Statesman, Diplomat and Entrepreneur of the St. Lawrence Seaway* (Montreal: Stanké, 1987), 167–70.

115 "Le Dr Laurin affirme que Dion doit être interné," *Le Soleil*, 9 December 1963.

116 Dion was tried only for the murder of Pierre Marquis, but Justice Gérard Lacroix permitted evidence concerning the other murders because it had been corroborated by the police. Dion, Volume 1804, volume 3, part 2.

117 Dr. Louis Charles Daoust, a psychologist attached to the Bordeaux Prison, was the Crown's expert.

118 Dion was convicted on 13 December 1963 and sentenced to death, his execution initially scheduled for 10 April 1964. On 28 January 1964, the Quebec Court of Appeal unanimously upheld the conviction. It reset the execution date to 28 November 1964 to allow an appeal to the Supreme Court, which dismissed the appeal on 7 October 1965. Cabinet Conclusions, Volume 6271, item 27129, 29 November 1965, 2–4.

119 Bertrand to Privy Council, 20 October 1965, in Dion, Volume 1804, volume 3, part 1. Bertrand's memo was a modified appeal argument, twenty-eight typed pages in length, accompanied by a table of contents.

120 Cabinet Conclusions, Volume 6271, Item 26999, 18 October 1965, 4.

121 Pennell, in ibid.

122 Before Favreau left office in June 1965, he tabled the research report on the death penalty he had commissioned: *Capital Punishment: Material Relating to Its Purpose and Value* (Ottawa: Information Canada, 1965). On his career, see John English, "The 'French Lieutenant' in Ottawa," in *National Politics and National Community in Canada*, ed. R. Kenneth Carty and W. Peter Ward (Vancouver: University of British Columbia Press, 1986), 184–200.

123 Cabinet Conclusions, Volume 6271, item 27102, 26 November 1965, 6.

124 Bienvenue to Christie, 18 October 1965, in Dion, Volume 1, part 1.

125 Assistant Deputy Minister T.D. MacDonald to Solicitor General Pennell, 26 November 1965, in Dion, Volume 1, part 1.

126 Cabinet Conclusions, Volume 6271, item 27102, 26 November 1965, 6, 7; item 27120, 29 November 1965, 4.

127 Cabinet Conclusions, Volume 6271, item 27102, 26 November 1965, 4.

128 The Rassemblement pour l'indépendance nationale was the first mainstream organization to promote independence in 1960, and it became a political party in 1964. The Front de libération du Québec, founded in 1963, used violence to further its more radical aims. In 1967, former Liberal and death penalty opponent René Lévesque established the broader Mouvement Souveraineté-Association. Paul-André Linteau, René Durocher, François Ricard, and Jean-Claude Robert, *Quebec Since 1930*, trans. Robert Chodos and Ellen Garmaise (Toronto: Lorimer, 1991), 550–6, 547–50.

129 "Hold Referendum on Death Decree, Wagner Urges," Toronto *Globe and Mail*, 23 December 1965.

130 R.J. Anderson, "Never Underestimate the Power of a Woman," Brandon *Sun*, 28 March 1966; Patrick Nicholson, "Capital Punishment Finds House Divided," Nanaimo *Daily Free Press*, 28 March 1966; Jack Batten, "The System that Convicted Steven Truscott Is Still the Best," Montreal *Gazette*, 23 April 1966.

131 William French, "Behind the Truscott Case: The Trial of Isabel LeBourdais," *Maclean's* 79, no. 11 (4 June 1966): 26b–26e, 26c. British publisher Victor Gollancz accepted the manuscript and granted McClelland & Stewart the Canadian rights.

132 McGee was directed to issue a resolution that would simply "seek the House's opinion" and would not "tie the government's hands." Cabinet Conclusions, Volume 2746, 27 January 1966, 2.

133 Arthur Maloney, quoted in Albert Warson, "Will Parliament Abolish Capital Punishment?" Toronto *Globe and Mail*, 28 December 1963.

134 In Britain, the Homicide Act, 1957, restricted the death penalty to murders of law enforcement officers and guards and to second murders. The Murder (Abolition of Death Penalty) Act, 1965 (proclaimed 8 November 1965), removed those exceptional categories, but it did not apply to Northern Ireland.

135 "Capital Punishment Favoured 58 to 34," Edmonton *Journal*, 23 March 1966. The numbers referred to the paper's own poll. It predicted that MPs were "almost evenly matched."

136 Coverage of the book began in January 1966. Albert Warson, "Author Believes Steven Truscott Not Guilty: Book Disputes Evidence On Which Boy Convicted of Murder," Toronto *Globe and Mail*, 27 January 1966.

137 Two weeks after the book's release, Diefenbaker urged the government to bring on the debate with "as little delay as possible." *Debates*, 15 March 1966, 2710.

138 In 1960, Ontario's Minister of Reform Institutions George C. Wardrope allowed a reporter from the "tear-jerking" Toronto *Telegram* to interview Truscott at the Guelph Reformatory. He publicly stated he thought the boy was innocent. Admonished, he retracted the statement one month later, explaining that he approached the matter on a "humanitarian basis." "Folly at Queen's Park," Toronto *Globe and Mail*, 1 April 1960.

139 The CSADP referred frequently to the Evans-Christie case in England, in which Timothy Evans was executed for the murder of his wife in 1950 on the evidence of John Christie, later exposed as the real murderer and a serial offender. Home Office, *The Case of Timothy John Evans: Report of an Inquiry by The Hon. Mr. Justice Brabin* (London: HMSO, 1966).

140 Brewin, *Debates*, 23 March 1966, 3076. In advance of the vote, cabinet decided that the minister of justice or the solicitor general should speak on the bills. Cabinet Conclusions, Volume 6321, 8 February 1966.

141 Brewin, *Debates*, 23 March 1966, 3077.

142 "Boy Innocent – MP," Ottawa *Journal*, 11 March 1966. Byrne pledged to "rectify what appears to be an astounding example of a miscarriage of justice in the courts of Ontario." *Debates*, 7 March 1966, 2289. In January 1966, Byrne drafted a private member's bill in favour of abolition, but the cabinet requested that he join in an all-party resolution. Cabinet Conclusions, Volume 6321, 2 January 1966.

143 *Debates*, 18 March 1966, 2858. Diefenbaker referred to the judicial inquiry, then underway in England, concerning Timothy Evans's conviction.

144 Pearson asked the solicitor general to report on what the government might consider "desirable." *Debates*, 18 March 1966, 2858.

145 Simons was charged with the murder of a Pennsylvania woman, Katherine Rupert (the wife of his employer), and their two-year-old son at a Lake Superior tourist lodge. He was nineteen years old when he was executed in Sault Ste. Marie on 21 January 1948. The Ruperts' hometown paper reported that the murder occurred in the course of a "rape attempt." "Youth Hanged for Murder of Mother, Son," Altoona *Tribune*, 22 January 1948.

146 "Wishart Unable to Order Retrial for Truscott," Toronto *Globe and Mail*, 15 March 1966.

147 Geoffrey Stevens, "Review Approved for Truscott Case: Decision Not Reached on Form of Inquiry," Toronto *Globe and Mail*, 20 April 1966. The article discussed each of the options Wishart had dismissed: a royal commission, a judicial inquiry, and a new trial.

148 Geoffrey Stevens, "Truscott Review Allowed to Hear Fresh Evidence," Toronto *Globe and Mail*, 27 April 1966; "Judges 'Unfettered' on Truscott Case," Toronto *Daily Star*, 27 April 1966. The *Daily Star*'s front-page story included a picture of the Truscott family (his parents plus his younger sister and brother) in their home, with an empty chair awaiting Steven's return.

149 The referral of a criminal case to the Supreme Court of Canada was issued under section 55 of the "Supreme Court Act," *Revised Statutes of Canada*, 1952, c. 259.

150 The vote was 143 against and 112 in favour. *Journals of the House of Commons of Canada*, 5 April 1966.

151 The sponsors of the resolution were the Liberal Byrne, Edmonton Progressive Conservative Terry Nugent, and Toronto New Democratic Party MP Reid Scott. "The Capital Punishment Debate," Ottawa *Citizen*, 23 March 1966.

152 In January 1966, at a federal-provincial conference on crime, Wagner clashed with Cardin, the federal minister of justice, and Pennell, the solicitor general, and used the commutation of Marcotte and Dion to accuse Ottawa of being "soft" on crime. Lewis Seale, "Federals Softies – Wagner," Montreal *Gazette*, 13 January 1966; "Spirit of Murderer Hangs Over Meeting," Brandon *Sun*, 6 January 1966.

153 Choquette, *Debates*, 24 March 1966, 3127.

154 Choquette, *Debates*, 7 February 1966, 771.

155 Caouette, *Debates*, 24 March 1966, 3123. Bombings and assassinations escalated in the mid-1960s. Ian Ross, "Attributes of Domestic Political Terrorism in Canada, 1960–1985," *Terrorism: An International Journal* 11, no. 3 (Fall 1988): 213–23.

156 Kropf, "'A Matter of Deep Personal Conscience,'" 42–5.

157 Valade, *Debates*, 5 April 1966

158 Scott asked the solicitor general on 7 February and 22 February to clarify the government's policy prior to the debate on the death penalty. Pennell claimed it would become clear during the course of the debate. *Debates*, 7 February, 809, and 22 February 1966, 1589; Geoffrey Stevens, "Abolitionist Tells of Sensing Defeat before the Roll Was Called. How Doubts about Alternatives Won the Noose the Day," Toronto *Globe and Mail*, 6 April 1966.

159 During the 1967 debate, the Liberal member for Maisonneuve Rosemont, Antonio Thomas, stated that the fifty-one Quebec members, some of whom were abolitionists, voted against the abolition bill in 1966 because they felt obliged to represent their electors' wishes. Thomas, *Debates*, 4 April 1966, 3834.

160 An editorial by a member of the Barreau d'Arthabaska condemned Wagner's decision to wait until the retentionists prevailed. This vengeful move encouraged "une hostilité qui peut aller jusqu'au lynchage." Jacques Gagné, "Le ministère de la justice a dans le case de Léopold Dion pris une decision monstreuse," *Le Devoir*, 31 May 1966.

161 "Dion Trial Date for 3 Murders May Be October," Toronto *Globe and Mail*, 26 April 1966. The forensic evidence relating to Pierre Maquis's murder was considered the most reliable. On 4 October 1966, the Crown prosecutor, Anatole Corriveau, decided not to prosecute Dion because the federal government would "act in the same way if a new death sentence is imposed." "Quebec Drops Charges against Dion," Toronto *Globe and Mail*, 4 October 1966.

162 Martin L. Friedland, *My Life in Crime and Other Academic Adventures* (Toronto: University of Toronto Press, 2007), 68. Since 1989, the Canadian Criminal Lawyers' Association has awarded the G. Arthur Martin medal annually to the member considered to have made the greatest contribution to criminal justice.

163 Friedland, who assisted Martin in preparing the Truscott appeal before the Supreme Court, recalls that Martin paid his assistant at the same rate of $30 per hour. Friedland, *My Life in Crime*, 301–3.

164 Because he knew the Parole Board assumed he was guilty, Truscott told them he wanted to prove he had never confessed. Farrell Crook, "Truscott Professes His Innocence, Denies 'One Dreadful Mistake,'" Toronto *Globe and Mail*, 7 October 1966.

165 Frank Adams, "Steven's Neighbors Are Taking Sides," Toronto *Globe and Mail*, 24 March 1966. Donnelly was the son of a wealthy Conservative Senator, J.J. Donnelly. His appointment to the bench on 3 October 1959, three days after the verdict, required that another lawyer (John O'Discoll) argue the case in appeal.

166 Efforts to shield female rape complainants from such questions were not translated into law until 1975. Constance Backhouse, *Carnal Crimes: Sexual Assault Law in Canada* (Toronto: Irwin Law for the Osgoode Society for Canadian Legal History, 2008), 294.

167 Geoffrey Stevens, "34 Witnesses Called for Truscott Review," Toronto *Globe and Mail*, 21 September 1966.

168 In William B. Common's written submission to the court, he stated it was "unreal that Truscott did not discuss with his father or lawyer his penis injuries to support his claim of innocence." "Truscott Case Arguments Filed," Ottawa *Journal*, 5 January 1967.

169 Julian Sher, *"Until You Are Dead": Stephen Truscott's Long Ride into History* (Toronto: Alfred A. Knopf, 2001), 422–3.

170 From 5–12 October 1966, twenty-six witnesses appeared before the justices, who held further hearings with the Crown and defence, 25–30 January 1967. RG2, Privy Council Office, Series A-5-a, Volume 6323, item 27735, 5.

171 Clyde Sanger, Manchester *Guardian*, 23 January 1967. The *Guardian* condemned Canada for subjecting persons under eighteen to the death penalty, and it criticized the delayed commutation. "Death Sentence at 14," *Guardian*, 1 December 1959; "Death Sentence on Canadian Boy, Mr. Fulton's Comment," *Guardian*, 3 December 1959.

172 On 5 June 1967, the trial judge, Ronald Ferguson, complained to Justice Minister Pierre Trudeau that the ruling should pave the way for LeBourdais to be "prosecuted for public mischief." Kirk Makin, "Truscott Judge Wanted Author Prosecuted," Toronto *Globe and Mail*, 31 January 2007.

173 On Canadian impressions of the US Supreme Court in this period, see James G. Snell and Frederick Vaughan, *The Supreme Court of Canada: History of the Institution* (Toronto: University of Toronto Press for the Osgoode Society for Canadian Legal History, 1985), 227–8.

174 Supreme Court of Canada, "Reference Re: Steven Murray Truscott," *Supreme Court Reports* (1967), 309–412, 384, 387, 402, 406.

175 Sher, *"Until You Are Dead,"* 484–7.

176 Chandler, *Capital Punishment*, 41.

177 Cabinet Conclusions, Volume 6321, item 28632, 12 May 1967, 4.

178 "Eloquent Plea Is Weakened by Bias," Toronto *Globe and Mail*, 21 March 1966.

179 Although the victims, three-year-old Ronald MacLeod and two-and-a-half-year-old Michael Atkinson, were "allowed to go out to play on nice days," there was little public criticism of their families. McCorkell was tried for the murder of the elder boy. "Charge Youth of 19 Murdered Boys, 2, 3," Toronto *Daily Star*, 19 April 1962.

180 R. v. McCorkell, transcript of evidence, 1612–33, in McCorkell, Volume 1795, volume 1, part 4.

181 "Charged in Murders to Get Mental Test," Toronto *Daily Star*, 17 May 1962. Toronto Magistrate S. Tupper Bigelow committed McCorkell for examination after he was formally charged.

182 "Man 'Not Mentally Ill' When Boy Smothered," Toronto *Globe and Mail*, 25 October 1962.

183 "Mercy or Gallows for Gary McCorkell: From Bible Class to Death Row," Toronto *Telegram*, 18 February 1963. McCorkell's mother had sent her son to Salvation Army Sunday School.
184 "Court Rejects McCorkell Plea Against Hanging," Toronto *Globe and Mail*, 14 February 1963. Maloney explained that he would request clemency because of "the Conservative Government's declared policy" on mercy recommendations.
185 Christie to Minister of Justice, 15 February 1963, in McCorkell, Volume 1795, volume 1, part 2. The memo supported clemency and confirmed that McCorkell's referral to Toronto's Forensic Psychiatry Clinic for treatment at the age of fifteen had failed to cure him.
186 The records of the 22 February 1963 meeting of the cabinet indicate the sentence was commuted principally on account of the recommendations to mercy. Cabinet Conclusions, Volume 6253, item 2347.
187 "Wants 'Life' Enforced If Death Penalty Goes," Ottawa *Journal*, 30 March 1966.
188 "Police Accused of Lobbying to Keep Gallows," Toronto *Daily Star*, 7 May 1965. On the compromises leading up to the 1967 legislation, see Carolyn Strange, "The Lottery of Death: Capital Punishment, 1867–1976," *Manitoba Law Journal* 23, no. 3 (January 1996): 594, 619, 618.
189 At their 1965 annual meeting, the Canadian Association of Chiefs of Police and QPP leadership voted unanimously (with two abstentions) in favour of retaining the death penalty. "Police Chiefs Urging Amendments to Code," Montreal *Gazette*, 17 January 1966.
190 Greg Marquis, *Policing Canada's Century: A History of the Canadian Association of Chiefs of Police* (Toronto: University of Toronto Press for the Osgoode Society for Canadian Legal History, 1993), 286–9. Support for the death penalty among Quebec law enforcement agencies centred on concerns over organized crime and separatist violence. Andrew S. Thompson, "Uneasy Abolitionists: Canada, the Death Penalty, and the Importance of International Norms," *Journal of Canadian Studies* 42, no. 3 (Fall 2008): 172–92, 176.
191 Cabinet Conclusions, Volume 6323, item 2997, 14 November 1967, 6.
192 Thompson, *Debates*, 9 November 1967, 4093.
193 Pennell stated his support for abolition was "a matter of deep personal conscience." *Debates*, 9 November 1967, 4077.
194 Pennell, *Debates*, 9 November 1967, 4081.
195 Lawrence T. Pennell, "Capital Punishment," *Alberta Law Review* 5, no. 2 (1966–67): 167–73, 170, 173.
196 "What Deterrent Now?" Montreal *Gazette*, 2 December 1967. The comment referred to the legislation as a "compromise bill." Since the

House of Commons had 265 members, less than half voted in favour of partial abolition.

197 "Eighteen Awaiting Gallows," Montreal *Gazette*, 21 October 1967. The number declined by January 1967 after two men were granted a new trial.

198 "Grave Digger Faces 2 Murder Charges," Toronto *Globe and Mail*, 12 May 1965. The girl was murdered in 1961, and police also charged Bernier with the 1962 murder of Laurette Beaudoin, aged thirty-nine. Bernier, Volume 1837, volume 1, part 1.

199 Laprise, *Debates*, 9 November 1967, 4092.

200 Justice LeSage to Minister of Justice, 14 June 1966, in Bernier, Volume 1825, volume 1, part 2.

201 Cabinet Conclusions, Volume 6338, item 3652, 4 January 1968. In this cabinet meeting, Pennell reassured his colleagues that none of the men on the list was guilty of killing a law enforcer.

202 Chandler, *Capital Punishment*," 88–135; Thompson, "Uneasy Abolitionists."

203 For a summary of research used in the lead-up to the second moratorium, see Ezzat A. Fattah, *A Study of the Deterrent Effect of Capital Punishment, with Special Reference to the Canadian Situation* (Ottawa: Information Canada, 1972).

204 Section 2 of the Act to Amend the Criminal Code of 1967 reiterated that persons sentenced to life imprisonment could not be released without prior approval of the Governor General in Council.

205 "Coroner Criticizes Inmate Care at Archambault," Montreal *Gazette*, 30 November 1972. Normand Champagne, convicted in 1970 for a rape murder, beat Dion to death on 17 November 1972. The coroner, Jean Louis Taillon, also criticized the penitentiary for its high number of suicides.

206 G. Arthur Martin, "The Abolition of Capital Punishment," *Chitty's Law Journal* 14, no. 2 (February 1966): 48–54, 53. The article was originally published in 1965, but demand from readers persuaded the editors to republish it just prior to the 1966 debates.

207 During the 1966 debates, MP Robert G.L. Fairweather stated: "The repeal of the death penalty for rape has not led to any increase in this offence, that is, in the ratio by population, which is the only way in which we can consider any of these issues." *Debates*, 24 March 1966, 3106. Similar remarks were made by Liberal Donald R. Tolmie. *Debates*, 5 April 1966, 3875.

208 LaMarsh, *Debates*, 28 March 1966, 3270. LaMarsh, a barrister, entered Pearson's cabinet as minister of national health and welfare in 1963 and then served as secretary of state from 1965 to 1968.

209 Martin, "The Abolition of Capital Punishment," 53.
210 Ottawa *Journal*, 24 November 1967.
211 C.H.S. Jayewardene, *After Abolition of the Death Penalty* (Ottawa: Crimcare, 1989), 44.

Epilogue: The Problem of Sex Murder in the Shadow of Abolition

1 A November 1977 national poll indicated that 73 per cent of Canadians supported capital punishment. Support was highest for cases involving child victims. "The Weekend Poll: Canadians Believe Murderers Should Die," Ottawa *Journal*, 19 November 1977.
2 C.H.S. Jayewardene, *After Abolition of the Death Penalty* (Ottawa: Crimcare, 1989), 46. In 1979, a national poll showed that support for capital punishment dropped to 70 per cent for law enforcement victims but remained at 68 per cent if victims were "innocent" (46).
3 Michael Petrunik, "Dangerousness and Its Discontents: A Discourse on the Socio-Politics of Dangerousness," *Ethnicities of Law and Social Change: The Sociology of Law Deviance and Social Control* 6 (March 2005): 49–74, 50.
4 Neil Boyd discusses how several sex murder cases in the late 1970s and early 1980s increased demands to restore the death penalty. Boyd, *The Last Dance: Murder in Canada* (Toronto: Prentiss Hall, 1988), 210–11.
5 The abolition bill received royal assent on 26 July 1976. Jaques went missing on 28 July 1977.
6 Laura Fraser, "Murder of Emanuel Jaques Changed the Face of Yonge Street and Toronto," CBC News, 22 June 2017, https://www.cbc.ca/news/canada/toronto/emanuel-jaques-yonge-street-sex-work-1.4172511. Large demonstrations, many dominated by members of the Jaques family's Portuguese community, conflated homosexuality and paedophilia. Michael Lynch, "Media Fosters Bigotry with Murder Coverage," *Body Politic* 36 (September 1977): 1, 4.
7 Saul David Betesh was convicted of first-degree murder; Wayne Robert Kribs pleaded guilty to the same charge; and Josef Woods was convicted of second-degree murder. A fourth man was acquitted.
8 Jelinek, in Canada, House of Commons, *Debates*, 5 August 1977, 8078 (hereafter *Debates*). Jelinek, the member for High Park–Humber Valley, made a similar call after the men's trials to "reinstate forthwith capital punishment in respect of sex-related killings as well as all other first degree, premeditated murders." *Debates*, 7 March 1978, 3509.
9 Gamble, *Debates*, 11 June 1981, 10515. The boy's surname was frequently misspelled.

10 Kent Roach, *Due Process and Victims' Rights: The New Law and Politics of Criminal Justice* (Toronto: University of Toronto Press, 1996), 280; Jo-Anne M. Wemmers, *Victimology: A Canadian Perspective* (Toronto: University of Toronto Press, 2017), 31–6. Some victims' rights groups (such as Canadians Against Violence Everywhere Advocating for Its Termination [CAVEAT], established by Priscilla De Villiers in 1991) focused on law reform and victim compensation.

11 "Victim's Father Threatens to Kill Olson," Montreal *Gazette*, 2 October 1987.

12 Terrance Wills, "The Debate: Both Sides of an Emotional Issue," Montreal *Gazette*, 16 March 1987. Daniels's organization lobbied MPs and held demonstrations, primarily in Alberta but also in Ottawa.

13 Prime Minister Mulroney opposed the death penalty, a conviction that began with his belief that Wilbert Coffin was wrongfully convicted. Brian Mulroney, *Memoirs, 1939–1993* (Toronto: McClelland & Stewart, 2007), 557.

14 The restoration bill was defeated, 148 against 127. Elizabeth Comack, "Law-and-Order Issues in the Canadian Context: The Case of Capital Punishment," *Social Justice* 17, no. 1 (Spring 1990): 70–97, 79.

15 Sharon F. Carton, "Canada's Faint Hope Statute: Clifford Olson, Master Manipulator in the Criminal Justice System," *Transnational Lawyer* 13, no. 1 (Spring 2000): 37–74, 62–4.

16 Jack Ramsay, "This Hearing Should Not Happen," *Maclean's* 110, no. 33 (18 August 1997): 20. Olson's application for parole was featured on the cover of this issue, which included several articles on the case and the faint hope clause.

17 Trevor Harrison, *Of Passionate Intensity: Right-Wing Populism and the Reform Party of Canada* (Toronto: University of Toronto Press, 1995). In the 1997 election, held on 2 June, the Reform Party won 52 seats to the Liberals' 177. Almost all of the Reform Party members held seats in Alberta and British Columbia, where Olson had committed most of his crimes.

18 Canada, "An Act to Amend the Criminal Code (Judicial Review of Parole Ineligibility) and Another Act," *Statutes of Canada*, chapter 34, 1996. The act was assented to on 18 December 1996.

19 Bill Gilmour, *Debates*, 10 March 1997, 8859. Gilmour was the Reform member for Comox–Alberni. He delivered his speech while wearing a ribbon that listed the names of Olson's victims.

20 For a critique of the meaning of public safety, see Edward L. Greenspan and Anthony N. Doob, "Putting Politics before Public Safety," Toronto

Globe and Mail, 29 August 2011. In 2003, the federal Ministry of the Solicitor General was replaced by the Ministry of Public Safety and Emergency Preparedness.

21 Dr. Stephen Hucker was the Crown psychiatrist. Bernardo admitted that he raped thirteen women in the late 1980s, which made it possible for the judge, Justice Patrick LeSage, to sentence him indefinitely as a dangerous offender. Kirk Makin, "Bernardo Judge Wants Him in Forever," Toronto *Globe and Mail*, 4 November 1995.

22 As of 2017, 69 per cent of federal prisoners incarcerated as dangerous offenders had committed at least one sexual offence. Canada, *Corrections and Conditional Release Statistical Overview, 2017* (Ottawa: Public Safety Canada, 2018), 107–8. See also James Bonta, Ivan Zinger, Andrew Harris, and Debbie Carriere, *The Crown Files Research Project: A Study of Dangerous Offenders* (Ottawa: Public Safety Canada, May 1996).

23 Tracy Tyler, "Why Would Bernardo Consent to 'Dangerous' Restriction?" Toronto *Star*, 4 November 1995. Bernardo claimed he did not wish to traumatize his victims.

24 Petrunik, "Dangerousness and Its Discontents," 68; Jonathan Simon, "Managing the Monstrous: Sex Offenders and the New Penology," *Psychology, Public Policy, and Law* 4, no. 1–2 (1998): 452–67.

25 Senate Bill S-6 repealed this provision in 2011. As of 2 December that year, persons sentenced to first-degree murder were ineligible to apply for parole prior to serving twenty-five years in prison. Julian V. Roberts, "'Faint Hope' in the Firing Line: Repeal of Section 745.6?" *Canadian Journal of Criminology* 51, no. 4 (2009): 537–45.

26 Justice LeSage told Bernardo: "You are a sexually sadistic psychopath." Toronto *Star*, 4 November 1995. He was initially slated to be sent to the "psychopath wing" at Ontario's Oak Ridge Mental Health Centre. "Psychiatric Ward May Be Bernardo Jail," Toronto *Star*, 9 September 1995.

27 Colin Perkel, "'There's No Cure for Psychopathy': Experts on Bernardo-Like Sexual Deviancy," CTV News, Toronto, https://toronto.ctvnews.ca/there-s-no-cure-for-psychopathy-experts-on-bernardo-like-sexual-deviancy-1.4142321. Dr. Bradford was on faculty at the University of Ottawa.

28 Quoted in Paul Kaihla, "No Conscience, No Remorse: A British Columbia Psychologist Praises the Inner Workings of Psychopaths' Brains," *Maclean's* 109, no. 4 (22 January 1996): 50–1, 51. See also Robert D. Hare, "Psychopathy: A Clinical Construct Whose Time Has Come," *Criminal Justice and Behavior* 23, no. 1 (1996): 25–64. Although Hare conceded that

the construct was a century old, he claimed that cognitive neuroscience and behavioural genetics could prove the condition was organic.

29 The report of the Parole Board's decision to deny Bernardo parole referred to recent psychometric tests. Joseph Bream, "Paul Bernardo Psychiatric Report Describes a Remorseless Killer – But Perhaps Not a Psychopath," *National Post*, 30 November 2018. On the history of the DSM's use to diagnose psychopathy, see Cristina Greco and Thomas A. Widiger, "Psychopathy and the DSM," *Journal of Personality* 83, no. 6 (December 2015): 665–77.

30 On clinical analysis of psychopaths' non-responsiveness to punishment, see Sarah Gregory, R. James Blair, Dominic Ffytche, Andrew Simmons, Veena Kumari, Sheilagh Hodgins, and Nigel Blackwood, "Punishment and Psychopathy: A Case-Control functional MRI Investigation of Reinforcement Learning in Violent Antisocial Personality Disordered Men," *Lancet Psychiatry* 2, no. 2 (February 2015): 153–60.

31 The Nova Scotia Court of Appeal ordered Marshall's acquittal in 1983. Michael Harris, *Justice Denied: The Law versus Donald Marshall* (Toronto: Macmillan, 1986). The province conducted an inquiry into the case and awarded Marshall $700,000 in compensation in 1989. Nova Scotia, *Royal Commission on the Donald Marshall, Jr., Prosecution: Commissioner's Report* (Halifax: Province of Nova Scotia, 1989).

32 Senator John Macdonald, quoted in Mary Janigan, "CAPITAL PUNISHMENT: THE DEATH VOTE," *Maclean's* 100, no. 11 (16 March 1987): 8–12, 11.

33 Peter Maser, "Eddie Greenspan's One-Man Fight to Untie the Noose," Ottawa *Citizen*, 4 April 1987. Greenspan became known as the "celebrity" defender of abolition by 1987.

34 Twelve-year-old Christine Jessup was sexually assaulted and murdered in October 1984. In January 1986, Morin, her neighbour, was acquitted of her murder, but the Crown appealed, and he was retried and convicted in 1992. In 1995, the Ontario Court of Appeal set aside the verdict and entered an acquittal. See Sarah Harland-Logan, "Guy Paul Morin," Innocence Canada, https://www.innocencecanada.com/exonerations/guy-paul-morin.

35 The Justice for Guy Paul Morin Committee funded Morin's successful appeal. Subsequently, the Ontario government authorized an inquiry into Morin's conviction. Ontario Ministry of the Attorney General, *Report of the Kaufman Commission on Proceedings Involving Guy Paul Morin: The Honourable Fred Kaufman, C.M., Q.C.*, 2 vols. (Toronto: Queen's Printer, 1998).

36 An exoneration campaign, supported by Innocence Canada, led to the Ontario Court of Appeal's ruling that Baltovitch's conviction be set aside. The Crown did not proceed with a second trial, and he was acquitted in 2008. On the history of this case, see Sarah Hartland-Logan, "Robert Baltovitch," Innocence Canada, https://www.innocencecanada.com/exonerations/robert-baltovich.

37 On 28 October 2004, the federal minister of justice, acting under section 693.3(a) (ii) of the Criminal Code, directed a reference to the Ontario Court of Appeal, asking again that it consider whether new evidence would have changed the 1959 verdict in Truscott's trial. The court quashed the conviction in 2007 "in the interests of justice." The attorney general called Truscott's conviction a "miscarriage of justice." Ontario Ministry of the Attorney General, *In the Matter of Stephen Truscott: Advisory Opinion on the Issue of Compensation*, section 3, "Reference to the Court of Appeal," https://www.attorneygeneral.jus.gov.on.ca/english/about/pubs/truscott/section3.php#2. In 2008, the government of Ontario awarded Truscott 6.5 million dollars in compensation. Sarah Harland-Logan, "Steven Truscott," Innocence Canada, https://www.innocencecanada.com/exonerations/steven-truscott/#ftnref22.

38 Maser, "Eddie Greenspan's One-Man Fight to Untie the Noose."

39 Greenspan made this claim in a debate sponsored by the Edmonton Criminal Trial Lawyers' Association. Jack Danylchuk, "Executing a Guiltless Man Tolerable Risk – Columnist," Edmonton *Journal*, 12 June 1987.

40 John Diefenbaker, *Debates*, 4 April 1966, 2799. On 13 April 1966, Diefenbaker restated this claim in an interview on the CBC radio program "The Nation's Business": "Diefenbaker Votes to Abolish Capital Punishment," CBC Radio, http://www.cbc.ca/archives/entry/dief-votes-to-abolish-capital-punishment.

41 John Weisdorf, director of Legal Aid in Toronto, alleged that Louis Isaacs, who was committed to a mental hospital in 1948, was insane when he defended Sydney Chambers, Frederick Bussey, and another accused murderer between 1946 and 1947. Alan Edmonds, "'Mad Lawyer' Defended 3 Who Hanged," Toronto *Daily Star*, 14 April 1965.

42 Canada, *Capital Punishment: Material Relating to Its Purpose and Value* (Ottawa: Department of Justice Canada, 1965), 37.

43 Reform MP Bob Ringma (Nanaimo–Cowichan) introduced his private member's bill (C-261) on 20 September 1996.

44 Al Gioa, "Noted Sociologist Scoffs at Value of Death Penalty," Pittsburgh *Post-Gazette*, 10 January 1961. Sellin published a major work on the

subject that summed up three decades of his research. Thorsten Sellin, *The Penalty of Death* (Beverley Hills, CA: Sage, 1980). On the Canadian government's acknowledgment of his authority, see Carolyn Strange, "The Undercurrents of Penal Culture: Punishment of the Body in Mid-Twentieth-Century Canada," *Law and History Review* 19, no. 2 (Summer 2001): 343–85, 371, 385.

45 Val Daniels, quoted in Janigan, "CAPITAL PUNISHMENT," 8.

46 Canada, "Canadian Victims Bill of Rights," *Statutes of Canada*, 2015, chapter 13, section 2.

47 The inquiry was launched in December 2015. See National Inquiry into Missing and Murdered Indigenous Women and Girls, http://www.mmiwg-ffada.ca.

48 Maryanne Pearce, "An Awkward Silence: Missing and Murdered Vulnerable Women and the Canadian Justice System" (LLD diss., University of Ottawa, 2013).

49 Canada, *Reclaiming Power and Place: Executive Summary of the Final Report, National Inquiry into Missing and Murdered Indigenous Women and Girls* (Ottawa: 2019), 3, https://www.mmiwg-ffada.ca/wp-content/uploads/2019/06/Executive_Summary.pdf. Annita Lucchesi (Southern Cheyenne) has produced a database of US and Canadian cases beginning in 1900. As of September 2019, she had found over 4,000 cases involving murdered and missing Indigenous women, girls, and two-spirit people, 10 per cent of whom were also victims of sexual assault. See MMIWG2 Database, Sovereign Bodies Institute, https://www.sovereign-bodies.org/mmiw-database. I am grateful to Annita for sharing her work in progress.

50 Some family members objected to the proposed healing garden's proximity to the murder site; some thought no mention should be made of the perpetrator, while others considered it essential. Angela Sterritt, "Serial Killer Robert Pickton's Murder Victims: Proposed Healing Garden Taking Shape," CBC News, 13 May 2016. https://www.cbc.ca/news/canada/british-columbia/healing-garden-pickon-memorial-port-coquitlam-1.3580342.

51 See, for instance, the community forum on the fiftieth anniversary of Emanuel Jaques's murder, which brought together members of the Portuguese community, historians, members of the LGBTQI community, and sex worker advocates. "Emanuel Jaques Remembered by Portuguese and LGBTQ Communities," York University, http://laps.yorku.ca/2017/10/postdoctoral-fellow-leads-portuguese-and-lgbtq-communities-in-remembering-emanuel-jaques.

52 In 2014, an Ontario child sexual abuse service centre was renamed the Kristen French Child Advocacy Centre Niagara. The executive director stated that the "renaming honours Kristen's memory and is a tribute to the French family." Lynn Jerchel, *Annual Report of the Kristen French Child Advocacy Centre Niagara, 2014*, 3, http://www.kristenfrenchcacn.org/our-story.

Reflection on Sources and Methods

1 See chapter one for a full account of death penalty historiography in Canada.
2 In 1991, I participated in the preliminary review of the then Public Archives of Canada's collection of capital case files. Funding was provided to transfer key data on a dBase data management system.
3 Spousal immunity from prosecution for rape was not removed until 1982. On the battle to change the law, see Theresa Fus, "Criminalizing Marital Rape: A Comparison of Judicial and Legislative Approaches," *Vanderbilt Journal of Transnational Law* 39, no. 2 (March 2006): 481–518, 496–503.
4 Copyright lies with the Crown. For the current provisions, see Library and Archives Canada, "Access to Information, Privacy, and Personnel Records," http://www.bac-lac.gc.ca/eng/transparency/atippr/Pages/access-information-privacy-records.aspx.
5 Personal information (for instance, references to third parties who may have been involved in criminal activities) is sometimes redacted from records. For the full list of the volumes in R.G. 13 (capital punishment case files) that are open (code 90) versus restricted (code 32), see Library and Archives Canada, "Collections and Fonds –133981, Capital Punishment Case Files," http://www.bac-lac.gc.ca/eng/CollectionSearch/Pages/record.aspx?app=FonAndCol&IdNumber=133981. The Regulations with Respect to Privacy (SOR/83-508) that annex the Privacy Act indicate that personal information may be disclosed once 110 years have passed after an individual's birth. Consequently, there is more information available on condemned criminals who were executed or who died than on those whose sentences were commuted. See "Privacy Regulations, SOR/83-508, Privacy Act," Justice Law Website, https://laws-lois.justice.gc.ca/eng/regulations/SOR-83-508/page-1.html#docCont.
6 See Lorraine Gadoury and Antonio Lechasseur, *Persons Sentenced to Death in Canada, 1867–1976: An Inventory of Case Files in the Fonds of the Department of Justice* (Ottawa: National Archives of Canada, 1994),

http://data2.archives.ca/pdf/pdf001/p000001052.pdf. Publications that anonymize victims' and convicted murderers' identities provide archival references that allow access to names and personal information through the online LAC database. For an example, see Jacqueline Briggs, "Exemplary Punishment: T.R.L. MacInnes, the Department of Indian Affairs, and Indigenous Executions, 1936–52," *Canadian Historical Review* 10, no. 3 (September 2019): 398–438. For debates over privacy considerations in Indigenous history, see Linda Tuhiwai Smith, *Decolonizing Methodologies: Research and Indigenous Peoples*, 2nd ed. (London: Zed Books, 2012); and Mary Jane McCallum, "Laws, Codes, and Informal Practices: Building Ethical Procedures for Historical Research with Indigenous Medical Records," in *Sources and Methods in Indigenous Studies*, ed. Chris Andersen and Jean O'Brien (New York: Routledge, 2017).

7 Currently, the records are accessible up to 1979. Michael Dufresne, "The Beginning of the Conclusions: Documenting the Exercise of Power," *Library and Archives Canada Blog*, 16 February 2018, https://thediscoverblog.com/2018/02/16/the-beginning-of-the-conclusions-documenting-the-exercise-of-power.

8 Carolyn Strange, "Capital Case Procedure Manual," *Criminal Law Quarterly* 41 (1998): 184–97, 185.

9 Canada, House of Commons, *Debates*, 14 January 1914, 496 (hereafter *Debates*). Graham served as minister of railways and canals in Prime Minister Laurier's Liberal cabinet, 1907–1911.

10 I did not undertake a systematic review of radio and television archives. However, the CBC and Radio-Canada have archived audiovisual coverage of high profile cases, including Dion's and Truscott's, as well as programs concerning the death penalty. For the CBC digital archives, see https://www.cbc.ca/archives; for Radio-Canada, see https://ici.radio-canada.ca/archives. I found no references to further cases through the LAC's online database of film, video, and sound. On the history of television in Canada, see Paul Rutherford, *When Television Was Young: Primetime Canada, 1952–1967* (Toronto: University of Toronto Press, 1990). The Steven Truscott case has received the greatest media coverage.

11 For England, see Peter King, "Making Crime News: Newspapers, Violent Crime, and the Selective Reporting of Old Bailey Trials in the Late Eighteenth Century," *Crime, History, Societies* 13, no. 1 (2009): 91–116; Ian Marsh, "Conceptualising Media Representations of Crime and Justice within Historical and Contemporary Criminology," *Law, Crime and History* 4, no. 3 (2014): 74–83; John Carter Wood, "Crime News and the Press," in *The Oxford Handbooks of the History of Crime and Criminal Justice*,

ed. Paul Knepper and Anja Johansen (New York: Oxford University Press, 2016), 301–19. On Canada, see Richard V. Ericson, Patricia M. Baranek, and Janet L.B. Chan, *Representing Law and Order: Crime, Law and Justice in News Media* (Toronto: University of Toronto Press, 1991); Julian Roberts, *Public Opinion, Crime, and Criminal Justice* (New York, Routledge, 2018).

12 On the impact of digitized newspapers and other historical sources on historical research and writing, see Ian Milligan, *History in the Age of Abundance? How the Web Is Transforming Historical Research* (Montreal: McGill-Queen's University Press, 2019).

13 I conducted keyword searches of the Toronto *Globe and Mail* and the Toronto *Daily Star* through ProQuest subscriptions. I also purchased subscriptions to newspapers.com, newspaperarchive.com, and Ancestry.ca. I conducted similar searches through the free Google News Archive. The Bibliothèque et Archives nationales du Québec was the most important source for French language newspapers. I used UBC's BC Historical Newspapers database and the University of Alberta's Peel's Prairie Provinces for coverage of Western Canada. Using key dates and locations for each capital case, I used microfilmed newspapers held by the LAC and the Archives of Ontario. I purchased copies of articles held by local archives, and I hired researchers to search microfilm collections in the Vancouver Public Library and the Provincial Archives of New Brunswick.

14 Non-lethal racial violence and intimidation of blacks, Indigenous persons, and ethnic minorities did occur in Canada, but not fatal lynchings. Brent M.S. Campney, "'Canadians Are Not Proficient in the Art of Lynching': Mob Violence, Social Regulation, and National Identity," in *Global Lynching and Collective Violence*, vol. 2, *The Americas and Europe*, ed. Michael J. Pfeifer (Urbana: University of Illinois Press, 2017), 115–45; Constance Backhouse, *Colour Coded: A Legal History of Racism in Canada, 1900–1950* (Toronto: University of Toronto Press, 1999), 181–225.

15 On the complementarity of quantitative and qualitative evidence in death penalty historiography, see Carolyn Strange, "Stories of Their Lives: The Historian and the Capital Case File," in *On the Case: Explorations in Social History*, ed. Franca Iacovetta and Wendy Mitchinson (Toronto: University of Toronto Press, 1998), 25–48.

16 *Debates*, 12 January 1954, 1029.

17 Canada, Joint Committee of the Senate and the House of Commons on Capital and Corporal Punishment and Lotteries, *Minutes and Proceedings of Evidence*, 12 (11 May 1954), 503, 507. On depictions of robbery and burglary murderers as public menaces, see Carolyn Strange and Tina Loo,

True Crime, True North: The Golden Age of Canadian True Crime Magazines (Vancouver, BC: Raincoast Books, 2004), 61–79.

18 The overall proportion of convicted sex murderers executed (63.9 per cent), compared with the proportion of males convicted of robbery and burglary murders (54.3 per cent) was substantial, though not statistically significant. Pearson's chi-square test determined a difference in proportions of .079 (p=.169). However, from 1873 to 1914 and from 1953 to 1959, the differences were statistically significant.

19 Fisher's exact test shows a statistically significant difference in proportions of .525 (p=.003), confirming the higher likelihood of commutation if convicts were youths.

20 Owen Carrigan, *Juvenile Delinquency in Canada: A History* (Toronto: Irwin Publishing, 1998); Cynthia Comacchio, *The Dominion of Youth: Adolescence and the Making of Modern Canada* (Waterloo, ON: Wilfrid Laurier Press, 2006); Mona Lee Gleason, *Normalizing the Ideal: Psychology, Schooling and the Family in Postwar Canada* (Toronto: University of Toronto Press, 1999); Xiaobei Chen, *Tending the Gardens of Citizenship: Child Saving in Toronto, 1880s–1920s* (Toronto: University of Toronto Press, 2005); Shahid Alvi, *Youth and the Canadian Criminal Justice System* (Cincinnati, OH: Anderson Publishing, 2000).

21 "Souvenirs d'un ex-juge de la cour supérieure," *Le Soleil*, 13 April 1977. Justice Lacroix said he resolved never to express his feelings in court again. He emphasized that Dion's conviction was upheld by the provincial Court of Appeal and the Supreme Court.

22 Tom Ford, "William Common: Gray Eminence," Toronto *Daily Star*, 21 November 1964. At the point of Common's retirement, he was deputy attorney general of Ontario.

Index

Note: page numbers in *italics* refer to illustrations.

PUBLICATIONS OF THE OSGOODE SOCIETY FOR CANADIAN LEGAL HISTORY

2020 Heidi Bohaker, *Doodem and Council Fire: Anishinaabe Governance through Alliance*

Carolyn Strange, *The Death Penalty and Sex Murder in Canadian History*

2019 Harry W. Arthurs, *Connecting the Dots: The Life of an Academic Lawyer*

Eric H. Reiter, *Wounded Feelings: Litigating Emotions in Quebec, 1870–1950*

2018 Philip Girard, Jim Phillips, and R. Blake Brown, *A History of Law in Canada, Volume One: Beginnings to 1866*

Suzanne Chiodo, *The Class Actions Controversy: The Origins and Development of the Ontario Class Proceedings Act*

2017 Constance Backhouse, *Claire L'Heureux-Dubé: A Life*

Dennis G. Molinaro, *An Exceptional Law: Section 98 and the Emergency State, 1919–1936*

2016 Lori Chambers, *A Legal History of Adoption in Ontario, 1921–2015*

Bradley Miller, *Borderline Crime: Fugitive Criminals and the Challenge of the Border, 1819–1914*

James Muir, *Law, Debt, and Merchant Power: The Civil Courts of Eighteenth-Century Halifax*

2015 Barry Wright, Eric Tucker, and Susan Binnie, eds., *Canadian State Trials, Volume 4: Security, Dissent, and the Limits of Toleration in War and Peace, 1914–1939*

David Fraser, *Honorary Protestants: The Jewish School Question in Montreal, 1867–1997*

C. Ian Kyer, *A Thirty Years War: The Failed Public/Private Partnership that Spurred the Creation of the Toronto Transit Commission, 1891–1921*

Dale Gibson, *Law, Life, and Government at Red River: Settlement and Governance, 1812–1872*

2014 Christopher Moore, *The Court of Appeal for Ontario: Defining the Right of Appeal, 1792–2013*

Paul Craven, *Petty Justice: Low Law and the Sessions System in Charlotte County, New Brunswick, 1785–1867*

Thomas G.W. Telfer, *Ruin and Redemption: The Struggle for a Canadian Bankruptcy Law, 1867–1919*

Dominique Clément, *Equality Deferred: Sex Discrimination and British Columbia's Human Rights State, 1953–84*

2013 Roy McMurtry, *Memoirs and Reflections*

Charlotte Grey, *The Massey Murder: A Maid, Her Master, and the Trial that Shocked a Nation*

C. Ian Kyer, *Lawyers, Families, and Businesses: The Shaping of a Bay Street Law Firm, Faskens 1863–1963*

G. Blaine Baker and Donald Fyson, eds., *Essays in the History of Canadian Law, Volume XI: Quebec and the Canadas*

2012 R. Blake Brown, *Arming and Disarming: A History of Gun Control in Canada*

Eric Tucker, James Muir, and Bruce Ziff, eds., *Property on Trial: Canadian Cases in Context*

Barrington Walker, ed., *The African Canadian Legal Odyssey: Historical Essays*

Shelley Gavigan, *Hunger, Horses, and Government Men: Criminal Law on the Aboriginal Plains, 1870–1905*

2011 Robert J. Sharpe, *The Lazier Murder: Prince Edward County, 1884*

Philip Girard, *Lawyers and Legal Culture in British North America: Beamish Murdoch of Halifax*

John McLaren, *Dewigged, Bothered, & Bewildered: British Colonial Judges on Trial, 1800–1900*

Lesley Erickson, *Westward Bound: Sex, Violence, the Law, and the Making of a Settler Society*

2010 Judy Fudge and Eric Tucker, eds., *Work on Trial: Canadian Labour Law Struggles*

Christopher Moore, *The British Columbia Court of Appeal: The First Hundred Years*

Frederick Vaughan, *Viscount Haldane: 'The Wicked Step-father of the Canadian Constitution'*

Barrington Walker, *Race on Trial: Black Defendants in Ontario's Criminal Courts, 1858–1958*

2009 William Kaplan, *Canadian Maverick: The Life and Times of Ivan C. Rand*

R. Blake Brown, *A Trying Question: The Jury in Nineteenth-Century Canada*

Barry Wright and Susan Binnie, eds., *Canadian State Trials, Volume III: Political Trials and Security Measures, 1840–1914*

Robert J. Sharpe, *The Last Day, the Last Hour: The Currie Libel Trial* (paperback edition with a new preface)

2008 Constance Backhouse, *Carnal Crimes: Sexual Assault Law in Canada, 1900–1975*

Jim Phillips, R. Roy McMurtry, and John T. Saywell, eds., *Essays in the History of Canadian Law, Volume X: A Tribute to Peter N. Oliver*

Greg Taylor, *The Law of the Land: The Advent of the Torrens System in Canada*

Hamar Foster, Benjamin L. Berger, and A.R. Buck, eds., *The Grand Experiment: Law & Legal Culture in British Settler Societies*

2007 Robert Sharpe and Patricia McMahon, *The Persons Case: The Origins and Legacy of the Fight for Legal Personhood*
Lori Chambers, *Misconceptions: Unmarried Motherhood and the Ontario Children of Unmarried Parents Act, 1921–1969*
Jonathan Swainger, ed., *The Alberta Supreme Court at 100: History and Authority*
Martin L. Friedland, *My Life in Crime and Other Academic Adventures*

2006 Donald Fyson, *Magistrates, Police, and People: Everyday Criminal Justice in Quebec and Lower Canada, 1764–1837*
Dale Brawn, *The Court of Queen's Bench of Manitoba, 1870–1950: A Biographical History*
R.C.B. Risk, *A History of Canadian Legal Thought: Collected Essays*, edited and introduced by G. Blaine Baker and Jim Phillips

2005 Philip Girard, *Bora Laskin: Bringing Law to Life*
Christopher English, ed., *Essays in the History of Canadian Law, Volume IX: Two Islands: Newfoundland and Prince Edward Island*
Fred Kaufman, *Searching for Justice: An Autobiography*

2004 Philip Girard, Jim Phillips, and Barry Cahill, eds., *The Supreme Court of Nova Scotia, 1754–2004: From Imperial Bastion to Provincial Oracle*
Frederick Vaughan, *Aggressive in Pursuit: The Life of Justice Emmett Hall*
John Honsberger, *Osgoode Hall: An Illustrated History*
Constance Backhouse and Nancy Backhouse, *The Heiress versus the Establishment: Mrs. Campbell's Campaign for Legal Justice*

2003 Robert Sharpe and Kent Roach, *Brian Dickson: A Judge's Journey*
Jerry Bannister, *The Rule of the Admirals: Law, Custom, and Naval Government in Newfoundland, 1699–1832*
George D. Finlayson, *John J. Robinette, Peerless Mentor: An Appreciation*
Peter Oliver, ed., *The Conventional Man: The Diaries of Ontario Chief Justice Robert A. Harrison, 1856–1878*

2002 John T. Saywell, *The Lawmakers: Judicial Power and the Shaping of Canadian Federalism*
Patrick Brode, *Courted and Abandoned: Seduction in Canadian Law*
David Murray, *Colonial Justice: Justice, Morality, and Crime in the Niagara District, 1791–1849*
F. Murray Greenwood and Barry Wright, eds., *Canadian State Trials, Volume II: Rebellion and Invasion in the Canadas, 1837–1839*

2001 Ellen Anderson, *Judging Bertha Wilson: Law as Large as Life*
Judy Fudge and Eric Tucker, *Labour before the Law: The Regulation of Workers' Collective Action in Canada, 1900–1948*
Laurel Sefton MacDowell, *Renegade Lawyer: The Life of J.L. Cohen*

2000 Barry Cahill, *The Thousandth Man: A Biography of James McGregor Stewart*
A.B. McKillop, *The Spinster and the Prophet: Florence Deeks, H.G. Wells, and the Mystery of the Purloined Past*
F. Murray Greenwood and Beverley Boissery, *Uncertain Justice: Canadian Women and Capital Punishment, 1754–1953*
Bruce Ziff, *Unforeseen Legacies: Reuben Wells Leonard and the Leonard Foundation Trust*

1999 Constance Backhouse, *Colour-Coded: A Legal History of Racism in Canada, 1900–1950*
G. Blaine Baker and Jim Phillips, eds., *Essays in the History of Canadian Law, Volume VIII: In Honour of R.C.B. Risk*
Richard W. Pound, *Chief Justice W.R. Jackett: By the Law of the Land*
David Vanek, *Fulfilment: Memoirs of a Criminal Court Judge*

1998 Sidney Harring, *White Man's Law: Native People in Nineteenth-Century Canadian Jurisprudence*
Peter Oliver, *'Terror to Evil-Doers': Prisons and Punishments in Nineteenth-Century Ontario*

1997 James W. St. G. Walker, *"Race," Rights and the Law in the Supreme Court of Canada: Historical Case Studies*
Lori Chambers, *Married Women and Property Law in Victorian Ontario*
Patrick Brode, *Casual Slaughters and Accidental Judgments: Canadian War Crimes Prosecutions, 1944–1948*
Ian Bushnell, *The Federal Court of Canada: A History, 1875–1992*

1996 Carol Wilton, ed., *Essays in the History of Canadian Law, Volume VII: Inside the Law: Canadian Law Firms in Historical Perspective*
William Kaplan, *Bad Judgment: The Case of Mr Justice Leo A. Landreville*
Murray Greenwood and Barry Wright, eds., *Canadian State Trials, Volume I: Law, Politics, and Security Measures, 1608–1837*

1995 David Ricardo Williams, *Just Lawyers: Seven Portraits*
Hamar Foster and John McLaren, eds., *Essays in the History of Canadian Law, Volume VI: British Columbia and the Yukon*
W.H. Morrow, ed., *Northern Justice: The Memoirs of Mr Justice William G. Morrow*
Beverley Boissery, *A Deep Sense of Wrong: The Treason, Trials, and Transportation to New South Wales of Lower Canadian Rebels after the 1838 Rebellion*

1994 Patrick Boyer, *A Passion for Justice: The Legacy of James Chalmers McRuer*
Charles Pullen, *The Life and Times of Arthur Maloney: The Last of the Tribunes*
Jim Phillips, Tina Loo, and Susan Lewthwaite, eds., *Essays in the History of Canadian Law, Volume V: Crime and Criminal Justice*
Brian Young, *The Politics of Codification: The Lower Canadian Civil Code of 1866*

1993 Greg Marquis, *Policing Canada's Century: A History of the Canadian Association of Chiefs of Police*
F. Murray Greenwood, *Legacies of Fear: Law and Politics in Quebec in the Era of the French Revolution*
1992 Brendan O'Brien, *Speedy Justice: The Tragic Last Voyage of His Majesty's Vessel Speedy*
Robert Fraser, ed., *Provincial Justice: Upper Canadian Legal Portraits from the Dictionary of Canadian Biography*
1991 Constance Backhouse, *Petticoats and Prejudice: Women and Law in Nineteenth-Century Canada*
1990 Carol Wilton, ed., *Essays in the History of Canadian Law, Volume IV: Beyond the Law: Lawyers and Business in Canada, 1830–1930*
Philip Girard and Jim Phillips, eds., *Essays in the History of Canadian Law, Volume III: Nova Scotia*
1989 Desmond Brown, *The Genesis of the Canadian Criminal Code of 1892*
Patrick Brode, *The Odyssey of John Anderson*
1988 Robert J. Sharpe, *The Last Day, the Last Hour: The Currie Libel Trial*
John D. Arnup, *Middleton: The Beloved Judge*
1987 C. Ian Kyer and Jerome Bickenbach, *The Fiercest Debate: Cecil A. Wright, the Benchers, and Legal Education in Ontario, 1923–1957*
1986 Paul Romney, *Mr Attorney: The Attorney General for Ontario in Court, Cabinet, and Legislature, 1791–1899*
Martin L. Friedland, *The Case of Valentine Shortis: A True Story of Crime and Politics in Canada*
1985 James Snell and Frederick Vaughan, *The Supreme Court of Canada: History of the Institution*
1984 Patrick Brode, *Sir John Beverley Robinson: Bone and Sinew of the Compact*
David Williams, *Duff: A Life in the Law*
1983 David H. Flaherty, ed., *Essays in the History of Canadian Law: Volume II*
1982 Marion MacRae and Anthony Adamson, *Cornerstones of Order: Courthouses and Town Halls of Ontario, 1784–1914*
1981 David H. Flaherty, ed., *Essays in the History of Canadian Law: Volume I*

www.ingramcontent.com/pod-product-compliance
Lightning Source LLC
LaVergne TN
LVHW090148080826
844660LV00013B/711/J

* 9 7 8 1 4 8 7 5 0 8 3 7 1 *